A·N·N·U·A·L E·D·I

Entrepreneurship 02/03

Fourth Edition

EDITOR
Robert W. Price

Senior Research Fellow, Global Entrepreneurship Institute

Robert W. Price is a Senior Research Fellow at the Global Entrepreneurship Institute. As a business adviser, he works with small- and medium-sized global entrepreneurial firms. As an adjunct professor, he teaches classes and seminars for entrepreneurial management programs and executive MBA programs in southern California. Mr. Price received his bachelor's degree from Ohio State University and master's degree from Pepperdine University's George L. Graziadio School of Business Management in Malibu, California.

McGraw-Hill/Dushkin
530 Old Whitfield Street, Guilford, Connecticut 06437

Visit us on the Internet
http://www.dushkin.com

Credits

1. **Mastering Entrepreneurship**
   Unit photo—© 2002 by PhotoDisc, Inc.
2. **Creating and Launching the Business Venture**
   Unit photo—TRW Inc. photo.
3. **Financing the New Venture**
   Unit photo—© 2002 by Sweet By & By/Cindy Brown.
4. **Managing Growth and Creating Harvest Options**
   Unit photo—© 2002 by PhotoDisc, Inc.

Copyright

Cataloging in Publication Data
Main entry under title: Annual Editions: Entrepreneurship. 2002/2003.
1. Entrepreneur. 2. New business enterprises. I. Price, Robert, *comp.* II. Title: Entrepreneurship.
ISBN 0–07–252911–3   658'.05   ISSN 1520–3956

Fourth Edition

Cover image © 2002 PhotoDisc, Inc.
Printed in the United States of America   1234567890BAHBAH5432   Printed on Recycled Paper

Editors/Advisory Board

Members of the Advisory Board are instrumental in the final selection of articles for each edition of ANNUAL EDITIONS. Their review of articles for content, level, currentness, and appropriateness provides critical direction to the editor and staff. We think that you will find their careful consideration well reflected in this volume.

EDITOR

Robert W. Price
Global Entrepreneurship Institute

ADVISORY BOARD

Fernando Alvarez
New York University

Zenas Block
New York University

Joseph L. Bonnici
Bryant College

Martin S. Bressler
Houston Baptist University

Duke K. Bristow
University of California - Los Angeles

Thomas Byers
Stanford University

Gary M. Cadenhead
University of Texas - Austin

William H. Crookston
University of Southern California

Alex F. DeNoble
San Diego State University

Monica Diochon
St. Francis Xavier University

Lynne Pierson Doti
Chapman University

Mikhail V. Gratchev
Case Western Reserve University

Robert D. Hisrich
Case Western Reserve University

Charles W. Hofer
University of Georgia

William C. Johnson
Nova Southeastern University

Jill R. Kickul
DePaul University

Roger D. Lee
Salt Lake Community College

Patricia P. McDougall
Indiana University

Thomas Mierzwa
University of Maryland

William Naumes
University of New Hampshire

Thomas F. Penderghast
Pepperdine University

Michael Peters
Boston College

Gerhard R. Plaschka
DePaul University

Hans Schollhammer
University of California - Los Angeles

Pamela K. Shay
Union College

Joseph R. Stasio
Merrimack College

Amita Suhrid
Keller Graduate School of Management

Elisabeth J. Teal
Baylor University

Karl H. Vesper
University of Washington

Staff

EDITORIAL STAFF

Ian A. Nielsen, Publisher
Roberta Monaco, Senior Developmental Editor
Dorothy Fink, Associate Developmental Editor
William Belcher, Associate Developmental Editor
Addie Raucci, Senior Administrative Editor
Robin Zarnetske, Permissions Editor
Marie Lazauskas, Permissions Assistant
Diane Barker, Proofreader
Lisa Holmes-Doebrick, Senior Program Coordinator

TECHNOLOGY STAFF

Richard Tietjen, Senior Publishing Technologist
Jonathan Stowe, Executive Director of eContent
Marcuss Oslander, Sponsoring Editor of eContent
Christopher Santos, Senior eContent Developer
Janice Ward, Software Support Analyst
Angela Mule, eContent Developer
Michael McConnell, eContent Developer
Ciro Parente, Editorial Assistant
Joe Offredi, Technology Developmental Editor

PRODUCTION STAFF

Brenda S. Filley, Director of Production
Charles Vitelli, Designer
Mike Campell, Production Coordinator
Laura Levine, Graphics
Tom Goddard, Graphics
Eldis Lima, Graphics
Nancy Norton, Graphics
Juliana Arbo, Typesetting Supervisor
Karen Roberts, Typesetter
Jocelyn Proto, Typesetter
Cynthia Vets, Typesetter
Cathy Kuziel, Typesetter
Larry Killian, Copier Coordinator

To the Reader

In publishing ANNUAL EDITIONS we recognize the enormous role played by the magazines, newspapers, and journals of the public press in providing current, first-rate educational information in a broad spectrum of interest areas. Many of these articles are appropriate for students, researchers, and professionals seeking accurate, current material to help bridge the gap between principles and theories and the real world. These articles, however, become more useful for study when those of lasting value are carefully collected, organized, indexed, and reproduced in a low-cost format, which provides easy and permanent access when the material is needed. That is the role played by ANNUAL EDITIONS.

As I write this at the end of September 2001, a terrible cloud of insecurity lingers over our business economy. Rebuilding the spirit of business through entrepreneurship will become more important than ever because the United States was founded and has thrived on the principles of entrepreneurship. The imagination, boldness, and boundless energy of entrepreneurs combined with the involvement and persistence of experienced professional service providers—angel investors, venture capitalists, attorneys and accountants—have created new technologies, that have in turn increased the productivity of the nation's economy and workers.

To provide a better understanding of entrepreneurship and the process of creating and growing a new venture, this fourth edition of *Annual Editions: Entrepreneurship* has been revised and updated to incorporate the most current information. It is divided into four major units: "Mastering Entrepreneurship," "Creating and Launching the New Venture," "Financing the New Venture," and "Managing Rapid Growth and Creating Harvest Options."

Looking back over the years since our first edition, I have noticed a big change. Entrepreneurship has become mainstream. More than 850,000 new small businesses are created each year—today, one in 12 American workers are self-employed. The number of small- and medium-sized businesses (SMBs) has soared 75 percent in the last 20 years to 25 million. If U.S. small businesses were a nation of their own, that nation would have the third-largest gross domestic product in the world.

Starting a business is never easy. But it once was a whole lot harder than it is today. People can take advantage of exciting new programs at universities and colleges to learn more about entrepreneurship. At the beginning of the last decade, business schools were not teaching the fundamentals of entrepreneurship. Currently more than 1,200 postsecondary institutions in the United States offer courses pertaining to entrepreneurship or related disciplines, and every major school has a business-planning contest.

Students are motivated to study entrepreneurship for a variety of reasons. This text is aimed at preparing them to initiate their own venture, work in an emerging venture, or be employed in a company that provides goods and services to emerging firms. *Annual Editions: Entrepreneurship 02/03* is the product of more than 21 years of experience. Intended to be a practical tool that accompanies other texts, handouts, speakers, and in-class business planning projects, this text will provide you with a view of the entrepreneurial process from idea to IPO.

You will discover that entrepreneurship is as dynamic as it is diverse. The topics you study in this book and course explore an exciting process of economic renewal that makes entrepreneurship hard to define, but it is also what makes the field so exciting to study. Let us hope that, in the years to come, entrepreneurship will be an essential part of rebuilding our great nation.

Robert W. Price
Editor

Contents

UNIT 1
Mastering Entrepreneurship

The eleven articles in this unit examine what goes into becoming an entrepreneur, and how some of the most famous self-starters assess their success.

The concepts in bold italics are developed in the article. For further expansion, please refer to the Topic Guide and the Index.

UNIT 2
Creating and Launching the Business Venture

The twelve selections in this section discuss the importance of understanding strategic planning, identifying good business opportunities, and creating successful marketing plans.

The concepts in bold italics are developed in the article. For further expansion, please refer to the Topic Guide and the Index.

UNIT 3
Financing the New Venture

Thirteen articles in this section consider the importance of obtaining funding for a new business through private-equity investments, venture capitalization, and fund raising.

The concepts in bold italics are developed in the article. For further expansion, please refer to the Topic Guide and the Index.

The concepts in bold italics are developed in the article. For further expansion, please refer to the Topic Guide and the Index.

UNIT 4
Managing Growth and Creating Harvest Options

Thirteen articles in this section discuss the importance of developing an effective and realistic business plan to organize ongoing growth, plan for an initial public offering, and improve the odds of a successful merger or acquisition.

The concepts in bold italics are developed in the article. For further expansion, please refer to the Topic Guide and the Index.

The concepts in bold italics are developed in the article. For further expansion, please refer to the Topic Guide and the Index.

Topic Guide

This topic guide suggests how the selections in this book relate to the subjects covered in your course. You may want to use the topics listed on these pages to search the Web more easily.

On the following pages a number of Web sites have been gathered specifically for this book. They are arranged to reflect the units of this *Annual Edition.* You can link to these sites by going to the DUSHKIN ONLINE support site at *http://www.dushkin.com/online/.*

ALL THE ARTICLES THAT RELATE TO EACH TOPIC ARE LISTED BELOW THE BOLD-FACED TERM.

Acquisitions
46. The Race to Embrace

Appendices
17. Outline for a Business Plan: A Proven Approach for Entrepreneurs Only
24. Will Venture Capital Come in From the Cold?
32. Jackpot!
33. Not All VCs Are Created Equal
42. The Decision,
43. The Initial Public Offering: Early Planning Considerations
47. The Flip Side of the Boom

Assessment policies
27. Venture Capitalists' Assessment of New Venture Survival

Brands
10. Go Global

Business plan
14. The Success Start-Up Guide
15. Preliminary Legal Considerations in Forming a New Enterprise
16. How to Write a Great Business Plan
17. Outline for a Business Plan: A Proven Approach for Entrepreneurs Only

Business start-ups
1. The Origin of the Entrepreneurial Species
3. How a Start-Up Evolves
4. What It Takes to Start a Startup
13. How Entrepreneurs Craft Strategies That Work
14. The Success Start-Up Guide
15. Preliminary Legal Considerations in Forming a New Enterprise

Business ventures
3. How a Start-Up Evolves
4. What It Takes to Start a Startup
13. How Entrepreneurs Craft Strategies That Work
14. The Success Start-Up Guide
22. Characteristics of a Successful Entrepreneurial Management Team
23. Going Outside
25. Basic Instinct

Cash flow
21. Solving the Puzzle of the Cash Flow Statement

Communication
39. Managing Global Expansion: A Conceptual Framework

Company description
2. Who Are the Self-Employed?
18. Finding Your Competitive Edge
25. Basic Instinct
37. "Are You Built to Grow?"
39. Managing Global Expansion: A Conceptual Framework
43. The Initial Public Offering: Early Planning Considerations

Company operations
3. How a Start-Up Evolves
13. How Entrepreneurs Craft Strategies That Work
14. The Success Start-Up Guide
38. Managing Growth
44. Harvesting Firm Value: Process and Results

Company organization
15. Preliminary Legal Considerations in Forming a New Enterprise

Competition
18. Finding Your Competitive Edge
27. Venture Capitalists' Assessment of New Venture Survival

Customers
39. Managing Global Expansion: A Conceptual Framework

Developing world
39. Managing Global Expansion: A Conceptual Framework

Economic trends
39. Managing Global Expansion: A Conceptual Framework

Entrepreneurs
3. How a Start-Up Evolves
4. What It Takes to Start a Startup
5. Top Ten Entrepreneurs
6. The Man and His Money
7. Michael Dell
8. Success Rules!
13. How Entrepreneurs Craft Strategies That Work
17. Outline for a Business Plan: A Proven Approach for Entrepreneurs Only
38. Managing Growth
44. Harvesting Firm Value: Process and Results

European Union
39. Managing Global Expansion: A Conceptual Framework

Executive summary
1. The Origin of the Entrepreneurial Species
5. Top Ten Entrepreneurs
6. The Man and His Money
7. Michael Dell
8. Success Rules!
10. Go Global
13. How Entrepreneurs Craft Strategies That Work
15. Preliminary Legal Considerations in Forming a New Enterprise
16. How to Write a Great Business Plan
23. Going Outside
28. Five Things to Remember When Raising Money
33. Not All VCs Are Created Equal
34. Money Order
36. The Do's and Don'ts of Fund Raising
44. Harvesting Firm Value: Process and Results
45. Choosing Your Exit Strategy

World Wide Web Sites

The following World Wide Web sites have been carefully researched and selected to support the articles found in this reader. The easiest way to access these selected sites is to go to our DUSHKIN ONLINE support site at *http://www.dushkin.com/online/*.

AE: Entrepreneurship 02/03

The following sites were available at the time of publication. Visit our Web site—we update DUSHKIN ONLINE regularly to reflect any changes.

General Sources

Harvard Business School
http://www.hbs.edu/educators.html

Surf through the many valuable links attached to this Educators and Research News site and preview upcoming issues of the *Harvard Business Review.* Entrepreneurs are bound to find valuable information here.

STAT-USA
http://www.stat-usa.gov/stat-usa.html

This essential site, a service of the U.S. Department of Commerce, contains daily economic news, frequently requested statistical releases, information on export and international trade, domestic economic news, and statistical series.

The Wall Street Journal
http://interactive.wsj.com

This is an Internet edition of the *Wall Street Journal,* the informative and always interesting newspaper that is read by managers the world over.

UNIT 1: Mastering Entrepreneurship

Business Resource Center
http://www.morebusiness.com

This site reports daily news related to entrepreneurship and presents tips and guides to starting and running a business. It also provides templates and worksheets such as sample business agreements and business and marketing plans.

Entrepreneur Magazine
http://www.entrepreneurmag.com

This site, self-described as "The Online Small Business Authority," addresses a number of entrepreneurship issues, from finding a location for your business to raising money.

International Page
http://www.cob.ohio-state.edu/ciberweb/

Surf this site for information about international business/trade organizations and emerging markets, and for news links to other topics of interest to budding entrepreneurs.

Krislyn's Favorite Advertising & Marketing Sites
http://www.krislyn.com/sites/adv.htm

This extensive list of Internet sites includes information on marketing research, marketing on the Internet, demographic sources, and organizations and associations. The site also features current books on business management and marketing.

Startup Biz/Do-It-Yourself Resources
http://www.startupbiz.com/Doit/seven.htm

This commercial site offers a simple yet handy guide to some basic issues related to entrepreneurship. The material can help you identify the steps needed to start a business.

United States Association for Small Business and Entrepreneurs (USASBE)
http://www.usasbe.org

This site of USASBE, the U.S. affiliate of the International Council for Small Business, answers questions about owning a business and has search capabilities.

William Davidson Institute/University of Michigan Business School
http://www.wdi.bus.umich.edu

The William Davidson Institute is dedicated to the understanding and promotion of economic transition. Consult this site for discussion of topics related to the changing global economy and globalization in general.

UNIT 2: Creating and Launching the Business Venture

Economics Research Associates
http://www.econres.com

This site provides many links that may be of interest to entrepreneurs, such as to the U.S. Census Bureau, international economic data via the CIA Data Penn World Tables, and regional economic information.

Fortune
http://www.fortune.com/indexw.jhtml?channel=editorial/site_map.html

What features make a company a desirable employer? *Fortune* magazine discusses the characteristics of the "100 Best Companies to Work For." Just click on that title when you reach *Fortune's* site map.

Internal Auditing World Wide Web
http://www.bitwise.net/iawww/

This site provides valuable news, resources, events, and associations related to business auditing, which every entrepreneur should become well acquainted with.

National Business Incubation Association
http://www.nbia.org

Business incubation is a process of business enterprise development. Explore this site to consider options intended to facilitate small business creation, funding, and expansion.

Stockholm University
http://www.psychology.su.se/units/ao/ao.html

Explore topics related to job design and other management organizational concerns through this interesting site presented by this Swedish university's Department of Psychology, Division of Work and Organizational Psychology.

U.S. Chamber of Commerce Small Business Institute
http://www.uschamber.org/Small+Business/default.htm

This site offers information on resources for growing businesses, and includes an online small business bookstore.

U.S. Department of Labor
http://www.dol.gov

This massive Department of Labor site will lead to information about the department and to a vast array of labor-related data and

www.dushkin.com/online/

discussions of issues affecting managers. It presents statutory and regulatory information.

U.S. Federal Trade Commission
http://www.ftc.gov

The home page of the FTC can direct you to many useful online links, covering such topics as consumer protection. Valuable business guidance is provided.

UNIT 3: Financing the New Venture

Entrepreneur Magazine/America's Business Funding Directory
http://www.entrepreneurmag.com

This site bills itself as "The First Business Capital Search Engine" and claims to compare your capital request to over 15,000 lending and investment sources. Learn about putting together financial information and searching out funding.

Internet Resources for International Economics & Business
http://dylee.keel.econ.ship.edu/econ/

Dr. Daniel Y. Lee of the College of Business at Shippensburg University maintains this site, which lists important Internet resources related to economics, management, and business in general, references, and specific business topics.

U.S. Small Business Administration
http://www.sba.gov

The home page of the SBA is a must-visit for entrepreneurs. It provides small business–related news and helpful information on starting, financing, and expanding a business. Hundreds, if not thousands, of links are available through this site.

UNIT 4: Managing Growth and Creating Harvest Options

American Civil Liberties Union
http://www.aclu.org/issues/worker/campaign.html

The ACLU provides this interesting page on workplace rights in its "Campaign for Fairness in the Workplace." Briefing papers cover such privacy issues as lifestyle discrimination, workplace drug testing, and electronic monitoring.

Center for Entrepreneurial Leadership Clearinghouse on Entrepreneurship Education
http://www.celcee.edu

These abstracts from CELCEE, an ERIC adjunct, direct people to sources of entrepreneurial materials. This site allows you to search the CELCEE database and click on a collection of links to the Web pages of organizations dealing with entrepreneurship and entrepreneurship education.

Edward Lowe Foundation
http://www.lowe.org

This site provides valuable and extensive bibliographies (though not the articles themselves) on numerous topics related to entrepreneurship, such as issues related to retirement, venture capital, and selling a company.

High Performance Team
http://rampages.onramp.net/bodwell/home.htm

Donald Bodwell's site on high performance teamwork is filled with valuable information about team concepts, team building, coaching high performance teams, and the evolving art and science of building teams, one of the newest ways to manage rapid growth and expansion.

Sheffield University Management School
http://www.shef.ac.uk/uni/academic/I-M/mgt/research/research.html

The Current Research page of this British management school will lead to links on a broad array of real-world management issues: economics, finance, technological change, labor economics, and industrial relations.

U.S. Equal Employment Opportunity Commission
http://www.eeoc.gov

The EEOC's mission "is to ensure equality of opportunity by vigorously enforcing federal legislation prohibiting discrimination in employment." Consult this site for small business information, facts about employment discrimination, and enforcement and litigation.

We highly recommend that you review our Web site for expanded information and our other product lines. We are continually updating and adding links to our Web site in order to offer you the most usable and useful information that will support and expand the value of your Annual Editions. You can reach us at: *http://www.dushkin.com/annualeditions/*.

UNIT 1
Mastering Entrepreneurship

Unit Selections

Key Points to Consider

- What is entrepreneurship? Why is studying entrepreneurship important? What is your definition of a typical entrepreneur?

- What is the typical path of a new business venture? How can entrepreneurs be more successful in their startup ventures?

- What are the different types of entrepreneurs? What characteristics will separate the winners from the losers?

- What are some of the problems and barriers to entrepreneurs "going global"?

 **Links: www.dushkin.com/online/**
These sites are annotated in the World Wide Web pages.

Business Resource Center
http://www.morebusiness.com

Entrepreneur Magazine
http://www.entrepreneurmag.com

International Page
http://www.cob.ohio-state.edu/ciberweb/

Krislyn's Favorite Advertising & Marketing Sites
http://www.krislyn.com/sites/adv.htm

Startup Biz/Do-It-Yourself Resources
http://www.startupbiz.com/Doit/seven.htm

United States Association for Small Business and Entrepreneurs (USASBE)
http://www.usasbe.org

William Davidson Institute/University of Michigan Business School
http://www.wdi.bus.umich.edu

What do entrepreneurs do? Who starts a business and becomes an entrepreneur? When and how do they do so? What makes an entrepreneur successful? Most will agree that the answers are not simple. Few will disagree that never in the history of business in the United States has the entrepreneurial spirit been more alive. As previously stated in the Preface, the SBA estimates that more than 850,000 new small businesses are created each year—joining some 25 million that already exist. The combined economic value to the nation is staggering.

Entrepreneurship begins with an idea and the implementation of that idea. Its meaning can be found in the exciting process of putting together a unique team of creative individuals in pursuit of a limited opportunity before anyone else does. But being an entrepreneur also means taking on risks. No "venture team" led by an entrepreneur can control all the necessary "critical capital resources," such as employees, equipment, raw materials, and startup money, because pursuing such opportunity requires a bridging of the resource gap. Prudent decision making requires that the entrepreneur act in a manner that is consistent with risk reduction and growth.

Entrepreneurs' firms are critical to the health of America's economy; they create two out of every three new jobs and are twice as innovative as large companies. Entrepreneurs in the United States have created an economic sector that is worth trillions. The entrepreneur has also become increasingly important in restoring the competitive position of many U.S. companies in the global marketplace. In theory, entrepreneurship includes several subdisciplines, including small business, women-owned business, high-technology startups, home-based business, joint ventures, global startups, and family business. In this unit entrepreneurship will include all of these subdisciplines.

The exciting lure of entrepreneurship draws a lot of people who really aren't prepared for it into trying to be entrepreneurs. In fact, this is one reason why so many new startups fail, and, obviously, not all startups are profitable. The average annual net income for the millions of sole proprietorships in the United States is less than $20,000. And about 25 percent of these ventures do not make a penny of profit during a typical year.

Faced with these odds, entrepreneurs exhibit many of the qualities of the early pioneers because they are prepared to take enormous risks. They innovate in areas where most say that it cannot be done. They work incredibly long hours over extended periods of time, and even suffer personal problems, all for the excitement of developing a product or building an enterprise. Their passion brings a concentrated focus to their projects. Most have an ability to sell themselves and their ideas, but few understand that they cannot do it all by themselves.

Entrepreneurs essentially start with nothing more than an idea. They create "venture teams" that have the ability and resources to develop ideas to the point at which the startup can sustain itself and internally generate a positive cash flow. Typically, they are starting from scratch; they have no offices, no salespeople, no computer, no suppliers, and no customers. Their job at hand is to quickly gain a "critical mass" by putting all the ideas and resources together and yet somehow make a profit as quickly as possible. Professional or "serial" entrepreneurs are masters of this process. They know how to overcome hurdles and they know how to bounce back from roadblocks and failures.

Essentially what they become good at is starting up new ventures. Some typical beliefs of entrepreneurs are: (1) they are in control of their own destiny, (2) they are capable of solving any problem, (3) the climb to becoming a CEO requires owning the ladder, (4) there are no limits on personal income, and (5) their internal strength and wisdom comes from overcoming risks.

An entrepreneur is someone who perceives a new idea and creates an organization to harvest the opportunity; the activity involved in that pursuit is called the entrepreneurial process, which is very much a series of fits, starts, and brainstorms. What makes an entrepreneur successful is the ability to navigate through uncharted waters and, when faced with a tough challenge, continue on. The economist Joesph Schumpeter said, "As the inventor produces ideas, the entrepreneur gets things done."

The education of potential entrepreneurs is a difficult task, one that is complicated due to the absence of any clear career patterns. Also, there is really no such thing as a "true entrepreneurial profile" from which to learn. Entrepreneurs come from a variety of educational backgrounds. It doesn't take an MBA graduate to start and harvest a business successfully. Entrepreneurs have a special way of thinking, reasoning, and obsessing with harvesting an opportunity. In a holistic approach, they create teams that are leadership balanced, injecting imagination, motivation, commitment, passion, teamwork, and vision. A definition of tomorrow's entrepreneur may be as follows: one who is involved in the process of finding, leading, and coaching a close-knit group of talented people committed to pursuing an idea, as well as providing, marshaling, and allocating the resources needed to take advantage of a limited opportunity.

Some say that entrepreneurship is like driving fast on an icy road. To survive the journey, it requires unique industry insight through domain expertise, anticipation, and "traction" with sales. More important, it is a matter of finding the right balance between the individual and the opportunity. Entrepreneurs are rewarded with the freedom to do what they want, the ability to selectively control and reduce risks; they are rewarded with the potential to generate unlimited amounts of income. To accomplish this requires a good, solid plan and a far-reaching vision.

the ORIGIN of the entrepreneurial SPECIES

Finally, an answer to the question, What's the secret of start-up success?

I CAN'T EVEN BEGIN TO CALCULATE HOW OFTEN PEOPLE WHO ARE THINKING ABOUT STARTING NEW BUSINESSES have asked me to name the one book that illuminates, more than any other, what it's essential to understand in order to create a successful start-up. For close to 20 years now, I've had to answer that there is no such animal. Don't get me wrong—there are lots of perfectly acceptable books about almost every imaginable aspect of starting and running a new venture, from writing a business plan to raising capital. The limitation of such books is that, important though those tasks may be, you can get them right and still fall flat on your entrepreneurial face. But with the recent publication of *The Origin and Evolution of New Businesses*, by Amar V. Bhidé (Oxford University Press), there is now a book I can recommend to anyone starting a business.

This is no *60-Second Entrepreneur*. The book is a demanding read and is based on research Bhidé conducted over a 10-year period at the Harvard Business School, research that sheds light on the mother of all entrepreneurial questions: What differentiates a successful start-up from the masses of new businesses that are created every year? During a series of interviews, Bhidé and I talked about that subject and discussed topics as diverse as his contention that risk taking is irrelevant to early-stage company building, and the implications of young Internet companies' skipping a crucial stage of entrepreneurial development. —*George Gendron*

Getting started

Inc.: So many of your findings challenge conventional wisdom about entrepreneurial success. I'm curious: What has surprised *you* the most?

Bhidé: I grew up with an entrepreneur. My father started a series of businesses and eventually built a fairly significant glass-related business. He was adventuresome, to use that old-fashioned word. The way he started his companies was ad hoc and improvised and not planned and not systematic. I had attributed his behavior to his own eccentricity. So I was very surprised at the extent to which the way he built his businesses was the same as was true of the founders of *Inc.* 500 companies. I was even more surprised that the improvisation was the natural, logical outcome of the sorts of opportunities that those individuals pursued, of the capital constraints that they faced, and of their relative lack of human capital. And that it all made sense.

Inc.: So much of your research focuses on the difference between ordinary start-ups and those gazelles, or "promising companies," that go on to achieve significant levels of success. Could you give us an overview of how successful companies get started?

Bhidé: Here it is in summary: Most successful entrepreneurs start without a proprietary idea, without exceptional training and qualifications, and without significant amounts of capital. And they start their businesses in uncertain market niches.

Inc.: What you're saying is, it's not the exceptional start-up that has those characteristics but most growth companies, right?

Bhidé: Right.

Inc.: Well, then, let's start with the notion of no proprietary idea, no novel product or service to offer, which will come as a surprise to many people. How do these promising businesses get started?

Bhidé: Most are started by someone who is working for another business, who sees a small niche opportunity—one in which the company he or she is working for is already taking advantage of, or one in which a supplier or customer is involved. And the person jumps in with very little preparation and analysis but with direct firsthand knowledge of the profitability of that opportunity—and pretty much does what somebody else is already doing, but does it better and faster. These entrepreneurs don't have anything that differentiates their business from other businesses in terms of technology or in terms of a concept. They just work harder, hustle for customers, and know that the opportunity may not last for more than six or eight months. But they expect to make a reasonable return on those six to eight months. And along the way they'll figure out something else that will keep the business going.

Inc.: The idea that you build a company around novelty—around a unique proprietary idea—is very ingrained in our culture.

Bhidé: You're right. All my students, when they think of how they're going to start a business, want to start with a clever idea. I have very few students who come to me and say, "I want to start a business—I see X do this, and he's incredibly profitable. I want to do the same thing." Yet that's the way people seem to think. Yet that's the way most successful entrepreneurs start up. They make a small modification in what somebody else is doing.

W hat surprised me is that irrationality is central to the successful start-up, but it's not the entrepreneur who acts irrationally.

Inc.: OK, so having a terrific idea for a business is not a requirement for success. Next, you say that most of these promising start-ups bootstrap their companies.

Bhidé: It's interesting but not that surprising when you consider that historically venture capitalists have funded only a few hundred start-ups every year.

Inc.: I agree. But what does seem to fly in the face of popular wisdom is the case you make—quite compellingly—that risk taking is totally *irrelevant* to start-up success.

Bhidé: I think we have to distinguish between risk taking and a tolerance for ambiguity. Going to Las Vegas and taking a bet on a roulette wheel requires a lot of risk taking, in the sense you must be prepared to lose what you put up. But a tolerance for ambiguity, which is a characteristic of successful start-up entrepreneurs, is a willingness to jump into things when it's hard to even imagine what the possible set of outcomes will be. It means going ahead in the absence of information and in the absence of having much capital and in the absence of having a novel idea. In fact, just by looking at the amount of capital that people put on the table, you can see that those entrepreneurs don't have a lot of financial risk, and because most of them are

young, their opportunity costs are not that great.

Inc.: But, wait. This is huge: great ideas and risk just aren't relevant to start-up success.

Bhidé: But it's true. Most founders of promising companies do not start out as innovators or risk bearers. Those roles do become salient at a later stage of the enterprise.

Inc.: I want to get into that, but before we do, there must be millions of undercapitalized start-ups with nonproprietary products. What distinguishes the promising ones from your everyday laundry or lawn-care company?

Bhidé: The elite start-ups, although on the surface they may look a lot like the laundry or the lawn-care company, are actually born under different circumstances. They seem to be dispersed across the economy, but in fact there are pockets in which they are found. Part of the great joy of discovery of this process for me was to be able to characterize the nature of those pockets through talking to the entrepreneurs at great length and finding recurring facts—facts such as most of these companies were serving other businesses rather than consumers. On the surface that's not a terribly exciting fact in and of itself, but it's one piece of the puzzle. Another clue is the sort of products and services they offer. They are not impulse buys. The products and services require days or weeks worth of selling rather than the 10-minute vacuum-cleaner sale.

What's the ticket price? What's the unit purchase? Well, it's usually not a million dollars, but it's not the $5 or $10 purchase either. It's a purchase that is in the five hundreds or the thousands or the few thousands. How are these things sold? Well, they're almost never sold through intermediaries. They're sold direct to the end user.

Who's the salesperson? The entrepreneur himself or herself is the salesperson. And if you pull all those facts together and you put the stories together, you begin to get a deeper level of understanding of what it is that makes those promising start-ups different from the great mass of start-ups.

Inc.: You talk about the entrepreneur as a salesperson and as someone who has a

high tolerance for ambiguity. Tell us about some of the other personal characteristics you've discovered that differentiate those who start successful companies from those who don't.

Bhidé: Well, of course, there's a certain amount of luck. You can't deny that. But from their stories you can begin to figure out a whole bunch of other things. In the face of uncertainty, for instance, the capacity to adapt becomes absolutely critical. You hear stories of "I went to try to sell *x* to my customers, but none of them would buy *x*, so I decided to sell *y*." And it's that capacity to make a quick switch that becomes important. And it's the capacity, in a sense, to use smoke and mirrors, to convince people that you are a more stable and long-lived enterprise than you actually are. That, too, becomes critical. The capacity just to listen well to what people are telling you—an essential element of salesmanship.

Inc.: In your book you say that not only are successful entrepreneurs not risk takers, but they get the people around them to take the real risks.

Bhidé: Absolutely. I mean, the biggest risk in many of these businesses is ultimately taken by the customer. So, in a sense, who is financing this business? It's customer revenues that are financing this business. And the risk that the customers are taking is much more than just the amount of money that they're putting up for the product or service. They're spending a lot of time, and they're incurring potentially quite substantial switching costs if the start-up goes under. There is this idea that the entrepreneur is a crazy, irrational person and that only someone who is overoptimistic and who doesn't have a good sense of the odds would go ahead and do these things. What surprised me is that irrationality is central to the successful start-up, but it's not the entrepreneur who acts irrationally. It's the people whom the entrepreneur uses to get the business going.

Inc.: The idea that entrepreneurs seem to possess this incredible innate or intuitive ability to lay off the risk against the customers and, to some extent, employees is fascinating. But to change directions a bit here, when you tell us that successful entrepreneurs are not doing anything particularly new but instead are improving on what others are doing, it makes starting a business sound so—well—mundane.

Bhidé: There may not be any big new ideas, but in our research we did hear about a lot of creativity at the tactical level. People were telling us, "I have to do this in order to just see someone or to overcome their concerns about whether we'd be in business for five months or not." So while the basic idea for the business may be mundane, the implementation or the execution of the idea—particularly the overcoming of the constraints of the lack of money or track record—involves a great deal of creativity.

The mind-set of people who spot and respond to opportunities quickly may interfere with their capacity to build a large company.

Inc.: You said that these companies start in uncertain market niches. What do you mean by that? Or, more practically, what should entrepreneurs look for in a niche?

Bhidé: Two things to look for: One is an area where there is a lot of external change going on. The computer industry has been a classic example of that. The second characteristic is a business in which customers don't quite know what they want. They have these amorphous needs and they can't really compare one vendor with another. That's where the entrepreneur's personal capabilities can affect the customer's perceptions of the product or service.

Inc.: Could you give us some examples?

Bhidé: Well, take a laundry. In a laundry, people have a pretty straightforward idea of what it is they want. They want their clothes cleaned. They want their buttons not broken. They want their coats not to get lost. And most of whether that gets done or not is pretty much out of the hands of the person who runs the store. But in fields such as entertainment or professional services, buyers place a high value on fuzzy attributes

that they cannot easily measure or define. If you look at the computer industry, in which you find many successful start-ups, you find that a significant proportion of them started out in arenas where there was a lot of hand-holding. That sort of niche allows entrepreneurs to differentiate their offerings by tapping into the psyche of their customers or by responding to their unspoken wants. That's where the entrepreneur's personal effort can make a big difference.

Inc.: Of the hundreds of thousands of businesses started each year, only a small percentage go on to become "promising companies," and very few of those promising companies go on to greatness.

Bhidé: I think it takes an unusual person to start a promising business. It takes a really extraordinary individual to build on that business—extraordinary in terms of someone who has an almost maniacal level of ambition. Not just ambition to make a comfortable living, to make a few million dollars, but someone who wants to leave a significant mark on the world.

It's people like Ford, people like Sam Walton. As Sam Walton says in his autobiography, lots of people started discount stores in the early 1960s because it was relatively easy to do. However, most people who started those businesses then sold out to the larger chains. And Walton was just not happy to do that. He wanted to leave a legacy and build something that would be on the scale of a Kmart. I think that very few businesspeople have the drive to do that.

Inc.: But it's not just motivation. You say it's also about how few people have the *capacity* to be improvisers at the start and then become strategic thinkers later on.

Bhidé: That's right. Think about the early 1980s. There were a lot of people who, without any great insight or any great creativity, figured out that there was quick profit to be had by reselling PCs, basically living off the IBM world. Now, of a thousand people who might have thought that was an interesting idea, only a hundred or so might have had the gumption to actually do it. And then of the hundred or so who had the gumption to do it—because they were opportunists, they were resourceful, they jumped

into the stream—very few had the capacity to say, This could be a springboard to building something like a Gateway or a Dell. So, I think, fundamentally, that the mind-set of people who are good at spotting opportunities quickly and responding to them quickly may actually interfere with the capacity to step back later on to ask, What's the big picture?

Inc.: So it is in that context that risk—so unimportant during the start-up stage—becomes a crucial factor?

Bhidé: Absolutely. Now you do have assets; you have something you can lose. And to grow the business, you have to make a lot more investments.

Inc.: One of the things that begins to be a prerequisite, if you will, to taking your business to that next level is the ability to take big risks. And the second is to learn to substitute planning for improvisations?

Bhidé: Absolutely. And to have a long-term view about how things will accumulate to add up to something. Many entrepreneurs start out in businesses in which the uncertainty is very high and you can do nothing but adapt. But for somebody like Michael Dell, establishing a long-lived business required a distinctive vision of what his business would be like.

Inc.: It's interesting, and ironic, that the traits that hold companies back at a crucial stage of their development are the only traits that founders tend to romanticize. Perhaps most common is the lack of any disciplined planning—the idea that plans are for large companies, that real entrepreneurs sketch out ideas on the back of an envelope and then go execute.

Bhidé: Yes, because early on you want to be incredibly adaptive. You want to be changing your mind a lot. And you want to be open-minded. But if you remain that open-minded, you won't have the constancy to principle that is needed to actually implement a long-term strategy. I think Bill Gates is a fantastic example of someone who has been able to do that.

Inc.: So the cliché is true then, that all those things that contributed to your success can become your undoing.

Bhidé: Absolutely. For example, you typically have the wrong set of employees. I have this lovely picture of Microsoft from 1980 or something, maybe

1979. There's only one person from that picture who is still with the company. The same thing is true of Cisco. It started off with friends. And then VCs and professional managers came and cleaned up, you don't become a large company. Unless you stop being opportunistic, you don't become large. By that I mean that unless you begin to say, "I'm going to give up some cash-flow opportunities, because I have this long-term view, and I'm, in fact, reducing current cash flow in order to build this company—and I'm not going to chase after every little opportunity that I see, because I have a vision of where I'm going—unless you can do that, you're not going to become a large, long-life company.

Wal-Mart and Microsoft started off in this undercapitalized and improvised fashion, and the way they became a success in the long term was to abandon the very policies that made them successful to start with.

Inc.: Let's talk a little bit about what you think your research tells us about how the Internet economy might evolve. What are the parallels and differences between the start-ups you document in your book and what's happening now in the Internet world? Why don't we start with bootstrapping, which has been a critical part of the start-up process as you describe it.

Bhidé: There probably are many Internet start-ups that are being bootstrapped as we speak: entrepreneurs providing Web creation and maintenance to large corporations, for instance. What's different is that the number of relatively inexperi-

enced individuals with fuzzy ideas who are getting significant amounts of funding from angel investors and venture capitalists is incredible. So, many of the ventures that would otherwise have been bootstrapped are not. Similarly, we see lots of uninformed companies go public at rather extraordinary valuations.

Inc.: And with so much capital—human and financial—going into Internet ventures, what effect do you think that will have on the economy? Not just the Internet economy, but overall.

Bhidé: I think the implications are disturbing. New technologies and markets usually emerge through many small adaptations rather than through one great leap forward. Innovation requires a lot of trial and error. The entrepreneur tries something on a small scale and if it works, scales it up, and if it doesn't, tries something else.

We find the same process in the building of companies: great organizations like Hewlett-Packard and Microsoft take decades to build: entrepreneurs have to undergo a lot of on-the-job learning before they can effectively scale up. The easy availability of capital and unquestioning beliefs in first-mover advantage jeopardize this process of trial and error. Entrepreneurs are taking expensive, big leaps into the unknown. They can't easily change direction and don't even have a compass for doing so.

Historically, bootstrapped entrepreneurs have had to change course if they didn't generate positive cash flow; profits represented the primary measure of the success of their experi-

ments. In Internet time everything is supposed to happen immediately—except the appearance of profit. I cannot believe this represents a sensible approach to durable innovation.

Similarly, I cannot believe that many of the companies going public without having shown any capacity to generate profit on a small scale will subsequently develop the capacity to generate profit on a large scale when they are exposed to the many pressures of operating as public companies. Would Federal Express have effectively refined its business model if it had been able to go public when it was still losing money rather than having to wait until it had turned the corner?

Inc.: And the long-term consequences?

Bhidé: In effect we have broken a critical link. Financial markets used to take their cue from the "real" markets and provide capital to companies that demonstrated some evidence of profitability. Some specialized intermediaries, namely venture capitalists, did underwrite the losses of a few glamorous ventures, but for relatively short periods of time. Companies like Go and Momenta that failed to get into the black in a few years used to be cut off. Now, in a strange twist, capitalist financiers have the same disregard for profits that the socialist governments of Europe did in the 1960s. Those governments poured taxpayer funds into "national champions" that turned out to be world-class losers. A healthy capitalist economy keeps its entrepreneurs on a tight leash—they live or die by the profits they make.

Who Are the Self-Employed?

Yannis Georgellis and Howard J. Wall

Self-employment, or entrepreneurship, is commonly held to provide an important avenue for individuals to advance up the income ladder. For some, it may provide a better route than paid employment, while for others, who may be disadvantaged when pursuing paid employment, it may provide the only route.[1] The perceived importance of self-employment is reflected in government programs such as the U.S. Small Business Administration's loan programs and the Self-Employment Assistance programs that several states have used to help the unemployed to open their own businesses.[2]

Despite the perceived importance of self-employment, there has not been a great deal of basic data analysis to identify who the self-employed are and what they do. As a partial remedy, this paper uses data from the 1998 March Supplement to the Current Population Survey (CPS) to provide a snapshot of self-employment in the United States, with particular focus on the differences between self-employed men and self-employed women. The purpose of this is to inform more-rigorous analyses that try to identify the determinants of self-employment. It supplements and updates earlier looks at CPS self-employment, particularly Bregger (1996), who looked at self-employed men and women combined, and Devine (1994a), who compared male and female self-employment for the years up to 1990.

Because men and women face vastly different costs and benefits to self-employment relative to other labor market options, the self-employment decisions of men and women differ a great deal. Unsurprisingly then, self-employed men and self-employed women tend to do different things and have different labor market characteristics. Nonetheless, most studies that try to explain the decision to be self-employed use data for men only or they combine men and women into one data set. The most recent study that uses combined data on men and women is Blanchflower (2000), which estimates the determinants of self-employment for 23 Organization for Economic Co-operation and Development (OECD) countries.[3] Of the few studies that examine women's decisions to become self-employed, the most prominent are Macpherson (1988), Connelly (1992), and Devine (1994b). To our knowledge, Georgellis and Wall (1999) is the only study that has direct comparisons of the determinants of men's and women's self-employment decisions.

There are many factors that make a woman's self-employment decision differ from a man's. First, differences in male and female labor-market opportunities due to things like discrimination, experience and skill differentials, and labor-market segmentation may be more pronounced in some types of self-employment than in others.[4] Also, due primarily to child-care concerns, a woman may have a different lifetime occupational strategy than a man with otherwise identical characteristics. Consequently, some types of self-employment may be more preferable to some women because they reduce the costs of child care or allow for more time-flexibility or work from home (Connelly, 1992, and Macpherson, 1988). To some extent, for women, self-employment can be considered a closer substitute for part-time paid employment or being out of the labor force than it is for men. This is consistent with Georgellis and Wall (1999), who found that German women are less responsive to the difference between the wages in paid employment and self-employment and are more likely to have been out of the labor force or in part-time paid employment immediately prior to becoming self-employed.

CPS SELF-EMPLOYMENT DATA

Before beginning our analysis of the self-employment data, we should be clear about how we define self-employment. First, because the self-

Table 1

U.S. Self-Employment Rates

	1987	1997
Total	9.3	8.6
Males	11.9	11.0
Females	6.3	6.0

Figure 1

Self-Employment Rates by Region, 1987 and 1997

employment rate in agriculture—typically around 45 percent of total industry employment—is much higher than in other industries, we look at non-agricultural self-employment only. Second, in the CPS March supplement the class of a worker is determined by the job that was held the longest during the previous year.[5] In contrast, the class of a worker in the monthly CPS is the job that is currently held, so the self-employment rates derived from the monthly surveys are usually higher than for the March supplement. This is because within a monthly survey there will be some people who are self-employed for only a short period and, therefore, would not be captured by the March supplement. As long as the difference between the two measures is consistent across the various demographic, occupation, and industry groupings, then the issue that we are interested in—the composition of the self-employed—is not sensitive to this distinction.

The CPS is idiosyncratic because persons who work for themselves, but have incorporated their businesses, are not considered self-employed. This is because, technically, they do not work for themselves, but for a corporation. Thus, the usefulness of the CPS measure for looking at the cross-sectional composition of self-employment depends on the extent to which the decision to incorporate differs across the groupings we consider. Similarly, its usefulness for making comparisons over time depends on the extent of year-to-year changes in the tendency for the self-employed to incorporate. Manser and Picot (1999) show that there was a large jump in the share of the incorporated self-employed after the 1994 revision of the CPS survey although it has not changed much since then. Therefore, comparisons of pre- and post-1994 self-employment should be taken with a grain of salt.

Keeping these caveats in mind, we will restrict ourselves, for the most part, to cross-sectional differences among the self-employed. Nonetheless, when they are of particular interest, we will refer to changes since the 1988 CPS.

AGGREGATE SELF-EMPLOYMENT RATES

As reported in Table 1, in 1997, 8.6 percent of those who were employed were self-employed, which was a decrease from the self-employment rate of 9.3 percent ten years earlier. However, as noted above, this decline may partly reflect a greater tendency for people to incorporate their businesses and not be counted as self-employed. More tellingly, Table 1 also shows that for 1987 and 1997: of those who were employed, men were much more likely to be self-employed, and this tendency changed very little between the two years.

There also are notable differences in self-employment when broken down according to region and race. Specifically, as shown by Figure 1, for 1987 and 1997, the self-employment rate for all regions but the West was below the national rate. While the Northeast and the South had self-employment rates only slightly below the national rate in 1997, the Midwest's had fallen to much below it. Further, although all regions saw declines in self-employment between 1987 and 1997, the Northeast experienced a large relative rise; its self-employment rate was nearly the same during 1997 as for the nation as a whole, having been much lower than the nation's ten years earlier. Explanations for these regional differences are hard to come by. To date, there are no studies of the regional differences in self-employment in the United States, although a study of British self-employment by Georgellis and Wall (2000) may shed some light. They found that, not surprisingly, regional self-employment rates tended to differ according to regional differences in labor-market conditions, labor-force composition, and industry composition. They also found that region-specific factors that are unobservable or difficult to quantify—such as entrepreneurial spirit—play a role. For the United States, differences in state policies such as taxes, support for small business, and bankruptcy laws also may be important.

As Figure 2 shows, two racial groups, whites and Asians or Pacific Islanders, had self-employment rates above the national average for both 1987 and 1997. Interestingly, although the fall in the tendency of whites to be self-employed mirrored that of the nation, the Asian self-employment rate rose over the period, and, by 1997, exceeded that of whites. The two other racial groups—blacks and Native Americans—had self-employment rates well below the national average. While the Native American self-employment rate plunged between 1987 and 1997, from 8.2 percent to 6.3 percent, the black self-employment rate went against the national trend and rose from 3 percent to 3.3 percent.

Note, however, that because the CPS relies on a sampling of the population, one should be careful about reading much into changes in self-employment among minority groups. For example, assume that there are 60,000 people in the CPS, blacks make up 12 percent of the sampled population, the average household has 1.5 adults, 60 percent of the black population is employed, and 3.3 percent of the employed blacks are self-employed. Under these realistic assumptions, the CPS sample would have only 214 blacks that were self-employed. Given this small number, large fluctuations in the aggregate black self-employment rate might be due simply to random sampling error. This also means that one should be wary of disaggregating the CPS categories according to race. It would not be particularly meaningful, for example, to split the 214 self-employed blacks from our example into the 29 detailed industry categories of the CPS. Obviously, such problems are even more severe when disaggregating data for smaller minority groups such as Native Americans and Asian or Pacific Islanders.

WHAT DO THE SELF-EMPLOYED DO?

As shown by Figure 3, during 1997 self-employed men and women were concentrated in a small number of occupations—87 percent of self-employed men were in one of four occupations and 94 percent of women were in one of five occupations.[6] Self-employed men and women were similar in that three occupations—sales; professional specialty; and executive, administrative, and managerial—had large shares of both. Nevertheless, there were large differences: Whereas nearly a quarter of self-employed men were in precision production, very few self-employed women were. Instead, large shares of self-employed women were in service or administrative support occupations, where self-employed men were not likely to be.

Compared with 1987, the 1997 occupational distribution of self-employed men was little changed, although shares for professional specialty and precision production were slightly higher (between 1 and 2 percentage points) and the share in sales was slightly

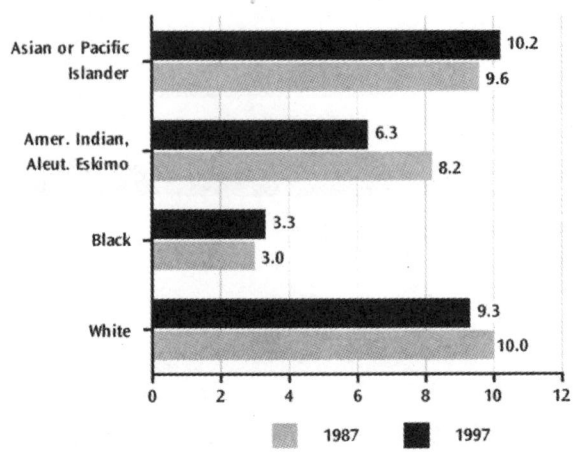

Figure 2

Self-Employment Rates by Race, 1987 and 1997

lower (3 percentage points). In contrast, the occupational distribution of women changed quite a bit. There were relatively large shifts of self-employed women toward professional specialty (6 percentage points higher) and executive, administrative, and managerial (4 percentage points higher); and away from service and sales occupations (both 4 percentage points lower). Thus, in common with women in paid employment, self-employed women appear to be moving away from traditional female service and sales occupations toward professional and executive ones. Because of this, the occupational distributions of self-employed men and women are becoming more similar over time.

Partly mirroring the differences in occupations, self-employed men and women are not always found in the same industries. As illustrated by Figure 4, during 1997, large shares of self-employed men and women worked in professional and related services, retail trade, and business and repair services industries. However, the shares of self-employed women in the first two of these industries were much higher than those for self-employed men. The construction industry was also a popular industry for self-employed men, although self-employed women were relatively scarce there. Instead, self-employed women were more likely to be in the personal services industry, which had relatively few of the self-employed men.

Self-employed men tended to be in the same industries during 1997 as they were in 1987, although there were slightly higher shares in construction and professional and related services during 1997 (1.7 and 1.5 percent, respectively). In contrast, during 1997, self-employed women were much more likely to be in professional and related services than during 1987, as their

Figure 3

Shares of the Self-Employed by Occupation, 1997

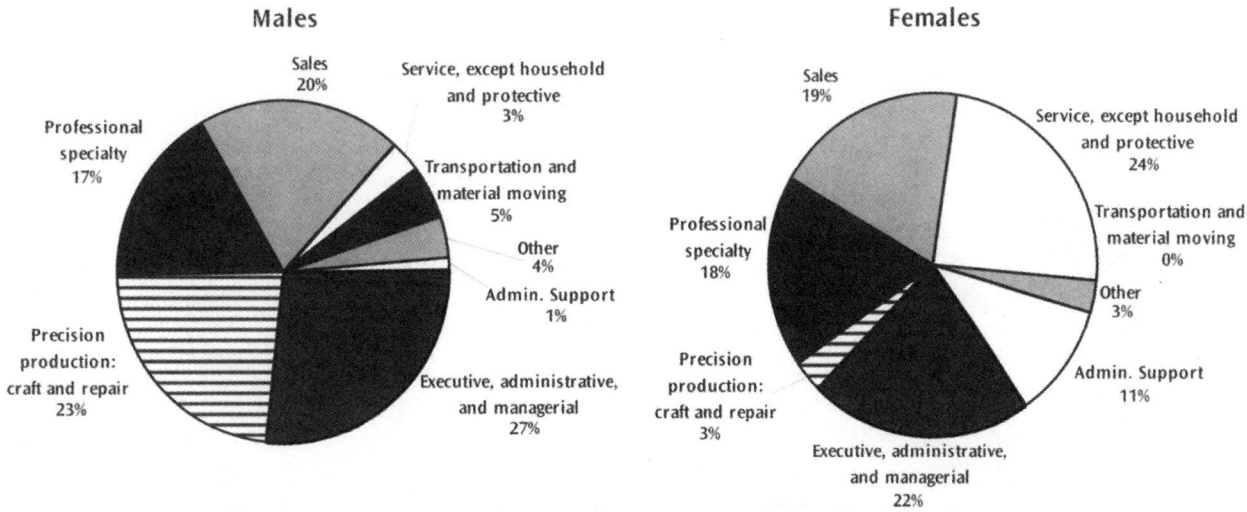

Figure 4

Shares of the Self-Employed by Industry, 1997

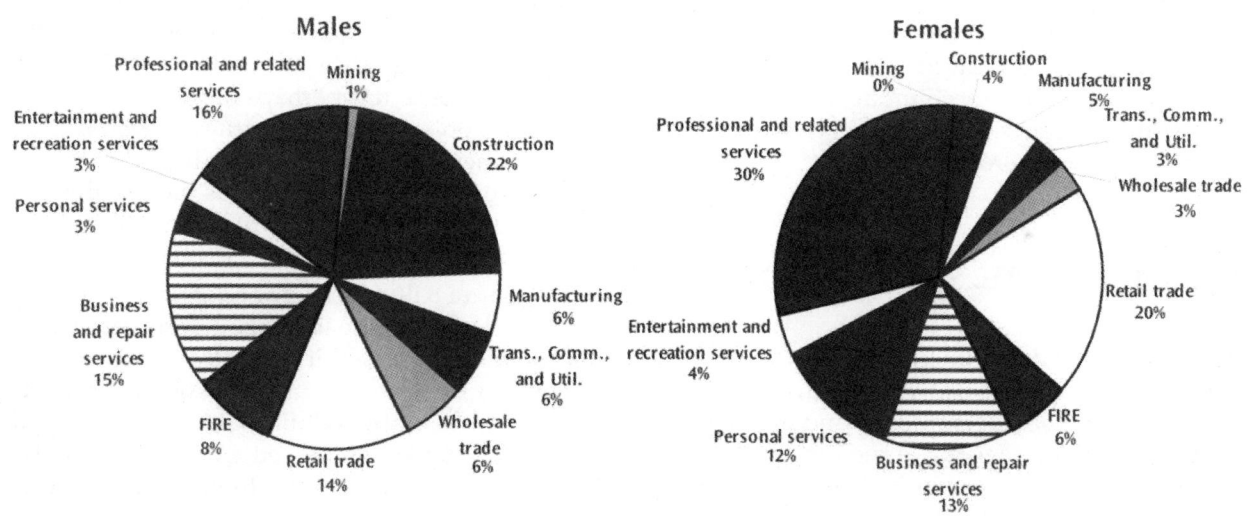

share in that industry rose by 13.2 percentage points over the period. This was made up for by large decreases in the shares of self-employed women in retail sales (5 percentage points lower) and personal services (10.6 percentage points lower).

On the face of it, the data indicate a trend toward self-employed men and women doing similar things in similar industries. However, a closer look reveals that this is not true, as men and women do very different things within the broad industry classifications discussed above. For example, as illustrated by Figure 5, if we disaggregate the retail trade industry we see that the only subindustry where self-employed men and women both tended to be

in similar numbers was eating and drinking places. Self-employed men and women were also both likely to be in grocery stores and miscellaneous retail, but men were much more likely to be in the former and women more likely to be in the latter. Self-employed men also tended to own motor vehicle dealerships and furniture and home furnishing stores, which were rarely owned by self-employed women. On the other hand, self-employed women were much more likely to be retail florists, be involved in direct selling, or own non-shoe apparel and accessory stores.

A similar disaggregation of the professional and related services industry reveals that there was only one

Figure 5

Detailed Shares of the Self-Employed in Retail Trade, 1997

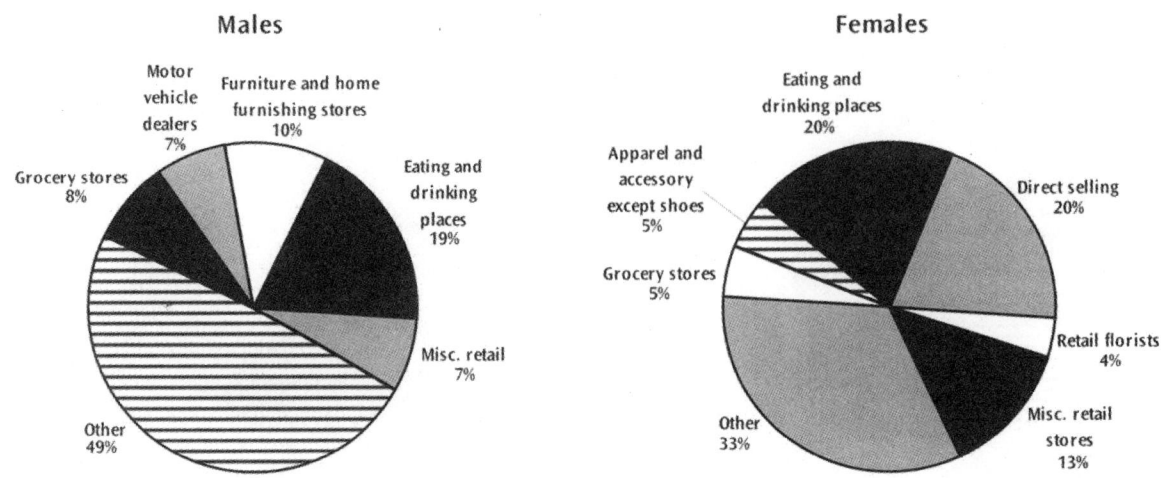

subindustry—management and public relations—for which the shares of self-employed men and women were both higher than 6 percent. Even there, the share of self-employed men was more than twice that of self-employed women. As illustrated by Figure 6, self-employed men in professional and related services tended to work in medicine, dentistry, legal services, engineering, architecture, or surveying. In contrast, self-employed women in the industry tended to be in accounting, auditing, and bookkeeping; education services; health services; and, most commonly child-care provision.

EDUCATION AND THE SELF-EMPLOYED

Many studies of the determinants of self-employment take a person's education to be an important factor in the decision to be self-employed and therefore include in their regressions a variable such as "years of education."[7] However, given the wide variety of occupations and industries where the self-employed are, the relationship between education and self-employment is not that simple. As Figure 7 shows, during 1997, 57 percent of self-employed men and women did not have a post-secondary degree, reflecting that some of the occupations and industries where the self-employed are prevalent provide relatively low returns to higher education. Other occupations popular with the self-employed, such as professional specialty and executive, administrative, and managerial, require a post-secondary diploma and thus provide high returns to education. Nonetheless, of the self-employed with post-secondary degrees, most have no more than a bachelor's degree.

To a large extent, Figure 7 simply reflects the shares of those who are employed according to education

groups, rather than the tendencies of the education groups to be self-employed. For instance, although those who have not had any education beyond high school account for 37 percent of the self-employed, they account for an even larger share of overall employment (44 percent). On the other hand, those with a bachelor's degree or higher account for 34 percent of the self-employed, although they account for only 29 percent of total employment. It is perhaps more instructive to look at the self-employment rates within a given education group. Rather than telling us who the self-employed are, as education shares do, they tell us the likelihood that a person with a given level of education will be self-employed.

As Figure 8 illustrates, the relationship between education level and the likelihood of self-employment was not monotonic, and it differed between men and women. For men, those with professional school degrees (M.D., D.D.S., D.V.M., L.L.B., and J.D.) were the ones most likely to be self-employed, as over 38 percent of such men were. The next highest self-employment rates for men were for those with doctorate degrees (Ph.D. and E.D.D.) and those with associate degrees. Men who held master's (M.A., M.S., M.ENG., M.ED., M.S.W., and M.B.A.) or bachelor's degrees were much less likely to be self-employed than were men with education levels either just higher or just lower. For men without a post-secondary degree, less education meant a lower likelihood of self-employment.

Consistent with their lower aggregate self-employment rate, women were less likely to be self-employed than were men with the same level of education. As with men, for those with an associate degree or less, self-employment rates were greater the higher the level of educational attainment. Also, for women with degrees, those with bachelor's or master's

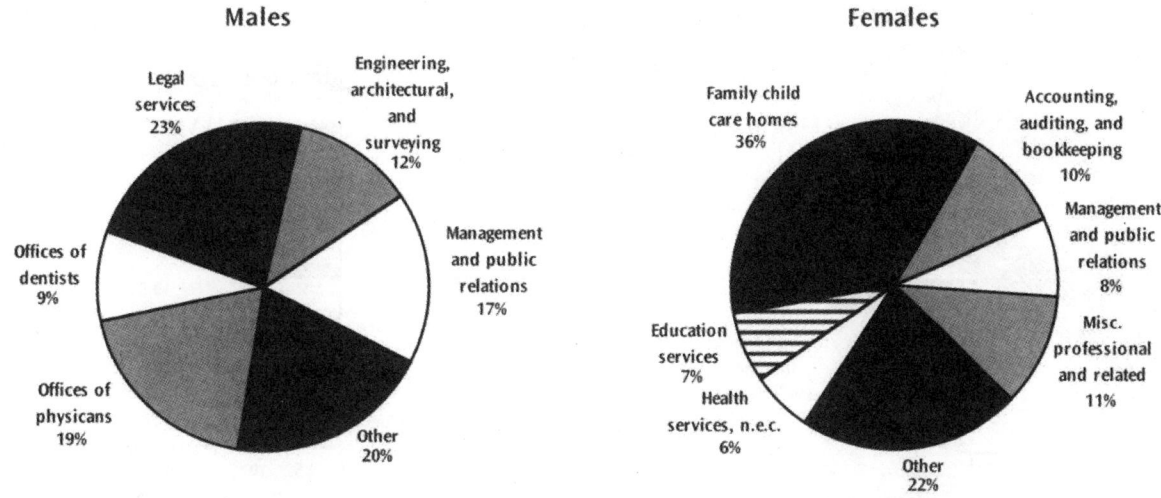

Figure 6

Detailed Shares of the Self-Employed in Professional and Related Services, 1997

degrees had the lowest self-employment rates. Here, the major difference between men and women is that women with professional degrees were only about one third as likely to be self-employed as were men with the same education level.

AGE AND THE SELF-EMPLOYED

The self-employed have a clear age profile, although there is very little difference between the age profile of self-employed women and that of self-employed men. As shown by Figure 9, during 1997, roughly equal numbers of the self-employed were either 35 to 44 years old or 45 to 54 years old, and these two age groups accounted for 58 percent of the self-employed. In contrast, there were relatively few of the self-employed who were between 25 and 34 years old, despite being almost as numerous in the workforce as 35- to 44-year-olds. To put this in perspective: About twice as many 35- to 44-year-olds were self-employed, even though there were only 13 percent more 35- to 44-year-olds in the work force. Even more telling is that there were more self-employed people between the ages of 55 and 64 than there were between the ages 25 and 34, even though 61 percent fewer of the older group are employed in any capacity.

A different perspective on the same phenomenon is provided by Figure 10, which reports the self-employment rates for men and women in the various age groups during 1997. The obvious pattern is that, for those who are employed, the tendency to be self-employed rises with age. The usual explanation for this is that success in self-employment is more dependent on experience than is success in paid employment. Because of this, older workers are more likely than younger workers to choose self-employment over paid

employment. This is likely to be a good explanation of the pattern at the low end of the age distribution. However, a tendency for the self-employed to retire later in life than those in paid employment would go a long way in explaining the positive link between age and self-employment rates among older workers.

For whatever reason self-employment rates rise with age, this effect was not as strong for women as it was for men. For the youngest three age groups, an employed man was between 60 to 70 percent more likely to be self-employed than was an employed woman. In contrast, for the oldest three age groups, an employed man was between 90 to 120 percent more likely than an employed woman to be self-employed.

CONCLUDING REMARKS

For researchers, this snapshot of U.S. self-employment reveals that there are many factors to keep in mind when studying the determinants of self-employment. These include differences in self-employment according to characteristics such as sex, race, region, age, and education. They also include differences in the occupations and industries in which self-employed men and women tend to be found. Because of these many differences, questions arise about whether policies designed to spur self-employment have different effects on the various categories: Are they more appropriate for occupations in which men or whites tend to be self-employed? Do they tend to favor certain types of self-employed people, such as those with professional degrees? Are they useful for home-based or part-time self-employment, which may be more amenable to women's career strategies because they decrease the costs

11

Figure 7

Shares of the Self-Employed by Education, 1997
Males and Females Combined

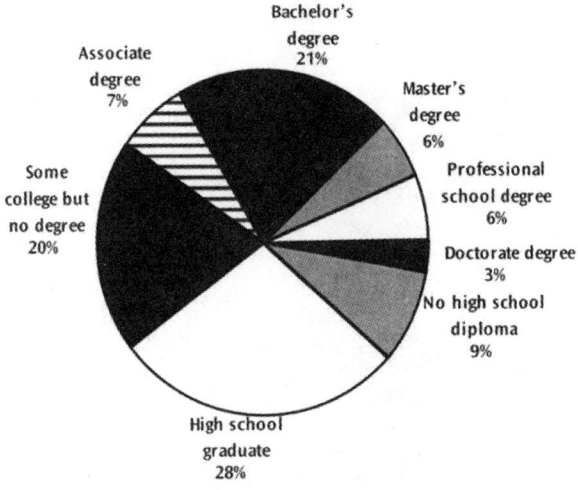

Figure 8

Male and Female Self-Employment Rates by Education, 1997

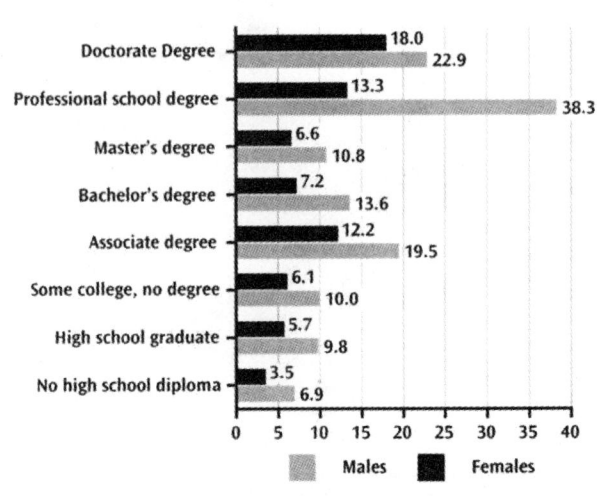

of childcare? Are they more useful for some states because of the states' industrial composition?

We do not attempt to answer these questions here, but they certainly indicate that there is much more to self-employment than has been addressed in previous studies which tend to ignore many of the differences outlined here.

NOTES

1. Holtz-Eakin, Rosen, and Weathers (2000) find evidence that self-employment can move low-income individuals ahead of those who pursue paid employment.
2. See Vroman (1997) for a description.
3. It also has an extensive literature review and reference list.

4. Devine (1994b) finds that for the period 1975–87, the rise in female self-employment was driven by an increasing tendency for high-skilled women to choose self-employment over paid employment.
5. The six non-agricultural job classes are private household, other private, government, self-employed, unpaid, and never worked.
6. This is out of 12 two-digit non-agricultural occupational classifications.
7. This includes Macpherson (1988), Connelly (1992), and Devine (1994b).

REFERENCES

Blanchflower, David G. "Self-Employment in OECD Countries," National Bureau of Economic Research Working Paper 7486, January 2000.

Figure 9

Shares of the Self-Employed by Age, 1997
Males and Females Combined

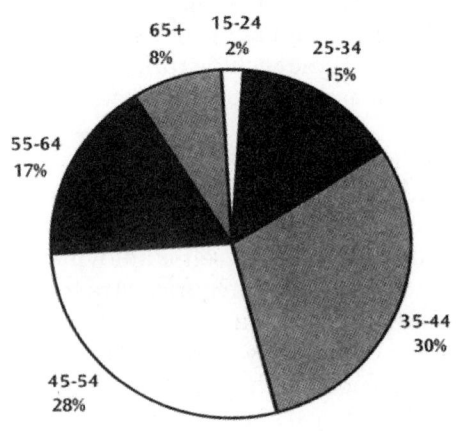

Figure 10

Male and Female Self-Employment Rates by Age, 1997

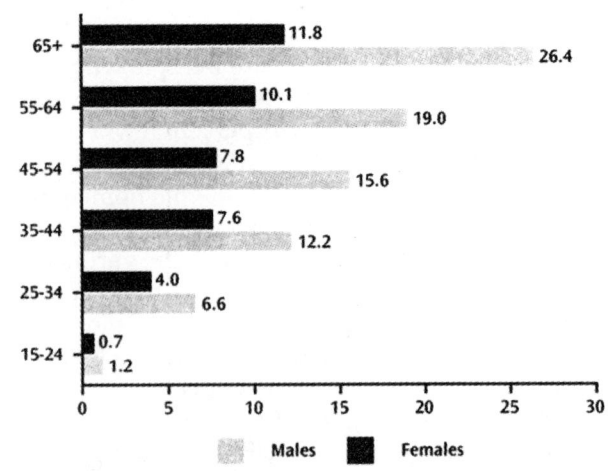

Bregger, John E. "Measuring Self-Employment in the United States," *Monthly Labor Review* (January/February 1996), pp. 3–9.

Connelly, Rachel. "Self-Employment and Providing Child Care," *Demography* (February 1992), pp. 17–29.

Devine, Theresa J. "Characteristics of Self-Employed Women in the United States," *Monthly Labor Review* (March 1994a), pp. 20–34.

____. "Changes in Wage-and-Salary Returns to Skill and the Recent Rise in Female Self-Employment," *American Economic Review* (May 1994b), pp. 108–13.

Georgellis, Yannis and Howard J. Wall. "What Makes a Region Entrepreneurial? Evidence from Britain," *Annals of Regional Science* (2000), pp. 385–403.

____ and ____. "Gender Differences in Self-Employment: Panel Evidence from the Former West Germany," Federal Reserve Bank of St. Louis Working Paper 99-008B, January 1999.

Holtz-Eakin, Douglas, Harvey S. Rosen, and Robert Weathers. "Horatio Alger Meets the Mobility Tables," National Bureau of Economic Research Working Paper 7619, March 2000.

Manser, Marilyn E. and Garnett Picot. "The Role of Self-Employment in U.S. and Canadian Job Growth," *Monthly Labor Review* (April 1999), pp. 10–25.

Macpherson, David A. "Self-Employment and Married Women," *Economics Letters* (1988), pp. 281–4.

Vroman, Wayne. "Self-Employment Assistance: Revised Report," The Urban Institute, December 1997.

Yannis Georgellis is a lecturer in the Department of Economics and Finance at Brunel University, United Kingdom. Howard J. Wall is a senior economist at the Federal Reserve Bank of St. Louis. Ling Wang provided research assistance.

How a Start-up Evolves

Businesses grow from start-up to conglomerate in three distinct phases, each of which is driven by a different type of person. The differences and conflicts between these waves of activity help explain why so many small companies self-destruct as they grow, and why so many large companies are so bad at doing anything new.

By Rob Landley

Chapter 12 of Robert X. Cringely's *Accidental Empires* gives an excellent analogy between the growth of a company and a military operation. He talks about three waves of expansion, each with its own characteristics and each one driven by people with very different sets of skills.

The first wave to hit the beach when entering new territory consists of commandos. These are people who, in Cringely's words, "Work hard, fast, and cheap.... Their job is to do lots of damage with surprise and teamwork, establishing a beachhead before the enemy is even aware that they exist." Simply put, they create something out of nothing, turning an idea into a product. A commando can literally do the work of a hundred normal employees when they've got the right problems to work on. A start-up without commandos has nothing to sell.

The second wave consists of infantry, exploiting the opportunity created by the commandos. These are the people who turn a promising start-up into a profitable business with systematic development, manufacturing, and sales efforts. They provide structure to the company that allows it to grow beyond an activity shared by a half-dozen friends into a real business. As Cringely says, "While the commandos make success possible, it's the infantry that makes success happen."

The third wave consists of police. Once the business has grown into its market niche, the third wave is an occupying force intent on holding territory. Author Eric Raymond describes middle managers as "conservators of the stability of the organization," which makes the presence of middle management a clear indicator that the third wave has arrived. A middle manager's job is to say no to ideas that don't originate from on high, somewhere near

the CEO. This prevents the enormous size of the company from tearing it apart. A mature third-wave corporation is full of bureaucrats defending the empire, approximately as interested in reducing expenses as growing sales. Third-wave gains come from economies of scale, incremental growth, and by simply remaining profitable quarter after quarter.

Yahoo!'s commandos were its founders, Jerry Yang and David Filo. Venture capital funded Yahoo!'s transition to a second-wave company with hundreds of employees, struggling toward profitability. It's still a second-wave company.

Earlier this year, VA Linux Systems bought Andover.net, primarily because Andover owned some interesting websites, including one it had bought only months earlier: Slashdot.org. Slashdot was also founded by two college students, Rob Malda and Jeff Bates. When Andover acquired Slashdot, Rob and Jeff handed off the administrative portion of their duties in order to concentrate on their creative work. They were amused that the jobs they used to do as a part-time sideline were now handled by more than a dozen full-time staff members at Andover. This is the normal productivity difference between commandos and infantry. The difference is you can hire more infantry fairly easily, and order the ones you have to do specific tasks. Commandos just don't work that way.

Although infantry and commandos can work together, there is some natural tension between the two groups. The founders of many companies leave after the IPO, commandos looking for fresh challenges rather than settling down to nurture old ideas. On the other hand, infantry can take much of the non-creative load off of commandos, giving them a protected environment in which to work free from distractions.

The third wave is fairly exclusive. Agents of change and facilitators of change don't mix with opponents of change. The only place second-wave people can survive in a third-wave company is at the executive level. The only way dynamic individuals can survive middle management is by outranking it. The problem here is that the company cannot promote from within easily. Middle management stifles visionaries, who leave the company or give up their creative ambitions. The company must hire executive talent from outside the company, or wind up as a paralyzed, reactionary zombie. This fate nearly befell AT&T, IBM, and many other large companies that gave middle managers executive power to suppress ALL change within the company.

Commandos categorically cannot STAND middle management. A third-wave company cannot keep commandos around. Period. Commandos create change, middle managers prevent change. When "the suits" take over, the commandos are outta there. The bureaucrats often don't value commandos during the brief times they have access to them (often in the brief period of time between buying a promising start-up and killing it). The commando's idiosyncratic nature, even outright unreliability, may be a minor price to pay to receive the benefits of their brilliance, but the unpredictability is all the bureaucrats can see, and it gives them hives.

Usually, commandos leave long before the third wave. When the second wave becomes too prominent, and building upon existing successes becomes more important to the company than creative new directions, the commandos simply get bored, take their stock options, and leave. This isn't a "lack of discipline" (a strange accusation to level at people who work 90 hours a week), this is just the way creative people ARE. Steve Wozniak of Apple, and Steve Jobs when he couldn't be CEO of a second-wave company. Mitch Kapor at Lotus. Netscape's Jamie Zawinski. The list is endless.

An interesting business model Robert Cringely recently covered in his PBS column is a private company founded by a couple of commandos with the intent of spinning off a continuous stream of new second-wave companies, each with its own IPO. The commandos come up with the new products, assemble a team of infantry around each one, and then release it into the wild. Meanwhile, the commandos are busy creating the next new product. You can read about it here.

Healthy companies need to mix the various waves. As they grow, they need to survive the transition from first wave to second wave, and later from second wave to third wave. At all costs, they need to isolate any commandos they need to have on staff from middle management. The case of the launch of IBM's PC is an instructive example of how a third-wave company can do this. (This is covered both in *Accidental Empires* and *The Innovator's Dilemma*—both perspectives are valuable.)

As investors, we tend to focus on second- and third-wave companies. First-wave companies aren't publicly traded, and most start-ups fail because their commandos can't handle the details of running and growing a business yet don't hand it off to competent infantry. Second-wave companies are Rule Breakers, most lucrative early in the second wave with plenty of room left to grow along their current lines. Third-wave companies with second-wave upper management are Rule Makers, stable and profitable with the potential for steady growth. Third-wave companies with third-wave executives are probably not a good investment.

RISK TAKERS

What It Takes
To Start A Startup

Entrepreneurs with the right stuff don't think much about taking risks or getting rich. Instead, they are obsessed with building a better mousetrap.

BY BRIAN O'REILLY

GETTING THE ENTREPRENEURIAL BUG, ARE YOU? TIRED OF reading about all these pubescent little CEOs who did nothing more clever than sell books or airline tickets over the Internet and made a billion? Meanwhile, you, despite 15 years at that same desk job, have been nursing this fabulous idea that could make you the richest and most powerful person in the entire brake-shoe industry.... Whoops. Better not tip your hand, or someone will steal the idea. But it's big. Big, big, big.

There's just one problem: Every time you think about pursuing that dream, your palms sweat. No steady paycheck! No dental plan! No time for golf! And those hungry venture capitalists expect you to take a second mortgage to help fund this scheme. If it bombs, you and Martha will spend your golden years in a trailer park, caddying at the country club. How, you wonder, do these entrepreneurs summon the brass ones to risk everything—income, lifestyle, self-esteem—on one crazy idea that probably won't work anyway? Are they thrill-seeking lunatics?

Better hunker down at that day job, bub. Entrepreneurially speaking, you ain't going nowhere.

Despite their image, entrepreneurs are not the Evel Knievels of the business world. Nor do they think much about risk, sweaty palms, wealth, power, or failure. All of that may come eventually, but words like "risk" and "failure"—even "power" and "money"—don't preoccupy the nascent Michael Dells or Larry Ellisons beavering away in the garage next door. If you are terrified at the prospect of becoming an entrepreneur, or are

busy dreaming of the money and power that success will bring, you're probably not cut out for this line of work.

People who spend time around the types eager to start the World's Next Great Company describe a very different person. Unlike Mr. Brake Shoe, he or she is wildly enthusiastic about the idea and utterly convinced of its success. Failure? Yeah, it's a theoretical possibility. But the consequences are insignificant compared to this great, great idea that will change the entire industry and maybe the world, and change how people live and create great value and a great company and... (breathless enthusiasm usually continues for several minutes).

MERRITT SHER, a retailing wizard, says of would-be entrepreneurs: "If you don't have an inspired idea, all you will see is the risk."

One reason entrepreneurs—the ones most likely to make it, at least—behave like men and women possessed is that they have experienced a flash of understanding known as "entrepreneurial insight," says professor Ian C. MacMillan, a guru of entrepreneurship at the Wharton School who has counseled innumerable startup wannabes. They have seen, in their mind's eye, the better mousetrap, the great unmet need, the changing tide, the big opportunity. Because they see it so clearly, they feel they know exactly what must be done to prevail. Entrepreneurial insight enabled Ken Olsen to grasp a way to make computers far more cheaply than IBM; he started Digital Equipment Corp. It helped retailing whiz Merritt Sher of San Francisco see that small specialty stores, often obscured by giant department stores at suburban shopping centers, would flourish in new, smaller "strip malls." And it has actor Robert De Niro convinced he can turn the Brooklyn Navy Yard into a successful East Coast movie studio. "I could be wrong a little bit here and there," De Niro told reporters recently. "But you cannot fail at this."

IRWIN JACOBS, one of the first hostile-takeover artists, says experience in the junk and salvage business gave him insight into the hidden value of ailing companies.

For some, entrepreneurial insight isn't a one-time flash but instead a unique way of viewing and valuing opportunities. Minnesota's Irwin Jacobs was practically the father of the hostile takeovers that began in the 1980s. What did he see in ailing companies that others didn't? He had been in the salvage business when he was young, and had learned to spot assets that could be spun off and sold. "My whole life I've been a junk man," he says. "That's how I look at things."

Some people call that insight "vision," but that's a spooky word, conjuring up people who think Jesus came to them in a dream and told them to make glow-in-the-dark sunglasses. To Merritt Sher it's pretty simple. "You suddenly understand how everything fits together. And then you want to demonstrate that you have the understanding." (People who've had that kind of epiphany generally don't need to attend "leadership" seminars; they know where they want to go and how to get there, and people instinctively rally behind them. It's the clueless CEO who needs leadership injections.)

If you don't have that insight—and the enthusiasm that comes with it—you won't get far. Venture capitalists look and sniff for it. Arthur Pappas, a former top executive at Glaxo who started a biotech venture capital firm near Research Triangle Park, N.C., a few years ago, says he leaves many of the early technical and financial details of business proposals to others on his staff. "I prefer to focus first on the character and commitment of the people on the management team," he says. "The people with vision or insight—they see something and are driven to its endpoint. You can hear it in their voices."

Pappas says he won't touch proposals from scientists who plan to keep their job at the local college and work on the startup part-time. That's because successful entrepreneurs need maximum enthusiasm and commitment. Explains Joel Hyatt, who started a chain of innovative legal clinics in the 1980s and now teaches entrepreneurship at Stanford: "It will take longer and require more money than you thought, and there will be problems you could not have anticipated." Some people think entrepreneurs are lunatics because of the way they spend years struggling to make an idea work. But Hyatt says the critics don't appreciate the optimism that drives the dreamers: "Bill McGowan [the founder of MCI] spent ten years working to end AT&T's monopoly of long-distance service. People would say to him, 'Ten years! How could you do that?' He would respond, 'Do you mean you think it was stupid? I never thought it would take that long. I thought I could do it tomorrow!'"

Falling in love with your idea is necessary, but not sufficient to make you an entrepreneur. Several years ago an MIT professor named Edward Roberts began studying MIT graduates who had gone on to start technology-related businesses. He found that 70% of the starter-uppers had parents who were entrepreneurs and that nearly all possessed a powerful drive for accomplishment.

It may seem obvious that people who accomplish things have a drive for accomplishment, but it's not that straightforward. In the 1930s, Harvard psychologist David McClelland described three needs (okay, besides sex, shelter, and chocolate) that drove human behavior: power, accomplishment, and affiliation. Power seekers want to make decisions others have to obey. Affiliators crave companionship. Achievers are intent on accomplishing something. The achievers don't seek "some intangible conceptual objective," says Roberts. "They're not devising brilliant ideas that only other brilliant people like themselves recognize. They want to create something significant and tangible—a building, a bridge, a company."

It's not clear whether the achievement urge is hard-wired before birth, but it seems to emerge early. McClelland played games with kindergarten children, having them toss rings onto an upright post. It is difficult, and most kids wound up standing over the post, dropping the rings straight down. Another group, content to rely on luck, flung the rings from across the room. A handful of children stood a foot away from the post, tossed until they made it, then stepped back to try again, and so forth. These kids turned out to be the achievers, eager to test themselves to see what they could accomplish. Says Roberts: "Achievers don't want to do something if it isn't a challenge, and they aren't interested in winning through luck, like the children who threw the ring from far away."

In his study of entrepreneurs, Roberts also looked at MIT graduates who had joined large companies, then left to start businesses. His findings puzzled him at first. When he tested for the achievement drive, the alums in startups didn't score much differently from grads who had remained in big corporations. "But when we looked further," says Roberts, "we found that successful entrepreneurs had a very high need for accomplishment. There was a big difference between those who just set up companies and those who made it big."

His research suggests that you don't need inkblots to determine which people in a large organization are most likely to go out on their own. Even before they quit Colossal Corp., says Roberts, the would-be entrepreneurs were "outperforming the people who stayed behind, in terms of the number of papers they published, number of patents they received, and ratings by former supervisors." The hyperachievers look around at their colleagues and decide they can succeed on their own. Explains Roberts: "They say to themselves, 'I'm pretty hot. I can do this.' "

Too much confidence, however, can be a problem. It's called arrogance, and it often trips up aspiring Edisons, especially hyperbright hyperachievers. The word "arrogance" came up repeatedly as venture capitalists, academics, and others ruminated on why so many promising people bomb as leaders of a startup. It may even answer that age-old question: "If you're so smart, why aren't you rich?"

RICHARD BRANSON,
believes the kicks he gets from ballooning and starting a new business are similar. It's about testing yourself, he says. "You're willing to go where most people won't dare."

A good entrepreneur is driven not by arrogance but by its close relative: a big ego. What's the difference? Mark Fraga, managing director of an entrepreneur development program at the Wharton School, explains: "The person with the big ego is committed to the venture and will do whatever it takes to succeed. His attitude is, 'I'm here, world. I'm going to turn air into gold. I'm going to make the impossible mundane.' The arrogant person is devoted to himself. He thinks he has all the answers, accepts no advice, and blames others for his failure." Pappas, the venture capitalist, looks for signs that the guy planning a startup can identify his own shortcomings. "It's evident in the team he wants to put together. A brilliant scientist will recognize that he needs a marketer or a financial manager." Hyatt at Stanford says he knows people with great ideas who say, "I need someone smarter than I am."

Nearly every entrepreneur is comfortable with—if not eager for—risky, unfamiliar situations. Jack Miller, who leads the U.S. Army's program to select candidates for high command, says the Army operates a crude but effective filter to weed out people who can't tolerate risk: It moves them to new locations every few years. Those who can't adjust to novel situations eventually leave, and, says Miller, "you are left with a reasonably flexible officer corps."

People who regard uncertainty as an adventure are far more likely to become entrepreneurs than those who see it as a threat to an orderly way of life. Richard Branson, the British billionaire, started Virgin Records and Virgin Atlantic Airlines. But he probably has gotten more attention for his efforts to circle the world in a hot-air balloon. He figures it's no coincidence that he likes risky balloon ventures and risky business ventures. "Being an adventurer and an entrepreneur are similar," he says. "You're willing to go where most people won't dare." When he decided to start the airline, his advisers called him crazy. "You know the joke," he says. "The easiest way to become a millionaire is to start with a billion and go into the airline business." He did it anyway. "It's not about making $2 billion or $3 billion. It's about not wasting one's life."

Some entrepreneurs are so comfortable with risk that they take deliberate steps to make their employees more daring. Joe Liemandt, who quit Stanford to form Trilogy Software in Austin, Texas, flies trainees to Las Vegas, where he encourages them to bet thousands of dollars (of their own money) on one spin of the roulette wheel. Too many successful companies become overcautious and risk-averse, explains Liemandt, and their growth rate slows. He believes that debating whether to bet money at roulette helps employees understand their attitude toward risk.

Paradoxically, entrepreneurs with the greatest appetite for risk also have a healthy respect for it. "In everything I do, I examine the downside, the danger, what can go wrong," says Branson. He bought just one plane when he started his airline: "And I had an agreement with Boeing to take it back if things didn't work out." Liemandt, for all his love of risk, makes employees who fail at one undertaking do something less risky for a while. "You don't want people placing a bigger second bet to make up for losses on the first one. That's very dangerous behavior." Shrewd entrepreneurs, says MacMillan, try to lay risk off on others while preserving as much upside potential as they can. It's not a taste for risk or money that motivates entrepreneurs, he insists. His advice: "Never buy what you can lease. Never lease what you can rent. Never rent what you can borrow. Never borrow what you can steal. The risk-seeking entrepreneur is a mythical beast."

Yeah, maybe. But I am still in awe of them. Years ago I came up with a device to help my nearly blind grandfather read. It was an ordinary videocamera mounted on a Plexiglas frame with wheels, with the lens set to close-up view. Words in the newspaper appeared an inch tall on the TV screen, and my grandfather was delighted. "Wow, a golden opportunity," I told myself. "Millions of old people would buy this." I fantasized about it for years and even researched miniature videocameras. But I never got the nerve to hock the house and start a factory. Eventually my cousin found a tiny version of my TV doodad, made by some company out west, and bought it for my grandfather. "Damn," I said to myself, "I was gonna do that." But I didn't.

REPORTER ASSOCIATE *Natasha A. Tarpley*

Reprinted from the June 7, 1999, issue of *Fortune*, pp. 135-140, by special permission. © 1999 by Time, Inc.

Top Ten Entrepreneurs

WE PRESENT OUR ANNUAL SELECTION OF TECHNOLOGY'S MOST INNOVATIVE ENTREPRENEURS.

Bill Nguyen, Seven Networks

SEEING MAGIC IN ONES AND SEVENS Bill Nguyen, founder, president, and chairman of wireless startup Seven Networks, proudly admits that he is "viciously focused on the numbers." He is not, however, referring to his company's enigmatic name, but rather to its bottom line. And numbers are an important reason for selecting Mr. Nguyen as our lead entrepreneur for 2001: in February of 1999, Mr. Nguyen sold his previous startup, Onebox.com, an Internet messaging provider, to Openwave Systems, a communications software company, for a cool $850 million. Exactly one month later, he left Openwave to begin work on Seven, a wireless software company that has already garnered $34 million in venture capital from Ignition and Greylock, retained British Telecommunications as a customer, and expects to be profitable by year-end. Mr. Nguyen sleeps three hours a night. He is 30 years old.

Mr. Nguyen has been a part of no fewer than six technology startups over the course of his young career, which goes a long way in explaining why he didn't have time to finish his undergraduate degree at Houston Baptist University. Speaking faster than most people think, Mr. Nguyen is at once self-effacing and eternally optimistic. He declines the label of serial entrepreneur and instead refers to himself as "serially lucky." However, luck had little to do with his ability to raise funding during a tight VC market.

"He's a rocket; you just strap in and try to hold on," says Brad Silverberg, CEO and partner at Ignition. Mr. Silverberg says that when Mr. Nguyen presented his idea for a software platform for wireless carriers that could provide companies with mobile access to their corporate data, Ignition told him, "Bill, we love you, but it's not going to work." Mr. Nguyen took the defeat in stride and went home to work on the idea's technical hurdles for three days straight, with no sleep. When he showed up at Ignition's offices with the new plan, he had not only solved the problems, but he had proved his mettle.

Seven's software makes it possible for wireless carriers to offer wireless data access directly to businesses, eliminating the need for expensive, custom-built software. However, building the highly reliable software demanded by carriers is no easy task. If Mr. Nguyen is successful, his company promises to help wireless carriers realize greater returns from their expensive new networks—something they are eager to do.

Mr. Nguyen's serial luck should take him far—it's in the numbers. Since its inception, Seven has burned through 30 to 40 percent less than it had budgeted, and is expecting revenue in the double-digit millions by year-end. Based in Redwood City, California, the company now employs 65 people and, unlike most of its Silicon Valley brethren, is now hiring.

—Dan Briody

Chris Stone, Tilion

SHEDDING LIGHT INTO DARKNESS The name of Chris Stone's company honors a character from J.R.R. Tolkien's *The Silmarillion*—Tilion, the steersman of the moon, who brought light to darkness. The 44-year-old Mr. Stone grandly seeks no less, though in the more pragmatic world of supply-chain event management.

He earned a computer-science degree and an executive MBA, worked his way up at Data General to become director of software products, then founded the Object Management Group to help create CORBA and other software standards. He next reinvented himself as second-in-command at Novell, a job that offered valuable experience with directories and a disconcerting view of how things can go wrong. When Novell took a $265 million hit in one quarter of 1997 because the company couldn't keep track of its inventory, Mr. Stone perceived a yawning gap. "We had no visibility into what our distributors were doing. It was a missing piece. So the lightbulb went off: I could solve this."

Tilion, founded in January 2000, is an Internet-based service that offers companies up-to-date supply-chain performance information. The company's software captures data from all supply-chain transactions, translates and encrypts it in Extensible Markup Language, then generates custom reports that users can access over the Internet. With real-time monitoring, companies can detect and correct inventory bottlenecks quickly and respond to changes in demand as they occur. "It's like switching from a typewriter to a word processor, where all of a sudden you can just delete the wrong word and put in the right one," Mr. Stone says.

Tilion has 89 employees; $46.5 million in venture funding from North Bridge Venture Partners, Venrock Associates, Lucent Ventures, and others; and four customers. This speaks to Mr. Stone's motivation: "I like watching a customer's eyes light up as he says, 'You can do that?!?'"

—*Thomas Maeder*

Klaus Wiemer, Communicant Semiconductor Technologies

AN INSURANCE POLICY FOR A NEW CLASS OF CHIP Klaus Wiemer doesn't mess around. He is raising $1.5 billion to fund his next startup, Communicant Semiconductor Technologies.

Mr. Wiemer is building a contract manufacturing chip factory—a foundry—in the former East Germany, capitalizing on big subsidies from the German government and the European Union to cover half the startup costs. He's raising the remaining $740 million from banks and strategic investors like Intel, and expects to begin minting chips in early 2003.

Mr. Wiemer has worked in chips for nearly three decades, running operations at Taiwan Semiconductor Manufacturing Company, as well as at Chartered Semiconductor Manufacturing in Singapore. He tried to start another foundry in Malaysia a few years ago, which failed when the Asian financial crisis struck.

'Our plan is to be a differentiated foundry. We decided it would be suicide to take the other players head on.'

Communicant will specialize in silicon germanium (SiGe) chips, which are ideal for communications applications like wireless phones and high-speed networking equipment.

The company will face tough competition from IBM, the leading SiGe chip maker. But Mr. Wiemer is betting that demand will be so strong that IBM won't be able to handle it all. Other chip makers are also expected to make their own SiGe chips, but, just as in other businesses, there are benefits in outsourcing.

"Our plan is to be a differentiated foundry," says Mr. Wiemer. "We decided it would be suicide to take the other players head on. We're like their insurance policy in case something goes wrong in their own factories."

—*Dean Takahashi*

Josh Coates, Scale Eight

LATTER-DAY SAINT OF STORAGE Scale Eight, a distributed storage startup, isn't Josh Coates's first company. He pirated games software in junior high and ran a T-shirt business in high school. And the 27-year-old's ambitions haven't waned since. As a software engineer at Inktomi, he saw that existing storage systems were expensive and poorly organized. He told himself, "I can totally build a storage system that will kick butt for way cheap, and it would be totally cool."

With data centers worldwide, Scale Eight stores rich-media files for the likes of Microsoft, MTVi, and Akamai, which can access and update files over the Internet, even while they are in use. The two-year-old company has raised more than $31.5 million and was a *Red Herring* 100 company for 2001.

A former missionary for the Church of Jesus Christ of Latter-day Saints, Mr. Coates vows Scale Eight won't be his last company. "I've got too many things cranking away in my mind."

—*Jennifer Lewis*

Peter Molyneux, Lionhead Studios

HELPING OTHERS PLAY GOD Peter Molyneux is a 41-year-old game developer with eight No. 1 titles to his name. He says he is "absolutely addicted to game design; it's like a drug." If it is, then two-year-old Lionhead Studios, his game development company in Guildford, England, is his never-ending source of pleasure.

Mr. Molyneux's first game company, Bullfrog Productions, was a runaway success. In 1987, it created Populous, which sold 4 million units. Other hits followed and in 1994, Bullfrog's sales were just under $20 million. The next year, Mr. Molyneux sold Bullfrog to Electronic Arts for an undisclosed sum of stock.

Two years later Mr. Molyneux cofounded Lionhead. The studio creates games and then partners with publishers for their marketing and distribution. Bankrolled with Mr. Molyneux's own riches, Lionhead's team of only 25 employees devoted the past three years to its latest title, Black & White, in which players assume the role of a god and battle other gods. "It's the best thing I've done in my life," Mr. Molyneux says of the game. Needless to say, when Black & White was released in April, it was an instant best-seller.

—Dean Takahashi

Teresa Meng, Atheros Communications

THE ACADEMIC ENTREPRENEUR Teresa Meng, professor of electrical engineering at Stanford University, never dreamed of starting her own company. But her academic career took an unexpected turn in 1998, when she discovered a technology that could make wireless networking cheap and powerful enough for use in businesses and homes.

But when she and John Hennessy (then dean of Stanford's School of Engineering) approached companies to develop this "radio on a chip," they found no takers. Thus, out of "half frustration, half ambition," Ms. Meng jokes, her entrepreneurial career began. She and Mr. Hennessy, now Atheros's chairman, assembled a team and raised $98.3 million from backers including Fidelity Management & Research, Bowman Capital, and August Capital.

Ms. Meng's career took an unexpected turn when she discovered a technology that could make wireless networking cheap and powerful.

Atheros is targeting a third-quarter release of its first chip set, with an eye on profitability by year-end 2002. Meanwhile, in addition to her Atheros duties, Ms. Meng is once again teaching a full course load. "I have students I need to take care of," she says, ever the dedicated academic.

—Julia Lawlor

Ray Ozzie, Groove Networks

CHANGING THE WAY WE GET THINGS DONE Ray Ozzie's latest venture, Groove Networks, hopes to improve upon his first creation, Lotus Notes. Groove combines the collaboration of

Notes with the communication of instant messaging to create a platform that will, for example, allow pharmaceutical maker GlaxoSmithKline's scientists to share information securely with outside researchers in real time.

The 45-year-old entrepreneur is betting that Groove's peer-to-peer collaboration platform, which bypasses a central server, is the next networking "killer app." Mr. Ozzie founded Groove in October 1997, bootstrapping it at first. Since then Groove has raised $63 million from Accel Partners, Intel Capital, and angels.

The always-modest Mr. Ozzie says his recipe for entrepreneurial success is simple: "Don't do the same thing everybody else is doing." Though it may be a while before Groove goes mainstream—version 1.0 shipped in April—he hopes it will create useful collaboration among people, technology, and organizations, improving the way we get things done.

—Michael Fitzgerald

Jagdeep Singh, Zepton Networks

NETWORKING MADE SIMPLE Jagdeep Singh is a prototypical networking entrepreneur—brilliant, shrewd, and very secretive. Two of his first three companies were network equipment makers. His fourth, Zepton Networks, is another one. "Equipment is a very straightforward business model; the only problem is technical execution," Mr. Singh says.

Cagey as ever, Mr. Singh says only that the six-month-old Zepton is an optical equipment maker based in Cupertino, California, that has a chance to eliminate the need for a so-called all-optical network. The company raised $37 million in first-round funding from Kleiner Perkins Caufield & Byers, Accel Partners, and Benchmark Capital.

What makes Mr. Singh so special is his track record. He entered the University of Maryland at 15 and joined Hewlett-Packard upon graduation. After stints at Sun Microsystems and as a VC, he got a master's in engineering from Stanford University, where he caught the entrepreneurial bug.

He sold his first two networking companies, AirSoft and Lightera Networks, for a total of $625 million. His third company is one-year-old OnFiber Communications, a metropolitan area networking services provider.

Earlier this year, Mr. Singh hired a new CEO for OnFiber, to allow himself time to pursue what he does best—invent hardware. To help him with this, Mr. Singh has tapped Drew Perkins, former chief technology officer of Lightera; David Welch, former chief technology officer of SDL; and Fred Kish, former research, development, and manufacturing manager at Agilent Technologies, to join him. Given his past success, it seems likely he is onto something big—again.

—Om Malik

Vani Kola, Nth Orbit

TAKING ENTERPRISE SOFTWARE TO NEW HEIGHTS For Vani Kola, building supply-chain startup Nth Orbit is very much like her climb to the summit of Mount Kilimanjaro this summer: a lot of fun, but also pretty damn serious. She trained to scale that famous mountain during a five-month "retirement" from her first startup, a B2B software company called RightWorks. Ms. Kola sold a majority stake in the four-year-old company in March 2000 to Internet Capital Group at a valuation of $1.25 billion. Although Ms. Kola enjoyed being with her husband and two daughters and devoting time to mountain climbing, she grew restless as she began to think about streamlining manufacturing supply chains. "I didn't really plan on coming back; it just happened," Ms. Kola says of entrepreneurship. "It sucks your soul into it and takes everything you've got."

In March 2001, she founded Nth Orbit, a supply-chain collaboration software company in San Jose, California. The company raised $7 million in venture funding from Sequoia Capital and individual investors—all of whom were early backers of RightWorks. The company is developing software to help business partners exchange orders for supplies and finished products in real time. Several of the company's 14 employees are Ms. Kola's former RightWorks colleagues.

While some entrepreneurs might be daunted by the complexities of creating supply-chain software that is always up-to-date, Ms. Kola is drawn to them. The 37-year-old native of Hyderabad, India, has spent most of her career developing enterprise software for manufacturers. Improving companies' supply chains is a ripe opportunity, she says. "This is where the most creativity comes out, because there are no answers, just chaos,"

says Ms. Kola. If successful, Nth Orbit will bring order to the manufacturing universe.

—*Julie Landry*

Bala Manian, Quantum Dot

PROOF THAT NO MAN CAN LIVE ON MOLECULES ALONE To get a sense of Bala Manian's genius and modesty, consider that the same person who developed the bar code, won an Academy Award for developing special effects for the Indiana Jones and Star Wars films, and holds some 30 nanotechnology patents also once had business cards that read: "I'm just an Indian, I'm no chief." Yeah, right.

Dr. Manian has hatched seven companies in fields ranging from biometrics to medical imaging, including Entigen, Lumisys, and Molecular Dynamics. Those that have been acquired have fetched prices ranging from $7 million to $250 million. His most recent creation is the nanotech-based genomics firm Quantum Dot, a 2001 *Red Herring* Ten to Watch selection that specializes in fluorescent tools used in drug discovery. Dr. Manian serves on the top-secret NASA-National Cancer Institute Mars Project, which sees nanotech as the key to getting astronauts to Mars and back in 2020.

—*Stephan Herrera*

THE ANTIENTREPRENEUR

J. Jovan Philyaw, CueCat

DUMB AND DUMBER This year's antientrepreneur requires a great deal of qualifying. Despite his obvious entrepreneurial zeal and a small degree of success, J. Jovan Philyaw is nonetheless our nominee for the next spectacular flameout. Unfortunately, his reality overtook our prediction, but not our deadline. The company laid off 110 of its 250 employees in mid-June.

Mr. Philyaw is the charismatic Texas businessman responsible for creating the CueCat. For the uninitiated, the CueCat is a poorly named mouselike device equipped with an infrared scanner that was distributed to more than 1 million subscribers of

Wired and *Forbes* last September. Mr. Philyaw's hope was that consumers would connect the "cat" to their PCs and use it to scan special bar codes from magazine advertisements, which would then steer their Internet browsers to the advertisers' Web pages. This was supposed to be an incentive for companies to advertise in the magazines. But of the 800,000 devices distributed to *Forbes* subscribers, only 100,000 were registered. Still, the lack of adoption hasn't dampened Mr. Philyaw's enthusiasm to bridge disparate media for advertising purposes.

In May, CueCat introduced CueTV in conjunction with NBC. The idea:

TV commercials emit an audio signal that directs a consumer's PC (connected to the TV with a free cable and proprietary software) to access, once again, an advertiser's Web site.

Despite being dumb ideas, these endeavors have helped CueCat raise about $180 million in venture funding since 1998. Companies like NBC, Coca-Cola, Radio Shack, and Sumitomo Electric have all backed Mr. Philyaw's screwball ideas. Obviously he knows about selling a concept—even a bad one.

—*Scott Tyler Shafer*

Where are they now?

A look back at our top ten entrepreneurs of 2000.

1. **Edward Tian**, CEO of China Netcom, a telecommunications carrier specializing in broadband Internet technology.

China Netcom is now China's third-largest telecom, after China Telcom and China Unicom. In March, News Corporation, the Goldman Sachs Group, Bank of China, China Construction Bank, and a group of unidentified companies agreed to pay $325 million for a combined 12 percent stake in the company.

2. **Steve Kirsch**, CEO of Propel Software, an Internet software company.

In July 2000, Propel raised a $36 million second round from big-name investors, including Marc Andreessen, Colin Powell, and Meg Whitman, as well as MSD Capital, the private investment firm for Michael Dell. To date, the company has raised $45 million.

3. **Judy Estrin**, president and CEO, and **Bill Carrico**, chairman of Packet Design, a networking startup.

The serial entrepreneurs are at it again. In March, they launched Vernier Networks, a wireless-local area networking startup that will develop hardware and software for the 802.11 and Bluetooth standards.

4. **K.B. Chandrasekhar**, chairman and CEO of Jamcracker, a network services company.

Jamcracker has more than 100 customers and, in the past year, has raised a second round of $100 million from Pivotal Asset Management, The Rolling Thunder Network, Morgan Stanley, Goldman Sachs, Credit Suisse First Boston, Robertson Stephens, and others.

5. **Kevin Wendle**, CEO of iFilm, an online movie and short film portal.

IFilm survived Hollywood's Internet shakeout and has built the largest online film library, with more than 15,000 short and feature films. In February, iFilm raised $10 million from investors like Sony Pictures Digital Entertainment, Vulcan Ventures, and Yahoo.

6. **Simon Foster**, CEO of SimonDelivers.com, a home-delivery grocery startup.

With more than 38,000 customers in Minneapolis and St. Paul, Mr. Foster has perfected the art of grocery distribution and delivery. The online grocer plans to add 27 neighborhoods to its coverage area.

7. **Daniel Aegerter**, CEO of the Armada Venture Group, a venture capital firm that invests in early-stage startups.

Mr. Aegerter is managing his $75 million fund and sits on the advisory board of CoreHarbor, a business-to-business e-commerce service provider.

8. **Wu-Fu Chen**, CEO of OptiMight Communications, an optical networking startup.

Mr. Chen is pursuing his next venture. As a founding partner, he has helped raise $40 million for Acorn Campus, a communications and networking incubator based in Cupertino, California.

9. **Martin Cooper**, chairman and CEO of ArrayComm, a wireless services company.

A busy year. ArrayComm secured an FCC license for a technology trial of its portable, broadband data system; closed a $34 million funding round; acquired 5 MHz of wireless spectrum in Australia; and recruited Joseph Hagan, chief financial officer of Ericsson's North American operations, to join ArrayComm as chief financial officer.

10. **Mory Ejabat**, chairman and CEO, and **Jeanette Symons**, chief technology officer and vice president of engineering of Zhone Technologies, a telecommunications equipment company.

In its first six months, Zhone raised $500 million and hired 500 employees. Zhone now has offices in more than a dozen cities worldwide and has partnerships with Ericsson, Qwest Communications, Texas Instruments, and Hughes Electronics.

—Jennifer Lewis

The **Man** and **His Money**

Excerpt from *Money and Power* charts Bill Gates's position among the great moguls of history.

Howard Means

With the computer and an Internet navigation system, every home could be not just an entertainment center but a learning center, a trading center, and a communication hub, to boot. While profitable brick-and-mortar companies shrank in market value, often profitless dot.com companies soared to price/earnings ratios that could make the Dutch tulipmania of the seventeenth century seem almost sane, and yet the market roared on and on, a bull on a record run. The old rules seemed to have been broken. Wealth had dematerialized. Physical content meant almost nothing. Intellectual content meant almost everything. Information, it seemed, was everywhere. And the great trailing fortune that embodied the Information Age belonged to an $80-billion Seattle nerd named William Henry Gates III.

Like Henry Ford with his Model T, Bill Gates envisioned the mass appeal of the personal computer, but unlike Ford, he didn't want to build it. Gates's genius was never in hardware; instead, he provided the brains—the software and operating systems—that made the hardware hum. Like J. P. Morgan, Gates also saw himself as creating order out of disarray. MS-DOS and Windows weren't just operating systems and software products; they were meant to be industry standards because a standardized industry would benefit everyone—Bill Gates most particularly. Gates understood brand, too: The various iterations of his Windows software, all named by year, were introduced at press conferences that wrapped high-tech in the glitz of a Miss Universe pageant. Be there or be square, the press conferences seemed to be saying, but there was a subliminal message as

well: Don't get in my way. Gates, in fact, had the ruthlessness of a John D. Rockefeller when it came to cutting down and co-opting his competition, and just as the government had broken up Rockefeller's Standard Oil, so it sought to dismantle Gates's Microsoft Corporation.

One more way that Gates resembles so many of the moguls who came before him: He began the business that was to make him the world's richest man out of nothing more than a dominating idea borne on an iron will. Henry Ford empowered his workers—and kept the unions at bay—by creating the $5 a day wage. Bill Gates empowered his workers—and kept them from fleeing to other software companies—by sharing the wealth through stock options. He wasn't the first to try the strategy, but no one had ever shared the wealth quite like this. As of the end of 1998, Microsoft had created more than twenty thousand in-house millionaires, from code writers to secretaries. Gates and all the others who helped launch the Information Age also shared the wealth in one more critical way that would remake the world as surely as the Industrial Revolution had done: They provided the infrastructure that anyone, anywhere on earth could use.

The Many Faces of Bill Gates

Moguls, magnates, the people who create and master industries, the ones who integrate them and bring them to their fullest fruition—such business meta-successes are always many different things to many different people. To some they are saints, promises that democratic capitalism nurtures a meritocracy of the naturally talented. Others laud the John D. Rockefellers for their generosity, even as they decry the ruthlessness that propels them to the top. To still others, moguls are evil incarnate, representatives of all that's wrong in a system that not only allows but sometimes seems to thrive on the economic disparity between top and bottom. Some of the biggest of the moguls have been all things at once: Henry Ford the first billionaire, Henry Ford the social innovator, Henry Ford the almost-president, Henry Ford the creator of the modern industrial order, Henry Ford the Fascist sympathizer and rabid antiunionist. The list of contradictions goes on and on. And so it is with Bill Gates.

No human has ever been so rich. Because Bill Gates is so heavily invested in his own company, his wealth at any given moment is tied intimately to the share price of Microsoft stock. That meant that in 1996, when the company's stock soared by 88 percent, Gates made nearly $11 billion on paper, or about $30 million a day. John D. Rockefeller was said to earn roughly $2 a second at his prime: At his company's prime, Gates was earning at a pace nearly 175 times that—roughly $347 a second, or enough every minute to buy a new Honda Accord. True to Gates's decree that Microsoft should always have enough cash in the bank to operate for a year without any revenues, his company at the time was carrying a balance of $8 billion. With his own money, Gates built a 40,000 square foot home sunk into a bluff overlooking Lake Washington, outside Seattle. The vaulted garage alone can hold 30 cars. Modern in the extreme, this house is also palatial in the extreme—an El Escorial for the Information Age.

"[Gates] doesn't look for win-win situations with others, but for ways to make others lose."

Rarely, too, has one human been quite so many conflicting things to quite so many people. Friends and colleagues like to talk—in the language of the digerati—about Gates's ability to "parallel process," his "unlimited bandwidth" and facility at "multitasking." They note that he works on two computers at once in his office at the sprawling Microsoft campus in Redmond, Washington: One computer sequences data coming in from the Internet, while the other handles the hundreds of daily

e-mail messages through which Gates keeps in touch with his own employees and the larger world. His mind, they say, has many of the problem-solving capacities of the best computers: a knack for turning enormous input into finely crafted answers. At least in part, Gates goes along with the idea.

Even Gates's famously contentious style is a positive, according to Microsoft executive Steve Ballmer, a former Harvard classmate (he graduated, Gates didn't) whom Gates lured to the company in 1980 from Procter & Gamble: "Conflict can be a good thing. The difference from P & G is striking. Politeness was at a premium there. Bill knows it's important to avoid that gentle civility that keeps you from getting to the heart of an issue quickly. He likes it when anyone, even a junior employee, challenges him, and you know he respects you when he starts shouting back."

As for Gates's softer, less binary side, supporters point to his philanthropy and to his friendship with the very low-tech billionaire, Warren Buffett, whom Gates superseded as America's richest citizen. Like Andrew Carnegie, Gates has expressed a desire to spend much of the second half of his life giving away his money, a process already underway. Through a foundation run by Gates's father, Gates and his wife, Melinda, have donated billions of dollars, mostly for education, libraries, and public health. For the year 1999, grants from the Bill & Melinda Gates Foundation included nearly $950 million for vaccines against preventable diseases and an even $1 billion to fund the Gates Millennium Scholars program, to enhance minority access to higher education. Among the points of attraction between Gates and Buffett, who is 25 years his senior, is a fascination with games of all sorts, and a marathon-like capacity to pursue them. The first time America's two richest men got together with their wives at Buffett's San Francisco home, they ended up playing nine straight hours of bridge.

The Microsoft Monstrosity

Where Bill Gates is concerned, though, such benign assessments never want for counterbalance. Gates and Microsoft spent most of the 1990s under almost constant legal assault: The antitrust suit filed by the Justice Department that led to Judge Thomas Penfield Jackson's order to break up the company was an outgrowth of a lengthy and inclusive investigation by the Federal Trade Commission. Next to the verbal and written assaults on Gates, though, the legal one seems almost tepid.

Rob Glaser, a former Microsoft executive who left to run an Internet sound system company, RealAudio, has called his former boss "Darwinian. He doesn't look for win-win situations with others, but for ways to make others lose. Success is defined as flattening the competition, not creating excellence." Thanks to Gates's contentious style, Glaser went on, the Microsoft "atmosphere was like a Machiavellian poker game where you'd hide things even if it would blindside people you were supposed to be working with."

Others like Silicon Valley lawyer Gary Reback maintain that Microsoft uses "its existing monopoly to retard introduction of new technology." The charge is a corollary of another longtime beef especially common among the most cutting-edge high-tech companies and their proponents: that both Gates and his company are evolutionary, not revolutionary. The same complaint could be made about moguls generally, from Cosimo de' Medici to Henry Ford. Just as Cosimo didn't invent banking, so Ford didn't invent the gasoline-powered automobiles; rather, their fortunes came from doing the job better. But in the digital, everything-must-be-new era the charge has gathered resonance.

"[Gates] is one part Albert Einstein, one part John McEnroe, and one part General Patton."

Gates's immediate rivals seem to take almost demonic glee in attacking the man, his products, and his company. Borland CEO Philippe Kahn once compared Microsoft to Germany under Adolph Hitler; another time, he likened Microsoft's Windows system to AIDS. Lotus founder Mitch Kapor looked around the landscape of the software industry and declared that Microsoft's dominance had left it "the kingdom of the dead." Oracle CEO Larry Ellison is probably the most antagonistic of Gates's many industry competitors. As the Justice Department was moving against Microsoft, Ellison told a May 1998 Harvard computer conference that the company's business practices were "patently illegal… more blatant than anything [John D.] Rockefeller ever did" and he accused Gates of "lying" about Microsoft's record of innovation. For good measure, Oracle also hired a Washington detective agency, Investigative Group International, to dig up dirt on its rival, literally going through Microsoft's trash.

In cyberspace, things only get worse. Half a year into the new millennium, you could use a Microsoft operating system and Microsoft Internet Navigator to find Web sites with names like Boycott Microsoft, Punch Bill Gates, the Microsoft Hate Page, Microsoft Boycott Campaign, IHateBillGates.com, and the Bill Gates Personal Wealth Clock, which tracks Gates's gross worth by the fractional second, based on the 141,159,990 shares of Microsoft he owned as of 1995, adjusted for splits in 1996, 1998, and 1999. As of Friday, December 15, 2000, at 13:45:47 p.m. Eastern Standard Time, with the Microsoft share price sitting at a chastened $48.875, Bill Gates was worth $55.1936 billion, the clock noted, or $199,738 for every living American. In case anyone missed the larger point, the clock also included an old Irish saying directly beneath its calculations: "If you want to know what God thinks about money, just look at the people He gives it to."

Birth of an Empire

The real Bill Gates is probably best described by a quote attributed to a competitor in the software business who also described himself as a friend of the Microsoft cofounder. Gates, this person said, is "one part Albert Einstein, one part John McEnroe, and one part General Patton"—one part, that is, scientific genius, one part the temperamental genius cum bad boy, and one part tactical genius. For good measure, this person might also have thrown in Thomas Edison, another genius but also an ultra-successful entrepreneur who knew how to turn technological innovation into sales.

Born to wealthy parents in Seattle—where his father was a prominent attorney and his mother a childhood friend of Meg Greenfield, the longtime editorial-page editor of the *Washington Post*—Gates attended the fashionable and academically rigorous Lakeside School. It was there that he and his friend Paul Allen first discovered computing, on a fossilized school terminal bought with the proceeds from a Mothers' Club cookie sale. By 1968, the two eighth graders had learned the BASIC computer language and produced their first programs. Soon, they were spending evenings debugging a computer for a Seattle company. By tenth grade, Gates was writing a program that handled class scheduling for Lakeside. About the same time, he, Paul Allen, and a third friend, Kent Evans, secured jobs writing a payroll system for a local firm and analyzing and graphing traffic data for the City of Seattle. (Evans, probably Gates's best friend from those days, was killed in a mountain climbing accident before the three of them had left high school.)

After graduating from Lakeside in 1973, Gates moved on to Harvard, while Allen went to work for Honeywell. Two years later, in January 1975, came the event enshrined in Microsoft mythology as the moment of conception. As the story goes, Allen, who had driven East to be near his computer pal, held up a copy of the new issue of *Popular Electronics* magazine and shouted at Gates, "It's about to begin!" What inspired Allen was a cover mockup of the MITS (for Micro Instrumentation and Telemetry Systems) Altair 8800, a kit computer that despite its primitive and often unworkable nature was to be the first personal computer. Gates and Allen immediately set out to write a BASIC language for the Altair, and on February 1 of that year, they sold it to MITS, their first customer. Thus it was that Bill Gates became Harvard's most famous dropout—he and Allen set up shop in Albuquerque, New Mexico, where MITS was headquartered—and Microsoft was launched. The conception turned into a very quick birth.

Micro-soft, as it was first spelled, ended 1975 with three employees and $16,005 in revenues, but Gates and Allen were well on their way to settling a fundamental question that was to make all the difference in the company's success: what part of the computing business they were going to be in. Allen, who would leave the company in the early 1980s after a bout with

Hodgkin's disease and go on to become a major venture capitalist as well as a sports team owner and the founder of a rock-and-roll museum, had favored a combination of software and hardware. Hardware, after all, was the business that nearly all the computing giants of the time were pursuing. Gates wanted to do software only, and luckily for Microsoft's eventual shareholders, he prevailed.

"When you have the microprocessor doubling in power every two years, in a sense you can think of computer power as almost free," Gates told a *Playboy* interviewer who asked about the rift. "So you ask, Why be in the business of making something that's almost free? What is the scarce resource? What is it that limits being able to get value out of that infinite computing power? Software. Another way to look at it is that I just understood a lot more about software than I did about hardware, so I was sticking to what I knew well—and that turned out to be something important."

Growth Spurts

By 1980, Microsoft had shed the hyphen, moved to Washington state, and was a 40-person company earning about $7.5 million in revenues. The company would end 1981 with three times as many employees and more than double the revenue. What happened in between was IBM. The computer giant had come calling with a request: Would Microsoft be willing to develop languages and an operating system for IBM's first personal computer? On August 12, 1981, IBM introduced with great fanfare its Personal Computer. Far less noticed at the time was the 16-bit brain inside the PC—Microsoft's Disk Operating System, or MS-DOS, for short—or the fact that Gates had pressured the industry behemoth into giving Microsoft sole rights to license MS-DOS. For Bill Gates and Microsoft, the train had left the station.

"We wanted to make sure only we could license it," Gates has said. "We did the deal with them at a fairly low price, hoping that would help popularize it…. We knew that good IBM products are usually cloned, so it didn't take a rocket scientist to figure out that eventually we could license DOS to others. We knew that if we were ever going to make a lot of money on DOS, it was going to come from the compatible guys, not from IBM."

And make a lot of money, Microsoft certainly would. Given an enormous leg up by IBM's failure to take control of its own operating system, Gates and company by the mid-1980s had won the personal-computer operating systems war and were turning their attention toward domination of what's known as the "office suite": the combination of word processing, spreadsheet, and presentation. Each new conquest further engrained MS-DOS and, later, its Windows successors as the industry standard. Happily for Microsoft, too, the company made money even when its operating system wasn't sold. Under an agreement that Gates's critics would come to deride as the "computer tax," all manufacturers of IBM personal computer clones had to pay Microsoft a royalty on every computer shipped, whether or not the machine was equipped with MS-DOS.

By the mid-1980s, Microsoft's market dominance was beginning to pay off in a serious fashion. Revenues for 1985 stood at over $140 million, more than nine times what they had been when the company's operating system was first introduced. The next year, on March 13, 1986, the company went public, at $21 a share with the price rising to $28 by the end of the trading day. (Fourteen years later, one of those original shares was worth $10,000, adjusting for stock splits.) It was, of course, only the beginning.

Capitalizing in Cyberspace

A second revolution in computing—this one led by Bob Kahn, Vint Cerf, and others—had been underway ever since the 1960s when the Defense Department's Advanced Research Projects Agency had authorized an experiment in networking known as the Arpanet. As the Arpanet evolved into the Internet, the digital interconnection of the world was launched, with all the new economic opportunities that entailed. To make certain that computer users would head into cyberspace using Microsoft products, the company gave away its Internet navigation software, called the MS Internet Explorer. It had the cash reserves to afford the luxury, and the killer competitive instincts to dry up its competitors' bottom lines. To make certain that its navigator would never fly far from its basic operating system and its users would never fly far from home, Microsoft bundled the Internet Explorer with Windows and created, in mid-1995, MSN—the Microsoft Network—as a full-service Internet portal. Within its first three months, MSN had enrolled more than half a million members. Thus what was by far the most popular personal computer operating software became by far the most popular Web exploration software. In time, Microsoft would spread itself all over the Internet and intranets, and into multimedia, on-line magazine publishing, Web TV, and just about anywhere else that a company with a limitless appetite and some $15 billion in annual revenues could take it.

Just as had been the case with Standard Oil almost nine decades earlier, the Justice Department and courts seemed unable to slow Gates's company down, even when the government appeared to have won. In February 1999, StatMarket, an Internet fact gatherer, reported that the Microsoft Internet Explorer was being used by nearly 65 percent of all Net surfers worldwide. By June 2000, after Judge Jackson had ruled against Microsoft in the antitrust case, more than 86 percent of global surfers were using the Internet Explorer—an increase of 32 percent in a scant 16 months that had been highlighted by a nonstop legal assault against the company. What's more, 93 percent of global Net surfers were also using a Microsoft licensed Windows operating system product, StatMarket found.

Bill Gates, who prefers to think of himself as a technologist, not a businessman, had become both one of the world's most admired men and one of its most despised men, as well as its richest citizen.

The Times They Are A-Changin'

John D. Rockefeller was in his early 70s when the breakup of Standard Oil ordered by the Supreme Court helped to triple his fortune in two short years to just under $1 billion. Henry Ford was 45 before he sold his first Model T and in his 60s before he became the world's first billionaire. By age 43, Bill Gates was a billionaire nearly 80 times over.

In the digital era, the speed at which information travels wasn't the only thing accelerating. So was the speed at which wealth accumulates, products seize their markets, and new ideas turn into the geese that lay golden eggs. Radio needed 20 years to garner 10 million listeners. Television halved that to 10 years. Netscape got to 10 million users in only 28 months, and Hotmail made it in a quarter of the time—a mere 7 months.

One year into the new millennium, 350 million people globally were expected to be using the Internet, according to *Computer Industry Almanac*. By the end of 2005, the wired worldwide population is predicted to hit 765 million people, and as the numbers grow, the digital wealth will spread. At the outset of the twenty-first century, about 43 percent of all Internet users were Americans; by 2005, that figure should drop to 28 percent. Almost overnight, Australia and Finland, the 11 time zones of the former Soviet Union, New Delhi, Madagascar, Rome, and New York City had all become just a log-on away. A web had been created—a literal web: Touch it anywhere and you are in touch with its whole being. And as the Web was spreading exponentially, opportunity was spreading with it. Microsoft, AOL, Macintosh, Lotus, Netscape, Bill Gates, Steve Case, Steve Jobs, Vint Cerf, Bob Kahn, and tens of thousands of others had all played a role in launching an opportunity machine such as the world had never known—one that spread the chance for a better economic life to places that can seem almost unimaginable.

From *Upside,* June 2001, pp. 133-137. © 2001 by Upside Media, Inc.

MICHAEL DELL has harnessed his discipline and focus to build a computer empire and become one of the most successful entrepreneurs in American history

BY RICHARD MURPHY

MICHAEL DELL was speaking to an entrepreneurship class at the University of Texas business school when a bold student stood up and asked the young multibillionaire why he still kept going to work. "You've got so much money," he blurted. "Why don't you just sell out, buy a boat, and sail off to the Caribbean?" Dell stared at him and said, "Sailing's *boring*. Do you have any idea how much fun it is to run a billion-dollar company?"

Few people could actually answer that question. But more important than the answer is what Dell's question reveals about the founder and CEO of Dell Computer Corp. and how this mega-entrepreneur was able to achieve so much, so fast. In 1984, Dell started his company with $1,000 and the premise that he could beat his competitors by building computers to order and selling them directly to consumers. It was a simple, radical idea, and it shook the computer world to its foundations. Fourteen years later, Dell's direct model guides an estimated $18 billion global corporation.

How did he do it? By keeping his mind firmly focused on doing business as opposed to making money. Walk into the hushed executive suite at Dell Computer Corp.'s headquarters in Round Rock, Tex., and you'll see a man standing behind a podium desk, both absorbed in and invigorated by his work. Michael Dell's office has chairs only for visitors. Dell works standing up, appropriately enough for the CEO of a manufacturing company that has slashed inventory turnover to an astonishing seven days, compared with 80 days or more for much of his competition. (In the computer industry, inventory loses 1 percent of its value every week that it sits on the shelf; Dell's world-beating inventory management is thus critical to the company's bottom line.)

Society expects visionaries and innovators to be eccentric. Consequently, Michael Dell's sheer normality is a bit deceiving. To put it mildly, Dell is not a wild or crazy guy. He is dark, soft-spoken, and reasonably handsome, with the slightly puffy look of one who puts in long hours running a multibillion-dollar company. He lives in an enormous house in the Austin hill country, guards the privacy of his wife, Susan, and their four young children, and gives generously to various charities. He is not especially keen on small talk; his only discernible quirk is that he is particular about his neckties—or so say sources close to Dell.

BYTE BY BYTE

But then consider that, like ties, entrepreneurs come in two basic styles. One is the peripatetic deal junkie, restlessly seeking new ventures and markets. The other is the methodical optimizer, who starts with a good idea and then tirelessly executes on that idea. "I'm not a deal junkie," Dell says. That may be his greatest understatement; it's also the secret of his success. Michael Dell is the methodical optimizer par excellence. In its history, Dell Computer has rarely deviated from the direct-sales model. When it has done so, business has suffered. In 1991, for example, the company tried selling through computer superstores and warehouse clubs; the experiment failed, and Dell got out of retail. Today, when asked whether he would consider taking some of his billions and branching out beyond the computer business, Dell simply replies, "I've learned from experience that a company can grow too fast. You have to be careful about expanding into new businesses because if you get into too many too quickly, you won't have the experience or the infrastructure to succeed."

To most small-business owners, speedy growth might not seem like such a bad problem. When you grow too fast, though, you run two risks: not only straying into the wrong businesses but also losing control of quality. Here again, Dell speaks from tough personal experience. In the second quarter of 1993 the company took a $94 million charge against earnings after a number of expansion problems, including the failure of a line of shoddy laptops. Dell responded by hiring a cadre of big-league professional managers to help structure the company's explosive growth (87 percent per year for the first eight years; 55 percent per year since 1992). The company has also coped with its rapid expansion by segmenting itself into home-office, small-business, education, government, and large-business/health-care divisions. According to Dell vice chairman Kevin B. Rollins, a 45-year-old former Bain consultant, "Michael realized that he needed professionals to run this company, so that he could continue to be a visionary."

A DORM-ROOM DYNASTY

At the tender age of 33, Michael Dell is not just the fourth-richest person in the country. Along with John D. Rockefeller, Henry Ford, and Bill Gates, he has entered American business mythology. Like all good myths, Dell's story is simple. As a 19-year-old freshman at the University of Texas, he borrowed $1,000 from his parents to start a business selling computer accessories out of his dorm room. The concept was straightforward: he would buy parts, assemble them into PC-upgrade kits, and sell the finished products directly to customers. By eliminating distributors, with their fat profit margins, he was immediately able to undersell far larger, more established competitors.

Dell quickly moved into designing and building his own line of

computers. On his way to grossing almost $6 million that first year, he dropped out of school. Three years later, Dell created the computer industry's first on-site-service program, which meant that if your computer was sick, you didn't put it in your car and go back to the store; Dell Computer came out to your house and fixed it. Says Dell, chuckling, "That was a pretty important plus because we didn't have any stores."

The lesson? Turn a negative situation (no stores) into a positive one by creating a sales model that's even more valuable to your customers.

Today Dell Computer still does essentially what Michael Dell started out doing by himself: it buys parts, builds custom computers, and sells them direct, only now Michael Dell has nearly 21,000 people working for him. Dell is the country's second-largest PC manufacturer, breathing down the neck of archrival Compaq, which recently started building custom computers in a belated attempt to copy Dell's direct model. The appeal of the direct model? Dell builds computers only in response to real orders that come in from end users, either by phone or via the company's benchmark Web site, which currently does about $6 million in sales every day. As a result, Dell sidesteps much of the hazard of trying to forecast market demand in the volatile computer industry. And the market has fed this strategy abundantly: today Dell builds computers on three continents and sells them all over the world.

GIVE 'EM WHAT THEY WANT

At Dell's "Metric 12" factory, in Austin, trucks pull up at a row of unloading docks, each one labeled with the name of a PC or server part: power supply, CD-ROM, cover, and so on. Inside, 1,500 purposeful workers assemble the parts according to specific customer instructions. And we do mean specific: customers can (and do) note where they want the

label stuck on the shipping box, not just the size of the hard drive, the amount of memory, or the software they wish to have installed in the computer itself. On average, it takes five hours for a finished, configured, tested, and boxed computer to leave the factory through loading docks at the other end of the assembly lines, according to proud line manager Sheri Arnaud.

Because customization is integral to Dell's manufacturing process, the company can provide unmatched levels of customer support. On October 27, 1997, for example, Nasdaq's Internet trading site was overwhelmed by massive trading volumes as the onset of Asia's economic crisis sent share prices on a 500-point dive. Nasdaq called Dell, which built eight custom-configured PowerEdge servers in just 36 hours; Nasdaq had them up and running three days later.

"AT THE ROOT OF IT, I WAS OPPORTUNISTIC… I SAW THAT YOU'D BUY A PC FOR ABOUT $3,000, AND INSIDE THAT PC WAS ABOUT $600 WORTH OF PARTS."

Stories like that help explain why Wall Street venerates Michael Dell. "He's very nimble," says Piper-Jaffray analyst Ashok Kumar. "His competitors are like sumo wrestlers. Dell is more like a kick boxer." Dell shares are up by 29,600 percent in the 1990s; they split like a methedrine-crazed amoeba and have a good chance of being crowned the stock of the decade. Michael Dell, consequently, is hailed a business genius. He smiles from national magazine covers, dines at the White House, and gives keynote speeches at industry conventions. Not surprisingly, he also has a book coming out: *Direct from Dell: Strategies That Revolutionized an Industry* (HarperBusiness, 1999).

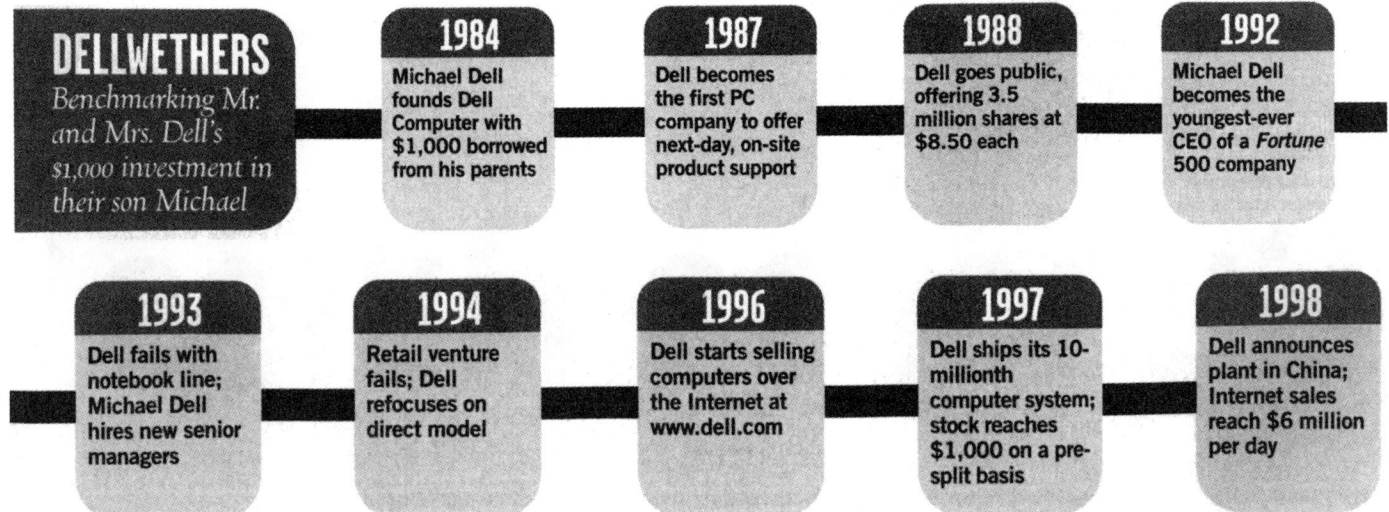

DELLWETHERS
Benchmarking Mr. and Mrs. Dell's $1,000 investment in their son Michael

1984
Michael Dell founds Dell Computer with $1,000 borrowed from his parents

1987
Dell becomes the first PC company to offer next-day, on-site product support

1988
Dell goes public, offering 3.5 million shares at $8.50 each

1992
Michael Dell becomes the youngest-ever CEO of a *Fortune* 500 company

1993
Dell fails with notebook line; Michael Dell hires new senior managers

1994
Retail venture fails; Dell refocuses on direct model

1996
Dell starts selling computers over the Internet at www.dell.com

1997
Dell ships its 10-millionth computer system; stock reaches $1,000 on a pre-split basis

1998
Dell announces plant in China; Internet sales reach $6 million per day

It's easy to marvel at Dell's success, but it's more important to understand the strategy that took him from the dorm room to the executive suite. When he talks about his beginnings as a University of Texas computer wonk, you realize that it all started with the basic entrepreneurial act of spotting a market niche. "At the root of it, I was probably just opportunistic," Dell says. "I had and still have a great interest in computers. There was a business opportunity [with] this product that I really liked, and it all kind of lined up together."

"I saw that you'd buy a PC for about $3,000, and inside that PC was about $600 worth of parts," he continues. "IBM would buy most of these parts from other companies, assemble them, and sell the computer to a dealer for $2,000. Then the dealer, who knew very little about selling or supporting computers, would sell it for $3,000, which was even more outrageous."

THE POWER OF "MASS CUSTOMIZATION"

When asked whether he understood at 19 how he was revolutionizing the marketplace, Dell responds, "Well, we started the company by building to the customer's order. And inter-estingly enough, we didn't do it because we saw some massive paradigm in the future. Basically, we just didn't have any capital [to mass-produce]."

So, Dell caught a lucky break in the beginning, but he hardly abandoned his business model once he got a few nickels together. Instead, he expanded it on a mass scale, using information technology to customize millions of computers individually. Today business pundits have anointed "mass customization" the industrial paradigm of the next century, just as mass production was the paradigm of the 20th century. And while many companies are turning to mass customization (anybody can now order made-to-measure jeans from Levi-Strauss or a personalized car from BMW), Dell's brilliant and, more important, consistent execution of this model sets the computer company apart from the crowd.

Even in the depths of the Asian economic crisis, Dell Computer has managed to make money in the Far East, where sales were up by 77 percent in fiscal 1998, compared with a 38 percent increase in fiscal 1997. Michael Dell takes this in stride: the cost and price advantages of the direct model, he argues, give the company room to profit in any kind of market. "We can gain share whether the market is growing or shrinking," he says. "Also, we're growing in Asia because we're not very big [in that market]. It's only 6 percent of our revenue. There are many global companies out there, and even though there may be economic turmoil and contraction, they're still buying PCs."

One hundred years ago, Thomas Alva Edison told *Success* magazine that the first requisite of success was the ability to concentrate on a single problem. "If you get up at seven and go to bed at eleven, you have put in sixteen good hours, and it is certain with most men that they have been doing something all the time," Edison said. "The only trouble is that they do it about a great many things, and I do it about one." Dell and Edison are kindred spirits in this regard. For the past 14 years, Michael Dell has concentrated his mind on one issue: building better computers and selling them at a lower price. While he may not be a world-altering inventor like Edison, Dell has managed to reinvent his industry, build a world–class company, and enrich thousands of employees and shareholders along with himself. For a 33-year-old college dropout, that's not too shabby.

Success Rules!

Succeed with these five rules from five entrepreneurs who have made it.

by THOMAS MELVILLE

Joe Mancuso, a burly sexagenarian with a white beard and an easy laugh, knows about success. He has founded seven businesses, along with the Center for Entrepreneurial Management and the Chief Executive Officers Club, written 24 business books, and is a much sought-out corporate motivational speaker. Mancuso, who is often called "the entrepreneur's entrepreneur," has spent a lifetime being successful and being around the successful.

"Entrepreneurs and CEOs accomplish more because they are always thinking," says Mancuso. "Success is not only about financial success, it is about a lifestyle—people doing what they want to do. It's a classic cliché, but people that make a lot of money are not always happy."

But are there definitive rules that someone could follow to success?

Ask the businessman's Buddha, Mancuso, who relishes his role as mentor, and he will give you his 20 commandments (see some of them in the sidebar included in this article).

Twenty is a lot to remember. SUCCESS went looking for five rules essential to startup success and found them in five entrepreneurs who have made it. Some are serial entrepreneurs who have

succeeded several times over, and some have nurtured one business for years, but all have one thing in common—they are winners.

"Don't cling to ownership. Give employees stock options."

—STEVEN CASH NICKERSON,
CEO, MUCHO.COM

---

1 ALWAYS START WITH THE EXIT IN MIND

Steven Cash Nickerson's mother may have been clairvoyant. She worked as a vacuum salesman at J.C. Penney in Philadelphia, while carrying Nickerson to term. After giving birth she wanted to name her son Cash, after James Cash Penny, but her husband talked her out of it. Instead Cash became Steven's middle name, literally and figuratively. Now a 41-year-old serial entrepreneur who has founded 11 and sold eight companies, Nickerson has proved his mother's psychic abilities correct.

"Everybody calls me Cash now," says Nickerson, who sold his last startup company, Workforce Strategies, for $8.4 million.

Currently Nickerson, based in Lafayette, Calif., is busy launching his latest venture, Mucho.com, an Internet portal designed to provide small business owners a single source for all business needs. But it was starting and running Workforce Strategies where Nickerson learned some valuable lessons.

He was a partner in a large law firm in Chicago in the 1990s, earning a nice paycheck and feeling quite secure when he decided to jump ship and start his own business. Workforce Strategies ended up bringing in $25 million in revenue before he sold it in 1997.

"My plan from the start was to sell it," he says. "Always start with the exit in mind, otherwise you work for 40 years and become a penny stacker."

Nickerson also advises owners to share equity. "Don't cling to ownership. Give employees stock options." Nickerson sets aside 10 percent of the stock for employees at the beginning.

"Another big rule is not to lie to yourself when things are not going well," he says. "Always be assessing—what are your stars and your dogs? It's like keeping score when you were a kid. If things

Highlights from Joe Mancuso's 20 Commandments

Joe Mancuso, founder of the Chief Executive Officers Club, created 20 commandments for CEOs. "I chose 20 rather than 10 in remembrance of my favorite scene in a Mel Brooks movie, *The History of the World, Part I*. As Moses came down from Mount Sinai with three inscribed stone tablets, he bellowed out to the masses: 'I have spoken directly to God, and he has given me these 15 commandments.' As he spoke, he slipped and one of the three tablets in his hand fell and shattered. Thank God!"

In honor of the shattered tablet, here are five of Mancuso's 20.

Beg for forgiveness rather than ask permission. When you discover you are in a hole, maybe it's time to stop digging. Ready. Fire. Aim.

Abdicate vs. Delegate. You can get anything you want if you help enough other people get what they want.

Avoid the "sandbox syndrome." A company's weakest vice president often shares the CEO's area of expertise. Pity the vice president for marketing who reports to a CEO who came up through the ranks in marketing. Whether by accident or design, it seems that vice presidents in a CEO's discipline are seldom as effective as those in other areas. It's the sandbox syndrome as the CEOs with certain skills just can't help meddling in their old favorite sandbox.

Use your company's mission statement as a touchstone. The mission statement of an organization is the most tangible measure of a CEO's effectiveness.

Make sure that all objectives are clear and attainable. Both the entrepreneurial and the professional CEO agree that every person in a well-run organization can say: "I know what I'm supposed to accomplish and by when. My boss has agreed to my objectives and has allocated to me the resources I need to attain them. If conditions change, I can shift my effort and still attain my objectives."

are not working, do not be afraid to cut loose. And always, hire slowly, but fire quickly. Swallow your pride, admit you made a mistake in hiring someone, and move on."

2 COMMUNICATE WITH EMPLOYEES AND BE FLEXIBLE

Last year Jeff Lawrence learned about truth from about 50 students at UCLA, and it has helped him run his business. He gave a two-hour lecture to a class on engineering ethics, and afterward the students wrote a one-page report on what they heard.

"You should be as fair as possible with employees and customers. And encourage creativity from employees. Creativity sets you apart from other businesses in the same industry."

—MARY ELLA GABLER,
CEO, PEACOCK ALLEY

"Fifty people had heard 50 different things," Lawrence says. "I read their reports and everyone had their own interpretations. You can have a set of facts and then everyone has his own point of view about it. Truth is relative."

Lawrence, who started Trillium Digital Systems, a $20 million-plus internetworking communications software company in Los Angeles, knows about facing truths. In 1988 he was laid off from Doelz Networks and decided to start his own company.

"My father was self-employed most of his life, so I always thought about it," says the soft-spoken Lawrence. "Getting laid off was the catalyst. Then it came down to assessing what I could do. I had knowledge in telecommunications software development. And I figured if it

Six Rules of How Not to Fail

by NICHOLAS HALL

Seek out quality, supportive relationships. Entrepreneurs go through more ups and downs than a roller coaster. Without the supportive relationships of a spouse, significant other, business coach, family, mentors, or friends it can be a lonely and confidence-shattering journey.

Pick a strategy for every step of the way. Entrepreneurs spend most of their time focusing on the projected growth of their company. They don't spend enough time thinking about how far they are willing to go, in terms of time and money, on their startup. Success may always be right around the corner, but knowing when to pull the plug can save you many sleepless nights.

Volunteer in your community. Building a successful company will depend heavily upon the quality and diversity of your relationships. I have found no better way to build personal relationships that ultimately lead to valuable business relationships than through my volunteer efforts in the community.

Maintain your health and well-being. Entrepreneurs tend to invest far too much of their time and energy into their business and forget about their own well-being.

Diversify your interests. Pursue your hobbies and interests as passionately as you pursue the growth of your startup. It will help your brain to relax and rest. You will also find that you will be a far more interesting person to others as well as to yourself.

Maintain a life vision. Too often, entrepreneurs have their entire future invested in their startup. By maintaining a vision for all areas of their life they will keep their mind focused on today and the future, not worried about what worked or didn't work in the past.

didn't work out I still had the skills to go back and work for someone else."

Lawrence's initial $1,000 investment with partner Larisa Chistyakov has spawned a 250-employee company that takes up most of the Trillium Building in west L.A., is projected to have $30 mil-

Making a Success of Failure

Nicholas Hall has had more comebacks than George Foreman. After his first three startups went under, the 30-year-old entrepreneur kept climbing back in the ring for more punishment. Hall's latest creation, startupfailures.com, has been a cult hit as people get sick of hearing about overnight dot-com millionaires.

The website, www.startupfailures.com, Hall says, is a service for the many who don't make it and need some support. "The reality is that most startups are going to go through some tough time or fail. Entrepreneurs who fail have an emotional need, and I thought I could provide some support for these people," says Hall, who as president of the Silicon Valley Association of Software Entrepreneurs has witnessed a few startups crash and burn. Not to mention his own failures (for what he's learned see Six Rules of How Not To Fail).

First, as a young man in Cincinnati, he started a financial services company. "I tried to build it myself. I was headstrong, but I realized you can't do it alone," he says. Next he took a bath in the beverage industry when his coffee/hard-cider shop plan was scuttled. "By the time we went out to raise capital, that coffee shop market got hammered. So it was bad timing." Hall then had an idea for an Internet community site and decided to move to the San Francisco Bay area to drum up some interest. But he couldn't raise enough money to keep going. "I should have gone out and found some partners and potential customers instead of spending all my time trying to raise money."

With the support of his wife, Jennifer, Hall keeps bouncing back. He recently completed *The Future Scrapbook: Having the Design of Your Life*, a book that helps people plan out their futures. He's taking music lessons and is trying out for a musical.

"I've had some success," he says. "I'm not focusing on what did not work or how I screwed up. I have a network of supportive people to lean on. I wasn't born with a silver spoon in my mouth, nor did I receive a big inheritance. I'm just trying to make it like a lot of people."

lion in revenues for 2000, and has a long list of Fortune 500 clients. And last year he raised $14 million in venture capital from Intel and Rader, Reinfrank & Co.

"I think we have been successful because we have good people, smart people, nice people," says Lawrence. "To be successful you have to listen to people and be willing to change. You need to communicate with your people so they know what is going on. Encourage their input."

3 HIRE SMART PEOPLE

He talks in an authentic you-know-what-I'm-talking-about New York accent straight out of the city that never sleeps' mean streets. Glenn Schlossberg was raised on the ultra-competitive streets of New York City's garment district. And at age 36, he has made it there and proved he can make it anywhere.

In 1989, Schlossberg, who at the time worked in the family business in the clothing industry, broke out on his own at age 25 and started Jump Apparel, which manufactures social-occasion dresses. By 1999, the company was making $70 million in revenue and Schlossberg had spun off one separate company, Onyx Nite, and co-founded two other affiliated apparel companies—Helen Blake and Danielle Casey.

"I found a financial backer, borrowed from my family and used my life savings to start," Schlossberg says. "I put my blood on the table next to theirs."

Schlossberg, who arrives at work in a chauffeured Bentley from his Manhattan apartment every morning at 6:30, believes that hiring the best people and providing top-notch service to his clients have led to his success. "You need to hire smart people. I have more than 200 employees, and they are my championship team. It's all about the people."

It is not about being scared to fail. "Never show fear," he says. "*Show no fear* are the words to live by. I have a big sign on the front of my desk that says 'It can be done.' You have to have the guts to take the shots. You miss 100 percent of the shots you do not take."

4 STICK TO A REALISTIC BUSINESS PLAN

Jeff Parker has been to battle on the two great stages of the 20th Century—in war and on Wall Street—and has survived and thrived. In the mid-1960s he worked in the Pentagon while in the Army, and through the 1970s he did his tour at Fidelity, becoming an extremely successful bond salesman.

Throughout the next 20 years he became an entrepreneur and founded six companies including his latest, CCBN.com, an Internet portal that organizes and delivers easy-to-use investment-related information for the corporate marketplace. It had $9 million in revenues in 1999 and is projected to bring in $25 million next year. Street-Events, a leading service of CCBN.com, allows users to track significant company events such as earnings release dates and investor conferences.

"When I left my high-paying job at Fidelity to start my own business, people said 'Is he nuts?'" Parker says. "But I had an innate desire to do something better, which is what makes someone an entrepreneur. But I was also at a time in my life where it wasn't that risky. I was a well-known bond salesman. I don't think entrepreneurs are great risk takers; they should have a fallback position."

Parker, who describes himself as so organized he is anal, knew he could provide a service that no one else had, but needed. "As a bond-selling professional, it was a service I wish I had." His first business, started in 1980, was one of the first to provide organized, detailed, and easy-to-use information about the bond market. It clicked—and has been a springboard for the rest of Parker's successes.

"A successful business is about execution," he says. "You need laser focus and then do everything you can possibly do to stay on your business plan. But you need to be realistic about your business plan. I see ridiculous numbers from these young entrepreneurs sometimes, where they expect to go from zero in the first year to $42 million in revenue the next year."

Then, after the plan is set, you must create revenue. "All my businesses have had a heavy sales and marketing side," Parker says. "If you sit around and count expenses you will go out of business. You have to go out and sell it. Remember that cash is king."

5 NEVER GIVE UP

In the late 1980s Mary Ella Gabler made one of the toughest decisions in her professional life. Should she give up, get out, and try something else, or should she sink her life savings into her dream and hope for the best? Gabler, who in 1964 was one of the first women to work on Wall Street and had seen her share of successes and failures, made the decision to stick it out.

"All of Texas had a big downturn in the economy in the late '80s, and I was right in it," says Gabler, who started the fine-linen company Peacock Alley 27 years ago in Dallas. "It was a great lesson in not giving up. I came very close to quitting." When the bank foreclosed on her note, Gabler, a single mother of two small children at the time, believed in herself and her business and decided to use her savings to retire the debt and keep the business afloat.

Now, she has retail stores in Dallas, New York City, and Los Angeles, 31 in-store boutiques across the country, 105 employees, $20 million in annual sales, and celebrity clients such as Kathie Lee Gifford, John Travolta, and Jimmy Buf-fet. Even Pope John Paul II sleeps on Peacock Alley's solo white sheets.

"I don't give up," Gabler says. "If one plan does not work I always try to find a plan B. I have a desire to achieve and have confidence in my decisions. I figured I was better than the competition, and I would persevere. It takes a toll on you and you do have setbacks, but you keep going forward."

Gabler grew up in an entrepreneurial family. Her father and his three brothers owned and ran a furniture store in Chambersburg, Pa. "Seeing their success was inspirational to me," she says. "It was a wonderful combination of family and business ethics."

Gabler also recommends spending money on professional strategic planning. "That is absolutely critical for a growing company. It is something you cannot afford *not* to do."

10 STUPID THINGS
ENTREPRENEURS DO!

BY SUPREET MANCHANDA

While watching the Late Show with David Letterman the other night, I began musing about how it would be if people—especially new executives—suddenly realized some of the crazy things that they do over and over again? To get us started, here are ten of them.

Number 10

Assume that their idea is the only new idea since sliced bread.
Too often, you may get so caught up in the passion and focus required to build the company that your idea emerges as the only one that deserves to be funded, and how dare could anyone turn that down! Keep in mind that if you thought of it, so, most likely, did someone else. If you acknowledge that, you won't be surprised, and you will be free to focus on spectacular execution.

Number 9

Assume financial, market and sales numbers that make Al Gore and George Bush's math look as good as Einstein's.
You only need one percent of the trillion-trillion-dollar market, and the current players will give it to you on a silver platter. Right. Building the market and acquiring it are two very different things. Just as nature

abhors a vacuum, so does a market, and current players will not give away even a piece of their market without a fight. So please, no more funny math. VC's don't pay attention to that anyway.

Number 8

Team? What do you mean that I need a team? Don't you know that my idea will materialize by itself? I am the team!
People make or break a company. The founder(s) need to realize that the team is the single most important contributing factor for success and for VC's considering whether or not to fund the company. I consider it to be the deciding factor between two business plans with similar attributes. And the leadership and maturity of the CEO is the key ingredient on that team.

Number 7

You mean someone has to buy what I make? The technology can sell itself. Its Super Technology!
Okay, I concede—who does not like new technology? Hey, for boys it is a statement of testosterone, and for women it is a way of telling men that they, too, can play the game just as well. However, technology is a fickle partner. I am not knocking it (as a former CIO, I should know), but rather la-

menting that the half-life of a technology seems to be growing steadily shorter and shorter. As a result, value has to come not only from a technological edge but also—very quickly—from the supply-chain and strategic partnerships that extend the half-life of a technology all the way to profitability.

Number 6

I am a CEO, and I already know it all, you can tell because I now have the title.
Underestimating the cost and energy required to build a company, as many an exuberant CEO has done, has led to many a downfall. Building companies is serious business, sort of like making a baked Alaska in Saudi Arabia. Everything has to be exactly right, and even then something may go wrong. Remember PointCast?

Number 5

I only need a small amount of money and don't worry, someone will buy us soon.
This assumption is related to fuzzy math and lack of maturity. You always need to raise more money than you think you do, as many an Internet company has discovered. As for being bought out, that, like all things in the future, can be planned for but

not anticipated with certainty. Remember Pets.com? R.I.P.

Number 4

Well, it's just a feature today, but everyone will want one of these watchamacallit's.

The days of the uncritical enthusiam for one-feature companies are over, so please stop. You need to have a product, not just one feature; remember, the 'build it and they will come' idea only worked as long as there were fewer than three competitors. Now, unless you have come up with something new, something to rival, say, Marc Andreeson's Netscape.com or Shawn Fanning's Napster, go back to the drawing board.

Number 3

I can't believe you won't give me the valuation! After all, you do GIVE away money, don't you?

Will you fund me, because we are very close to a deal.... Right, and we also have a nice bridge we can sell you. Look, you don't get paid if you don't make money, and it's not about the valuation. Good VC's tend to be fair and will give you decent valuations. Focus on the plan and concentrate on negotiating like the good businesspersons you are.

Number 2

What do you mean I have to solve a problem and not just create something?

Focus closely on solving a specific problem. Too many people are busy making vitamins, but not focusing on current pain points. The companies that seem to focus on the pain points have no problem raising money and being successful.

Number 1

Letting their egos get in the way of truly running a company.

The ego factor is the difference between the right CEO and the wrong CEO. To assist all of you who have or will sweat blood for the sake of your idea, make sure that you take a hard look at who leads the company. Remember also, as the company grows, that you may need to call on different people to lead the way. Focus on the company's success first. Yes, you may grow, but typically the people who create companies are not the same kind of people who can lead after the company has become a stable entity. Even large, successful companies like Sun Microsystems and Oracle have had leadership changes.

Supreet Manchanda was until recently a General Partner with New York based venture firm Adler Partners. Write to him at: supreet@corp.siliconindia.com.

GO
GLOBAL

**If you're not doing business overseas,
you're ignoring a multibillion-dollar market.
Here's how to get your cut.**

By Wendy M. Grossman

For Bill Rozier picking the right number was worth more than a million-dollar jackpot. He staked the future of his newly minted company on the number 12.

Rozier, vice president of global marketing at Salt Lake City- and Dublin, Ireland-based Twelve Horses, and David Malone, the company's founder, wanted to create a brand with positive connotations around the world. They picked 12—a strong number in most cultures.

They also wanted a brand that did more than merely describe the company's initial product (which automates delivery of marketing literature) and one that didn't depend on words alone. So they developed an iconography that weaves positive imagery with the company's distinctive name. The logo leaves out black, a color that's popular in the United States and Europe but has negative connotations in Asian countries. Multiple colors connect to form a globally appealing horse—reinforcing the company name.

Will the cultural research pay off? Time will tell, as the company's MessageMaker service, launched in July, takes on the international market.

Rozier sweated the details about the worldwide implications of branding. But most American businesses don't share his con-

cerns. Even in the age of the global economy, few U.S. companies are doing business abroad. Only 1 percent of small and midsize American businesses export overseas, according to the Census Bureau, U.S. Department of Commerce. Even e-commerce hasn't made real-world borders disappear: Nearly half of U.S. Web sites turn away international orders because they are unable to process them—a move that forfeits an estimated $10 million in annual sales. At the same time, 60 percent of the online population will live outside the United States by 2003, making the market too large to ignore.

Expanding globally requires cross-cultural understanding, which doesn't come easily in a country with a huge and largely homogeneous domestic market. But one thing's for sure: If you don't seize the international opportunity, you're leaving a multibillion-dollar market to your competitors.

Location, Location

When you're trying to crack new markets, the first question is where to start. For most companies Europe—particularly Britain and Ireland, with their familiar language and legal systems—is the most likely port of call. The European Union is a sizable market: It has a population of 375 million and a gross domestic product of $8.4 trillion, slightly below the United States' GDP of $8.5 trillion.

And when it comes to e-commerce, although Europeans spent only $2.8 billion online in 1998, Jupiter Research projects that by 2003 that figure will increase to a whopping $33.6 billion. Add the introduction of the euro and the deregulation of the telecommunications, air travel, postal service, and energy markets, and it's a compelling proposition.

But Europe is a big target. Focus is key, and that requires market research. Larry Levy, founder of Protégé Econet, a network of companies working to build European Internet businesses, has helped dozens of American firms expand into Europe since starting his company in 1996. He typically works with Internet infrastructure players, including Vignette, AvantGo, and iCat, and he concentrates on Britain and Scandinavia. His reasoning? Those regions have a high percentage of English-speaking Internet users.

For many companies, the United Kingdom is the likely choice. It has a sound infrastructure; an educated, English-speaking workforce; a cordial relationship with the United States; and a long tradition of hosting American businesses.

During the past decade, Ireland, which has the same advantages and is a member of the EU, has also been a prime candidate. It doesn't hurt that Ireland offers substantial financial incentives to entice foreign investment, transforming itself from a tiny country with Third World-sized debt into one with the fastest-growing economy in Europe. Two booming high-tech areas have led this change, one in Limerick, where Dell Computer has two factories, and one south of Dublin, where Microsoft, Lotus, and Gateway all maintain facilities. In addition, Bray hosts many of Europe's call centers.

Dell had small operations in Bracknell, England, and Limerick when in 1991 the company started planning to take advantage of the European consolidation set for the next year. Dell considered a number of locations and in the end selected Limerick, where it took over an abandoned Atari factory. Now, Dell's Irish manufacturing space has grown to 700,000 square feet—and the company has become one of the leading personal computer manufacturers in Europe.

At the time, Dell noted that Limerick manufactured all the service industry pieces the company needed, including corrugated cardboard boxes and blocks of plastic foam packing. Because Ireland was experiencing a job shortage, Dell knew it could easily staff the factory.

"The 1980s weren't a pretty time for Ireland," says Tim McCarthy, country manager for Dell Ireland, who quotes figures from the Industrial Development Agency. "There was a lot of emigration. But the 1990s have really turned it completely on its head."

Clothing retailer Lands' End, which has been in the catalog business since 1963, also did its homework before going global in 1991. The company picked the United Kingdom first because it's an English-speaking region and Japan next because it's the second largest retail market. From there Lands' End moved to Germany, where families spend more on catalog shopping than in any other country.

For Lands' End the discovery process is ongoing, says Sam Taylor, vice president, international. The Japanese market has taught the company about the value of thinking globally. Japanese women, he says, are more fashion-conscious than Americans. "They look at Paris and quickly follow," he says. What Americans think of as specialty fabrics are big sellers in Japan.

How Do You Get There?

After companies decide on a target market, they need to choose a method for reaching it. Those with the time and resources can build from scratch overseas with a local team. Many well-established computer companies, such as Dell, IBM, and Hewlett-Packard, have gone this route. But for other businesses, this isn't a practical solution.

A popular approach is to take on partners to help build up a truly local product or service. That's what America Online did. (Overseas the company calls itself simply AOL to de-emphasize its American roots.) Its main challenges were not only to create content that would be relevant to local users but also to deal with markets where the Internet was not widely used. AOL teamed with local companies that often had nothing to do with the Internet but brought local expertise and talent to the table.

Rich D'Amato, a spokesman for AOL, explains, "In Australia we want to build a service that is truly Australian. Our partner [AAPT, a telecommunications company] helps us localize content, billing, and management." Having local staff helps the company introduce widespread global use of the Internet by tailoring services and content to each region.

AOL's future plans include expanding into Mexico and Argentina. Its biggest challenges there will be to teach local populations about the Internet and create affordable access. To help make decisions about entry into a market with few established Internet portals, AOL teamed with Cisneros Group, a large conglomerate based in Venezuela.

D'Amato believes partnering is the best strategy for companies like AOL because "our service is about creating local services relevant to consumers, and that really does require knowledge of that marketplace and business relationships and marketing expertise."

Easy Way In

Many dot-coms have taken an even quicker route to building a global presence, by buying an existing company that otherwise might become a stalwart competitor. For example, sky-high stock prices let Amazon.com buy Britain's Bookpages, now better known as Amazon.co.uk. Amazon bought a similar operation in Germany, as well as the British-based Internet Movie Database.

Other businesses expand overseas by exporting products to a local distributor, or by franchising or licensing their business and products. This is a common tactic among food and retail chains, including Burger King, Holiday Inn, and Tower Records.

eBay didn't settle on a single approach to export its wildly successful auction site. But Susanna Kass, chief operating officer for international operations, says some routes are easier than others. Instead of going out on its own, as it did in the United Kingdom, eBay prefers the strategy it adopted in Germany: acquiring other businesses.

Kass says, however, that eBay was somewhat wary of acquiring a local company in Germany. "We were worried that German employees may not stay, but it turns out that they were very committed. We spend a lot of time bringing employees over here and flying our employees out there." She says what made the U.K. project so difficult was having to staff all the positions and build up a team. While the site there is doing well, Kass doubts the company will use the same strategy in the future—especially in places like France where a market leader already exists.

Which countries the company targets and how it enters depends on the existing market for online auctions in that region. Kass explains, "We are not looking to be in 24 markets all at the same time. We are looking to have a very successful community for every market we enter. So it's more important to us to be the leader in the market we are in vs. being in every continent."

No matter which strategy you choose, you still face the challenge of managing customers' expectations—and that can be difficult in the global economy. It's disconcerting to a customer to buy a familiar product—say, Crest toothpaste—overseas and find it tastes different from what he's used to at home. When Borders Books opened in London, it stocked the sports section with books about American games from baseball to ice hockey—but omitted books featuring any of the big British sports like soccer and rugby. Even distinctive brand names, chosen for the local market, can also be confusing to consumers abroad. Oil of Olay, for example, was marketed in Europe as Oil of Ulay until recently, when globalization led the company to adopt a single brand name.

Separated by A Common Language

Understanding how local tastes and attitudes influence people's reactions to products and companies is a key issue for American companies moving overseas. "The obvious error," says Steve Walker, a British independent consultant who has worked for a number of American companies abroad, "is the lack of understanding of the importance of language to people. America as I've seen it is not only monolingual but very solipsistic. The next problem is culture, for example, the difference between Swiss German and Austrian German, or French and Belgian French."

Twelve Horses' Bill Rozier agrees: "A problem Americans have is they may get the branding or color right, but then they ship in U.S. English. Just as I don't want to read the Taiwanese manual for my lawnmower, respect has to be given to a language."

David Katz, senior commercial officer at the International Marketing Center at the U.S. Embassy in London, says these problems are less common today. "I think American companies are a lot more savvy now than they were 20 years ago," he says. "Are they as internationally savvy as European or Asian companies? No, because the U.S. domestic market is so unbelievably large. But compared to where they were 20 to 30 years ago.…"

GLOBAL RESOURCES

The most important factor for succeeding globally? Doing your homework beforehand. Here's where to get started.

BASIC GUIDE TO EXPORTING
www.unzco.com/basicguide/index.html
Everything you need to know to export goods and services.

eTRANSLATE www.etranslate.com
Web site globalization services will help you translate your site, set up international billing systems, and develop an overall global strategy.

GOING GLOBAL www.going-global.com
A fine place to start, with the most comprehensive list of resources available.

LERNOUT AND HAUSPIE www.lhsl.com
Better known for its voice recognition software, this company also provides comprehensive translation services for materials and sites.

INTERNATIONAL NEWS
dir.yahoo.com/News_and_Media/By_Region/Countries/
Get a handle on the daily news in world markets through Yahoo's comprehensive listing.

INVEST IN EUROPE www.investineurope.com
Find out what you need to know to invest and do business in individual countries.

THUNDERBIRD www.thunderbird.edu
Continue your global education at the well-known graduate school for international management—or just tap into its vast resources.

UNIVERSITY OF KANSAS, SCHOOL OF BUSINESS, INTERNATIONAL BUSINESS RESOURCE CONNECTION
www.ibrc.bschool.ukans.edu/resources/articles/articles.htm
Great source of articles and global information.

U.S. COMMERCIAL SERVICE www.usatrade.gov
Don't miss its commercial guides to every country, highlighting opportunities and local conditions.

Another common mistake companies make when going global is not thinking enough about pricing. The same products frequently cost substantially more in Europe than in the United States. In Britain, for example, computer hardware or software pricing often seems to be calculated by simply switching the dollar sign to a pound sign—a 51 percent markup at today's exchange rates.

True, the cost of doing business in Europe is higher, and value-added tax takes a substantial bite. Even so, it's hard to explain why a British consumer can buy a DVD of, say, *Being John Malkovich* for $18.71 from Amazon.com but will pay £18.99 ($28.67) for the British DVD from Amazon.co.uk. The upshot, thanks to the Web and the new ease of international ordering, is a steady stream of American DVDs flowing eastward.

"Consumers are smart," says Sam Taylor, who has had to deal with precisely this kind of issue as vice president, international, for Lands' End. "If companies are not pricing fairly, [consumers will] figure out ways to get around it."

The best advice for avoiding these kinds of mistakes? It's the same principle you followed when you launched your product: Know your market. For a broad perspective, look to the Department of Commerce (www.doc.gov), which publishes reports on virtually every country. And specialists such as Levy or major consultancy firms like Ernst & Young, Pricewaterhouse-Coopers, the Yankee Group, and the Boston Consulting Group offer globalization services. (For more help, see "Global Resources,").

They Do Things Differently There

Changes abroad are also making it easier for American companies to do business internationally. The euro, for example, paves the way toward easier cross-border trading among the 15 member states of the EU, as well as American businesses. The dropping of national customs controls within Europe will also ease international trade.

But you'll still have to deal with very different independent legal and tax systems in each country. One problem is the value-added tax, the European equivalent of sales tax. VAT rates vary widely across Europe—ranging from 15 percent to 25 percent—as do exempt items, which can include children's clothing and books.

VAT administration is complicated because each country has a threshold of sales; if a company falls below this threshold, it doesn't have to report its earnings for tax purposes. But the advent of e-commerce makes it easier than ever to pass that threshold without planning to. Requirements for VAT registration vary too; in some countries you need a local representative and office. To make matters worse, VAT agents from the various countries you'll deal with might not agree on how the system works.

That's what happened to Moda1to1, a U.S.-based Web site selling Italian custom-made men's clothing. When the company tried to determine how to calculate taxes for sales to Britain initially, both the British and the Italian tax officials insisted the money should be paid to them (though eventually they worked it out and paid only the Italians). Typically, a business pays VAT to the country it's based in, but there are exceptions depending on the class of goods you're selling.

Your best bet? Always get information from the tax office in writing if possible, as different tax officials may give conflicting answers. The EU is hoping to standardize VAT regulations, but changes will take several years. The EU is also considering a proposal that requires U.S. businesses selling to Europe on the Web to charge VAT.

WENDY M. GROSSMAN *is a freelance technology writer based in London. Additional reporting by* RENUKA RAYASAM.

SMART ANSWERS

Lights Amid the Gloom

As America prepares for war, entrepreneurs are recognizing opportunities in the fields of security and defense

By Karen E. Klein

Uncertainty about the future descended thickly in the days following Sept. 11. Will there be a war? Where? For how long? How safe are we here at home? Opinion polls show that increasing numbers of Americans now believe the economy, already slipping, is sliding toward full-blown recession. Small-business owners, insecure and scared, are not sure what their next move should be.

Not everyone sees doom on the horizon, however. In fact, there are optimists among us who believe that entrepreneurial opportunities will abound, even at a time when the cost of doing business may rise. When corporations merge and downsize, they say, small and medium-sized companies provide the perfect solution: outsourcing. In the spirit of bolstering the entrepreneurial outlook, this column discusses a few of the sectors where tragic circumstances have provided new possibilities.

Security systems for buildings, personnel, school campuses, and corporations are going to become serious priorities, experts say. Before Sept. 11, Matthew Simmons, owner of security identification badge company OneCard, averaged 200 unique visitors per day to his Web site. The day after the terrorist attacks, the site logged more than 350 unique visitors, and he has averaged more than 300 per day since. "Security is transforming identification badges from a luxury to a requirement. Companies are calling up with a sense of urgency," Simmons says. "I got a call from a Jewish community center that used OneCard for their membership identification cards, and now the police strongly urged them to have employee badges made up, too."

Videoconferencing is quickly becoming an appealing alternative to in-person business meetings, and technological advances that once seemed too much hassle to master are now looking more appealing. Martin Shum, CEO of engineering software firm Aprisa, hosted two online trade shows last year for his industry niche. While exhibitor participation and traffic to the sites were good, the company put the virtual shows on hold after they realized that hosting them cost more than the company could recoup in fees. Now, all that may change. "Given today's environment, we may go back to that idea and make it a profit center rather than a cost exercise," Shum says.

CHEAPER AND SAFER. Information technology is going to grow in importance all around, experts say. "This portends great things for technology as it displaces traditional transportation," says Rob Frankel, a branding and new-media expert. "In my own case, I likely will not be able to speak at a conference scheduled for later this month in the Persian Gulf. However, there's a good chance that that venue will continue by videoconference." The use of technology to bring people in scattered locations together will grow exponentially over the next year, Frankel predicts. "A year from now, they'll ask for videoconferencing first, before they ask for personal appearances, but they won't mention the security aspect. It will be perceived as a cost efficiency."

Obtaining more services over the wire, rather than in person, will appeal to large corporations, as well. Establishing workers in telecommuting positions will be only natural for companies worried about the vulnerability of placing all their employees, projects, and records in one huge headquarters location. And outsourcing some of their operations to small companies will make both safety and dollar sense. "Why have someone sitting in an office crunching numbers or doing billing all day, when a company can hire a small outsourcer who works at home and can transmit all the figures and forms online, and also has the time to get other business contracts?" asks Barry Allen, whose International Fieldworks management consulting firm urges its clients to rely on telecommuting and outsourcing.

The defense industry, with infusions of government spending after many years of smaller budgets and base closures, will surely make plans for security investments in the coming months. As a result, Mary Ann Mitchell is gearing up for increased business—by perhaps as much as 25%—at her Culver City, Calif.-based company, CC-OPS, which works for military and defense contractors and expects to net $25 million this year. Though Mitchell, like all the entrepreneurs interviewed for this column, is loath to contemplate profits in the wake of tragedy,

she anticipates that her systems automation and integration firm will be hired for new projects.

Mitchell says that she is gearing up her employees for an expected increase in the need for computer security. "I'm thinking about the value we can add to secure our country. The fact that we have relationships in place with the [Dept. of Defense] and many of the contractors, and we have had security clearances for many years, will make it likely that we can help, I'm sure," she says. If more small companies are contracted by the military, they will wind up forming strategic alliances with larger corporations like Raytheon and Northrup, she says, giving them additional benefits down the line.

"It's to [the government's] advantage… using smaller companies, because we can offer more competitive prices and more specialization," adds Mitchell. "They don't have to go out and hire 60 people—they can outsource much more efficiently."

UNIT 2

Creating and Launching the Business Venture

Unit Selections

Key Points to Consider

- How can inventors increase their chance of creating a viable business venture? What marketing research should the entrepreneur use to analyze new opportunities?

- How can the entrepreneur use strategic planning to reduce risks? What information should a good business plan contain?

- What are the characteristics of a successful entrepreneurial management team?

 **Links: www.dushkin.com/online/**
These sites are annotated in the World Wide Web pages.

Economics Research Associates
http://www.econres.com
Fortune
http://www.fortune.com/indexw.jhtml?channel=editorial/site_map.html
Internal Auditing World Wide Web
http://www.bitwise.net/iawww/
National Business Incubation Association
http://www.nbia.org
Stockholm University
http://www.psychology.su.se/units/ao/ao.html
U.S. Chamber of Commerce Small Business Institute
http://www.uschamber.org/Small+Business/default.htm
U.S. Department of Labor
http://www.dol.gov
U.S. Federal Trade Commission
http://www.ftc.gov

Entrepreneurs see opportunity where others see risks. They generate lots of ideas as they pursue business opportunities. But for professional or "serial" entrepreneurs with eyes on limited resources, launching a new business means more than just "scratching the cerebral itch." Very seldom do they act on impulse. Experts say that an entrepreneur can never be too prepared—screening out unpromising ventures requires a methodology based on experience, judgment, and internal reflection, but not always upon mounds of new data. With a little insight and diligent preparation, people who yearn for their own business can feel confident of forthcoming success or, at the very least, can decide rationally that they should not start one.

The key to creating and starting the new business venture successfully is to look at the new business strategy and the window of market opportunity, and then measure the appropriate risk and consider whether or not the opportunity fits personal goals and needs. Assessing viability requires analyzing a venture's ability to profitably win customers, employees, resources, and to secure financing. This unit discusses the legal issues entrepreneurs face and creating the business and marketing plans. Subsequent units cover financing issues and managing rapid growth.

The opportunity should be based on a distinct "competitive advantage" that creates a "barrier to entry," preventing others from following. A competitive advantage may be based on an invention, unique "intellectual property" like software code, or the entrepreneur may be a "domain expert" having unique insight about solving a particular problem in a sector of a large industry. In fact, 60 percent of the *Inc.* 500 CEOs say that the idea for their company came while working in the same industry. No venture will have the resources or ability to compete against all competitors and should not attempt to do so. Instead, an entrepreneur should target a few key competitors and act to ensure success against them. The opportunity should be a niche with potential for plenty of growth and high-gross margins in order to make sure that the startup has enough capital to achieve long-term viability.

What form should the new business venture take? One of the key issues that an entrepreneur must resolve very early in the entrepreneurial process is what legal form of organization the venture should adopt. Creating the legal entity that best supports the opportunity is almost always a challenge. It is very important that the entrepreneur carefully evaluate the pros and cons of the various legal forms when organizing the new venture. This requires the entrepreneur to determine the priority of each of the factors mentioned in this unit. Variations, and their advantages and disadvantages, are numerous. Finally, these decisions about the legal entity must be made prior to the submission of a business plan and the request for venture capital, loans, lines of credit, and joint ventures.

Successful entrepreneurs don't take risks blindly. They carefully craft strategies that work. But still, reports indicate that 90 percent of small businesses don't have a business plan or business strategy. Some claim that they lack the time and money to research business opportunities. Others indicate that they don't understand the value of strategic planning and consider it a waste of time. But all are in a race with time because by the time an opportunity is investigated fully, they know that it may no longer exist. If done wisely though, strategic planning can help entrepreneurs reach a higher level of success in their ventures.

Few areas of entrepreneurship attract as much attention as the business plan. Professional entrepreneurs, advisers, educators, and consultants know that writing a business plan is part art, part science. The business plan is probably the single most important document to any entrepreneur at the startup stage because it is the preferred mode of communication between entrepreneurs and potential investors, and it also becomes a selling document that conveys a level of excitement and promise to any potential investor or stakeholder.

Preparing a business plan that needs to both guide the growth of the new venture and attract interest from outside stakeholders requires a great amount of skill, time, and analysis. A well-prepared business plan is used internally to help the venture team decide what choices are to be made about startup costs and to help figure out how the venture will be managed. Most important, the plan should help the team to identify the resources required to pursue the opportunity, explain how the team will gather the resources required, and, finally, propose methodologies for controlling and allocating critical capital resources. A business plan can also be used externally for raising financing. The plan should be able to convince and communicate to investors that the new venture has identified an opportunity, the venture team has the entrepreneurial talent to exploit that opportunity, and the management has the needed skills for achieving positive cash flow targets on time. Note that our *topic guide* at the beginning of this text is framed around the business plan outline we have presented in this unit.

Finally, the selection of stakeholders and organizational structure for any business venture requires some major decisions that will affect long-term effectiveness and profitability. When it comes to successful entrepreneurs and entrepreneurial teams, most investors will agree that they prefer a grade A entrepreneur with a grade B business idea to a grade B entrepreneur with a grade A idea. In other words, they prefer to bet on the jockey and not the horse. Since no one individual can possess all the attributes that venture capitalists and academics say are important for success, it is generally a strong entrepreneurial management team, not a lone entrepreneur, that investors will back. Regardless of how great the opportunity may seem to be, it will not become a successful venture unless it is developed by a venture team with strong entrepreneurial and management skills.

ONE MORE TIME... SHOULD SMALL COMPANIES ATTEMPT *STRATEGIC* PLANNING?

ABSTRACT *Most entrepreneurs and small company owners agree they need a strategic plan. Pursued for an explanation, many envision a business plan that enables a relationship with a bank, investor or supplier. Beyond that, they often view the plan having little real value. They see successful venturing as a combination of good ideas and persistence, not a plan or roadmap. Sadly, these are necessary but not sufficient conditions for success. What is needed and often ignored is a strategy—a logic for competing and a logic for organizing. Tight integration of the these two concepts lays the foundation for competitive advantage—the basis of superiority over rivals in serving a particular market. And creating a logic for competing and a logic for organizing is the job of simple strategic planning, the rudiments of which are discussed in this article along with simple reasons you should do it and a few references you might use to get started.*

William R. Sandberg, University of South Carolina
Richard Robinson, University of South Carolina
John A. Pearce II, Villanova University

INTRODUCTION

Most entrepreneurs and small company owner/managers agree they need a plan. Pursued for an explanation, they allow that some form of a business plan, or company description and financial projections, has proven essential to establishing a line of credit, getting a loan, or attracting an investor. They often clarify their position by adding that the plan has little real value, and that it indeed has been ignored since the loan was received, the line of credit was established, or the investor brought on board.

As we have studied and worked with thousands of entrepreneurs and their businesses over the last 20 years, this perspective has begun to make sense. Admonitions to plan aside, a business or financial "plan" that serves only as a resource solicitation document is just that! Created to accomplish that objective, it is set aside so that tomorrow's efforts and undertakings may be focused on tomorrow's new objectives. So admonishing entrepreneurs with the importance of their "plan" accomplishes little and brings immediately to their minds a stale document that has served its purpose and, not surprisingly, has little contemporary relevance.

The admonition to plan could gain an audience if we simply change the semantics of the conversation to *planning*.

Adding the "ing" adds the notion of action... doing... which begins to gain a bit of a raised eyelid from the entrepreneur. General Eisenhower's famous dictum, *"it's not the plan, it's the process of planning,"* has a certain relevance here. He had in mind the discipline of figuring things out and a management team's give and take during that process, which gives this simple notion some credibility in the entrepreneur's mind. Unfortunately, that spark of credibility is satisfied in many entrepreneurs' minds with the follow-on notion that *yes, that planning process was useful, and the next time we need to create a business plan or financial plan for our banker or investor the process will be more appreciated as a meaningful activity.* Or, for the more humorous entrepreneur, it is synonymous with the notion that *planning by the seat of your pants usually means you end up with torn pants.* Both such follow-on notions are sadly incomplete.

IDEAS AND PERSISTENCE ARE NOT ENOUGH

What's missing from this contemplation and discussion of the lasting value of planning, or even of a plan, may still be a matter of semantics. At the risk of oversimplifying something that may truly be profound, the issue may boil down to the word *strategic* and what it means, or should mean, to the entrepreneur or small business when coupled to the word *plan*, or more importantly, *planning*.

Most of us are familiar with common arguments-by-analogy in favor of *strategic* planning by small businesses. They often sound something like the following: *"No strategic plan? Would you travel through unfamiliar territory without a map?"* We've heard this one countless times, and it sounds reasonable to us—

but then we already believe in the value of strategic planning to small businesses.

Many owners and managers of small businesses, on the other hand, are less convinced of its value. They object that the road to success isn't waiting, paved and marked, for the entrepreneur who remembered to bring the map—and they're right! And they're right again when they add that successful entrepreneurs start out with an idea, a concept, or an urge, and combine it with persistence. The sad fact is, however, that these ingredients are necessary but not sufficient conditions for success.

Research and experience show that nearly all entrepreneurs—successful and failed—start with an idea, concept, or urge. Many of them persist, some even when failure should be obvious. A few are "lucky" but hardly enough to account for the majority of successes. Besides, as football coach Ara Parseghian used to tell his teams, "Luck is when preparation meets opportunity." In business, preparation comes through *strategic* planning.

THE VALUE OF A STRATEGY

Many owners and managers of small businesses routinely plan their day-to-day operations but don't believe that *strategic* planning applies to them. Mention strategic planning, and they think of elaborate bound documents resting on bookshelves in the offices of large companies, or of the detailed plans used in project management. That's where many small businesses go wrong. No business is too small to require a sound strategy, and few strategies are so simple that they need not be developed into a strategic plan. Our hope in writing this article is briefly to explain why small businesses need a strategic plan and to suggest several sources of detailed guidance for readers who wish to learn more.

A strategy spells out three elements that are essential to any business: (1) its *goals*, (2) the *policies* or rules that guide its decisions, and (3) the *actions* intended to accomplish its goals. This seems cut-and-dried, but actually developing and executing a strategy is far from a routine, connect-the-dots process. The thinking behind a strategy need not be sophisticated, but nevertheless must be thorough and careful.

A firm's strategy should serve as its *logic for competing*—a coherent encapsulation of its products and services, the markets and types of customers it serves, and the benefits they derive. From this logic come the firm's decision on how to position itself against rivals, on which markets to focus, and which opportunities to pursue. A strategy also should summarize the firm's *logic for organizing*—an identification of key activities and how they will be carried out to realize the logic for competing. From the logic for organizing come decisions on which activities are critical to the firm's success, how the tasks required by these activities should be grouped into jobs, and what criteria are appropriate in evaluating the performance of those jobs. Tight integration of the logics for competing and for organizing lays the foundation for the firm's *competitive advantage*—the basis of its superiority over rivals in serving a particular market or market segments.

THE PERIL OF HAVING *NO* STRATEGY

Over the past twenty years we have worked with over 1,000 small businesses, either supervising teams of students who consulted to them or on a personal consulting basis. Our observations of these and other small businesses square with what experts have written: *At least half of small businesses do not have a strategy.* The consequences vary in their particulars, but the pattern of increased failure is clear among these companies.

Without a strategy's *logic for competing*, a florist clambered vainly after each specialized market developed by her successful rivals, never identifying a market opportunity suited to her own resources and location. A home-inspection service struggled to survive, seeking business directly from homeowners through small advertisements and business cards posted on bulletin boards while rivals developed productive relations with leading realtors. The partners in a startup venture to produce an industrial product drained their capital in securing a production site, equipment, and component parts prior to identifying a target market or the distribution channel to reach one.

Without a strategy's *logic for organizing*, a graphic arts partnership identified one market as its primary target but devoted most of its sales efforts to two other markets. Lacking knowledge of its own costs-by-products, a producer of consumer commodities vigorously promoted items on which, at best, it broke even and neglected items that earned robust margins. A restaurateur attempted to combine large-volume, off-site catering and a diverse, sit-down luncheon menu from one small kitchen.

Each of these businesses benefitted from an entrepreneur's idea, concept, or urge, and each entrepreneur labored with total devotion to make it succeed. And ofttimes that devotion to success can be documented though one or more "plans" that became dust-collecting reminders of loans won or investments sold. Yet each of these businesses failed or came perilously close to failure because it lacked a coherent strategy, expressed in a *strategic* plan. Their entrepreneurs' close attention to daily operations and immediate tactics, as well as their occasional business plans, were not sufficient to ensure survival, let alone success, in the absence of a logic for competing or of a logic for organizing.

GETTING STARTED ON STRATEGIC PLANNING

We don't mean to suggest that any strategy is better than none. We have seen companies killed by strategies so wrongheaded that they probably were worse that unguided, reactive decisions. With that experience in mind, we urge owners and managers of small companies to do strategic planning, and do it well.

Many good sources of advice and guidance are available. We will recommend several that can get you started. Complete reference information for each book is provided at the end of this article.

For an introduction to *strategic* planning and related issues in the small business, we suggest that you consider two books. *Simplified Strategic Planning: A No-Nonsense Guide for Busy People Who Want Results Fast!* is the product of extensive work by its authors with small and medium-sized businesses. The book presents straightforward, concise guidance (including planning templates) and a logical sequence for developing a strategic plan without a large staff. While it draws heavily on the academic work of leading researchers James Brian Quinn (Dartmouth/Tuck) and Michael Porter (Harvard), the book has a firm grounding in the environment of businesses that cannot ignore daily operational requirements for the sake of planning. A second introductory book, *Applied Strategic Planning: How to Develop a Plan That Really Works*, was written by three consultants and trainers and offers a clear, effective way to identify and implement strategic objectives. It covers all phases of the strategic planning process, including determining if an organization is ready for strategic planning. The book offers numerous charts, diagrams, and checklists to aid readers in applying its ideas to their businesses. It is particularly appropriate for the beginning strategic planner.

The entrepreneur or small company builder who wants to take strategy development to its highest level might consider one of the following books. *Leading the Revolution*, by Gary Hamel, is a recent, important best seller that integrates the arguments of many leading thinkers into one set of procedures for constantly establishing and superbly implementing improved business models for customers interfaces, core strategy, using strategic resources, and value networks. *Corporate Strategy: A Resource-Based Approach*, by David Collis and Cynthia Montgomery, gives small company owners several conceptual tools, built around the notion of a company's strategy being crafted from a unique understanding of its true strategic resources, with which to guide quality strategic thinking and analysis of their company and shape sound strategies. Finally, Michael Porter offers a time-tested set of three classic books to guide your strategic thinking: *Michael Porter on Competition, Competitive Strategy*, and *Competitive Advantage*. Martyn Richard Jones, founder of Iniciativas, a management consulting firm, had this to say in an Amazon.com book review (March 3, 2001) about Porter's books: "You can always tell when it's time to dust off the old Michael E. Porter books and to start to frantically search for better and sounder ways to do business and compete, it's when the economy starts to get a little tighter and begins to show signs of taking a down-turn, like about now. So, before you fork out good money and time to read the next grandiose book on how to make a fast few million bucks on the internet read this first, and you will still be in business this time next year, and after that—maybe."

A final set of reading recommendations involves strategy implementation. As important as the competitive logic behind a strategy can be, it is execution of those ideas that determine success. One new book, *The Strategy-Focused Organization: How Balanced Scorecard Companies Thrive in the New Business Environment*, by Robert Kaplan and David Norton, offers an impressive framework building upon their "balanced score-

board" approach for the implementation of strategy. Their research suggests that 90% of strategic plans fail due not to formulation but to implementation difficulties. This book suggests ways to align and link all parts of an organization to its strategy and offers numerous examples to help managers adapt their ideas. In short, it addressed the logic of organizing. A second book, *Formulation, Implementation and Control of Competitive Strategy*, by Jack Pearce and Richard Robinson, offers broad coverage of a variety of concepts and models for implementing and controlling strategy execution.

John Naisbett's book, *Global Paradox*, predicted that the larger and more interconnected the world economy becomes, the more important become the smallest players in that economy. We mention this book in closing because Naisbett's evidence is compelling: the rate of change, the impact of technology, the importance of speed, and the ability to reach anywhere in the world—all create the opportunity for competitive advantage among smaller companies. And large companies are rapidly deconstructing and reorganizing to respond to this critical advantage that's inherent to their smaller competitors. With so much 21st century opportunity, many entrepreneurs with excellent ideas, concepts, or urges will labor with total devotion to build new companies. Yet history suggests that many of these exciting new businesses will fail or come perilously close to failure because they lack a coherent *strategy*, expressed in a *strategic* plan. The entrepreneurs' close attention to daily operations and immediate tactics, as well as their occasional business plans, will not be sufficient to ensure survival, let alone success. In this historical period of global opportunity for small business, that will be a shame.

REFERENCES

The texts were referenced in the following sequence by the authors:

Bradford, R. W., Duncan, J. P., Duncan, P. & B. Tracey. (1999). *Simplified Strategic Planning: A No-Nonsense Guide for Busy People Who Want Results Fast!* New York: Chandler House Press.

Goodstein, L., Nolan, T. & J. W. Pfeiffer. (1992). *Applied Strategy Planning: How to Develop a Plan That Really Works*. New York: McGraw-Hill.

Hamel, G. (2000). *Leading the Revolution*. Cambridge: Harvard Business School Press.

Collis, D. J. & C. A. Montgomery. (1997). *Corporate Strategy: A Resource-Based Approach*. Chicago: McGraw-Hill Higher Education.

Porter, M. (1998). *Michael Porter on Competition*. Cambridge: Harvard Business School Press.

Porter, M. (1998). *Competitive Strategy: Techniques for Analyzing Industries and Competitors*. New York: The Free Press.

Porter, M. (1998). *Competitive Advantage: Creating and Sustaining Superior Performance*. New York: The Free Press.

Pearce, J. A. & R. B. Robinson. (2000). *Formulation, Implementation and Control of Competitive Strategy*. Chicago: McGraw-Hill Higher Education.

Naisbett, J. (1994). *Global Paradox*. New York: William and Morrow.

Entrepreneurs adopt the approaches that work —and they're quick, cheap and timely.

How Entrepreneurs Craft Strategies That Work

By Amar Bhidé

However popular it may be in the corporate world, a comprehensive analytical approach to planning doesn't suit most start-ups. Entrepreneurs typically lack the time and money to interview a representative cross section of potential customers, let alone analyze substitutes, reconstruct competitors' cost structures, or project alternative technology scenarios. In fact, too much analysis can be harmful; by the time an opportunity is investigated fully, it may no longer exist. A city map and restaurant guide on a CD may be a winner in January but worthless if delayed until December.

By the time an opportunity is investigated fully, it may no longer exist.

Interviews with the founders of 100 companies on the 1989 *Inc.* "500" list of the fastest growing private companies in the United States and recent research on more than 100 other thriving ventures by my MBA students suggest that many successful entrepreneurs spend little time researching and analyzing. [See the box, "Does Planning Pay?"] And those who do often have to scrap their strategies and start over. Furthermore, a 1990 National Federation of Independent Business study of 2,994 start-ups showed that founders who spent a long time in study, reflection, and planning were no more likely to survive their first three years than people who seized opportunities without planning. In fact, many corporations that revere comprehensive analysis develop a refined incapacity for seizing opportunities. Analysis can delay entry until it's too late or kill ideas by identifying numerous problems.

Yet all ventures merit some analysis and planning. Appearances to the contrary, successful entrepreneurs don't take risks blindly. Rather, they use a quick, cheap approach that represents a middle ground between planning paralysis and no planning at all. They don't expect perfection—even the most astute entrepreneurs have their share of false starts. Compared to typical corporate practice, however, the entrepreneurial approach is more economical and timely.

What are the critical elements of winning entrepreneurial approaches? Our evidence suggests three general guidelines for aspiring founders:

1. Screen opportunities quickly to weed out unpromising ventures.

2. Analyze ideas parsimoniously. Focus on a few important issues.

3. Integrate action and analysis. Don't wait for all the answers, and be ready to change course.

Screening Out Losers

Individuals who seek entrepreneurial opportunities usually generate lots of ideas. Quickly discarding those that have low potential frees aspirants to concentrate on the few ideas that merit refinement and study.

Screening out unpromising ventures requires judgment and reflection, not new data. The entrepreneur should already be familiar with the facts needed to determine whether an idea has prima facie merit. Our evidence suggests that new ventures are usually started to solve problems the founders have grappled with personally as customers or employees. (See the diagram "Where Do Entrepreneurs Get Their Ideas?") Companies like Federal Express, which grew out of a paper its founder wrote in college, are rare.

Profitable survival requires an edge derived from some combination of a creative idea and a superior capacity for execution. (See the diagram "Tipping the Competitive Balance.") The entrepreneur's creativity may involve an innovative product or a process that changes the existing order. Or the entrepreneur may have a unique insight about the course or consequence of an external change: the California gold rush, for example, made paupers of the thousands caught in the frenzy, but Levi Strauss started a company— and a legend—by recognizing the opportunity to supply rugged canvas and later denim trousers to prospectors.

But entrepreneurs cannot rely on just inventing new products or anticipating a trend. They must also execute well, especially if their concepts can be copied easily. For example, if an innovation cannot be patented or kept secret, entrepreneurs must acquire and manage the resources needed to build a brand name or other barrier that will deter imitators. Superior execution can also compensate for a me-too concept in emerging or rapidly growing industries where doing it quickly and doing it right are more important than brilliant strategy.

Ventures that obviously lack a creative concept or any special capacity to execute—the ex-consultant's scheme to exploit grandmother's cookie recipe, for instance—can be discarded without much thought. In other cases, entrepreneurs must reflect on the adequacy of their ideas and their capacities to execute them.

Successful start-ups don't need an edge on every front. The creativity of successful entrepreneurs varies considerably. Some implement a radical idea, some modify, and some show no originality. Capacity for execution also varies among entrepreneurs. Selling an industrial niche product doesn't call for the charisma that's required to pitch trinkets through infomercials. Our evidence suggests that there is no ideal entrepreneurial profile either: successful founders can be gregarious or taciturn, analytical or intuitive, good or terrible with details, risk averse or thrill seeking. They can be delegators or control freaks, pillars of the community or outsiders. In assessing the viability of a potential venture, therefore, each aspiring entrepreneur should consider three interacting factors:

There is no ideal profile. Entrepreneurs can be gregarious or taciturn, analytical or intuitive, cautious or daring.

1. Objectives of the Venture. Is the entrepreneur's goal to build a large, enduring enterprise, carve out a niche, or merely turn a quick profit? Ambitious goals require great creativity. Building a large enterprise quickly, either by seizing a significant share of an existing market or by creating a large new market, usually calls for a revolutionary idea. Launching Home Depot, for example, called for a

new retailing concept of immense proportions; opening a traditional hardware store does not. Revolutionary enterprises usually require new processes or manufacturing techniques; competitive markets rarely fail to provide valuable products or services unless providing them involves serious technological problems.

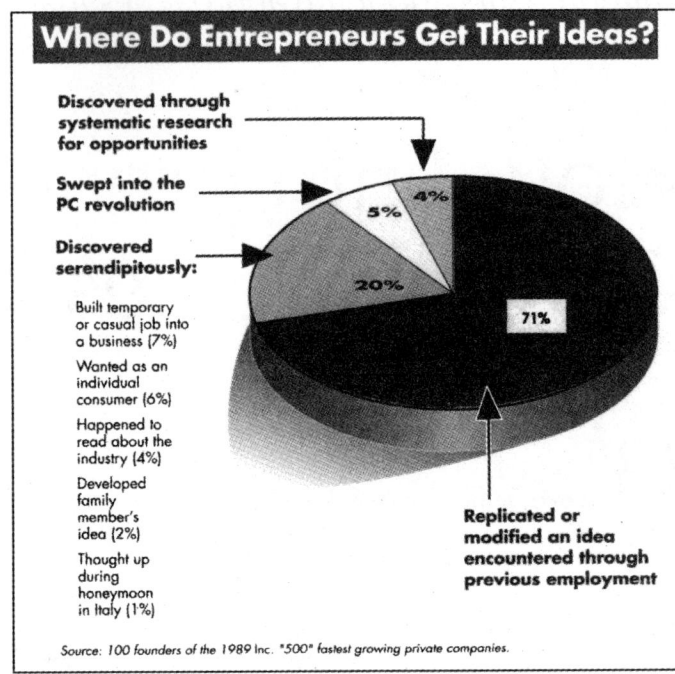

Where Do Entrepreneurs Get Their Ideas?

Discovered through systematic research for opportunities — 4%

Swept into the PC revolution — 5%

Discovered serendipitously: — 20%
- Built temporary or casual job into a business (7%)
- Wanted as an individual consumer (6%)
- Happened to read about the industry (4%)
- Developed family member's idea (2%)
- Thought up during honeymoon in Italy (1%)

71% Replicated or modified an idea encountered through previous employment

Source: 100 founders of the 1989 Inc. "500" fastest growing private companies.

Requirements for execution are also still. Big ideas often necessitate big money and strong organizations. Successful entrepreneurs, therefore, require an evangelical ability to attract, retain, and balance the interests of investors, customers, employees, and suppliers for a seemingly outlandish vision, as well as the organizational and leadership skills to build a large, complex company quickly. In addition, the entrepreneur may require considerable technical know-how in deal making, strategic planning, managing overhead, and other business skills. The revolutionary entrepreneur, in other words, would appear to require almost superhuman qualities: ordinary mortals need not apply.

Consider Federal Express founder Fred Smith. His creativity lay in recognizing that customers would pay a significant premium for reliable overnight delivery and in figuring out a way to provide the service for them. Smith ruled out using existing commercial flights, whose schedules were designed to serve passenger traffic. Instead, he had the audacious idea of acquiring a dedicated fleet of jets and shipping all packages through a central hub that was located in Memphis.

As with most big ideas, the concept was difficult to execute. Smith, 28 years old at the time, had to raise $91 million in venture funding. The jets, the hub, operations in 25 states, and several hundred trained employees had to be in place before the company could open for business. And Smith needed great fortitude and skill to prevent the fledgling enterprise from going under: Federal Express lost over

Does Planning Pay?

Interviews with the founders of 100 companies on the 1989 *Inc.* "500" list of the fastest growing companies in the Untied States revealed that entrepreneurs spent little effort on their initial business plan:

41% had no business plan at all.

26% had just a rudimentary, back-of-the-envelope type of plan.

5% worked up financial projections for investors.

28% wrote up a full-blown plan.

Many entrepreneurs, the interviews suggested, don't bother with well-formulated plans for good reasons. They thrive in rapidly changing industries and niches that tend to deter established companies. And under these fluid conditions, an ability to roll with the punches is much more important than careful planning.

The experiences of two *Inc.* "500" companies, Attronica Computers and Boh dan Associates, illustrate the limitations of planning in entrepreneurial ventures. Carol Sosdian and Atul Tucker, who had worked together in a large corporation, started Attronica in 1983 to retail personal computers in Washington, D.C. Carol recalls that Atul "wrote a one-paragraph business plan and brought it to me, and I turned it into a real business plan. It took about one month, and then we bantered back and forth over the next three months. We got to where we thought it might work, and then we showed it to some friends. It passed the 'friends test.'"

Heartened, Carol and Atul conducted almost two years of market research,

which led them to purchase a Byte franchise for $150,000. Soon after they opened their first store, however, Byte folded. They then signed on as a franchisee of World of Computers, which also folded, and in 1985, Attronica began to operate as an independent, direct dealer for AT&T's computers. This partnership clicked, and Attronica soon became one of AT&T's best dealers. Attronica also changed its customer focus from people off the street to corporate and government clients. They found large clients much more profitable because they valued Attronica's technical expertise and service.

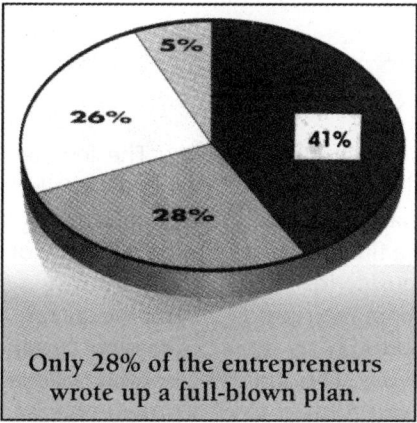

Only 28% of the entrepreneurs wrote up a full-blown plan.

Peter Zacharkiw founded Bohdan Associates in a Washington, D.C., suburb in the same year that Atul and Carol launched Attronica. Peter did not conduct any research, however. He was em-

ployed by Bechtel and invested in tax shelters on the side. He bought a computer for his tax shelter calculations, expecting to deduct the cost of the machine from his income. When Peter discovered that he was overdeducted for the year, he placed an ad in the *Washington Post* to sell his computer. He got over 50 responses and sold his machine for a profit. Peter figured that if he had had 50 machines, he could have sold them all and decided to begin selling computers from his home. "At first, I just wanted to earn a little extra Christmas money," he recalls. "My wife put systems together during the day, and I delivered them at night. We grew to $300,000 per month, and I was still working full-time. I made more then than I would have made the entire year at Bechtel."

Like Attronica, Bohdan evolved into serving corporate clients. "First, we sold to individuals responding to ads. But these people were working for companies, and they would tell their purchasing agents, 'Hey, I know where you can get these.' It was an all-referral business. I gave better service than anyone else. I would deliver them, install them, and spend time teaching buyers how to use them." In 1985, after customers started asking for Compaq machines, Bohdan became a Compaq dealer, and the business really took off. "We're very reactive, not proactive," Peter observes. "Business comes to us, and we react. I've never had a business plan."

$40 million in its first three years. Some investors tried to remove Smith, and creditors tried to seize assets. Yet Smith somehow preserved morale and mollified investors and lenders while the company expanded its operations and launched national advertising and direct-mail campaigns to build market share.

In contrast, ventures that seek to capture a market niche, not transform or create an industry, don't need extraordinary ideas. Some ingenuity is necessary to design a product that will draw customers away from mainstream offerings and overcome the cost penalty of serving a small market. But features that are too novel can be a hindrance; a niche market will rarely justify the investment required to educate customers and distributors about the benefits of a radically new product. Similarly, a niche venture cannot support too much production or distribution innovation; unlike Federal

Express, the Cape Cod Potato Chip Company, for example, must work within the limits of its distributors and truckers.

And since niche markets cannot support much investment or overhead, entrepreneurs do not need the revolutionary's ability to raise capital and build large organizations. Rather, the entrepreneur must be able to secure others' resources on favorable terms and make do with less, building brand awareness through guerrilla marketing and word of mouth instead of national advertising, for example.

Jay Boberg and Miles Copeland, who launched International Record Syndicate (IRS) in 1979, used a niche strategy, my students Elisabeth Bentel and Victoria Hackett found, to create one of the most successful new music labels in North America. Lacking the funds or a great innovation to compete against the major labels, Boberg and Miles promoted "alternative" music—undiscovered British

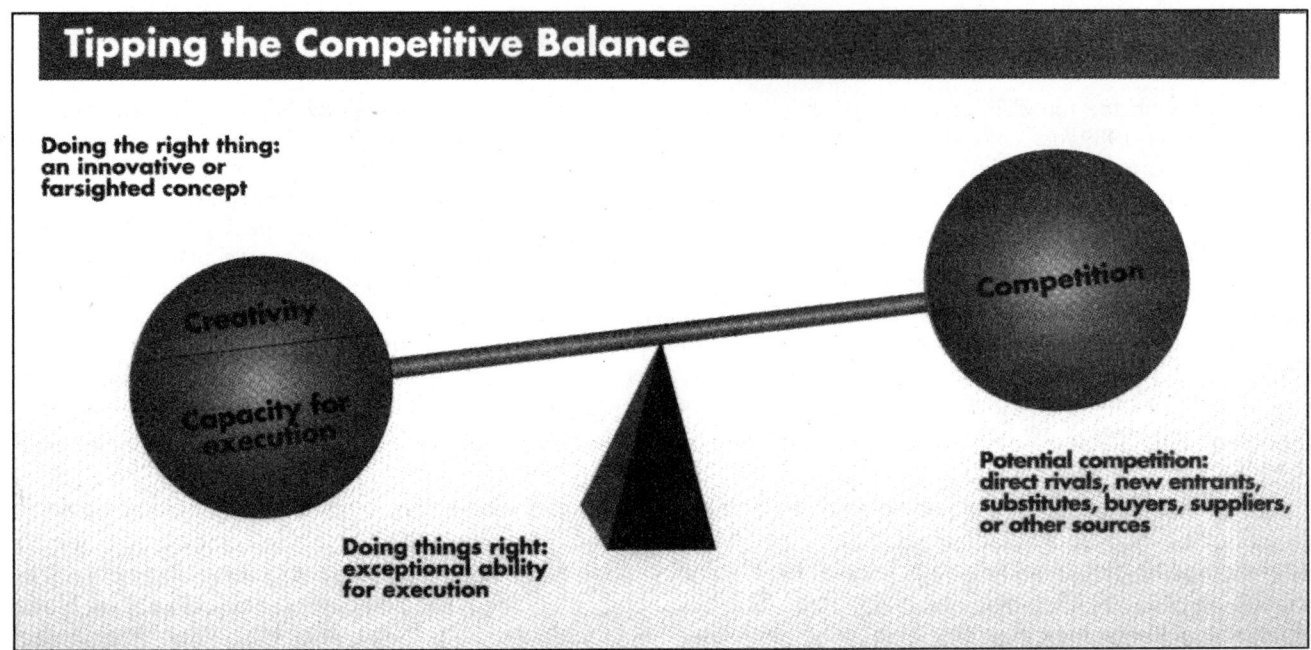

Tipping the Competitive Balance

Doing the right thing:
an innovative or
farsighted concept

Creativity

Capacity for
execution

Doing things right:
exceptional ability
for execution

Competition

Potential competition:
direct rivals, new entrants,
substitutes, buyers, suppliers,
or other sources

groups like the Buzzcocks and Skafish—which the major labels were ignoring because their potential sales were too small. And IRS used low-cost, alternative marketing methods to promote their alternative music. At the time, the major record labels had not yet realized that music videos on television could be used effectively to promote their products. Boberg, however, jumped at the opportunity to produce a rock show, "The Cutting Edge," for MTV. The show proved to be a hit with fans and an effective promotional tool for IRS. Before "The Cutting Edge," Boberg had to plead with radio stations to play his songs. Afterward, the MTV audience demanded that disc jockeys play the songs they had heard on the show.

2. Leverage Provided by External Change. Exploiting opportunities in a new or changing industry is generally easier than making waves in a mature industry. Enormous creativity, experience, and contacts are needed to take business away from competitors in a mature industry, where market forces have long shaken out weak technologies, strategies, and organizations.

But new markets are different. There start-ups often face rough-around-the-edges rivals, customers who tolerate inexperienced vendors and imperfect products, and opportunities to profit from shortages. Small insights and marginal innovations, a little skill or expertise (in the land of the blind, the one-eyed person is king), and the willingness to act quickly can go a long way. In fact, with great external uncertainty, customers and investors may be hesitant to back a radical product and technology until the environment settles down. Strategic choices in a new industry are often very limited; entrepreneurs have to adhere to the emerging standards for product features, components, or distribution channels.

The leverage provided by external change is illustrated by the success of numerous start-ups in hardware, software, training, retailing, and systems integration that emerged from the personal computer revolution of the 1980s. Installing or fixing a computer system is probably easier than repairing a car; but because people with the initiative or foresight to acquire the skill were scarce, entrepreneurs like Bohdan's Peter Zacharkiw built successful dealerships by providing what customers saw as exceptional service (see "Does Planning Pay?"). As one Midwestern dealer told me, "We have a joke slogan around here: We aren't as incompetent as our competitors!"

Bill Gates turned Microsoft into a multibillion-dollar company without a breakthrough product by showing up in the industry early and capitalizing on the opportunities that came his way. Gates, then 19, and his partner Paul Allen, 21, launched Microsoft in 1975 to sell software they had created. By 1979, Microsoft had grown to 25 employees and $2.5 million in sales. Then in November 1980, IBM chose Microsoft to provide an operating system for its personal computer. Microsoft thereupon bought an operating system from Seattle Computer Products, which it modified into the now ubiquitous MS-DOS. The IBM name and the huge success of the 1–2–3 spreadsheet, which only ran on DOS computers, soon helped make Microsoft the dominant supplier of operating systems.

Microsoft won the operating system battle without clockwork execution and amidst considerable organizational turmoil. According to author Scott Lewis, during the early 1980s, "The firm was doubling in size every year and had not yet adapted to being a large company. Gates, whose volatile temperament was well-known in the computer industry, had exacerbated Microsoft's chaos by abruptly changing product specifications and moving developers around."[1]

External changes can provide great leverage for creative and nimble entrepreneurs.

External changes, such as collapses in the price of real estate or energy, also create opportunities for entrepreneurs who speculate in out-of-favor assets. Sam Zell, the self-described "grave dancer," and his now deceased partner, Robert Lurie, built a multibillion-dollar real estate and industrial empire through such opportunities. Their first big success followed the collapse of the real estate investment trusts in the early 1970s. Later they picked up millions of square feet of office space and shopping centers and tens of thousands of apartments and trailer-park spaces for mobile homes. During the early 1980s, the partners sold a number of buildings in the booming Southwest and invested in Rust Belt cities like Buffalo and Chicago.

His approach, Zell concedes, doesn't call for the sort of creativity that's involved in building a business.[2] Contrarian speculators don't innovate much; the entrepreneur merely anticipates that the confusion or panic that has depressed prices will pass. Nor does successful execution require much managerial capacity. Organizational development, engineering, or marketing abilities add little value when an entrepreneur buys assets at a low price, expecting to sell them at a high price. Rather, good execution requires the ability to move quickly, negotiate astutely, and raise funds under favorable terms.

Microsoft's Bill Gates built a multibillion-dollar business without a breakthrough product.

3. Basis of Competition: Proprietary Assets Versus Hustle. In some industries, such as pharmaceuticals, luxury hotels, and consumer goods, a company's profitability depends significantly on the assets it owns or controls—patents, location, or brands, for example. Good management practices like listening to customers, maintaining quality, and paying attention to costs, which can improve the profits of a going business, cannot propel a start-up over such structural barriers. Here a creative new technology, product, or strategy is a must.

Companies in fragmented service industries, such as investment management, investment banking, head hunting, or consulting cannot establish proprietary advantages easily but can nonetheless enjoy high profits by providing exceptional service tailored to client demands. Start-ups in those fields rely mainly on their hustle.[3] Successful entrepreneurs depend on personal selling skills, contacts, their reputations for expertise, and their ability to convince clients of the value of the services rendered. They also have the capacity for institution building—skills such as recruiting and motivating stellar professionals and articulating and reinforcing company values. Where there are few natural economies of scale, an entrepreneur cannot create a going concern out of a one-man-brand or ad hoc ensemble without a lot of expertise in organizational development.

McKinsey & Company grew out of a simple idea: high-quality advice for top managers.

Marvin Bower, who cofounded McKinsey & Company in 1939, created a premier management consulting firm through the relentless execution of a simple idea: providing high-quality business advice to the top managers of large companies. Bower was very skilled in developing and serving his clients and was dogged in building organizational capabilities. He preached constantly the virtues of putting clients' interests first. Under his leadership, McKinsey started recruiting from top business schools, adopted an up-or-out policy to eliminate employees who didn't make the mark, declined studies that didn't fit the firm's mission of serving top management, and opened international offices to better serve chosen clientele. Bower didn't dictate policy, however, and had the patience to work on bringing partners around to his point of view. Also, he was willing to sell his stock at book value so that the equity of the firm was shared widely.[4]

Gauging Attractiveness

Entrepreneurs should also screen potential ventures for their attractiveness—their risks and rewards—compared to other opportunities. Several factors should be considered. Capital requirements, for example, matter to the entrepreneur who lacks easy access to financial markets. An unexpected need for cash because, say, one large customer is unable to make a timely payment may shut down a venture or force a fire sale of the founder's equity. Therefore, entrepreneurs should favor ventures that aren't capital intensive and have the profit margins to sustain rapid growth with internally generated funds. In a similar fashion, entrepreneurs should look for a high margin for error, ventures with simple operations and low fixed costs that are less likely to face a cash crunch because of factors such as technical delays, cost overruns, and slow buildup of sales.

Other criteria reflect the typical entrepreneur's inability to undertake multiple projects: an attractive venture should provide a substantial enough reward to compensate the entrepreneur's exclusive commitment to it. Shut-down costs should be low: the payback should be quick, or failure soon recognized so that the venture can be terminated without a significant loss of time, money, or reputation. And the entrepreneur should have the option to cash in, for example, by selling all or part of the equity. An entrepreneur locked into an illiquid business cannot easily pursue other opportunities and risks fatigue and burnout.

These criteria cannot be applied mechanically like, say, a textbook rule of backing all projects with positive net present value (NPV). Ventures that shine by one measure are often questionable by another. For example, a successful biotech venture whose parents provide sustainable advantages can be taken public more easily than an advertising agency. But biotech entrepreneurs need to raise significant capital and may be locked into a venture whose success can't be ascertained for many years.

Ventures must also fit what the individual entrepreneur values and wants to do. Surviving the inevitable disappointments and near disasters one encounters on the rough road to success requires a passion for the chosen business. Entrepreneurs should evaluate a potential new venture against what they're looking for and the sacrifices they're willing to make. Do they want to make a fortune, or will a small profit be sufficient? Do they seek public recognition? Is the stimulation of working with exciting technologies, customers, or colleagues important to them? Are they prepared to devote their lives to a business, or do they want to cash out quickly? Can they tolerate working in an industry that has questionable ethical standards? Or an industry where there is high uncertainty? What financial and career risks are they prepared to take and for how long?

These deeply personal preferences determine the types of ventures that will enthuse and fortify an entrepreneur. For example, ambitious undertakings like Federal Express fit people who are ready to win or lose on a grand scale. Success can create dynastic fortunes and turn the entrepreneur into a near-cult figure. But the risks also are substantial. Visionary schemes may fail for any number of reasons: the product is flawed, cannot be made or distributed cost-effectively, serves no compelling need, or requires customers to incur unacceptable switching costs. Worse, the failure may not be apparent for several years, locking the entrepreneur into an extended period of frustrating endeavor. Even businesses that succeed may not be financially rewarding for their founders, especially if they encounter delays en route. Investors may dump the visionary founders or demand a high share of the equity for additional financing. The entrepreneur must therefore anticipate recurring disappointments and a high probability that years of toil may come to naught. Unless entrepreneurs have a burning desire to change the world, they should not undertake revolutionary ventures.

Surprisingly, small endeavors often hold more financial promise than large ones. Often the founders can keep a larger share of the profits because they don't dilute their equity interest through multiple rounds of financings. But entrepreneurs must be willing to prosper in a backwater; dominating a neglected market segment is sometimes more profitable than intellectually stimulating or glamorous. Niche enterprises can also enter the "land of the living dead" because their market is too small for the business to thrive but the entrepreneur has invested too much effort to be willing to quit.

Speculators like Zell, who don't build a company or introduce an innovation to the world, can take pleasure from showing up the crowd. Their financial risks and returns depend on the terms of the deal, the capital at risk, the conditions and amount of borrowing, and, or course, the price of the asset acquired. Risks are generally not staged; the entrepreneur is fully exposed when the asset is acquired. Liquidity or exit options often turn on the success of the speculation: if, as hoped, prices rise, the speculator can expect many buyers for the asset owned, but if prices decline or stay depressed, market liquidity for the asset will be generally poor. All things considered, such ventures appeal most to entrepreneurs who enjoy making deals and rolling the dice.

A new company that is based on hustle in, say, consulting or advertising can provide the satisfaction of working with talented colleagues in a dynamic and competitive market. Capital requirements are low, and investments can be staged as the business grows. Entrepreneurs can therefore avoid significant personal risk and meddling by outside investors. But although such businesses can provide attractive current income, great wealth in those situations is elusive: hustle businesses, which lack a sustainable franchise, cannot be easily sold or taken public at a high multiple of earnings. The entrepreneur must therefore savor the venture enough to make a long-term career of it rather than enjoy the fruits of a quick harvest.

Parsimonious Planning and Analysis

To conserve time and money, successful entrepreneurs minimize the resources they devote to researching their ideas. Unlike the corporate world, where foil mastery and completed staff work can make a career, the entrepreneur only does as much planning and analysis as seems useful and makes subjective judgment calls when necessary.

As Harvard's Michael Porter has pointed out, a start-up faces competition not only from rivals offering the same goods but also potentially from substitutes, suppliers, buyers, and other new entrants. A start-up even competes with companies outside its industry for employees and capital. A complete analysis, therefore, would cover many industry participants and probe internal core competencies and weaknesses. But the astute entrepreneur isn't interested in completeness. He or she understands that returns from additional analysis diminish rapidly and avoids using spreadsheet software to churn out detailed but not particularly insightful analyses of a project's break-even point, capital requirements, payback period, or NPV.

Surviving the inevitable disappointments on the rough road to success requires passion for the chosen business.

In setting their analytical priorities, entrepreneurs must recognize that some critical uncertainties cannot be resolved through more research. For example, focus groups and surveys often have little value in predicting demand for products that are truly novel. At first, consumers had dismissed the need for copiers, for instance, and told researchers they were satisfied with using carbon paper. With issues like this, entrepreneurs have to resist the temptation of endless investigation and trust their judgment.

The parsimonious analyst should also avoid research that he or she can't act on. For example, understanding broad market trends and the strategies of the industry leaders is unlikely to affect what a start-up in a hustle business like advertising does and therefore isn't worth bothering with. Entrepreneurs should concentrate instead on issues that they can reasonably expect to resolve through analysis and that determine whether and how they will proceed. Resolving a few big questions—understanding what things *must* go right and anticipating the venture-destroying pitfalls, for instance—is more important than investigating many nice-to-know matters.

Standard checklists or one-size-fits-all approaches don't work for entrepreneurs. The appropriate analytical budget and the issues that are most worthy of research and analysis depend on the characteristics of each venture.

Ambitious endeavors like Federal Express, for example, require significant capital and must be better researched and documented than ventures that can be self-financed. Professional investors usually ask for a written business plan because it provides clues about the entrepreneur's seriousness of purpose, concern for investors, and competence. So entrepreneurs must write a detailed plan even if the are skeptical about its relationship to the subsequent outcomes.

Revenues are notoriously difficult to predict. At best, entrepreneurs may satisfy themselves that their novel product or service delivers considerably greater value than current offerings do; how quickly the product catches on is a blind guess. Leverage may be obtained, however, from analyzing how customers might buy and use the product or service. Understanding the purchase process can help identify the right decision makers for the new offering. With Federal Express, for instance, it was important to go beyond the mailroom managers who traditionally bought delivery services. Understanding how products are used can also help by revealing obstacles that must be overcome before consumers can benefit from a new offering.

Visionary entrepreneurs must guard against making competitors rich from their work. Many concepts are diffi-

cult to prove but, once proven, easy to imitate. Unless the pioneer is protected by sustainable barriers to entry, the benefits of a hard-fought revolution can become a public good rather than a boon to the innovator. Sun Microsystems and Apple, for example, won big from pathbreaking innovations that had been developed at Xerox's Palo Alto Research Center.

Entrepreneurs who hope to secure a niche face different problems: they often fail because the costs of serving a specialized segment exceed the benefits to customers. Entrepreneurs should therefore analyze carefully the incremental costs of serving a niche and take into account their lack of scale and the difficulty of marketing to a small, diffused segment. And especially if the cost disadvantage is significant, entrepreneurs should determine whether their offering provides a significant performance benefit. Whereas established companies can vie for share through line extensions or marginal tailoring of their products and services, the start-up must really wow its target customers. A marginally tastier cereal won't knock Kellogg's Cornflakes off supermarket shelves.

Inadequate payoffs also pose a risk for ventures that address small markets. For example, a niche venture that can't support a direct sales force may not generate enough commissions to attract an independent broker or manufacturers' rep. Entrepreneurs will eventually lose interest too if the rewards aren't commensurate with their efforts. Therefore, the entrepreneur should make sure that everyone who contributes can expect a high, quick, or sustainable return even if the venture's total profits are small.

Entrepreneurs who seek to leverage factors like changing technologies, customer preferences, or regulations should avoid extensive analysis. Research conducted under conditions of such turbulence isn't reliable, and the importance of a quick response precludes spending the time to make sure every detail is covered.

Standard checklists or one-size-fits-all approaches don't work. The appropriate analytical priorities vary for each venture.

The entrepreneur has to live with critical uncertainties, such as the relative competencies of rivals or the preferences of strategic customers, which are not easy to analyze. Who could have forecast, for example, that Sun Microsystems's four 27-year-old founders, who had virtually no business or industry experience, would beat more than a dozen start-ups, including Apollo, a textbook venture launched by industry superstars? Or that IBM would turn to Microsoft for an operating system, gain dominance for its hardware, and go on to dethrone Digital Research's entrenched CP/M operating system? Entering a race requires faith in one's ability to finish ahead of whoever else might happen to play.

Analyzing whether or not the rewards for winning are commensurate with the risks, however, can be a more feasible and worthwhile exercise. In some technology races, success is predictably short-lived. In the disk-drive industry, for example, companies that succeed with one generation of products are often leap-frogged when the next generation arrives. In engineering workstations, however Sun enjoyed long-term gains from its early success because it established a durable architectural standard. If success is unlikely to be sustained, entrepreneurs should have a plan for making a good return while it lasts.

Ventures in fast-changing markets are more likely to fold because they can't design, produce, or sell a timely, cost-effective product that works than because they pursued a poor strategy. Successful entrepreneurs, therefore, usually devote more attention to operational analysis and planning than strategic planning. Sun's business plan, one founder recalls, was mainly an operating plan, containing specific timetables for product development, opening sales and service offices, and hiring engineers.

For speculators like Zell who seek to purchase assets at depressed prices, two sets of analysis are crucial. One relates to the market dynamics for the asset being acquired or, more specifically, why the prices of the asset may be expected to rise. Entrepreneurs should try to determine whether prices are temporarily low (due to, say, an irrational panic or a temporary surge in supply), in secular decline because of permanent changes in supply or demand, or merely correcting after an irrational prior surge. Also important to analyze is the entrepreneur's ability to hold or carry the asset until it can be sold at a profit because it is difficult to predict when temporarily depressed prices will return to normal. Carrying capacity depends on the extent of borrowing used to purchase the asset, the conditions under which financing may be revoked, and the income produced by the asset. Rental properties or a producing well that provides ongoing income, for example, can be carried more easily than raw land or drilling rights. For certain kinds of assets, mines and urban rental properties, for example, the entrepreneur should also consider the risks of expropriation (through, for example, rent control) and windfall taxation.

Start-ups with powerful competitors must wow their customers. A marginally tastier cereal won't knock Kellogg's Cornflakes off supermarket shelves.

In ventures based on hustle rather than proprietary advantages, a detailed analysis of competitors and industry structure is rarely of much value. The ability to seize short-lived opportunities and execute them brilliantly is of far more importance than a long-term competitive strategy. Analysis of specific clients and relationships dominates general market surveys. Partnership agreements, terms for offering equity to later employees, performance measurement criteria, and bonus plans are important determinants of company success and are best thought through before launch rather than hastily improvised later on. And although projections of long-term cash flows are not meaningful, back-of-the-envelope, short-term cash forecasts and analyses of breakevens can keep the entrepreneur out of trouble. Overall, though, the analytical preparation required for such ventures is modest.

Integrating Action and Analysis

Standard operating procedure in large corporations usually makes a clear distinction between analysis and execution. In contemplating a new venture, managers in established companies face issues about its fit with ongoing activities: Does the proposed venture leverage corporate strengths? Will the resources and attention it requires reduce the company's ability to build customer loyalty and improve quality of core markets? These concerns dictate a deliberate, "trustee" approach: before they can launch a venture, managers must investigate an opportunity extensively, seek the counsel of people higher up, submit a formal plan, respond to criticisms by bosses and corporate staff, and secure a headcount and capital allocation.[5]

Entrepreneurs who start with a clean slate, however, don't have to know all the answers before they act. In fact, they often can't easily separate action and analysis. The attractiveness of a new restaurant, for example, may depend on the terms of the lease; low rents can change the venture from a mediocre proposition into a money machine. But an entrepreneur's ability to negotiate a good lease cannot be easily determined from general prior analysis; he or she must enter into a serious negotiation with a specific landlord for a specific property.

Acting before an opportunity is fully analyzed has many benefits. Doing something concrete builds confidence in oneself and in others. Key employees and investors will often follow the individual who has committed to action, for instance, by quitting a job, incorporating, or signing a lease. By taking a personal risk, the entrepreneur convinces other people that the venture *will* proceed, and they may believe that if they don't sign up, they could be left behind.

Early action can generate more robust better informed strategies too. Extensive surveys and focus-groups research about a concept can produce misleading evidence: slippage can arise between research and reality because the potential customers interviewed are not representative of the market, their enthusiasm for the concept wanes when they see the actual product, or they lack the authority to sign purchase orders. More robust strategies may be developed by first building a working prototype and asking customers to use it before conducting extensive market research.

The ability of individual entrepreneurs to execute quickly will naturally vary. Trial and error is less feasible with large-scale, capital-intensive ventures like Orbital Sciences, which had to raise over $50 million to build rockets for NASA, than with a consulting firm start-up. Nevertheless, some characteristics are common to an approach that integrates action and analysis:

• *Handling Analytical Tasks in Stages.* Rather than resolve all issues at once, the entrepreneur does only enough research to justify the next action or investment. For example, an individual who has developed a new medical technology may first obtain crude estimates of market demand to determined whether it's worth seeing a patent lawyer. If the estimates and lawyer are encouraging, the individual may do more analysis to investigate the wisdom of spending money to obtain a patent. Several more iterations of analysis and action will follow before the entrepreneur prepares and circulates a formal business plan to venture capitalists.

• *Plugging Holes Quickly.* As soon as any problems or risks show up, the entrepreneur begins looking for solutions. For example, suppose that an entrepreneur sees it will be difficult to raise capital. Rather than kill the idea, he or she thinks creatively about solving the problem. Perhaps the investment can be reduced by modifying technology to use more standard equipment that can be rented instead of bought. Or under the right terms, a customer might underwrite the risk by providing a large initial order. Or expectations and goals for growth might be scaled down, and a niche market could be tackled first. Except with obviously unviable ideas that can be ruled out through elementary logic, the purpose of analysis is not to find fault with new ventures or find reasons for abandoning them. Analysis is an exercise in what to do next more than what not to do.

• *Evangelical Investigation.* Entrepreneurs often blur the line between research and selling. As one founder recalls, "My market research consisted of taking a prototype to a trade show and seeing if I could write orders." Software industry "beta sites" provide another example of simultaneous research and selling; customers actually pay to help vendors test early versions of their software and will often place larger orders if they are satisfied with the product.

Entrepreneurs must be smart enough to recognize mistakes and change strategies.

From the beginning, entrepreneurs don't just seek opinions and information, they also look for commitment from other people. Entrepreneurs treat everyone whom they talk to as a potential customer, investor, employee, or supplier,

or at least as a possible source of leads down the road. Even if they don't actually ask for an order, they take the time to build enough interest and rapport so they can come back later. This simultaneous listening and selling approach may not produce truly objective market research and statistically significant results. But the resource-constrained entrepreneur doesn't have much choice in the matter. Besides, in the initial stages, the deep knowledge and support of a few is often more valuable than broad, impersonal data.

• *Smart Arrogance.* An entrepreneur's willingness to act on sketchy plans and inconclusive data is often sustained by an almost arrogant self-confidence. One successful high-tech entrepreneur likens his kind to "gamblers in a casino who know they are good at craps and are therefore likely to win. They believe: 'I'm smarter, more creative, and harder working than most people. With my unique and rare skills, I'm doing investors a favor by taking their money.'" Moreover, the entrepreneur's arrogance must stand the test of adversity. Entrepreneurs must have great confidence in their talent and ideas to persevere as customers stay away in droves, the product doesn't work, or the business runs out of cash.

But entrepreneurs who believe they are more capable or venturesome than others must also have the smarts to recognize their mistakes and to change their strategies as events unfold. Successful ventures don't always proceed in the direction on which they initially set out. A significant proportion develop entirely new markets, products, and sources of competitive advantage. Therefore, although perseverance and tenacity are valuable entrepreneurial trails, they must be complemented with flexibility and a willingness to learn. If prospects who were expected to place orders don't, the entrepreneur should consider reworking the concept. Similarly, the entrepreneur should also be prepared to exploit opportunities that didn't figure in the initial plan.

The evolution of Silton-Bookman Systems illustrates the importance of keeping an open mind. The venture's original plan was to sell general-purpose, PC-based software for human resource development. But established competitors who already sold similar software on mainframes were beginning to develop products for PCs. So the company adopted a niche strategy and developed a training registration product. And although the founders had initially targeted small companies that couldn't afford mainframe solutions, their first customer was someone from IBM who happened to respond to an ad. Thereafter, Silton-Bookman concentrated its efforts on large companies, where they had considerable success. "The world gives you lots and lots of feedback," cofounder Phil Bookman observes. "The challenge is to take advantage of the feedback you get."

The apparently sketchy planning and haphazard evolution of many successful ventures like Silton-Bookman doesn't mean that entrepreneurs should follow a ready-fire-aim approach. Despite appearances, astute entrepreneurs do analyze and strategize extensively. They realize, however, that businesses cannot be launched like space shuttles, with every detail of the mission planned in advance. Initial analyses only provide plausible hypotheses, which must be tested and modified. Entrepreneurs should play with and explore ideas, letting their strategies evolve through a seamless process of guesswork, analysis, and action.

References

1. Scott Lewis, "Microsoft Corporation," in *International Directory of Company Histories*, ed. Paula Kepos (Detroit, Michigan: St. James Press, 1992), p. 258.

2. Erik Ipsen, "Real Estate: Will Success Spoil Sam Zell?" *Institutional Investor*, April 1989, pp. 90–99.
3. See Amar Bhidé, "Hustle as Strategy," HBR September-October 1986.
4. See "McKinsey & Company [A]: 1956," Harvard Business School Case No. 393–066, 1992.
5. See Howard Stevenson and David Gumpert, "The Heart of Entrepreneurship," HBR March-April 1985.

Amar Bhidé teaches entrepreneurship at the Harvard Business School, where he is associate professor. His last HBR article was "Bootstrap Finance: The Art of Start-ups" (November-December 1992).

The SUCCESS
Start-up Guide

Have a great idea but don't know what to do next? Take these five steps, and you'll end up with more than a great idea; you'll have your own business

JACK CHEN AND Fernando Espuelas were willing to risk it all: their high-powered careers, their life's savings, their future security. They were boyhood friends who wanted to make a name for themselves—and a nice chunk of change—by starting the equivalent of the next America Online. Their idea was to offer Spanish and Portuguese versions of the Internet to all of Latin America.

Fueled by that high-octane dream, Chen quit his hotshot job as a securities analyst at Credit Suisse First Boston in the summer of 1990, and Espuelas kissed his lucrative position as an AT&T marketing executive goodbye. With $100,000 they'd saved, they launched StarMedia Network on September 1, 1996, out of a dilapidated house they rented for a song in Riverside, Conn. (The house was slated for demolition.)

The gamble paid off, big-time, for the two 32-year-old entrepreneurs. They now run the largest Internet network targeted in Latin America; it has 2.5 million visitors per month from Mexico to Brazil. With the company's valuation estimated at several hundred million dollars during its most recent round of financing, they've attracted prominent investors, including David Rockefeller and Henry Kravis, as well as such strategic partners as Intel, GE Capital, and Morgan Stanley. "If StarMedia continues to be successful, we will make a lot of money both for initial investors and for the Henry Kravises of this world," says Espuelas.

STARMEDIA NETWORK

JACK CHEN AND FERNANDO ESPUELAS, COFOUNDERS

Everyone wants to start a lucrative Internet business. What allowed Chen and Espuelas to succeed was their systematic strategy for attracting investors—and for parlaying the $96.1 million that they raised into a world-class venture.

Espuelas and Chen undoubtedly had impeccable timing, but the real secret to their achievement was their systematic approach to building their business. They had the discipline to follow the five steps that are essential to starting up any successful company: they are analyzing an idea and its potential market, writing a compelling business plan, raising capital to make and distribute the product, putting out a solid service or commodity, and getting the wares to market quickly.

The rules that Espuelas and Chen followed will work just as well for your business. Here's a crash course in how to make your start-up a success.

STEP 1 Evaluate your idea.

ESPUELAS AND CHEN knew a lot about Latin America before they started their business. For one thing, Espuelas, a native of Uruguay, had specialized in the region at AT&T; Chen was an investment banker at Goldman Sachs, where he acquired a broad knowledge of world markets. Even with all their expertise, though, they recognized their limitations. They understood that their hunch that use of the Web was about to explode in Latin America was not a strong enough foundation for a business.

So, for two months, the partners pored over demographic figures. They learned that 20 percent of the population in Central and South America—around 100 million people—controlled 65 percent of the wealth. These folks were, naturally, the most likely to try the Web. Bingo! StarMedia Network had found its target customers.

The lesson? If you're hoping to achieve the kind of success that Chen and Espuelas did, it's essential to set aside some time to evaluate your idea coolly before you set up shop. Ask yourself these two key questions before you proceed:

IS THERE A MARKET FOR MY PRODUCT?

Jim Lowe and his friend Polly Nelson thought they were onto a profitable idea when they dreamed up Hog's Head Beer Cellars, a company that would sell its gourmet micro-brewed beers through a mail-order club like Beer Across America. But they didn't know whether there'd be enough customers out there to support a whole company.

Thus, before the two beer-loving engineers from Greensboro, N.C., quit their day jobs, they spent a year taking evening business courses at a local community college, conferring with business associates, reading trade magazines about the beer industry, and talking with the brew masters at many of the nearly 1,000 specialty breweries across the nation. This research helped them take in the market thoroughly, refine their niche in the industry further, shape their business plan, and provide accurate yearly sales projections for their venture. Their five-year-old company is now one of the leading custom-beverage service providers in the United States.

HOW WILL THIS IDEA MAKE ME MONEY?

"Just because you have a great recipe for butterscotch sauce doesn't mean you can be successful," says George Dawson, business consultant and the author of *Borrowing to Build Your Business* (Dearborn, 1997). "You have to know all the costs involved, the size of the audience, and the right pricing structure to make a profit." If you can't address these issues, do not pass "Go" until you can.

STEP 2 Write a great business plan.

AT THE SAME time Chen and Espuelas were researching their target market, they crafted their business plan. Chen, as an investment banker, had seen hundreds of similar documents, so he knew what a good one looked like. The plan had to be exciting enough to hook investors by the first page but chock-full of financial details that would convince outsiders that the company was worth their time and money.

The partners ultimately decided to play up the fact that they were pioneers in a huge, undeveloped market. The rest of the plan explained their business model. They would offer free Web access to establish a large audience. Most revenue would be earned by the sale of advertising and through commissions on goods sold on their network. "We showed it to each other and debated it until we felt we had the right strategy," recalls Espuelas.

But there's more to writing a business plan than making investors salivate—really. As Espuelas and Chen will attest, writing one is also about focusing on your organization's goals and making sure you can turn them into reality. "I'm still amazed that 80 percent of the plans we made in the summer of 1996 are still on target," says Espuelas.

A compelling and focused business plan must include five elements:

PASSION

If it doesn't come across that your heart and soul are dedicated to this venture, then no one else is going to buy into your concept. "One potential investor asked me, 'What would you do if you didn't get this money?'" recalls Susan Willett Bird, founder of American Mediation Council LLC in New York, her fourth successful start-up company. "If my answer had been 'I guess I won't start the business,' then he wouldn't have invested."

A MARKET DESCRIPTION

"Too often, the entrepreneur focuses on the nature of the product rather than on how that product can satisfy a market need," says R. Duane Ireland, director of the Entrepreneurship Studies Program at Baylor University's Hankamer School of Business in Waco, Tex. Prove to investors that you really can sell your merchandise by showing them the market research you've been so diligently amassing. Don't forget to tell them exactly how you plan to connect with potential customers.

"I look at some 1,500 business plans a year, and I've learned to go straight to the management bios."

—JERRY COLONNA,
FLATIRON PARTNERS

MANAGEMENT BIOS

Your investors are, in the end, investing in you and your team. "I look at some 1,500 business plans a year," says Jerry Colonna, a venture capitalist and managing partner of Flatiron Partners, a New York firm specializing in early-stage Internet software and media companies, "and I've learned to go straight to the management bios. If the CEO of a new software company says he also plans to sell advertising for the company, even though he never has done this, that's an immediate red flag. I look for a well-rounded management team, not one person who says he will perform most of the tasks."

FINANCIALS

"While balance sheets and income statements are crucial, the cash-flow statement is typically the most important financial document," says Ireland. "Investors will want to know if the business has the capacity to create a good rate of return or cover the loan," notes Dawson.

AN EXIT PLAN

"Looking ahead five years, are you planning to sell the company, take it public, or hold on to it?" asks Bird. "Each of those has different implications for the investor, who wants to know when and how he's going to get his money out." Be careful here, though. You don't want investors to question your dedication to the venture.

STEP 3 Raise the money you need.

CHEN AND ESPUELAS started out relatively small when it came to financing. After raiding their $100,000 life's savings, they sold shares of the company to their friends and family, coming up with $500,000. That enabled them to hire a small research-and-development team to build their network, which they ran on a limited basis for two months to lay down a track record.

Once the company was up and running, they were in a better position to approach venture capitalists and big companies that could be strategic partners. Nonetheless, says Espuelas, "it was very, very difficult. Very few people believed Latin Americans were ready for the Internet. They didn't believe the people had phones."

Finally, they turned to two institutional investors with experience in both Latin America and the Internet: Chase Capital Partners and Flatiron Partners in New York. A couple of months later, Chen and Espuelas had a little over $3.5 million at their disposal. "We persuaded very few venture capitalists to invest," says Espuelas. "But we just happened to persuade the right ones."

Having those heavy hitters behind them made raising capital much easier. In January 1998 they drew $12 million in a private placement. As an encore, they raised another $80 million in September. "It was the largest private placement by an Internet company," crows Espuelas. Their latest plan: to go public this year.

The strategy that Chen and Espuelas used to raise money for their company makes a lot of sense for even the smallest ventures. Start with money from people you know; then branch out to larger private investors and venture capitalists. Here are the basics.

SHAKE THE FAMILY TREE

Matthew Magnozzi followed this rule when he opened Forest Saver Inc., a Ronkonkoma, N.Y.-based company that converts recycled maps into a range of products, such as stationery and wrapping paper. Determined to maintain full control of his business, he turned to his dad for his $5,000 in initial start-up capital. When he moved his company from his basement to an actual factory, he tapped Grandma for an additional $5,000. That small war chest has been enough to keep the company going for the past six years. Today the company generates about $250,000 in annual sales.

TRY PLASTIC SURGERY

Before they received their first venture-capital bonanza, Espuelas and Chen borrowed $200,000 on 18 credit cards just to stay in business. Although it was very expensive money, it kept the company alive until the VCs administered CPR. A note of caution: Espuelas and Chen were lucky; others have sunk their ventures by drowning in credit-card debt.

"Anyone who's selling any product and who's not looking at Internet opportunities is stuck in the last century."

—GARY CADENHEAD,
UNIVERSITY OF TEXAS AT AUSTIN

APPEAL TO THE HEAVENS

Once you've exhausted friends, family, and your own financial resources, consider tapping the private investors known as angels. In many cities, well-to-do people form investment networks. You can find them through local entrepreneurs or by consulting *Where to Go When the Bank Says No*, by David Evanson (Bloomberg Press, 1998), which has one of the best listings of angel and venture-capital groups across the country.

STEP 4 Build your product.

EVEN WHEN THE MONEY started pouring in to StarMedia Network, Chen and Espuelas continued fine-tuning their product, expanding their research-and-development team to 100 people. "The name of the game is that you are never finished with the product," says Espuelas. "Once users find us, they have to like us enough to return."

The rules are a little different if your goal is to manufacture a product outside of the extremely dynamic Internet. Here are some guidelines.

DEFINE YOUR LEVEL OF INVOLVEMENT

Are you after quick cash or committed for the long haul? This is one of the first questions to ask yourself, says Kathleen Allen, professor of entrepreneurship at the University of Southern California. Commitment-phobes can sell their product concept outright for a lump sum or license it in return for a percentage of the royalties. Middle-of-the-roaders might consider manufacturing the product themselves and hiring distributors to sell it. And those in for the long haul can take responsibility for bringing the product to the retailer or become the retailer themselves. "As you come down the pyramid, the cost of doing business is higher and the time involved is higher, but the return is also higher," says Allen.

NETWORK

The best way to find a great manufacturer is to go to your state's business-development agency, your chamber of commerce, or an industry association for recommendations. Ask others whether they have found anyone who makes quality and on-time shipments. "You can talk about your product, process, or service without giving away the guts of your idea," says David Livingstone, director of the Center for Entrepreneurship at Brigham Young University.

LOOK BEYOND NATIONAL BORDERS

One entrepreneur, who wanted to manufacture and sell plush toy animals, chose to have the toys designed in Korea because of the workmanship offered by one company there. But he went to southern China to have them produced because the manufacturing costs were lower. "The telephone and the Internet give ready access to resources around the world," says Livingstone.

RECYCLE

When Gerald Ritthaler, founder of Ritz Foods International Inc., needed a new factory in Cantaura, Venezuela, to manufacture the chips he makes from South American yuca, he converted an idle processing plant. He got a deal on machinery from an overequipped, underutilized Detroit-based factory.

STEP 5 Sell your wares.

WHEN ALL IS SAID and done, you won't have much of a business if you can't get your product or service to your customers. The strategy at StarMedia Network was to develop a high-profile network that was easy to access. Here are some other tactics you can try.

THINK BACKWARD

Start at the place where you hope to finish—your customer's reaching into his wallet and laying out cold, hard cash for your product. "Ask yourself, Who is my ultimate customer? How would they acquire the product?" says Phil Gross, entrepreneur in residence at the University of Maryland's Dingman Center for Entrepreneurship. Then examine the channels for getting your product to that place. For example, if you're selling a new service to nursing homes, start by contacting the American Nursing Home Association or buying a full-page ad in its newsletter. To capture their massive audience, Espuelas and Chen advertised online, on network television, and in publications all over Latin America—and continue to do so.

SCOPE OUT THE COMPETITION

Studying the successes and failures of your competitors will not only give you a good idea of what works but also spark notions for more innovative marketing strategies. "Start where the other guy is doing well," advises Fred Kiesner, professor of management and entrepreneurship at Loyola Marymount University in Los Angeles.

FORM AN ALLIANCE

Find a person or company with a vested interest in your success—for example, a salesperson who sells related but not competing products. Jerry Buck of Innovative Solutions Group Inc. in Sterling, Va., knew exactly whom to contact about selling a program that extracts map features from digital and aerial imagery—the company that sells the industry-leading map systems. "They are a major player in the business and have access to about 286,000 customers," says Buck. "Now they can go out and sell our products to their core base as an enhancement."

GET WIRED

If someone said that he had the means to distribute your product or service globally and that, for a very low start-up cost, the distribution channel would run itself for free, would you be interested? Of course you would. Well, Gary Cadenhead, senior lecturer in entrepreneurship at the University of Texas at Austin, says that's exactly what the Internet can do. "Anyone who's selling any product and who's not looking at Internet opportunities is stuck in the last century," says Cadenhead. "That clearly is the future, and it's growing enormously. You're going to see entrepreneurs figure out how best to use it, and it's going to be a huge advantage."

Just ask Espuelas and Chen.

EDITED BY ELAINE POFELDT Reporting by Gerald Secor Couzens, Sara Eckel, Colum Lynch, Rebecca Saunders, and Dina Ingber Stein.

Preliminary Legal Considerations in Forming a New Enterprise

Michael P. Ridley, Esq.

The following article is a summary of the key legal concerns of the entrepreneur in the planning stages and start-up of a business.

Form of Enterprise

Prior to the Tax Reform Act of 1986, the normal form of business entity would be a corporation. With the repeal of General Utilities, founders should consult with counsel to determine whether S Corp. status, partnership, limited partnership, proprietorship, or a limited liability company may be appropriate during the pre-venture capital period of the entity's existence. If founders operate as a limited partnership or limited liability company, care must be taken to follow statutory formalities to avoid personal liabilities on behalf of limited partners, or to avoid classification as a corporation if a limited liability company is chosen. Unfortunately, S Corp. status, which would be ideal from a liability standpoint and a pass through of income and losses at individual rates without tax at the corporate level, will not be available if venture capital investors are other than individuals or certain trusts (most venture capital funds are limited partnerships) or if there is more than one class of security (most venture capital funds would take preferred stock or convertible debt). In order to minimize out-of-pocket expenses, founders should determine name availability before purchasing stationery, directory listings, brochures, etc.

Relations with Prior Employers

Venture capitalists typically invest in enterprises headed by superior managers with prior track records. It is therefore likely that founders and key employees in a new business will have recently left or are considering leaving their present employment. As such, it will be important during the formation process to ensure that the founders and key employees do not misappropriate the trade secrets of prior employers or otherwise engage in unfair competition with the prior employer.

Trade Secrets

Although employees are free to leave employment and start a competing enterprise, they are not free to utilize their employer's trade secrets or compete while still employed. Most litigation involving the improper use by a departing employee of an employer's trade secrets will center on whether the information used by a departing employee is in fact a trade secret. Definitions of what constitutes a trade secret will vary from state to state. As a general rule, a trade secret means "information, including a formula, pattern, computation, program, device, method, technique or process that (1) derives independent economic value, actual or potential, from not being generally known to the public or to other persons who can obtain economic value from its disclosure or use; and (2) is the subject of efforts that are reasonable under the circumstances to maintain its secrecy." Uniform Trade Secret Act.

It will be important for the new enterprise to avoid situations in which it is involved in the misappropriation of trade secrets of prior employers for several reasons: (a) certain jurisdictions make it a criminal offense to misappropriate trade secrets, e.g., California Penal Code Section 499(c) makes it a misdemeanor punishable by up to one year in prison and up to $5,000 in fines to steal, copy or use without authorization trade secrets; (b) the prior employer has legal recourse to enjoin the new enterprise's use of the employer's trade secrets and to seek damages, including royalties and, where appropriate, punitive damages, which recourse could very well mean the termination of the start-up's activities and, at a minimum, the incurrence in a very short period of time of substantial legal fees and management time diverted from the enterprise; and, last, but not least, (c) venture capitalists, depending upon their respective involvement in formulating the start-up and whether they knew or should have known that the start-up they were financing had misappropriated trade secrets, may themselves be liable for damages to the prior employer.

Although one can never obtain complete assurance that a start-up or a departing employee will not be sued by a prior employer, the departing employees should follow certain steps:

1. Review all nondisclosure and assignment of invention agreements executed by founders and new employees, particularly those sections relating to prior discoveries. Certain jurisdictions provide that inventions developed on an employee's own time not relating to the employer's business constitute the property of the employee. Any work on technology to be utilized by a start-up should be done on the employee's time with the employee's own resources. Employment agreements should be reviewed to determine the existence of and enforceability of covenants not to compete.
2. Prepare the business plan on the employee's individual time.
3. Do not use the prior employer's premises or equipment in preparing the business plan or doing preparatory work in setting up the new venture. Calls to future suppliers, employees and funding sources should be done at home or during the employee's free time. Utilizing E-mail at the employer will leave a trail that is readily discoverable as "deleted."
4. Turn in all customer lists, product specifications, marketing plans, etc. Do not bring copies of proprietary information to the start-up.
5. A problem area will exist where the founder is not merely an employee but rather an officer or director of the former employer. The fiduciary relationship to the former employer may be breached by failing to offer the opportunity to the employer. Corporate opportunity problems may be solved by having the prior employer decline to pursue the opportunity or invention which the start-up is formed to pursue.
6. The safest course of action is for the employee to depart from the employer prior to competing with the employer and to disclose preparations to compete if such failure to disclose preparation would be harmful to the employer. Departing employees should inform the prior employer of plans rather than have the prior employer learn of plans from reference checks of venture capitalists or in a newspaper.

Solicitation of Fellow Employees

The general rule is that, absent unfair or deceptive means, the public interest of the mobility of employees enables the start-up to hire employees, after departure, of the former employer. A problem arises if the solicitation occurs while the founders are still employed by the former employer or if the employees are hired not for their skills but rather to obtain the prior employer's trade secrets.

Solicitation of Business of Former Employer

The general rule is that, absent a valid noncompetition agreement, employees may solicit customers of former employers after departing unless proprietary customer lists or confidential information, such as pricing, is used. A problem area is the difficulty of defining what constitutes customer lists. To the extent that the identity of customers, purchasing agents, required terms a vendor must meet, etc., are known to the public, the more likely a customer list will not be found.

Ownership and Protection of Technology

If technology will be important to the success of the start-up, steps should be implemented on formation to acquire and protect the technology, to the extent that technology or intellectual property is being contributed to prior to the raising of funds. There are several alternatives to follow in protecting technology—trade secrets, patents and copyrights. The best method to be used is dependent on the type of technology involved.

Trade Secrets

The general rule is that a trade secret is lost if it is disclosed to the general public or competitors or if the person seeking to protect a trade secret does not take reasonable steps under the circumstances to ensure its confidentiality. A start-up should require that all employees and founders, prior to and as a condition of employment, execute nondisclosure and assignment of invention agreements that (a) set forth recognition of employee of the nature of the importance of trade secrets to the company and contain an agreement to keep all such information in confidence; (b) set forth the prior inventions that are being brought by the employee to the company; (c) represent that no trade secrets of prior employers are being brought to the new enterprise and require that the employee will not disclose to the company trade secrets which may have been obtained as a result of prior employment; and (d) assign all inventions to be used by the company or which are developed during the course of employment, except those inventions which are developed entirely on an employee's own time and do not relate either to the business of the employer or to the employer's actual or anticipated research or development or do not result from any work performed by the employee for the employer; and (e) require such individual to execute and deliver any and all documents necessary to perfect company's ownership rights in and to such intellectual property.

The company should seek a proper balance between the cost to implement certain procedures designed to restrict the flow of information to protect the confidentiality of trade secrets and the necessity for information to flow within the enterprise. At minimum, the company should consider the following:

1. Sensitive areas should be under lock and key with only specified employees having access and that access should be logged. Access to computer files should similarly be controlled. Visitors to the facility should not be shown sensitive areas containing trade secret information, such as a manufacturing process or computer programs. Visitors, consultants or possible purchasers, suppliers or providers of capital should sign nondisclosure and confidentiality agreements. Confidential documents should not be left in open view or unattended in areas in which employees or other persons not authorized to have access to the information would have access. Courts are often impressed with a lock box for blue prints or source and object codes.

2. Proprietary information stored on magnetic or paper media is subject to recovery from such discarded media. Trash should not be an inadvertent conduit of trade secrets to third parties.

3. Proprietary documents and information should be legended as such with restrictions on copying or disseminating the same. Trade secrets and privileged or confidential commercial or financial information disclosed to the federal government should be marked as such to prevent disclosure under the Freedom of Information Act.

4. Departing employees should be interviewed to determine identity of future employer or plans, to ensure no trade secrets are being withdrawn or in the possession of the departing employee and to reiterate the company's claim of trade secrets. Caution

should be used in the form of any communications to a departing employee's new employer concerning trade secrets.

5. Employees must be made aware of the fact that they are dealing with trade secrets, that such trade secrets are the property of the employer and are of vital importance to that employer, and that the company will prevent the improper use of the company's trade secrets.

6. To the extent that the company contracts with the federal government and delivers trade secrets such as computer software agreements, it should comply with applicable Federal Acquisition Regulations, Federal Procurement Regulations System, or Defense Federal Acquisition Regulations to limit use.

Patent

A 20-year monopoly created by statute for "new and useful process, machine, manufacture or composition of matter, or any new and useful improvement thereof." The invention must be "new" to be patentable. 35 U.S.C. 102(b) prevents issuance of patent if the invention has been in public use for over a year or if the invention has been described in a publication that has been published for over a year prior to the application. It is important for the company to see patent counsel early to determine patentability, particularly on the issues of (i) when public use has occurred, (ii) whether a patent would be the most appropriate method of protection, (iii) the scope of the license to be granted by the inventor and (iv) whether federal research or contract funds have been utilized in conjunction with the proposed invention. Patent protection extends only to jurisdictions in which it is filed. Major disadvantages relate to the fact that the invention must be disclosed after issued or denied, patent litigation is expensive, and, until recently, most inventors were not successful in patent claims. Patent protection is afforded only in the jurisdiction in which it is issued. In today's global economy advice should be procured with respect to the advisability of filing for patent protection in foreign jurisdictions.

Copyright

A limited monopoly is granted for the term of the individual author's life plus 50 years for an original work of authorship, including computer software, but not ideas, principles, concepts or discoveries. Difficulties will arise in the area of whether "non-employees" are creating copyrightable material and are developing "work for hire" which would grant authorship and copyright protection to the company. New regulations provide that to perfect, an author must deposit a copy of the work with the Library of Congress and the Copyright Office. An author may deposit the first and last 10 or 25 pages of a computer program depending on presence of trade secrets with ability to block out trade secret portions which may prevent disclosure of integral workings of the program. Material must be marked to indicate copyright protection.

Trademark

The company should, at a very early stage after determining its name and the names of its proposed products, conduct name and a trademark availability search. It makes no sense to incur significant advertising, printing and marketing costs only to find that a desired name has been registered by a third party as a trademark. As of November 16, 1989, it is now possible to register a federal trademark prior to consummating a sale in interstate commerce. Evidence of sale must be filed thereafter within six months subject to extensions up to 30 months and affidavits of use must be filed subsequently. Federal registration gives right of holder of trademark to seek damages, including treble damages, for infringement of trademark. Pending registration, a company should not indicate the existence of a trademark on its products. Trademark needs to be renewed every 10 years.

Securities Issues

Shares Issued for Compensation

It will be critical to reduce to writing the proposed ownership split of company by founders. Founders, hopefully, should receive shares in the start-up at a fraction of what the venture capitalists are paying. As such, the company should be organized and shares issued as soon as possible during the formation process. The founders should avoid situations in which the founders are incorporating the enterprise on day one at a low valuation, and capitalists are being issued shares at a much higher valuation.

If shares are issued for services and will be subject to a risk of forfeiture, regardless of whether the founder is paying fair market value, employees and founders should file 83(b) elections with the Internal Revenue Service within 30 days of issuance of such shares to elect to have the value of the securities in excess of the cost to the employee (which should be zero) treated as income in year of issuance. Failure to file will mean that when the risk of forfeiture lapses, the employee will be taxed at the difference between what was paid for the shares and their value at the date the restrictions lapse. If the company is successful, the effect will be disastrous to the founders and employees, since the shares may not then be marketable but may have great value.

An emerging area of the law is wrongful termination of employment. All stock purchase or option agreements should provide that no employment agreement is in-

tended and that the company has the right to terminate employment and repurchase any nonvested shares. Similarly, technology transfer agreements should be independent of ability of company to terminate employee.

Shareholder Agreements

The founders should execute rights of first refusal giving the company and the other founders rights of first refusal in the event of any transfer to a third party. Founders should also consider (i) granting to company and founders rights to purchase in event of founder's death, disability or dissolution of marriage, (ii) imposing restrictions upon transfer by any of the founders during the first years of the enterprise of any significant percentage of shares and (iii) vesting of shares based on length of service with the company and granting to the company of a right to repurchase unvested shares at cost. Venture capitalists will typically insist upon such restrictions and a vesting requirement; it is far better to obtain them while the only value of the company is as perceived in the business plan or in an untested prototype as opposed to after the financing is in place and value is more apparent. Although the founding team, at the onset, may appear quite compatible, as the enterprise grows it is entirely possible that certain elements of that team will not be up to the task and, as such, a portion of those shares should be made available to bring in new people. If the initial funding is from friends and families and includes notes, such persons should be made aware of venture capitalists' typical demands that such notes either should be contributed to capital at closing or subject to deferred pay-out. As such, the founders should ensure that amendments to such notes be made by other than unanimous consent of the note holders. As such, the founders should avoid granting preemptive rights or antidilution rights to such initial funding sources.

Regulatory Compliance

Securities issued to the founders and pre-venture capital sources of funds should be issued in compliance with applicable state blue sky laws and the Securities Act of 1933. Failure to do so gives rights of rescission and may delay and/or hinder a subsequent public offering. The general rule for state purposes is that no securities may be issued without a permit unless an exemption is otherwise available. Exemptions will vary from state to state but will be predicated on the type of security, the qualifications of the purchaser and/or the amount of financing or number of purchasers. Even if an exemption is available for the issuance of securities to sophisticated individuals, the company may wish to issue shares or options to all employees, regardless of their sophistication. In such case, very early in the formation process the company should implement a restricted stock purchase plan or nonqualified or qualified incentive stock option plan (recent tax law changes make qualified incentive stock option plans less desirable for the company) and obtain permit for the same. Promises to new employees for securities should not be made in absence of permit or exemption.

Under the Securities Act of 1933, securities may not be issued unless registered or unless an exemption from registration is available. The typical exemption would be Regulation D adopted by the SEC on April 15, 1982, which sets forth a means wherein an issuer may issue securities without the need for registering the same.

Rule 504: $1 million limit in 12 months preceding issue, no requirement of disclosure (caveat: fraud rules still applicable), no advertising, restrictions on resale.

Rule 505: $5,000,000 limit in 12 months preceding issue, no more than 35 unaccredited purchasers, no requirement of disclosure to accredited investors but if to nonaccredited investors, Part II of Form 1–A and financial statement information required under Item 310 of SB–2 (only balance sheet) if less than $2 million and the financial information required in Form SB–2 Part 1 of 5–18 if less than $5 million, no advertising, restrictions on resale.

Rule 506: No limit as to dollar size, no more than 35 nonaccredited investors (nonaccredited investor must be able to evaluate merits and risks), no requirement of disclosure to accredited investors but disclosure of information on Part 1 of form SB–2 if nonaccredited and less than $7,500,000 and financial statement as required in a registration statement if over $7,500,000, no advertising, restrictions on resale. The issuer must complete and file Form D with SEC with 15 days of first sale.

Rule 701: Securities issued to employees, directors, consultants or advisers pursuant to written compensatory plan or agreement, shall not exceed in 12 months the greater of $500,000 or 15% of total assets or outstanding securities.

Employment Relationships

Due Diligence

Venture capitalists can be expected to perform extensive reference checks on key people in the company. Misleading or fraudulent resumes may be sufficient grounds for withdrawing a proposed funding. Nondisclosed criminal convictions or existing SEC consent decrees may be disastrous to the company in the future. The chief executive officer should investigate backgrounds of key personnel consistent with statutory and constitutional prohibitions on invasion of privacy.

Wrongful Termination

Ability of employer to terminate at will without "cause" is being eroded in many jurisdictions. Employment agreements, employer handbooks and manuals, personnel files and interview notes should all indicate absence of any implied or oral understanding of continual employment, particularly in cases where new employees are being asked to terminate existing employment and relocate.

Miscellaneous

Insurance: Have in force necessary general liability, casualty, workers' compensation. If certain individuals are key to success of the venture, company should acquire key man life insurance which is usually inexpensive. Venture capitalists will also want it in place.

Permits: Nature of critical governmental permits required to operate business will depend on nature of business and jurisdictions; examples are resale certificate to avoid sales tax on sales, permits to discharge hazardous waste, permits to possess goods, export licenses needed to export high technology products. Company should apply early and have in force prior to obtaining venture capital. Failure to obtain could delay funding or result in fines, penalties or shutdown of business.

Conclusion

These are just a few of the potential problem areas to consider prior to commencing a new business and seeking capital. It is wise to consult with an attorney experienced in new company formations very early in the planning process to avoid future difficulties.

Michael P. Ridley *is a principal of the Orange County office of the law firm of Arter, Hadden, Lawler, Felix & Hall, specializing in venture capital and corporate finance. He and his firm represent numerous venture capital funds and small business investment companies and a large number of companies that have been financed by venture capital sources. Mr. Ridley is a graduate of Stanford University and Yale Law School.*

Which information belongs—and
which doesn't—may surprise you.

How to Write a Great Business Plan

by William A. Sahlman

Few areas of business attract as much attention as new ventures, and few aspects of new-venture creation attract as much attention as the business plan. Countless books and articles in the popular press dissect the topic. A growing number of annual business-plan contests are springing up across the United States and, increasingly, in other countries. Both graduate and undergraduate schools devote entire courses to the subject. Indeed, judging by all the hoopla surrounding business plans, you would think that the only things standing between a would-be entrepreneur and spectacular success are glossy five-color charts, a bundle of meticulous-looking spreadsheets, and a decade of month-by-month financial projections.

Nothing could be further from the truth. In my experience with hundreds of entrepreneurial start-ups, business plans rank no higher than 2—on a scale from 1 to 10—as a predictor of a new venture's success. And sometimes, in fact, the more elaborately crafted the document, the more likely the venture is to, well, flop, for lack of a more euphemistic word.

What's wrong with most business plans? The answer is relatively straightforward. Most waste too much ink on numbers and devote too little to the information that really matters to intelligent investors. As every seasoned investor knows, financial projections for a new company—especially detailed, month-by-month projections that stretch out for more than a year—are an act of imagination. An entrepreneurial venture faces far too many unknowns to predict revenues, let alone profits. Moreover, few if any entrepreneurs correctly anticipate how much capital and time will be required

to accomplish their objectives. Typically, they are wildly optimistic, padding their projections. Investors know about the padding effect and therefore discount the figures in business plans. These maneuvers create a vicious circle of inaccuracy that benefits no one.

Don't misunderstand me: business plans should include some numbers. But those numbers should appear mainly in the form of a business model that shows the entrepreneurial team has thought through the key drivers of the venture's success or failure. In manufacturing, such a driver might be the yield on a production process; in magazine publishing, the anticipated renewal rate; or in software, the impact of using various distribution channels. The model should also address the break-even issue: At what level of sales does the business begin to make a profit? And even more important, When does cash flow turn positive? Without a doubt, these questions deserve a few pages in any business plan. Near the back.

What goes at the front? What information does a good business plan contain?

If you want to speak the language of investors—and also make sure you have asked yourself the right questions before setting out on the most daunting journey of a businessperson's career—I recommend basing your business plan on the framework that follows. It does not provide the kind of "winning" formula touted by some current how-to books and software programs for entrepreneurs. Nor is it a guide to brain surgery. Rather, the framework systematically assesses the four interdependent factors critical to every new venture:

The People. The men and women starting and running the venture, as well as the outside parties providing key services or important resources for it, such as its lawyers, accountants, and suppliers.

The Opportunity. A profile of the business itself—what it will sell and to whom, whether the business can grow and how fast, what its economics are, who and what stand in the way of success.

The Context. The big picture—the regulatory environment, interest rates, demographic trends, inflation, and the like—basically, factors that inevitably change but cannot be controlled by the entrepreneur.

Risk and Reward. An assessment of everything that can go wrong and right, and a discussion of how the entrepreneurial team can respond.

The assumption behind the framework is that great businesses have attributes that are easy to identify but hard to assemble. They have an experienced, energetic managerial team from the top to the bottom. The team's members have skills and experiences directly relevant to the opportunity they are pursuing. Ideally, they will have worked successfully together in the past. The opportunity has an attractive, sustainable business model; it is possible to create a competitive edge and defend it. Many options exist for expanding the scale and scope of the business, and these options are unique to the enterprise and its team. Value can be extracted from the business in a number of ways either through a positive harvest event—a sale—or by scaling down or liquidating. The context is favorable with respect to both the regulatory and the macroeconomic environments. Risk is understood, and the team has considered

BUSINESS PLANS:
FOR ENTREPRENEURS ONLY?

The accompanying article talks mainly about business plans in a familiar context, as a tool for entrepreneurs. But quite often, start-ups are launched within established companies. Do those new ventures require business plans? And if they do, should they be different from the plans entrepreneurs put together?

The answer to the first question is an emphatic yes; the answer to the second, an equally emphatic no. All new ventures—whether they are funded by venture capitalists or, as is the case with intrapreneurial businesses, by shareholders—need to pass the same acid tests. After all, the marketplace does not differentiate between products or services based on who is pouring money into them behind the scenes.

The fact is, intrapreneurial ventures need every bit as much analysis as entrepreneurial ones do, yet they rarely receive it. Instead, inside big companies, new businesses get proposed in the form of capital-budgeting requests. These faceless documents are subject to detailed financial scrutiny and a consensus-building process, as the

project wends its way through the chain of command, what I call the "neutron bomb" model of project governance. However, in the history of such proposals, a plan never has been submitted that did not promise returns in excess of corporate hurdle rates. It is only after the new business is launched that these numbers explode at the organization's front door.

That problem could be avoided in large part if intrapreneurial ventures followed the guidelines set out in the accompanying article. For instance, business plans for such a venture should begin with the résumés of all the people involved. What has the team done in the past that would suggest it would be successful in the future, and so on? In addition, the new venture's product or service should be fully analyzed in terms of its opportunity and context. Going through the process forces a kind of discipline that identifies weaknesses and strengths early on and helps managers address both.

It also helps enormously if such discipline continues after the intrapreneurial

venture lifts off. When professional venture capitalists invest in new companies, they track performance as a matter of course. But in large companies, scrutiny of a new venture is often inconsistent. That shouldn't or needn't be the case. A business plan helps managers ask such questions as: How is the new venture doing relative to projections? What decisions has the team made in response to new information? Have changes in the context made additional funding necessary? How could the team have predicted those changes? Such questions not only keep a new venture running smoothly but also help an organization learn from its mistakes and triumphs.

Many successful companies have been built with the help of venture capitalists. Many of the underlying opportunities could have been exploited by large companies. Why weren't they? Perhaps useful lessons can be learned by studying the world of independent ventures, one lesson being: Write a great business plan.

ways to mitigate the impact of difficult events. In short, great businesses have the four parts of the framework completely covered. If only reality were so neat.

The People

When I received a business plan, I always read the résumé section first. Not because the people part of the new venture is the most important, but because without the right team, none of the other parts really matters.

I read the résumés of the venture's team with a list of questions in mind. (See the insert "Who Are These People, Anyway?") All these questions get at the same three issues about the venture's team members: What do they know? Whom do they know? and How well are they known?

What and whom they know are matters of insight and experience. How familiar are the team members with industry players and dynamics? Investors, not surprisingly, value managers who have been around the block a few times. A business plan should candidly describe each team member's knowledge of the new venture's

type of product or service; its production processes; and the market itself, from competitors to customers. It also helps to indicate whether the team members have worked together before. Not played—as in roomed together in college—but *worked*.

Investors also look favorably on a team that is known because the real world often prefers not to deal with start-ups. They're too unpredictable. That changes, however, when the new company is run by people well known to suppliers, customers, and employees. Their enterprise may be brand new, but they aren't. The surprise element of working with a start-up is somewhat ameliorated.

Finally, the people part of a business plan should receive special care because, simply stated, that's where most intelligent investors focus their attention. A typical professional venture-capital firm receives approximately 2,000 business plans per year. These plans are filled with tantalizing ideas for new products and services that will change the world and reap billions in the process—or so they say. But the fact is, most venture capitalists believe that ideas are a dime a dozen: only execution skills count. As Arthur Rock, a venture capital

legend associated with the formation of such companies as Apple, Intel, and Teledyne, states, "I invest in people, not ideas." Rock also has said, "If you can find good people, if they're wrong about the product, they'll make a switch, so what good is it to understand the product that they're talking about in the first place?"

Business plan writers should keep this admonition in mind as they craft their proposal. Talk about the people—exhaustively. And if there is nothing solid about their experience and abilities to herald, then the entrepreneurial team should think again about launching the venture.

The Opportunity

When it comes to the opportunity itself, a good business plan begins by focusing on two questions: Is the total market for the venture's product or service large, rapidly growing, or both? Is the industry now, or can it become, structurally attractive? Entrepreneurs and investors look for large or rapidly growing markets mainly because it is often easier to obtain a share of a growing market than to fight with entrenched competitors for a share of a mature or stagnant market. Smart investors, in fact, try hard to identify high-growth-potential markets early in their evolution: that's where the big payoffs are. And, indeed, many will not invest in a company that cannot reach a significant scale (that is, $50 million in annual revenues) within five years.

Who Are These People, Anyway?

Fourteen "Personal" Questions Every Business Plan Should Answer

- Where are the founders from?
- Where have they been educated?
- Where have they worked—and for whom?
- What have they accomplished—professionally and personally—in the past?
- What is their reputation within the business community?
- What experience do they have that is directly relevant to the opportunity they are pursuing?
- What skills, abilities, and knowledge do they have?
- How realistic are they about the venture's chances for success and the tribulations it will face?
- Who else needs to be on the team?
- Are they prepared to recruit high-quality people?
- How will they respond to adversity?
- Do they have the mettle to make the inevitable hard choices that have to be made?
- How committed are they to this venture?
- What are their motivations?

As for attractiveness, investors are obviously looking for markets that actually allow businesses to make some money. But that's not the no-brainer it seems. In the late 1970s, the computer disk-drive business looked very attractive. The technology was new and exciting. Dozens of companies jumped into the fray, aided by an army of professional investors. Twenty years later, however, the thrill is gone for managers and investors alike. Disk-drive companies must design products to meet the perceived needs of original equipment manufacturers (OEMs) and end users.

Selling a product to OEMs is complicated. The customers are large relative to most of their suppliers. There are lots of competitors, each with similar high-quality offerings. Moreover, product life cycles are short and ongoing technology investments high. The industry is subject to major shifts in technology and customer needs. Intense rivalry leads to lower prices and, hence, lower margins. In short, the disk-drive industry is simply not set up to make people a lot of money; it's a structural disaster area.

The information services industry, by contrast, is paradise. Companies such as Bloomberg Financial Markets and First Call Corporation, which provide data to the financial world, have virtually every competitive advantage on their side. First, they can assemble or create *proprietary* content—content that, by the way, is like life's blood to thousands of money managers and stock analysts around the world. And although it is often expensive to develop the service and to acquire initial customers, once up and running, these companies can deliver content to customers very cheaply. Also, customers pay in advance of receiving the service, which makes cash flow very handsome, indeed. In short, the structure of the information services industry is beyond attractive: it's gorgeous. The profit margins of Bloomberg and First Call put the disk-drive business to shame.

The market is as fickle as it is unpredictable. Who would have guessed that plug-in room deodorizers would sell?

Thus, the first step for entrepreneurs is to make sure they are entering an industry that is large and/or growing, and one that's structurally attractive. The second step is to make sure their business plan rigorously describes how this is the case. And if it isn't the case, their business plan needs to specify how the venture will still manage to make enough of a profit that investors (or potential employees or suppliers, for that matter) will want to participate.

Once it examines the new venture's industry, a business plan must describe in detail how the company will build and launch its product or service into the marketplace.

Again, a series of questions should guide the discussion. (See the insert "The Opportunity of a Lifetime—or Is It?")

Often the answers to these questions reveal a fatal flaw in the business. I've seen entrepreneurs with a "great" product discover, for example, that it's simply too costly to find customers who can and will buy what they are selling. Economically viable access to customers is the key to business, yet many entrepreneurs take the *Field of Dreams* approach to this notion: build it, and they will come. That strategy works in the movies but is not very sensible in the real world.

It is not always easy to answer questions about the likely consumer response to new products or services. The market is as fickle as it is unpredictable. (Who would have guessed that plug-in room deodorizers would sell?) One entrepreneur I know proposed to introduce an electronic newsclipping service. He made his pitch to a prospective venture-capital investor who rejected the plan, stating, "I just don't think the dogs will eat the dog food." Later, when the entrepreneur's company went public, he sent the venture capitalist an anonymous package containing an empty can of dog food and a copy of his prospectus. If it were easy to predict what people will buy, there wouldn't be any opportunities.

The Opportunity of a Lifetime—or Is It?

Nine Questions About the Business Every Business Plan Should Answer

- Who is the new venture's customer?
- How does the customer make decisions about buying this product or service?
- To what degree is the product or service a compelling purchase for the customer?
- How will the product or service be priced?
- How will the venture reach all the identified customer segments?
- How much does it cost (in time and resources) to acquire a customer?
- How much does it cost to produce and deliver the product or service?
- How much does it cost to support a customer?
- How easy is it to retain a customer?

Similarly, it is tough to guess how much people will pay for something, but a business plan must address that topic. Sometimes, the dogs will eat the dog food, but only at a price less than cost. Investors always look for opportunities for value pricing—that is, markets in which the costs to produce the product are low, but consumers will still pay a lot for it. No one is dying to invest in a company when margins are skinny. Still, there is money to be made in inexpensive products and services—even in commodities. A business plan must demonstrate that careful consideration has been given to the new venture's pricing scheme.

The list of questions about the new venture's opportunity focuses on the direct revenues and the costs of producing and marketing a product. That's fine, as far as it goes. A sensible proposal, however, also involves assessing the business model from a perspective that takes into account the investment required—that is, the balance sheet side of the equation. The following questions should also be addressed so that investors can understand the cash flow implications of pursuing an opportunity:

•When does the business have to buy resources, such as supplies, raw materials, and people?

•When does the business have to pay for them?

•How long does it take to acquire a customer?

•How long before the customer sends the business a check?

•How much capital equipment is required to support a dollar of sales?

Investors, of course, are looking for businesses in which management can buy low, sell high, collect early, and pay late. The business plan needs to spell out how close to that ideal the new venture is expected to come. Even if the answer is "not very"—and it usually is—at least the truth is out there to discuss.

The opportunity section of a business plan must also bring a few other issues to the surface. First, it must demonstrate and analyze how an opportunity can grow—in other words, how the new venture can expand its range of products or services, customer base, or geographic scope. Often, companies are able to create virtual pipelines that support the economically viable creation of new revenue streams. In the publishing business, for example, *Inc.* magazine has expanded its product line to include seminars, books, and videos about entrepreneurship. Similarly, building on

the success of its personal-finance software program Quicken, Intuit now sells software for electronic banking, small-business accounting, and tax preparation, as well as personal-printing supplies and on-line information services—to name just a few of its highly profitable ancillary spin-offs.

Whatever the reason, better-mousetrap businesses have an uncanny way of malfunctioning.

Now, lots of business plans runneth over on the subject of the new venture's potential for growth and expansion. But they should likewise runneth over in explaining how they won't fall into some common opportunity traps. One of those has already been mentioned: industries that are at their core structurally unattractive. But there are others. The world of invention, for example, is fraught with danger. Over the past 15 years, I have seen scores of individuals who have devised a better mousetrap—newfangled creations from inflatable pillows for use on airplanes to automated car-parking systems. Few of these idea-driven companies have really taken off, however. I'm not entirely sure why. Sometimes, the inventor refuses to spend the money required by or share the rewards sufficiently with the business side of the company. Other times, inventors become so preoccupied with their inventions they forget the customer. Whatever the reason, better-mousetrap businesses have an uncanny way of malfunctioning.

Another opportunity trap that business plans—and entrepreneurs in general—need to pay attention to is the tricky business of arbitrage. Basically, arbitrage ventures are created to take advantage of some pricing disparity in the marketplace. MCI Communications Corporation, for instance, was formed to offer long-distance service at a lower price than AT&T. Some of the industry consolidations going on today reflect a different kind of arbitrage—the ability to buy small businesses at a wholesale price, roll them up together into a larger package, and take them public at a retail price, all without necessarily adding value in the process.

Taking advantage of arbitrage opportunities is a viable and potentially profitable way to enter a business. In the final analysis, however, all arbitrage opportunities

evaporate. It is not a question of whether, only when. The trick in these businesses is to use the arbitrage profits to build a more enduring business model, and business plans must explain how and when that will occur.

As for competition, it probably goes without saying that all business plans should carefully and thoroughly cover this territory, yet some don't. That is a glaring omission. For starters, every business plan should answer the following questions about the competition:

•Who are the new venture's current competitors?

•What resources do they control? What are their strengths and weaknesses?

•How will they respond to the new venture's decision to enter the business?

•How can the new venture respond to its competitors' response?

•Who else might be able to observe and exploit the same opportunity?

•Are there ways to co-opt potential or actual competitors by forming alliances?

Business is like chess: to be successful, you must anticipate several moves in advance. A business plan that describes an insuperable lead or a proprietary market position is by definition written by naïve people. That goes not just for the competition section of the business plan but for the entire discussion of the opportunity. All opportunities have promise; all have vulnerabilities. A good business plan doesn't whitewash the latter. Rather, it proves that the entrepreneurial team knows the good, the bad, and the ugly that the venture faces ahead.

The Context

Opportunities exist in a context. At one level is the macroeconomic environment, including the level of economic activity, inflation, exchange rates, and interest rates. At another level are the wide range of government rules and regulations that affect the opportunity and how resources are marshaled to exploit it. Examples extend from tax policy to the rules about raising capital for a private or public company. And at yet another level are factors like technology that define the limits of what a business or its competitors can accomplish.

Context often has a tremendous impact on every aspect of the entrepreneurial process, from identification of opportunity to harvest. In some cases, changes in some contextual factor create opportunity. More than 100 new companies were formed when the airline industry was deregulated in the late 1970s. The context for financing was also favorable, enabling new entrants like People Express to go to the public market for capital even before starting operations.

Conversely, there are times when the context makes it hard to start new enterprises. The recession of the early 1990s combined with a difficult financing environment for new companies: venture capital disbursements were low, as was the amount of capital raised in the public markets. (Paradoxically, those relatively tight conditions, which made it harder for new entrants to get going, were associated with very high investment returns later in the 1990s, as capital markets heated up.)

Sometimes, a shift in context turns an unattractive business into an attractive one, and vice versa. Consider the case of a packaging company some years ago that was performing so poorly it was about to be put on the block. Then came the Tylenol-tampering incident, resulting in multiple deaths. The packaging company happened to have an efficient mechanism for installing tamper-proof seals, and in a matter of weeks its financial performance could have been called spectacular. Conversely, U.S. tax reforms enacted in 1986 created havoc for companies in the real estate business, eliminating almost every positive incentive to invest. Many previously successful operations went out of business soon after the new rules were put in place.

One of the great myths about entrepreneurs is that they are risk seekers. All sane people want to avoid risk.

Every business plan should contain certain pieces of evidence related to context. First, the entrepreneurs should show a heightened awareness of the new venture's context and how it helps or hinders their specific proposal. Second, and more important, they should demonstrate that they know the venture's context will inevitably change and describe how those changes might affect the business. Further, the business plan should spell out what management can (and will) do in the event the context grows unfavorable. Finally, the business plan

should explain the ways (if any) in which management can affect context in a positive way. For example, management might be able to have an impact on regulations or on industry standards through lobbying efforts.

Risk and Reward

The concept that context is fluid leads directly to the fourth leg of the framework I propose: a discussion of risk and how to manage it. I've come to think of a good business plan as a snapshot of an event in the future. That's quite a feat to begin with–taking a picture of the unknown. But the best business plans go beyond that; they are like movies of the future. They show the people, the opportunity, and the context from multiple angles. They offer a plausible, coherent story of what lies ahead. They unfold possibilities of action and reaction.

The best business is a post office box to which people send cashier's checks.

Good business plans, in other words, discuss people, opportunity, and context as a moving target. All three factors (and the relationship among them) are likely to change over time as a company evolves from start-up to ongoing enterprise. Therefore, any business plan worth the time it takes to write or read needs to focus attention on the dynamic aspects of the entrepreneurial process.

Of course, the future is hard to predict. Still, it is possible to give potential investors a sense of the kind and class of risk and reward they are assuming with a new venture. All it takes is a pencil and two simple drawings. (See the insert "Visualizing Risk and Reward.") But even with these drawings, risk is, well, risky. In reality, there are no immutable distributions of outcomes. It is ultimately the responsibility of management to change the distribution, to increase the likelihood and consequences of success, and to decrease the likelihood and implications of problems.

One of the great myths about entrepreneurs is that they are risk seekers. All sane people want to avoid risk. As Harvard Business School professor (and venture capitalist) Howard Stevenson says, true entrepreneurs want to capture all the re-

ward and give all the risk to others. The best business is a post office box to which people send cashier's checks. Yet risk is unavoidable. So what does that mean for a business plan?

It means that the plan must unflinchingly confront the risks ahead—in terms of people, opportunity, and context. What happens if one of the new venture's leaders leaves? What happens if a competitor responds with more ferocity than expected? What happens if there is a revolution in Namibia, the source of a key raw material? What will management actually *do*?

Those are hard questions for an entrepreneur to pose, especially when seeking capital. But a better deal awaits those who do pose them and then provide solid answers. A new venture, for example, might be highly leveraged and therefore very sensitive to interest rates. Its business plan would benefit enormously by stating that management intends to hedge its exposure through the financial-futures market by purchasing a contract that does well when interest rates go up. That is the equivalent of offering investors insurance. (It also makes sense for the business itself.)

Finally, one important area in the realm of risk/reward management relates to harvesting. Venture capitalists often ask if a company is "IPOable," by which they mean, Can the company be taken public at some point in the future? Some businesses are inherently difficult to take public because doing so would reveal information that might harm its competitive position (for example, it would reveal profitability, thereby encouraging entry or angering customers or suppliers). Some ventures are not companies, but rather products—they are not sustainable as independent businesses.

Therefore, the business plan should talk candidly about the end of the process. How will the inventor eventually get money out of the business, assuming it is successful, even if only marginally so? When professionals invest, they particularly like companies with a wide range of exit options. They like companies that work hard to preserve and enhance those options along the way; companies that don't, for example, unthinkingly form alliances with big corporations that could someday actually *buy* them. Investors feel a lot better about risk if the venture's endgame is discussed up front. There is an old saying, "If you don't know where you are going, any road will get you there." In crafting

Visualizing Risk and Reward

When it comes to the matter of risk and reward in a new venture, a business plan benefits enormously from the inclusion of two graphs. Perhaps *graphs* is the wrong word; these are really just schematic pictures that illustrate the most likely relationship between risk and reward, that is, the relationship between the opportunity and its economics. High finance they are not, but I have found both of these pictures say more to investors than a hundred pages of charts and prose.

The first picture depicts the amount of money needed to launch the new venture, time to positive cash flow, and the expected magnitude of the payoff.

This image helps the investor understand the depth and duration of negative cash flow, as well as the relationship between the investment and the possible return. The ideal, needless to say, is to have cash flow early and often. But most investors are intrigued by the picture even when the cash outflow is high and long—as long as the cash inflow is more so.

The second picture complements the first. It shows investors the range of possible returns and the likelihood of achieving them. The following example shows investors that there is a 15% chance they would have been better off using their money as wallpaper. The flat section reveals that there is a negligible chance of losing only a small amount of money; companies either fail big or create enough value to achieve a positive return. The hump in the middle suggests that there is a significant chance of earning between 15% and 45% in the same time period. And finally, there is a small chance that the initial outlay of cash will spawn a 200% internal rate of return, which might have occurred if you had happened to invest in Microsoft when it was a private company.

Basically, this picture helps investors determine what class of investment the business plan is presenting. Is the new venture drilling for North Sea oil—highly risky with potentially big payoffs—or is it digging development wells in Texas, which happens to be less of a geological gamble and probably less lucrative, too? This image answers that kind of question. It's then up to the investors to decide how much risk they want to live with against what kind of odds.

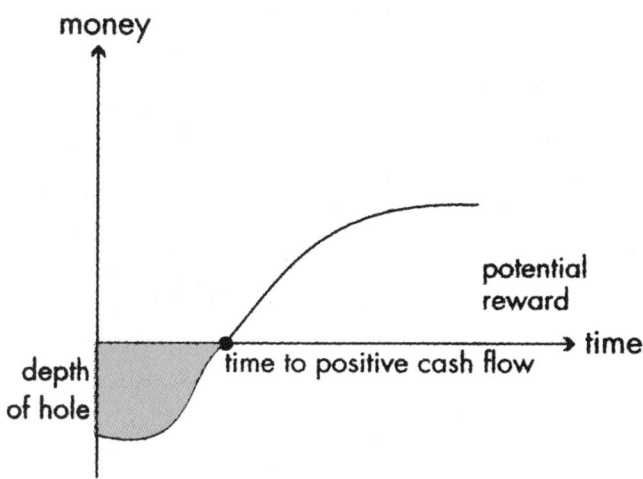

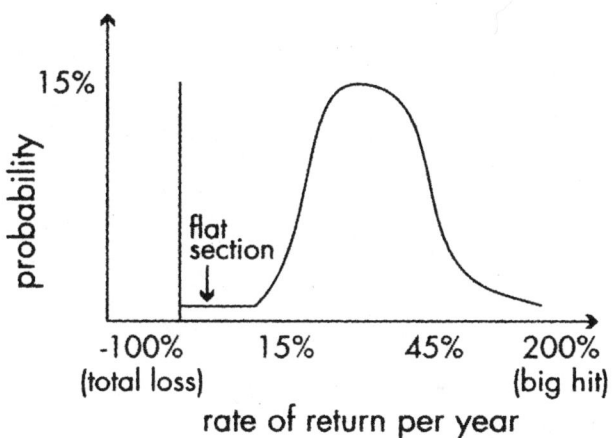

Of course, since the world of new ventures is populated by wild-eyed optimists, you might expect the picture to display a shallower hole and a steeper reward slope than it should. It usually does. But to be honest, even that kind of picture belongs in the business plan because it is a fair warning to investors that the new venture's team is completely out of touch with reality and should be avoided at all costs.

Again, the people who write business plans might be inclined to skew the picture to make it look as if the probability of a significant return is downright huge and the possibility of loss is negligible. And, again, I would say therein lies the picture's beauty. What it claims, checked against the investor's sense of reality and experience, should serve as a simple pictorial caveat emptor.

sensible entrepreneurial strategies, just the opposite is true: you had better know where you might end up and have a map for getting there. A business plan should be the place where the map is drawn, for, as every traveler knows, a journey is a lot less risky when you have directions.

The Deal and Beyond

Once a business plan is written, of course, the goal is to land a deal. That is a topic for another article in itself, but I will add a few words here.

When I talk to young (and old) entrepreneurs looking to finance their ventures, they obsess about the valuation and terms of the deal they will receive. Their explicit goal seems to be to minimize the dilution they will suffer in raising capital. Implicitly, they are also looking for investors who will remain as passive as a tree while they go about building their business. On the food chain of investors, it seems, doctors and dentists are best and venture capitalists are worst because of the degree to which the latter group demands control and a large share of the returns.

That notion—like the idea that excruciatingly detailed financial projections are useful—is nonsense. From whom you raise capital is often more important than the terms. New ventures are inherently risky, as I've noted; what can go wrong will. When that happens, unsophisticated investors panic, get angry, and often refuse to advance the company more money. Sophisticated investors, by contrast, roll up their sleeves and help the company solve its problems. Often, they've had lots of experience saving sinking ships. They are typically process literate. They understand how to craft a sensible busi-

A Glossary of Business Plan Terms

What They Say...	and What They Really Mean
We conservatively project...	We read a book that said we had to be a $50 million company in five years, and we reverse-engineered the numbers.
We took our best guess and divided by 2.	We accidentally divided by 0.5.
We project a 10% margin.	We did not modify any of the assumptions in the business plan template that we downloaded from the Internet.
The project is 98% complete.	To complete the remaining 2% will take as long as it took to create the initial 98% but will cost twice as much.
Our business model is proven...	If you take the evidence from the past week for the best of our 50 locations and extrapolate it for all the others.
We have a six-month lead.	We tried not to find out how many other people have a six-month lead.
We only need a 10% market share.	So do the other 50 entrants getting funded.
Customers are clamoring for our products.	We have not yet asked them to pay for it. Also, all of our current customers are relatives.
We are the low-cost producer.	We have not produced anything yet, but we are confident that we will be able to.
We have no competition.	Only IBM, Microsoft, Netscape, and Sun have announced plans to enter the business.
Our management team has a great deal of experience...	Consuming the product or service.
A select group of investors is considering the plan.	We mailed a copy of the plan to everyone in *Pratt's Guide*.
We seek a value-added investor.	We are looking for a passive, dumb-as-rocks investor.
If you invest on your terms, you will earn a 68% internal rate of return.	If everything that could ever conceivably go right does go right, you may get your money back.

ness strategy and a strong tactical plan. They know how to recruit, compensate, and motivate team members. They are also familiar with the Byzantine ins and outs of going public—an event most entrepreneurs face but once in a lifetime. This kind of know-how is worth the money needed to buy it.

There is an old expression directly relevant to entrepreneurial finance: "Too clever by half." Often, deal makers get very creative, crafting all sorts of payoff and option schemes. That usually backfires. My experience has proven again and again that sensible deals have the following six characteristics:

•They are simple.
•They are fair.
•They emphasize trust rather than legal ties.
•They do not blow apart if actual differs slightly from plan.
•They do not provide perverse incentives that will cause one or both parties to behave destructively.
•They are written on a pile of papers no greater than one-quarter inch thick.

But even these six simple rules miss an important point. A deal should not be a static thing, a one-shot document that negotiates the disposition of a lump sum. Instead, it is incumbent upon entrepreneurs, before they go searching for funding, to think about capital acquisition as a dynamic process—to figure out how much money they will need and when they will need it.

How is that accomplished? The trick is for the entrepreneurial team to treat the new venture as a series of experiments. Before launching the whole show, launch a little piece of it. Convene a focus group to test the product, build a prototype and watch it perform, conduct a regional or local rollout of a service. Such an exercise reveals the true economics of the business and can help enormously in determining how much money the new venture actually requires and in what stages. Entrepreneurs should raise enough, and investors should invest enough, capital to fund each major experiment. Experiments, of course, can feel expensive and risky. But I've seen

them prevent disasters and help create successes. I consider it a prerequisite of putting together a winning deal.

Beware the Albatross

Among the many sins committed by business plan writers is arrogance. In today's economy, few ideas are truly proprietary. Moreover, there has never been a time in recorded history when the supply of capital did not outrace the supply of opportunity. The true half-life of opportunity is decreasing with the passage of time.

A business plan must not be an albatross that hangs around the neck of the entrepreneurial team, dragging it into oblivion. Instead, a business plan must be a call for action, one that recognizes management's responsibility to fix what is broken proactively and in real time. Risk is inevitable, avoiding risk impossible. Risk management is the key, always tilting the venture in favor of reward and away from risk.

A plan must demonstrate mastery of the entire entrepreneurial process, from identification of opportunity to harvest. It is not a way to separate unsuspecting investors from their money by hiding the fatal flaw. For in the final analysis, the only one being fooled is the entrepreneur.

We live today in the golden age of entrepreneurship. Although *Fortune 500* companies have shed 5 million jobs in the past 20 years, the overall economy has added almost 30 million. Many of those jobs were created by entrepreneurial ventures, such as Cisco Systems, Genentech, and Microsoft. Each of those companies started with a business plan. Is that why they succeeded? There is no knowing for sure. But there is little doubt that crafting a business plan so that it thoroughly and candidly addresses the ingredients of success—people, opportunity, context, and the risk/reward picture—is vitally important. In the absence of a crystal ball, in fact, a business plan built of the *right* information and analysis can only be called indispensable.

William A. Sahlman is Dimitri V. d'Arbeloff Professor of Business Administration at the Harvard Business School in Boston, Massachusetts. He has been closely connected with more than 50 entrepreneurial ventures as an adviser, investor, or director. He teaches a second-year course at the Harvard Business School called "Entrepreneurial Finance," for which he has developed more than 100 cases and notes.

Outline for a **Business** Plan

A proven approach for entrepreneurs only

… a written representation of where a company is going, how it will get there, and what it will look like once it arrives

Ernst & Young LLP

Business plans are the preferred mode of communication between entrepreneurs and potential investors. Experienced owners and managers of closely held businesses know that business plans can also be an indispensable management tool. Many have found that just completing the steps required to develop a business plan forces them to introduce discipline and a logical thought process into all of their planning activities. They have found that a properly prepared business plan can greatly improve their company's ability to consistently establish and meet goals and objectives in a way that best serves the company's owners, employees, and investors.

A business plan can take many forms, from a glossy, professionally produced document to a handwritten manuscript in a three-ring binder that serves as the documentation for the goals, objectives, strategies, and tactics of a company.

In any form, a business plan is simply a written representation of where a company is going, how it will get there, and what it will look like once it arrives.

Uses of a **Business Plan**

A business plan is a valuable management tool that can be utilized in a wide variety of situations.

In most companies, business plans are used at a minimum to:

- *Set the goals and objectives for the company's performance.*
- *Provide a basis for evaluating and controlling the company's performance.*
- *Communicate a company's message to middle managers, outside directors, lenders, and potential investors.*

When utilized most efficiently, the same business plan, with slight modification, can be used for all three actions.

Setting Goals and Objectives

The business plan for an early-stage company is, in many ways, a first attempt at strategic planning. An entrepreneur should use a business plan as a tool for setting the direction of a company over the next several years, and a plan should set the action steps and processes to guide the company through this period. Many entrepreneurs say that the pressures of the day-to-day management of a company leave them little time for planning, and this is unfortunate because, without it, an owner runs the risks of proceeding blindly through the rapidly changing business environment. Of course, writing a business plan is not a guarantee that problems will not arise. But, with a thoroughly thought-out plan, a business owner can better anticipate a crisis situation and deal with it up front. Further, a well-constructed plan can help avoid certain problems altogether. All in all, business planning is probably more important to the survival of a small and growing company than a larger, more mature one.

Performance Benchmarks

A business plan can also be used to develop and document milestones along your business's path to success. In the heat of daily operations, you may find that taking an objective look at the performance of your business is difficult. Often, the trees encountered daily obscure your view of the forest in which your company operates. A business plan can provide you and your management team with an objective basis for determining if the business is on track to meet the goals and objectives you have set.

Internal and External Communications

Your company's story must be told and retold many times to prospective investors, potential and new employees, outside advisors, and potential customers. And the most important part of the story is the part about the future, the part featured in a business plan.

Your business plan should show how all the pieces of your company fit together to create a vibrant organization capable of meeting its goals and objectives. It must be able to communicate your company's distinctive competence to anyone who might have an interest.

Steps in Preparing Your Business Plan

This booklet presents a generalized outline for writing a business plan. The outline is intended to be used with *Ernst & Young's Business Plan Guide*, published by John Wiley & Sons. The Guide can be purchased at many bookstores. . . .

Listed below are the steps you should follow in preparing your business plan, whether you are writing it for the first time or rewriting it for the twentieth.

STEP 1—IDENTIFY YOUR OBJECTIVES

Before you can write a successful business plan you must determine who will read the plan, what they already know about your company, what they want to know about your company, and how they intend to use the information they will find in the plan. The needs of your target audience must be combined with your communication objectives—what you want the reader to know. Once you have identified and resolved any conflicts between what your target audience wants to know and what you want them to know, you are ready to begin preparing a useful business plan.

STEP 2—OUTLINE YOUR BUSINESS PLAN

Once you have identified the objectives for your business plan, and you know the areas that you want to emphasize, you should prepare an outline based on these special requirements. The outline can be as general or detailed as you wish, but typically a detailed outline will be more useful to you while you are writing your plan.

STEP 3—REVIEW YOUR OUTLINE

Review your outline to identify the areas that, based on your readers and objectives, should be presented in detail or summary form in your business plan. Keep in mind that your business plan should describe your company at a high level and that extremely detailed descriptions are to be avoided in most cases. However, you must be prepared to provide detailed support for your statements and assumptions apart from your business plan if necessary.

STEP 4—WRITE YOUR PLAN

The order in which the specific elements of the plan are developed will vary depending on the age of your company and your experience in preparing business plans.

You will probably find it necessary to research many areas before you have enough information to write about them. Most people begin by collecting historical financial information about their company and/or industry, and completing their market research before beginning to write any part of their plan. Even though you may do extensive research before you begin to develop your plan, you may find that additional research is required before you complete it. You should take the time to complete the required research because many of the assumptions and strategies described in the plan will be based on the findings and analysis of your research.

Initial drafts of prospective financial statements are often prepared next, after the basic financial and market research and analysis are completed.

By preparing these statements at this time, you will have a good idea which strategies will work from a financial perspective before investing many hours in writing a detailed description of them. As you develop your prospective statements, be certain that you keep detailed notes on the assumptions you make to facilitate preparation of the footnotes that must accompany the statements, as well as the composition of other business plan elements.

The last element of a business plan to be prepared is the Executive Summary. Since it is a summary of the plan, its contents are contingent on the rest of the document, and it cannot be written properly until the other components of the plan are essentially complete.

While preparing each element of your plan, refer to the outline in this booklet to be certain that you have covered each area thoroughly.

STEP 5—HAVE YOUR PLAN REVIEWED

Once you have completed and reviewed a draft of your plan, have someone familiar with business management and the planning process review it for completeness (by referring to the outline in this publication), objectivity, logic, presentation, and effectiveness as a communications tool. Then, modify your plan based on your reviewer's comments.

STEP 6—UPDATE YOUR PLAN

Business plans are "living" documents and must be periodically updated, or they become useless. As your environment and your objectives—and those of your readers—change, update your plan to reflect these changes. Refer to this booklet each time your plan is updated to be certain that all areas are properly covered.

Outline for a **Business Plan**

I. Executive Summary

The Executive Summary should not be a mere listing of topics contained in the body of your business plan but should emphasize the key issues presented.

A critical point that must be communicated in the Executive Summary is your company's distinctive competence—the factors that will make your business successful in a competitive market.

A. The Purpose of the Plan

1. Attract investors
2. Document an operational plan for controlling the business

B. Market Analysis

1. The characteristics of your target market (demographic, geographic, etc.)
2. The products or services you will offer to satisfy those needs

C. The Company

1. The needs your company will satisfy
2. The products or services you will offer to satisfy those needs

D. Marketing and Sales Activities

1. Marketing strategy
2. Sales strategy
3. Keys to success in your competitive environment

E. Product or Service Research and Development

1. Major milestones

2. Ongoing efforts

F. Organization and Personnel

1. Key managers and owners
2. Key operations employees

G. Financial Data

1. Funds required and their use
2. Historical financial summary
3. Prospective financial summary (including a brief justification for prospective sales levels)

Note—In total, your Executive Summary should be less than three pages in length and provide the reader with a succinct overview of your entire business plan.

The Executive Summary should be followed by a brief table of contents designed to assist readers in locating specific sections in the plan. Detailed descriptions of the plan's contents should be avoided in the table of contents.

 If your company is new, you could be sending your business plan to potential investors who review hundreds of them each year. More often than not, these individuals do not get past the Executive Summary of the plans they receive. Your Executive Summary must therefore give the reader a useful understanding of your business and make the point of most interest to them: "What is in it for the investor?"

II. Market Analysis

The Market Analysis section should reflect your knowledge of your industry, and present highlights and analysis of your market research. Detailed market research studies, however, should be presented as appendices to your plan.

A. Industry Description and Outlook

1. Description of your primary industry
2. Size of the industry
   a. Historically
   b. Currently
   c. In five years
   d. In ten years
3. Industry characteristics and trends (Where is company in its life cycle?)
   a. Historically
   b. Currently
   c. In the future

4. Major customer groups
   a. *Businesses*
   b. *Governments*
   c. *Consumers*

B. Target Markets

1. Distinguishing characteristics of your primary target markets and market segments. Narrow your target markets to a manageable size. Efforts to penetrate target markets that are too broad are often ineffective.
   a. *Critical needs*
   b. *Extent to which those needs are currently being met*
   c. *Demographics*
   d. *Geographic location*
   e. *Purchasing decision-makers and influencers*
   f. *Seasonal/cyclical trends*
2. Primary/target market size
   a. *Number of prospective customers*
   b. *Annual purchases of products or services meeting the same or similar needs as your products or services*
   c. *Geographic area*
   d. *Anticipated market growth*
3. Market penetration—indicate the extent to which you anticipate penetrating your market and demonstrate why you feel that level of penetration is achievable based on your market research
   a. *Market share*
   b. *Number of customers*
   c. *Geographic coverage*
   d. *Rationale for market penetration estimates*
4. Pricing/gross margin targets
   a. *Price levels*
   b. *Gross margin levels*
   c. *Discount structure (volume, prompt payment, etc.)*
5. Methods by which specific members of your target market can be identified
   a. *Directories*
   b. *Trade association publications*
   c. *Government documents*
6. Media through which you can communicate with specific members of your target market
   a. *Publications*
   b. *Radio/television broadcasts*
   c. *Sources of influence/advice*
7. Purchasing cycle of potential customers
   a. *Needs identification*
   b. *Research for solutions to needs*
   c. *Solution evaluation process*
   c. *Final solution selecting responsibility and authority (executives, purchasing agents, engineers, etc.)*

8. Key trends and anticipated changes within your primary target markets
9. Secondary target markets and key attributes
   a. *Needs*
   b. *Demographics*
   c. *Significant future trends*

C. Market Test Results

1. Potential customers contacted
2. Information/demonstrations given to potential customers
3. Reaction of potential customers
4. Importance of satisfaction of targeted needs
5. Test group's willingness to purchase products/ services at various price levels

D. Lead Times (amount of time between customer order placement and product/service delivery)

1. Initial orders
2. Reorders
3. Volume purchases

As your market analysis provides the only basis for your prospective sales and pricing estimates, make sure that this section clearly demonstrates that there is a market need for your product or service, that you as owner not only understand this need but can meet it, and that you can sell at a profit. This section should also include an estimate of your market penetration annually for the next five years.

E. Competition

1. Identification (by product line or service and market segment)
   a. *Existing*
   b. *Market share*
   c. *Potential (How long will your "window of opportunity" be open before your initial success breeds new competition? Who will your new competitors likely be?)*
   d. *Direct*
   e. *Indirect*
2. Strengths (competitive advantages)
   a. *Ability to satisfy customer needs*
   b. *Market penetration*
   c. *Track record and reputation*
   d. *Staying power (financial resources)*
   e. *Key personnel*
3. Weaknesses (competitive disadvantages)
   a. *Ability to satisfy customer needs*
   b. *Market penetration*

c. Track record and reputation

d. Staying power (financial resources)

e. Key personnel

4. Importance of your target market to your competition

5. Barriers to entry into the market

a. Cost (investment)

b. Time

c. Technology

d. Key personnel

d. Customer inertia (brand loyalty, existing relationships, etc.)

e. Existing patents and trademarks

F. Regulatory Restrictions

1. Customer or governmental regulatory requirements

a. Methods for meeting the requirements

b. Timing involved

c. Cost

2. Anticipated changes in regulatory requirements

III. Company Description

The Company Description section must provide an overview of how all of the elements of your company fit together without going into detail, since most of the subjects will be covered in depth elsewhere in the plan.

A. Nature of Your Business

1. Marketplace needs to be satisfied

2. Method(s) of need satisfaction (products and services)

3. Individuals/organizations with the needs

B. Your Distinctive Competencies (primary factors that will lead to your success)

1. Superior customer need satisfaction

2. Production/service delivery efficiencies

3. Personnel

4. Geographic location

IV. Marketing and Sales Activities

Both general and specific information must be included in this part of your plan. Your objective here is to describe the activities that will allow you to meet the sales and margin levels indicated in your prospective financial statements.

A. Overall Marketing Strategy

1. Marketing penetration strategy

2. Growth strategy

a. Internal

b. Acquisition

c. Franchise

d. Horizontal (providing similar products to different users)

e. Vertical (providing the products at different levels of the distribution chain)

3. Distribution channels (include discount/profitability levels at each stage)

a. Original equipment manufacturers

b. Internal sales force

c. Distributors

d. Retailers

4. Communication

a. Promotion

b. Advertising

c. Public relations

d. Personal selling

e. Printed materials (catalogues, brochures, etc.)

B. Sales Strategies

1. Sales Force

a. Internal vs. independent representatives (advantages and disadvantages of your strategy)

b. Size

c. Recruitment and training

d. Compensation

2. Sales activities

a. Identifying prospects

b. Prioritizing prospects

c. Number of sales calls made per period

d. Average number of sales calls per sale

e. Average dollar size per sale

f. Average dollar size per reorder

Writing this section is the first real test of your ability to communicate the essence of your business. The lack of a clear description of the key concepts of your company will indicate to the reader that you have not yet clearly defined it in your own mind. Therefore, you must be certain that this section concisely and accurately describes the substance of your new business.

V. Products and Services

Special attention should be paid to the users of your business plan as you develop this section. Too much detail will have a negative impact on most external users of the plan. Avoid turning this section of your business plan into a policies and procedures manual for your employees.

A. Detailed Product/Service Description (from the user's perspective)

1. Specific benefits of product/service
2. Ability to meet needs
3. Competitive advantages
4. Present stage (idea, prototype, small production runs, etc.)

 Do not underestimate the importance of presenting a well-conceived sales strategy here. Without an efficient approach to beating a path to the doors of potential customers, companies with very good products and services often fail.

B. Product Life Cycle

1. Description of the product/service's current position within its life cycle
2. Factors that might change the anticipated life cycle
   a. Lengthen it
   b. Shorten it

C. Copyrights, Patents, and Trade Secrets

1. Existing or pending copyrights or patents
2. Anticipated copyright and patent filings
3. Key aspects of your products or services that cannot be patented or copyrighted
4. Key aspects of your products or services that qualify as trade secrets
5. Existing legal agreements with owners and employees
   a. Nondisclosure agreements
   b. Noncompete agreements

D. Research and Development Activities

1. Activities in process
2. Future activities (include milestones)
3. Anticipated results of future research and development activities
   a. New products or services
   b. New generations of existing products or services
   c. Complementary products or services
   d. Replacement products or services
4. Research and development activities of others in your industry
   a. Direct competitors
   b. Indirect competitors

c. Suppliers
d. Customers

VI. Operations

Here again, too much detail can detract from the rest of your plan. Be certain that the level of detail included fits the specific needs of the plan's users.

A. Production and Service Delivery Procedures

1. Internal
2. External (subcontractors)

B. Production and Service Delivery Capability

1. Internal
2. External (subcontractors)
3. Anticipated increases in capacity
   a. Investment
   b. New cost factors (direct and indirect)
   c. Timing

C. Operating Competitive Advantages

1. Techniques
2. Experience
3. Economies of scale
4. Lower direct costs

D. Suppliers

1. Identification of the suppliers of critical elements of production
   a. Primary
   b. Secondary
2. Lead-time requirements
3. Evaluation of the risks of critical element shortages
4. Description of the existing and anticipated contractual relationships with suppliers

VII. Management and Ownership

Your management team's talents and skills are some of the few truly unique aspects of your company. If you are going to use your plan to attract investors, this section must emphasize your management's talents and skills, and indicate why they are a part of your company's distinctive competence that cannot easily be replicated by your competition. Remember that individuals invest in people, not ideas.

Do not use this section of the plan to negotiate future ownership of the company with potential investors. Simply explain the current ownership.

A. Management Staff Structure

1. Management staff organization chart

2. Narrative description of the chart

The emphasis in this section should be on your company's unique ability to satisfy the needs of the marketplace. Avoid criticizing your competition's products too severely in this section because the natural tendency of a reader who is not part of your organization will be to empathize with the unrepresented party —your competition.

Concentrate on the positive aspects of your product's ability to meet existing market needs and allow your readers to come to their own conclusions about your competition based on the objective information presented here and in the Market Analysis section.

B. Key Managers (complete resumes should be presented in an appendix to the business plan)

1. Name
2. Position
3. Brief position description, including primary duties
4. Primary responsibilities and authority
5. Unique skills and experiences that add to your company's distinctive competencies
6. Compensation basis and levels (be sure they are reasonable—not too high and not too low)

C. Planned Additions to the Current Management Team

1. Position
2. Primary responsibilities and authority
3. Requisite skills and experience
4. Recruitment process
5. Timing of employment
6. Anticipated contribution to the company's success
7. Compensation basis and levels (be sure they are in line with the market)

Because many of the aspects of your new business are still theoretical at this point, special care must be taken to be sure the specifics of your operations do not conflict with the information included in your prospective financial statements. Any inconsistencies between those two areas will result in some unpleasant surprises as your company begins operations.

D. Legal Structure of the Business

1. Corporation
   a. C corporation
   b. S corporation
2. Partnership
   a. General
   b. Limited
3. Proprietorship

E. Owners

1. Names
2. Percentage ownership
3. Extent of involvement with the company
4. Form of ownership
   a. Common stock
   b. Preferred stock
   c. General partner
   d. Limited partner
5. Outstanding equity equivalents
   a. Options
   b. Warrants
   c. Convertible debt
6. Common stock
   a. Authorized
   b. Issued

F. Board of Directors

1. Names
2. Position on the board
3. Extent of involvement with the company
4. Background
5. Contribution to the company's success
   a. Historically
   b. In the future

VIII. Funds Required and Their Uses

Any new or additional funding reflected in your prospective financial statements should be discussed here. Alternative funding scenarios can be presented if appropriate, and corresponding prospective financial statements are presented in subsequent sections of your plan.

A. Current Funding Requirements

1. Amount
2. Timing
3. Type
   a. Equity
   b. Debt
   c. Mezzanine
4. Terms

B. Funding Requirements over the Next Five Years

1. Amount
2. Timing
3. Type

a. Equity

b. Debt

c. Mezzanine

4. Terms

C. Use of Funds

1. Capital expenditures
2. Working capital
3. Debt retirement
4. Acquisitions

D. Long-Range Financial Strategies (liquidating investors' positions)

1. Going public
2. Leveraged buyout
3. Acquisition by another company
4. Debt service levels and timing
5. Liquidation of the venture

Note—Ernst & Young's Guide to Financing for Growth contains a detailed discussion of various alternatives for raising capital and may provide you with some of the ideas and information you may need to write this portion of your business plan. The Guide, written by E&Y partners and published by John Wiley & Sons, can be purchased at many bookstores.

IX. Financial Data

The Financial Data section contains the financial representation of all the information presented in the other sections. Various prospective scenarios can be included, if appropriate.

 Because your management team is unique, make sure that you stress members' backgrounds and skills, and how they will contribute to the success of your product/service and business. This is especially important to emphasize when you are looking for financing.

A. Historical Financial Data (past three to five years, if applicable)

1. Annual statements
   a. Income
   b. Balance sheet
   c. Cash flows
2. Level of CPA involvement (and name of firm)
   a. Audit
   b. Review
   c. Compilation

 Remember that because the rate of return is their most important consideration—and that the initial public offering market is sometimes not available—investors will be looking for alternative exit strategies. Therefore, be flexible and creative in developing these opportunities, taking into consideration such recent trends as merger/acquisitions and strategic partnering. Although details can be worked out later, investors need to know that you understand their primary objectives as you develop your overall business strategy.

B. Prospective Financial Data (next five years)

1. Next Year (by month or quarter)
   a. Income
   b. Balance sheet
   c. Cash flows
   d. Capital expenditure budget
2. Final four years (by quarter and/or year)
   a. Income
   b. Balance sheet
   c. Cash flows
   d. Capital expenditure budget
3. Summary of significant assumptions
4. Type of prospective financial data
   a. Forecast (management's best estimate)
   b. Projection ("what-if" scenarios)
5. Level of CPA involvement
   a. Assembly
   b. Agreed-upon procedures
   c. Review
   d. Examination

C. Analysis

1. Historical financial statements
   a. Ratio analysis
   b. Trend analysis with graphic presentation
2. Prospective financial statements
   a. Ratio analysis
   b. Trend analysis with graphic presentation

X. Appendices or Exhibits

Any additional detailed or confidential information that could be useful to the readers of the business plan but is not appropriate for distribution to everyone receiving the body of the plan can be presented here. Accordingly, appendices and exhibits should be bound separately from the other sections of the plan and provided on an as-needed basis to readers.

 The Financial Data section of your business plan is another area where specialized knowledge can be invaluable. If you do not have someone with sufficient financial expertise on your management team, you will probably need to utilize an outside advisor.

A. Resumes of Key Managers

B. Pictures of Products

C. Professional References

D. Market Studies

E. Pertinent Published Information

1. Magazine articles
2. References to books

F. Patents

G. Significant Contracts

1. Leases
2. Sales contracts
3. Purchase contracts
4. Partnership/ownership agreements
5. Stock option agreements
6. Employment/compensation agreements
7. Noncompete agreements

8. Insurance
   a. *Product Liability*
   b. *Officers' and directors' liability*
   c. *General liability*

Administrative **Considerations**

The copies of your plan should be controlled and a distribution record should be kept. This process will allow you to update your distributed plans as needed and help to ensure that your plan is not more widely distributed than you intend. In fact, many plans include ethical disclaimers that limit the ability of individuals distributing or otherwise copying the plan without the consent of the company's owners. Remember too that an appropriate private placement disclaimer should be included if the plan is being used to raise capital.

 In some instances, the thicker the business plan, the less likely a potential investor is to read it thoroughly. However, you do want to be able to demonstrate to potential funding sources that you have done a complete job in preparing your plan and that the comments made within it are well documented. By properly utilizing appendices and exhibits, you can keep the size of your business plan palatable to its users and still have the additional information they may require readily available.

finding your competitive edge

HOW TO DETERMINE YOUR UNIQUE SELLING PROPOSITION AND PUT IT TO WORK FOR YOUR BUSINESS

By Sid Davis

IT'S A TOUGH WORLD OUT THERE. Competition has never been so intense for small business. All the more reason to figure out your "USP."

Say what?

A USP is your "Unique Selling Proposition." That's marketing-speak for whatever it is that sets your small business apart from the thundering herds.

Every business has one. You just have to know where to look—and then put it to work for your business. For small business owners just starting out, finding a competitive edge early, and then building the biz around it, will be a tremendous advantage. First ask yourself:

Who is your competition, what are they doing and how are they doing it?

A quick check of the yellow pages, trade association memberships, Internet business directories or Dun & Bradstreet listings will give you a good idea of who and how many are going to be on the playing field trying to sack you.

Next, just as sports teams study game films of each other looking for weaknesses, you'll need to find out how your competition operates. What is their marketing approach? How do they advertise their product or service? Study their sales literature. Call to request a brochure. Get on their mailing lists, attend their trade shows and ask lots of questions. The objective is to become an expert on your competition and learn their playbook.

Curtis Snow followed this route when he created his Salt Lake City consulting firm, Organizational Solutions Network, which specializes in human resources and government compliance.

After studying the market, Snow realized that most small business owners are too busy building their operations to keep track of complex and changing regulations. The big consulting firms went after the larger companies and tended to ignore small business. That left a niche that Snow felt he could fill with a unique approach. His company would sell a package of on-site training and a hotline service that a company's owner or employees could tap for instant solutions or help with problems as they occurred.

Snow's approach worked. Organizational Solutions Network fills a need and, as a result, is growing at an impressive pace. "The key is to study the market you're interested in," says Snow. "Look for problems you can solve that no one else is going after because that's where you'll find your niche. Then work up a plan of action and go out and sell it."

What can you do better or differently?

Once you've studied the competition—know thoroughly what they're doing and how they're doing it—make a list of their strengths and weaknesses. Be objective and make your list as complete as possible.

Note what strengths or special benefits your competitors stress in their sales literature because this is where they're focusing their resources. Since no company has unlimited time, funds and talent, their market coverage will be like a slice of Swiss cheese. It's going to be up to you to find the holes and then develop a strategy to capitalize on them.

As marketing guru Jay Abraham points out in his book, *Getting Everything You Can Out of All You've Got: 21 Ways You Can Out-Think, Out-Perform, and Out-Earn the Competition* (St. Martin's Press, 2000), "The possibilities for building a USP are unlimited. It's best, however, to adopt a USP that dynamically addresses an obvious void in the marketplace that you can fill."

In your search for a USP, ask yourself if your business can offer:

- Faster service, faster delivery or shorter turn-around?
- More experience, knowledge or reputation that translates into a benefit for the customer?
- Better location or more convenient access?
- A superior selection or better quality?
- Price advantages?

• A better warranty, customer support or guarantee?

Keep your USP simple. You should be able to explain it to a novice in one short, clear paragraph.

A USP can also be a unique approach, advertising strategy or perceptual advantage. For example, you may be selling the same product as your competitors. But, if you're the only one aggressively promoting or advertising a special offer, you've created a USP.

Jo Casper, a Sandy, UT, real estate broker, found this out when she was trying to secure "for-sale-by-owner" listings and losing out to agents from the big franchise offices.

To succeed, Casper knew she would need to come up with something different to offset the "bigger is better" pitch of her competitors. Also knowing that homeowners who try to sell without a broker are deluged with cold calls from other agents, she felt that a simple but professional letter might be the best way to cut through the clutter and get her own message across.

Her USP was this: if a home seller would list with her, but found a buyer on their own within the first 30 days, there would be no commission. Since many for-sale-by-owners try to sell on their own for a few weeks before they give up and list with an agent, she felt this would give them a strong incentive to go with her. As an added benefit, if they did find a buyer during this time period, she would do the paperwork and put the deal together for $500 instead of the usual six percent commission.

Casper's approach proved successful, but with an unforeseen twist. "Most sellers who list with me don't even try to take advantage of the 30-day free ride. It appears they just need an excuse to list without a lot of hype and pressure and are relieved to get rid of the stress and have me take over."

Getting the most out of your USP

Your product or service may not be all that different from your competition's. But when you hit a hot button and a potential client believes that you can solve their problem better than anyone else, that's when you really have something.

As Lynda Falkenstein says in her book, *Nichecraft: Using Your Specialness To Focus Your Business, Corner Your Market, and Make Customers Seek You Out* (HarperBusiness), "Everyone has pressure points. Hot buttons typically produce emotional instead of strictly intellectual responses. Strong niches connect with the consumer's hot buttons."

Once you've found your competitive niche you must nurture it, protect it and keep it shiny by performing on whatever you advertise. If you do, clients will identify with your unique approach and come back again and again. They'll also tell others about you.

Here are five ways to supercharge your USP to attract clients and keep them coming back:

1. Make sure you can deliver what you promise. People come to you because you offer something different. If you don't deliver it, you're history. Delivering on what you promise by itself will often set you apart from the pack.

Consider Tom and Carol Keljo, who took over Security Signs in Portland, OR, in 1997. The 72-year-old company was in serious debt when Tom, who worked for the company in sales, saw an opportunity.

The Keljo's USP is to give the customer killer, one-stop service. If they have to develop alliances with competitors to get a job done, they'll do it. For instance, when West Coast Bank needed 41 electric signs changed and operating in 60 days, Security Signs was the only company willing to take on the project. They had to bring in two other sign companies to help out, but they got it done on schedule.

This "get the job done no matter what" creed helped the Keljos build their business from 9 to 18 employees in under three years.

2. Focus your thinking. One way to do that is to keep working on your USP until you have it in a single, concise sentence, focused on *client benefits*. That means you'll avoid pronouns such as I, we, me and our. Instead, focus on the rapport-building words: you, your and yours. When you do this you'll be forced to express your statement from the client's point of view and your sales letters will be much more effective.

For example, instead of saying "We will give you a free tote bag with every order," write, "You will receive a free tote bag with every order."

3. Use your USP as the center of your advertising, marketing materials, letterhead, business cards, signs and all communications. This will keep both you and your clients focused on what you have to offer that no one else has.

4. When writing sales letters, flyers and brochures, incorporate your USP statement in the lead paragraph and build your letter around it. This will help you zero in on client benefits rather than getting stuck on reciting product or service features—or worse, giving in to the temptation of simply bragging about your biz.

5. Always offer a generous warranty or money-back guarantee. It's a powerful tool that tells potential clients that you're here to stay and you're serious about earning their business.

Awesome Computers, a northern Utah company selling desktop computers, uses a warranty to create a market niche. The firm touts unlimited tech support and a lifetime warranty as its USP. This approach capitalizes on many computer buyers' fear of being on their own if they need tech help or a problem develops.

Awesome Computers aggressively pushes its warranty in all its advertising. The business strives to give buyers a warm feeling that they will be taken care of as long as they have the computer. And it works. Business is booming and Awesome is opening additional stores throughout the region.

Sid Davis is a freelance business writer based in Farmington, UT.

Bear Opportunities

An economic slowdown doesn't mean abandoning marketing plans—it means being clever enough to take advantage.

BY JENNIFER GILBERT AND JANE HODGES

The news from Wall Street in recent months has not exactly helped the cause of marketing departments. It is difficult enough to craft an effective advertising campaign without being sideswiped by headlines such as "Wall Street Shuns Dot-Coms" and "Bearish Investors Flee to Blue Chips."

Headlines like these are now a part of the New Economy business climate. And while it is impossible to forecast the impact of a sustained downturn on corporate marketing budgets, one thing is certain: Conditions are going to be different for a while than they were in the late 1990s.

But take heart. An economic downturn need not signal drastic reductions in the scope of marketing plans. Think of it instead as the birth of *smart* marketing. What's more, bear market marketing may pay off better in the long run than all those pricey ads and gimmicks did way back in 1999.

"Things that might not have been very powerful before a recession become very powerful in a recession," says Bob Atkins, a vice president of Mercer Management Consulting in New York. "You've got to revisit the tools you've been using to attract and retain customers. And systematic in-vestment in the brand during a recession can be extremely powerful when the economy snaps out of it. Those who continue to invest in brand advertising in bad times can potentially widen their lead over the competition."

Where to begin? Here are four strategies that are helping About.com, Northwest Airlines, FTD.com, and Family.com make the most of their marketing dollars while the economy is in the doldrums:

1. Leverage your relationships.

Last fall, magazine publisher Primedia bought About.com, a network of more than 700 topic, shopping, and community sites. The $690 million deal enables About—which previously spent much of its ad money on guerrilla marketing—to advertise in Primedia publications such as *American Baby, New York, Seventeen*, and *Soap Opera Digest*.

Being part of the Primedia family gives the company the opportunity to leverage more than 274 print publications, and book-jacket covers in elementary and high schools, to target the appropriate audience. John Caplan, president of About's networks group, says it enables About to gain market share, get attractive ad-placement rates, and do a better job of addressing an appropriate audience. "When marketing budgets are cut but revenue goals remain the same, you have to make sure you find an audience that is large enough and will react to your messages," Caplan says.

About.com plans to spend more than $12 million on in-house-created advertising this year. That is down from the $25 million it spent last year on marketing and advertising. But About is attracting more customers by spending less. Last November, according to Media Metrix, About was the Web's seventh most-trafficked online property site. By December, it had jumped to sixth place, with 21.3 million U.S. viewers.

"About's leveraging [of] Primedia's properties makes a lot of sense," says David Smith, president and media director of Mediasmith, a media agency in San Francisco. He says Primedia has a lot of vertical-market magazines that "match up very nicely with About, which is really a series of vertical market minisites." And there is a lot of synergy in that deal, he says: "This could launch About into a whole new area of success."

> "Systematic investment in the brand during a recession can be **extremely powerful** when you come out of a recession."

2. Advertise value propositions.

Northwest Airlines' original ads promoting its online entity failed to tell consumers what its Website could do for them. Now, after revamping its advertising to better reflect its services, Northwest is emphasizing value propositions, particularly the ability to download boarding passes.

"We had the epiphany that we have made huge strides in customer convenience, and we took that and decided the commercials needed to be updated to reflect our new identity," says Beth Shultis, vice president of worldwide advertising and marketing programs at the airline. She says it is important now to identify and advertise something your customer base actually wants. Her firm's strategy, she says, is to focus on applications rather than aspirations. "Aspirational is fine," she says, "but customer desires will sell a business a million times faster."

The more-focused approach is reflected in all of Northwest's television, print, radio, and outdoor advertising, created by Carmichael Lynch of Minneapolis, and first introduced in the third quarter last year. It has no tagline, but the advertising's theme is "We remove obstacles away from travel," Shultis says. Northwest spent $44.2 million on advertising during the first 10 months of last year, according to Competitive Media Reporting.

Already, Northwest's new marketing message appears to be working: Online check-ins at the airline's site were nearly nonexistent in early December; but by early January, that number had hit 120,000. "It proves the fact that this is functionality people are looking for," Shultis says, "and the advertising, instead of giving a shopping list of service offerings, spends its 60 seconds well."

"We will continue to run advertising that focuses on our 'value proposition'," adds Craig Braasch, managing director of advertising for Northwest. "Advertising needs to be simple, very focused, and singular."

3. Control costs.

Michael Soenen, CEO of online florist FTD.com in Downers Grove, Ill., defied the conventional dot-com wisdom last year. Soenen decided to slash his company's marketing budget in half, slow the business's growth, and divert much of FTD.com's marketing funds from mass-media advertising into efforts to retain customers.

Last June, the beginning of FTD.com's fiscal year, Soenen took a step back and decided that his company would no longer overspend on advertising to attract customers. Before then, the online company spent $43 million on marketing to pursue typical dot-com hyper-growth—adding 80 percent to 90 percent more revenues year-over-year as it signed new customers. There was a hefty price to pay for that growth, though—and not just metaphorically speaking. "It wasn't going to continue to work to lose $30 million a year," Soenen says.

Working with a budget of roughly $20 million and a new strategy—where spending is divided evenly between acquisition and retention efforts such as catalog marketing, email programs, and personalized interactive tools such as a calendar that reminds shoppers of special occasions—Soenen reckoned the company could survive any pending shakeout.

By January 2001, midway through FTD's fiscal year and the dot-com Armageddon, Soenen seemed prescient. By merely trimming mass media advertising and shifting investment into direct marketing methods, the company's cost of customer acquisition nose-dived to $16 earlier this year from $67 last year.

Now, FTD.com is growing at a slower but sustainable rate of 25 percent—while turning what Soenen calls a "modest" profit. "We like to think it's a balanced effort between acquiring and retaining customers," he says.

> "Identify and advertise something your **customer base actually wants.** You should focus on applications rather than aspirations."

4. Pursue traditional marketers.

Family.com, part of the Walt Disney Internet Group, has been courting —and convincing—traditional companies to advertise on its site. It is a natural fit for many offline companies, particularly packaged goods firms, since the site is geared toward families and moms, with topics ranging from "PMS busters" to "bread-baking basics."

Traditional advertisers aren't necessarily increasing their individual spending at the site, says Beth Collins, vice president and general manager of Family.com. But the number of traditional advertisers interested in getting involved has grown substantially. "There's no question that there has been a shift in the market," she says.

Family.com now works with Procter & Gamble, Campbell Soup, and Nestlé. And last year, it entered a multiyear marketing program with Pillsbury that Family.com hopes will become a model for deals with other traditional marketers.

As part of the partnership, Pillsbury ads will be placed at Family.com's recipes section. Site content, such as a recipe guide, will also be branded with the Pillsbury name. Family.com, on the other hand, gains valuable visibility without additional cash outlays, because Pillsbury will market its affiliation

Tenets of Two Markets

Bull marketing	Bear marketing
Big spending wins eyeballs.	Smart spending wins customers.
Customer acquisition is a priority.	Customer retention is a priority.
Companies merge to look big.	Companies merge in order to survive.
"We'll be the next Yahoo!"	"We're not the next Yahoo!"
Free offers lure new customers.	Reward programs benefit good customers.
It's an ad seller's market: "You need us, we're a portal."	It's an ad buyer's market: "I'll buy on performance metrics."
Services firms take equity as a form of payment.	Services firms take cash, thanks.
Cool factor marketing: Big parties, big budgets, Super Bowl ads.	Cash factor marketing: Case studies, frugal budgets, email marketing.
Reactive direct marketing—occasionally contacting registrants or members.	Proactive direct marketing—using tools to figure out the right customer offer.
Partnerships help you build buzz— you are who your partners are.	Partnerships help you expand your value proposition— customers get a new service. —*JH*

with the dot-com on 10 million food packages this year.

There is plenty of room for other dot-coms to cash in on the trend. While Forrester Research, in Cambridge, Mass., estimates that dot-com marketing accounted for 69 percent of all digital marketing spending last year, that share is expected to drop to 16 percent by 2005. Traditional advertisers are predicted to spend the other 84 percent.

"General Motors , Coca-Cola, PepsiCo, and Procter & Gamble are all spending more online during the second half of the year," says Jim Nail, a senior analyst for Forrester Research. "And Volvo Cars has launched a car ad campaign online with AOL."

Nail identifies three types of traditional advertisers as ready to make an online play: those that went online early and will spend as much as 23 percent of their budgets online by 2005; mainstream advertisers that hung back but will begin to commit this year; and the still-cautious companies, which will likely begin by selecting strategic marketing deals

JENNIFER GILBERT (JGILBERT@BUSINESS2.COM) IS A STAFF WRITER IN THE NEW YORK OFFICE OF BUSINESS 2.0
JANE HODGES (JANEHODGES@HOTMAIL.COM) IS A CONTRIBUTING WRITER FOR BUSINESS 2.0.

MARKETING

Get Smart Fast– Or Else

All sorts of entrepreneurs are scrambling to keep their companies afloat amid the shockwaves that have followed the terrorist attacks

In the seven years since Ellen Bristol started her sales-consulting business in Miami, Bristol Strategy Group, she never had a zero-revenue month. Until September. She had to postpone a large project because it required flying just a couple days after hijackers crashed airplanes into the World Trade Center and the Pentagon. All the other clients she had planned to work with called to say: "'We're too confused, we're too frightened, we have to delay it.' What could I say?" Bristol asks.

Like many other small-business owners who are seeing revenue vanish in the wake of the Sept. 11 attacks, Bristol knows she has to get real smart real fast. Unlike some of her clients, she can't afford to be frightened. "Now, more than ever, I have no excuse not to sit down and design the best possible marketing campaign that I can possibly come up with. I have never had a greater need.... I can't be confused about this or not ready or ineffectual. That's pointless. That's wasteful."

Other small-business owners also say smart, focused marketing is their key strategy for climbing out of the sudden revenue trough and negotiating the recession and wartime terrain that now seem certain to lie ahead.

RIPPLE EFFECT. David Cohn, who owns seven restaurants in the heart of San Diego, is working on a new print and TV ad campaign with two main themes: "Celebrate life" and "Come to our house." Now that the tourists and conventioneers are gone (and not expected to return anytime soon), Cohn is trying to persuade locals to become tourists in their own community. The Visitors and Convention Bureau is taking a similar approach, says Cohn, one of its elected officers. "We're not marketing to Europeans and New Yorkers right now, but to people within a couple hours of San Diego, trying to get them to spend a weekend here."

Fear of flying is not what's hurting Edward's Steak House, a family-owned business in El Monte, outside Los Angeles. It's fear of spending money. The lunch business, which accounts for at least a third of the restaurant's revenue, is much slower since Sept. 11, says Ken Rausch, manager.

One group of Edward's regulars that's a lot less regular these days works for a company that heat-treats metal. A big chunk of their business came from Boeing, which is canceling business because plane orders are being canceled. Another group Rausch doesn't see as often employees of a construction company that specializes in digging trenches for fiber-optic cable. Its big project for AT&T has been put on hold indefinitely as the telecom company concentrates on restoring East Coast operations.

"It's a ripple effect all across the country," Rausch says, adding: "Anybody who doesn't think so is crazy." To fill his seats, he has resorted to traditional marketing—a postcard coupon redeemable for a free pint of chili, which he expects will bring in 500 patrons over the next couple of weeks. Even so, he had to cut his lunchtime staff from seven waitresses to five. Overall, the National Restaurant Assn. estimates 65,000 restaurant jobs will be lost as tourism and the general economy slump.

STAYING AHEAD. Sheila Brooks says she has no plans to lay off employees at her TV and video production company, SRB Productions in Washington, even though a $500,000 contract was canceled the day after the attacks. However, Brooks has directed her business manager to prepare a recession budget for the fourth quarter and is taking a hard look at her marketing strategy.

"Instead of saying we're still going to cover the world, we need to see what's really going to sell in the next 3, 6, 9 months and focus on that," she says. That means letting people know about SRB's new interactive audio-video Web service, which permits far-flung people to meet via the Internet. "It's a good market right now for that," says Brooks, who founded her company 14 years ago. "The only way to survive bad times is to stay ahead of the business environment."

That's a tall order when business conditions are unlike any that company owners have ever been through. No one yet fully knows what it will be like doing business after such devastation. Many companies find it difficult, although necessary, to consider marketing at a time like this.

"No one wants to capitalize on this," says Brian Walker, head of marketing at Creative Realities, a Boston-based consulting firm. At the same time, he says, "certain things are happening to the American psyche that companies should be thinking through." Now, he says, people will want to be closer to home and will be embracing tradition, nostalgia, patriotism, charitable giving, and comfort food.

TOUGHEST CHALLENGE. Businesses in Long Beach, Calif., planned to have a firefighter or police office outside every business on Pine Street—the main shopping strip—the weekend of Sept. 28–30. "People want to give and they want to see you give," says Jeff King, a Long Beach businessman who owns 11 restaurants in California. In business since 1945, he has "never been more challenged" to keep customers coming in the door. "Any business that doesn't have a survival strategy will be gone by the end of the year," says King, whose receipts are off about 15%, forcing him to shed some part-time workers.

At Creative Realities, Walker estimates business will be off about 20% for the rest of the year as corporations slash budgets. The firm, which specializes in helping companies implement innovations, is tailoring its message to the times. Innovation, Walker is emphasizing, isn't just about new products or services—it is containing costs while doing things better, quicker, and cheaper. Heeding a page from its own play book, the firm is finishing the redesign of its Web site to make it more interactive and give potential clients an opportunity to sample its services. That redesign, talked about for some time, became a higher priority after the mass murders in New York, Washington, and Pennsylvania. Those attacks, says Walker, "raised our awareness of the urgency to focus on doing a few things well."

Procrastination, like confusion, is an unaffordable luxury right now. As Bristol, the Miami sales consultant, puts it: "Right now, people need to climb out from underneath the bed. Then they need to realize it's going to be tougher than ever."

The stereotypical entrepreneur is a gutsy, creative risk-taker. Ready or not, many are finding it crucial to live up to that image.

By Theresa Forsman in New York
Edited by Robin J. Phillips

Solving The Puzzle Of The Cash Flow Statement

Julie H. Hertenstein and Sharon M. McKinnon

The cash flow statement is one of the most useful financial statements companies prepare. When analyzed in a rational, logical manner, it can illuminate a treasure trove of clues as to how a company is balancing its receivables and payables, paying for its growth, and otherwise managing its flow of funds. But many readers seem to bypass the cash flow statement and head only for the old, familiar, comfortable income statement and balance sheet—despite the fact that the cash flow statement may provide considerable information about what is really happening in a business beyond that contained in either of the other two statements.

A Business Horizons tutorial.

There are several reasons why the cash flow statement may not get the attention it deserves. First, although it has been around in its present format since mid-1988, it is still considered the "new statement"; many managers were not exposed to it during their business schooling in financial analysis. If they were, they may have been taught how to prepare one but not how to interpret the story it tells.

Second, the format of the "Cash Flow from Operating Activities" section of the statement can be challenging to

follow if presented in what is known as the "indirect" method. But perhaps most daunting to many is the mistaken idea that it takes a very sophisticated analysis of complicated ratios and relationships to use a cash flow statement effectively.

Contributing to this notion are numerous business journal articles that have appeared in the past decade. They promote the value of this statement when appropriate cash flow ratios are used in statistical packages, such as those used to predict bankruptcy. Present day textbooks, when not merely teaching students to prepare the statement, also concentrate on describing how ratios such as "free cash flow to net income" can be derived, but say little about what truly useful information these ratios or other information from the cash flow statement may provide.

Analyzing this statement should not present a formidable task when reviewed in the manner we are advocating here. Instead, it will quickly become obvious that the benefits of understanding the sources and uses of a company's cash far outweigh the costs of undertaking some very straightforward analyses. Executives want to know if the cash generated by the company will be sufficient to fund their expansion strategy; stockholders want to know if the firm is generating enough cash to pay dividends; suppliers want to know if their customers will be able to pay if offered credit; investors want to evaluate future growth potential; and employees are interested in the overall viability of their employer as indicated by its ability to fund its operations. These are just a few of the valuable insights to be gained from the cash flow statement.

The method we suggest for studying this valuable statement contains several steps, with the preliminary step consisting of gaining a basic understanding of the format of the cash flow statement. Once a certain "comfort level" with the structure of the statement has been attained, individual companies' statements should be examined to gain practice in using the stepwise approach described shortly. These steps consist of:

1. scanning the big picture;
2. checking the power of the cash flow engine;
3. pinpointing the good news and the bad news; and
4. putting the puzzle together.

Pay attention, for you will be tested on your new expertise at the end of this article!

Format Of The Cash Flow Statement

The cash flow statement is divided into three sections: operating activities, investing activities, and financing activities. **Figure 1** presents an example of a simple cash flow statement with the three sections delineated in bold letters. Each section shows the cash inflows and outflows associated with that type of activity.

Cash flow from operating activities shows the results of cash inflows and outflows related to the fundamental operations of the basic line or lines of business in which the company engages. For example, it includes cash receipts from the sale of goods or services and cash outflows for purchasing inventory and paying rent and taxes. You will notice it does not show these items directly. It assumes that most of these cash inflows and outflows are already summarized in the "Net Income" figure, so it starts at that figure and makes an adjustment for everything that is not a true representation of "cash in and out" in net income. This approach is the "indirect format" of presenting cash flows from operating activities and is the one chosen by most companies. The indirect format can be confusing, and a longer explanation of "direct versus indirect" formats is provided in **Figure 2** for readers who desire more information.

Regardless of how the cash flow from operating activities section is formatted, it is important to remember that this is the most important of the three sections because it describes how cash is being generated or used by the primary activities of the company. To picture activities that affect cash flow from operations, think of the cash receipts and payments that make most working capital accounts on the balance sheet increase or decrease. For example, accounts receivable decreases when cash is collected from customers, inventory increases when goods are purchased, and accounts payable decreases when suppliers are paid for their goods.

The next section is called *cash flow from investing activities*. Here you see the cash flows associated with purchases and sales of non-current assets, such as building and equipment purchases, or sales of investments or subsidiaries. An easy way to picture what activities would be here is to think again of a balance sheet. If you assume current assets are associated with operations,

then the activities associated with all the rest of the assets are in this section.

Figure 1
Statement of Cash Flows

Cash Flow from Operating Activities

Net Income	XXX,XXX
Adjustments to reconcile net income to net cash provided by operating activities:	
Depreciation and amortization	XX,XXX
Changes in other accounts affecting operations:	
(Increase)/decrease in accounts receivable	X,XXX
(Increase)/decrease in inventories	X,XXX
(Increase)/decrease in prepaid expenses	X,XXX
Increase/(decrease) in accounts payable	X,XXX
Increase/(decrease) in taxes payable	X,XXX
Net cash provided by operating activities	XXX,XXX

Cash Flow from Investing Activities

Capital expenditures	(XXX,XXX)
Proceeds from sales of equipment	XX,XXX
Proceeds from sales of investments	XX,XXX
Investment in subsidiary	(XXX,XXX)
Net cash provided by (used in) investing activities	(XXX,XXX)

Cash Flow from Financing Activities

Payments of long-term debt	(XX,XXX)
Proceeds from issuance of long-term debt	XX,XXX
Proceeds from issuance of common stock	XXX,XXX
Dividends paid	(XX,XXX)
Purchase of treasury stock	(XX,XXX)
Net cash provided by (used in) financing activities	(XX,XXX)
Increase (Decrease) in Cash	**XX,XXX**

The third section is called *cash flow from financing activities*. Again, the balance sheet provides a handy way of discerning what would be in this section. If you eliminate the current liabilities associated with operations, then the activities of all the rest of the liabilities and the stockholders' equity accounts are summarized here.

These are all the flows associated with financing the firm, everything from selling and paying off bonds to issuing stock and paying dividends.

Warning! There are exceptions to everything and the cash flow statement format has a few to watch out for. Two working capital accounts, one asset and one liability, are dealt with outside the cash flow from operating activities section. Short-term marketable securities are treated as long-term investments and appear in cash flow from investing activities; similarly, short-term debt is treated as long-term debt and appears in cash flow from financing activities.

Another anomaly is the treatment of interest and dividends. Although dividends are handled as a cash outflow in the cash flow from financing activities section, interest payments are considered an operating outflow, despite the fact that both are payments to outsiders for using their money! In some countries, such as the United Kingdom, interest payments are included in the financing activities section. But in the United States, the Financial Accounting Standards Board (FASB) voted that interest payments should be in the operating activities section instead. In such a situation, one might have to adjust somewhat if one were trying to compare a UK company like British Petroleum to a U.S. company like Exxon.

Step 1: Scanning The Big Picture

Now, sit back with your favorite company's annual report and follow these steps to understanding its cash flow picture. You can think of this as a big puzzle exercise. All the pieces are there in the statement; your task is to put them in the proper context to form a mosaic from which a picture of the firm's cash flow health emerges. If you don't have an annual report handy, you can use **Figure 3**, which shows the cash flow statements for the Colgate-Palmolive Company for the years ending 1992, 1993, and 1994. We chose Colgate-Palmolive because it represents one of the best annual reports in the country and the positive trends are clear for illustrative purposes. Other reports may not contain such "rosy scenarios," as you will discover shortly.

Scanning the big picture involves several substeps. The first is to place your company in context in terms of its age, industry, and size. We expect mature companies to have different cash flows from start-up companies, and service industries to look different from heavy manufacturing industries. Big corporations may experience declining cash flows in certain years, but the sheer immensity of their cash flows may ameliorate concerns, whereas the declining trend might be much more worrisome if they were small firms without such vast resources.

Colgate-Palmolive certainly qualifies as a mature company. It is huge (figures are rounded to millions), and it operates primarily in consumer product markets throughout the world. A firm like this should be involved in complex activities on a global scale. Colgate-Palmolive certainly is, but its cash flow statement is not much more complex than what one might expect from a much smaller, perhaps simpler, company.

Continue your big picture scan by flipping through the annual report to determine how management believes the year has progressed. Was it a good year? Perhaps a record-breaking year in terms of revenues or net income? Or is management explaining how the company has weathered some rough times?

A key part of the big picture scan is to look at a key summary figure of financial health—net income. If the cash flow statement has been prepared using the indirect method for operating cash flows, as Colgate-Palmolive's has, you can find this at the top of the cash flow statement. Otherwise you'll have to use the reconciliation of net income and operating cash flows that accompanies the cash flow statement, or take a peek at the income statement itself. What is the bottom line? Does it show income or losses over the past few years? Is income (or loss) growing or shrinking? Keep these points in mind as you examine the cash flows. In addition, scan the comparative numbers for the past three years for unusual items you'd like to have explained eventually.

Colgate-Palmolive shows positive net income for all three years—a promising start. The three-year trend appears to be positive, but a big drop in 1993 raises a few questions. The statement also reveals a few items that need to be checked out. In the operating activities section, what is that "cumulative effect on prior years of accounting changes" in 1993? And what are those "restructured operations"? File those away to examine later. Note any line items that are vastly different from year to year. Colgate-Palmolive has a few of those, including changes in its working capital accounts, the proceeds from issuance of debt, and its purchases of treasury stock.

Step 2: Checking The Power Of The Cash Flow Engine

The cash flow from operating activities section is the cash flow engine of the company. When this engine is working effectively, it provides the cash flows to cover the cash needs of operations. It also provides cash necessary for routine needs, such as the replacement of worn-out equipment and the payment of dividends. There are exceptions, of course. Start-up companies, for example, usually have negative cash flows from operating activities because their cash-flow engines are not yet up to speed. Companies in cyclical industries might have negative operating cash flows in a "down" year; a company that has experienced an extensive strike could also be expected to have negative cash flow from operating activities. Although occasional years of negative cash flow from operating activities do not spell disaster, on the average we should expect it to be positive.

Figure 2 Cash Flow From Operating Activities: Direct and Indirect Formats

The cash flow from operating activities section of a cash flow statement can be presented using the direct format or the indirect format. The bottom line is the same, but the two begin at different points. Companies are free to choose either format.

A is an income statement, followed by (*B*) the cash flow from operating activities section for the same company presented in the two different formats.

A. Income Statement	
Sales	$412,000
Cost of goods sold	(265,000)
Other expenses	(133,000)ᵃ
Net income	$30,000

ᵃ *Other expenses includes $25,000 depreciation expense.*

The direct method is just like a cash tax return: how much cash came in the door for sales and how much cash went out the door for the inventory and other operating expenditures. Many believe the direct format is better, because it is easier to understand at first glimpse. However, if companies choose the direct format, they must also present a reconciliation between cash flow from operating activities and net income—which is precisely what the indirect format shows! Consequently, most firms simply choose to present the indirect format.

The indirect method starts with net income as a figure that summarizes most of the cash transactions for operating activities in a firm. However, net income also includes transactions that were not cash, so we must eliminate the non-cash transactions from the net income figure to arrive at an accurate presentation of cash flows from operating activities.

A common, typically major expense that does not involve the expenditure of any cash at all is depreciation. Depreciation is always added back to net income under the indirect method. Do not be confused by this presentation into thinking depreciation somehow provides cash. It is only added back because it was subtracted to get to net income in the first place, and it must now be added back to get to cash. If there are other expenses that did not involve cash, these too will be added back to net income.

For most income statement items, the cash paid (or received) could be a little more, or a little less, than the income statement item. For example, cash received from customers could be a little more than revenues, especially if we collected large amounts owed to us from prior years, or it could be a little less if we made significant credit sales this year. Changes in operating working capital accounts reveal whether or not the amounts included in net income for sales, inventory costs, and other expenses really reflect the actual cash inflows and outflows. Changes in these accounts are added back to or subtracted from net income to reveal the true cash inflows and outflows.

Say the total sales number on our income statement was $412,000. But if we examined accounts receivable, we would find that receivables increased by $12,000, which customers essentially "put on their bill," and only $400,000 was actually collected in cash. So the deduction of $12,000 for "increase in receivables" in the indirect format adjusts the sales number of $412,000 down to $400,000, the actual cash received.

The inventory decrease reveals that we used some inventory purchased in prior years for sales this year. Our cost of goods sold figure in net income is therefore too high as an indicator of cash paid this year for inventory.

Similarly, it looks as if we paid some of last year's bills this year, because our payables went down by $8,000. So we must subtract an additional $8,000 to adjust the net income figure for the additional, actual cash expenditures.

There is a simple rule by which accounts should be added to or subtracted from net income: *Increases in current assets are subtracted, and increases in current liabilities are added.* The simplest approach to remember this is to pick a single account that is easy to figure out when it changes in one direction. For example, you might remember that increases in accounts receivable represent goods sold on account, but not for cash; so increases in accounts receivable must be subtracted from net income to reflect cash flows from operating activities. Once you know this, you know that a decrease in accounts receivable must be treated the opposite way: it will be added. Now you can deduce the remaining working capital accounts. The asset accounts will be treated just like accounts receivable. And the liability accounts will be exactly the opposite. Once you know one working capital account, you know them all.

Although initially it takes practice to become familiar with the indirect format, you will discover that it actually shows quite a bit of useful information you might need to search for otherwise. The quickest way to find the company's total depreciation, for example, is on the cash flow statement. In addition, it directly displays the changes in the working capital accounts. If you were to use the balance sheet for this information, you would have to perform the subtraction yourself.

B. Cash Flow from Operating Activities (two formats)

Direct		Indirect	
Cash received from customers	$400,000	Net Income	$30,000
Cash paid to suppliers	(260,000)	Adjustments to reconcile net income to net cash provided, by operating activities:	
Cash paid to employees	(70,000)	Depreciation	25,000
Other cash operating expenditures	(30,000)		
Net cash provided by operating activities	$40,000		
		Changes in other accounts affecting operations:	
		(Increase) in receivables	(12,000)
		Decrease in inventory	5,000
		(Decrease) in payables	(8,000)
		Net cash provided by operating activities	$40,000

Figure 3
Consolidated Statements of Cash Flows: Colgate-Palmolive

(In millions)	1994	1993	1992
Operating Activities			
Net Income	$ 580.2	$ 189.9	$ 477.0
Adjustments to reconcile net income to cash provided by operations:			
Cumulative effect on prior years of accounting changes	---	358.2	---
Restructured operations, net	(39.1)	(77.0)	(92.0)
Depreciation and amortization	235.1	209.6	192.5
Deferred income taxes and other, net	64.7	53.6	(25.8)
Cash effects of these changes:			
(Increase) in receivables	(50.2)	(103.6)	(38.0)
(Increase)/decrease in inventories	(44.5)	31.7	28.4
(Increase)/decrease in current assets	(7.8)	(4.6)	10.6
Increase/(decrease) in payables	90.9	52.6	(10.0)
Net cash provided by operations	829.4	710.4	542.7
Investing Activities			
Capital expenditures	(400.8)	(364.3)	(318.5)
Payment for acquisitions	(146.4)	(171.2)	(170.1)
Sale of securities and investments	58.4	33.8	79.9
Investments	(1.9)	(12.5)	(6.6)
Other, net	33.0	61.7	17.4
Net cash used for investing activities	(457.7)	(452.5)	(397.9)
Financing Activities			
Principal payments on debt	(88.3)	(200.8)	(250.1)
Proceeds from issuance of debt	316.4	782.1	262.6
Proceeds from outside investors	15.2	60.0	---
Dividends paid	(246.90)	(231.4)	(200.7)
Purchase of treasury stock	(357.9)	(657.2)	(20.5)
Proceeds from exercise of stock options	18.5	21.8	22.6
Net cash used for financing activities	(343.0)	(225.5)	(186.1)
Effect of exchange rate changes on cash	(2.9)	(6.2)	(9.3)
Net increase (decrease) in cash	$ 25.8	$ 26.2	$(50.6)

To check the cash flow engine, first observe whether cash flow from operating activities is greater than zero. Also check whether it is growing or shrinking. Assuming it is positive, the next question is whether or not it is adequate for important, routine expenditures. Just as we do not expect a start-up company to have positive cash flow from operating activities, we also do not expect a

company still in a very rapid growth phase to generate enough cash flow from operating activities to cover the investments required to rapidly expand the firm. However, we do expect the operations of a mature company to generate enough cash to "keep the company whole." This would include the amount of investment required to replace those fixed assets that are used up, worn out, or technologically obsolete as well as cash required to pay the annual dividend shareholders have come to expect.

It is difficult to know precisely how much cash is required to keep the company's fixed assets "whole," because the cash flow statement does not separate capital expenditures for replacement and renewal from those for expansion and growth. However, the annual depreciation amount provides a very rough surrogate for the amount of fixed assets that need to be replaced each year. In periods when prices are rising, the cost to replace assets should be somewhat greater than the cost of older assets that are being depreciated. So to ensure that the firm is kept whole and is not shrinking, we should expect the portion of investing activities related to the purchase of fixed assets to exceed depreciation.

Important information about the cash flow engine is also revealed by examining the operating working capital accounts. In the Colgate-Palmolive operating activities section, these are shown under "cash effects of these changes." In a healthy, growing company, we would expect growth in operating working capital accounts such as inventory and accounts receivable as well as in accounts payable and other operating payables. Obviously there can be quite a bit of variability in working capital accounts from period to period. Streamlining a collections policy or implementing a Just-In-Time inventory system could shrink accounts receivable or inventory in a growing company. But on the average, inventories, receivables, and accounts payable usually grow in expanding companies. Beware of situations in which all working capital accounts increase net cash from operating activities. This likely would not happen randomly in a healthy, growing company. It normally results from deliberate management action and could indicate a company in such a cash flow crisis that managers have been forced to raid the working capital accounts to survive.

With these ground rules, let's check Colgate Palmolive's cash flow engine. In all three years, cash flow from operating activities is greater than zero, reaching over $800 million in 1994. It increases steadily every year, unlike net income. Annual depreciation is in the vicinity of $200 million each year, and the yearly dividend is also around $200 million. Colgate-Palmolive's cash flow engine is not only generating enough cash to cover "keeping the company whole," it is also able to throw off around $400 million annually for growth and investment, and the amount of excess cash has been increasing each year.

This is a powerful cash flow engine. A glance at the working capital account differences indicates that receivables, other assets, and payables have grown (net) over the three years, while inventories have shrunk slightly. This picture is consistent with a global company increasing its scope through acquisitions and new product development.

Step 3: Pinpointing The Good News And The Bad News

This step involves looking at the total cash flow statement to find where the rest of the "good news" and "bad news" lie. What you are looking for is the story the statement is trying to tell you. It will not come simply by divine revelation, but by systematic observation of the items on the statement and their trends over the years presented for your comparison.

Begin with cash flow from investing activities. What is this section trying to tell you? One systematic observation is to check whether the company is generating or using cash in its investing activities. Whereas we expect positive cash flow from operating activities, we also expect a healthy company to invest continually in more plant, equipment, land, and other fixed assets to replace the assets that have been used up or have become technologically obsolete, as well as to expand and grow. Although companies often sell assets that are no longer of use to them, they would normally purchase more capital assets than they sell. As a result, we generally expect negative cash flows from investing activities. As with operating activities, exceptions do occur, especially if the firm divests a business or subsidiary. However, watch for companies that are beginning to shrink substantially because they are generating much of their cash by selling off chunks of the business!

Colgate-Palmolive exhibits the signs of a "good news from investing activities" company. Capital expenditures are nearly 1.5 times the amount of depreciation, so they are clearly at a level well beyond that required to keep the company whole. In addition, Colgate-Palmolive makes significant expenditures for acquisitions in each year—another growth indicator. These numbers remain consistent or increase from year to year and paint a picture of a steadily growing company, with enough cash flow from operating activities to cover these expenditures and more.

Cash flows from financing activities could as easily be positive as negative in a healthy company. Moreover, they are likely to change back and forth, so finding the "good" and "bad" is more challenging. It requires viewing the cash flows from financing activities in conjunction with other information on the cash flow statement and basing your conclusions on the weight of the evidence and your own judgment. Assume a company has borrowed cash or issued stock. A "good news" scenario might be that the firm has carefully analyzed its leverage and cost of capital and chosen to finance itself through debt or equity rather than from cash from operations. Another "good news" scenario might be that a new start-up is doing well enough to issue an Initial Public Offering. On the other hand, a "bad news" scenario might be that the company has low (or negative) cash flows from operations and is being forced to generate funds from other sources. You must look at the entire package to evaluate whether your cash flows from financing are in the "good news" or "bad news" categories.

One systematic way to begin is to compare borrowing and payments on debt with each other across the years and note the trends. Colgate-Palmolive has been consistently borrowing more than it has paid back, and to a very substantial degree in 1993. Good news or bad? We have already seen the incredible amount of cash being thrown off from operations, so this increase in debt financing is probably the result of a conscious management decision and not the actions of a company desperately borrowing to survive. Nevertheless, it might be worth another more detailed look if we wanted to consider whether continued borrowing provides a likely source of funds for future growth, or whether the firm is nearing its debt capacity.[1]

A second systematic step in uncovering the news in this section is to check the activities in the stock accounts. Colgate-Palmolive is not issuing much stock; instead, it seems to be buying back substantial amounts of treasury stock. In fact, that is the single largest use of cash outside of capital expenditures.[2] This is probably a "good news" scenario, because the company may be cashing in on what it considers a low price for its stock, or perhaps protecting itself from takeover attempts. In either event, Colgate Palmolive appears to have sufficient cash available to make this large, non-routine investment. A little digging in the rest of the financial statements might present the whole story.

Step 4: Putting The Puzzle Together

In evaluating the cash flow statement, you are evaluating many pieces of evidence to produce an overall picture. However, it would be rare to find a company in which all of the evidence is positive, or in which all of the evidence is negative. To make a balanced evaluation, you must use both the good news and the bad news identified in each section of the statement. To reach an overall conclusion, you need to judge the relative importance of each piece of evidence and assess its relationship to the overall picture. As in a legal case, your conclusion needs to be based on the "weight of the evidence."

Before proceeding with the overall evaluation, one loose end to tie up at this point might be any unusual line items you spotted in your scan of the big picture. Sometimes these demand that you ask an expert, but frequently you can think them through or search for illumination elsewhere in the annual report. Earlier we identified two unusual line items for Colgate-Palmolive. One was the "cumulative effect on prior years of an accounting change" in 1993. Without the deduction of this $358 million item from income in 1993, Colgate-Palmolive had a healthy income figure of $548 million; but after subtracting it, income fell to $190 million. The explanation is that when Colgate-Palmolive made this accounting change, all of its effects prior to 1993 were charged to income in 1993. In reality, there was not actual expenditure of cash in 1993, which is why we added this back on the cash flow statement.[3] This is good to know, because if we ignore the accounting change and the associated charge, net income has steadily increased.

<table>
<tr><td colspan="4">Figure 4
Jones Company: Statements of Cash Flows
For Year Ending December 31</td></tr>
<tr><td>Millions of Dollars</td><td>1995</td><td>1994</td><td>1993</td></tr>
<tr><td>Cash Flow from Operating Activities</td><td></td><td></td><td></td></tr>
<tr><td>Net income (loss)</td><td>$ (43)</td><td>$ (189)</td><td>$ (134)</td></tr>
<tr><td>Depreciation</td><td>230</td><td>271</td><td>350</td></tr>
<tr><td>(Increase) in receivables</td><td>(121)</td><td>(25)</td><td>(4)</td></tr>
<tr><td>Decrease in inventories</td><td>50</td><td>42</td><td>30</td></tr>
<tr><td>Changes in other current accounts</td><td>16</td><td>(8)</td><td>(12)</td></tr>
<tr><td>Net cash provided by operating activities</td><td>132</td><td>91</td><td>230</td></tr>
<tr><td>Cash Flow from Investing Activities</td><td></td><td></td><td></td></tr>
<tr><td>Capital Expenditures</td><td>(200)</td><td>(260)</td><td>(300)</td></tr>
<tr><td>Disposal of plant assets</td><td>204</td><td>200</td><td>180</td></tr>
<tr><td>Disposal of business segment</td><td>134</td><td>51</td><td>---</td></tr>
<tr><td>Net cash (used in)/provided by investing activities</td><td>138</td><td>(9)</td><td>(120)</td></tr>
<tr><td>Cash Flow from Financing Activities</td><td></td><td></td><td></td></tr>
<tr><td>Proceeds of long-term debt</td><td>200</td><td>450</td><td>215</td></tr>
<tr><td>Reductions of long-term debt</td><td>(460)</td><td>(480)</td><td>(322)</td></tr>
<tr><td>Dividends paid</td><td>---</td><td>---</td><td>(30)</td></tr>
<tr><td>Net cash used for financing activities</td><td>(260)</td><td>(30)</td><td>(137)</td></tr>
<tr><td>Increase (decrease) in cash</td><td>$10</td><td>$52</td><td>(27)</td></tr>
</table>

The other unusual line item was called "restructured operations," which Colgate-Palmolive subtracted from net income. This means that the cash flows associated with restructuring operations occurred in a different year from when these costs were expensed on the income statement. In all three years presented by Colgate-Palmolive, it had more cash outflows for restructuring than it expensed in the income statement.

Good news or bad news? When a company restructures some of its operations, there is both. The bad news is that there was some kind of problem that required the restructuring. The good news is that the company recog-

nized the problem and took action it hopes will be effective. Whether the restructuring cash costs are more or less than the restructuring expense is simply a timing issue. Because expenses are recognized as soon as reasonably possible, it typically requires several years after the expense has been recorded for all of the cash costs to be incurred. Colgate-Palmolive probably recognized these restructuring expenses in prior years and this is just the anticipated cash outflows catching up with them. Moreover, the amount on the cash flow statement is declining each year.

Whether or not to chase down explanations for unusual or unknown items is a subjective call. For example, if Colgate-Palmolive's restructuring charge differences were bigger or growing, it might be worthwhile to search for more information. However, the "weight of the evidence" so far indicates that this issue is not particularly relevant in getting at the big picture. If you encounter something you do not understand, consider its materiality. If it has a major effect on cash flow from operating activities, or if it ranks as one of the major sources or uses of cash, you should probably search for an explanation. Otherwise it may be more efficient to ignore it and concentrate on the many items you know.

Now let's summarize what we've learned by examining Colgate-Palmolive's cash flow statement. First, the good news. Net income has been positive for all three years and, if we eliminate the effects of the accounting change, has been steadily increasing. Operating cash flows have also been positive for three years; they, too, have been steadily increasing. Operating cash flows have significantly exceeded the sum of depreciation and dividends, so Colgate-Palmolive is generating enough cash from operations to expand the business. By making capital expenditures that significantly exceed depreciation, and also by making fairly large acquisitions, Colgate-Palmolive shows that it is grooming the business for the future. There are no large-scale sales of fixed assets or divestitures that indicate any downsizing or shrinking of the business. The company has increased its dividend payments annually, an expression of management's confidence in the firm's future cash-generating capability. It also has sufficient excess cash to repurchase large amounts of its stock.

Now the bad news. The presence of charges for "restructured operations" indicates that Colgate-Palmolive has experienced problems in some portions of the business. It has borrowed significantly, in excess of repayment, which could increase leverage. The repurchase of stock could indicate management concerns with possible takeovers. And acquisitions sometimes create problems for firms; it is difficult to integrate them successfully into the company's business to ensure adequate returns.

The good news in the Colgate-Palmolive cash flow story is quite compelling. The bad news is more at the level of "concerns" rather than major cash flow problems.

So considering the weight of the evidence, Colgate-Palmolive appears to have a strong positive cash flow story.

Now it's your turn. The best way to learn about cash flow statements is to study some carefully using the four steps described above. You may not become an expert but you will be able to spot the big trends and important issues involved with the management of cash in most companies.

Figure 4 provides you with the opportunity to test your newfound skills. It is similar to the puzzles you encountered as a child in which you spot the things that are wrong with the picture. Poor Jones Company is having some rough times, as illuminated by their cash flow statements for 1993, 1994 and 1995. See how many of these troubling developments you can identify by putting together the Puzzle of the Cash Flow Statement! (Some possible answers are listed at the end of the article.[4])

Opportunities for applying your new expertise are many. As an employee curious about your company's ability to cover your paycheck, you can check out the health of cash flow from operating activities. Or suppose you are a supplier whose customer has just announced a loss for the year and you are wondering whether to continue to extend credit. An analysis of the customer's cash flow from operating activities can provide you with evidence that the firm does or does not have strong enough cash flows from operating activities to pay its bills despite losses on the income statement.

If you are a stockholder, you may be interested in whether cash flow from operating activities is large enough to invest in the capital expenditures required to keep the company whole and make it grow while still paying the dividend you have come to expect. As an executive, you might examine the cash flow statement to determine whether it is likely that all of the major sources of cash—operating activities, issuing stock, and borrowing—will be sufficient to fund a major expansion program you plan to undertake. As your expertise increases, many other useful applications may appear to you.

The information contained in a cash flow statement cannot replace the information from the traditional income statement and balance sheet. But it does provide valuable input for understanding the relationships between income and its short- and long-term ability to generate cash.

Notes

1. This might be the time to go looking for clues in the rest of the annual report. Where to look? A footnote on long-term debt might seem logical, but it is often almost impossible to truly understand unless you are a Chief Financial Officer. Easier and sometimes more illuminating is to do some simple ratios on the balance sheet and income statement. How has debt changed as a percentage of total liabilities and stockholders' equity? For Colgate-Palmolive, the percentage of debt to total liabilities and stockholders' equity is quite high and has gotten higher, from 67% in 1993 to 70% in 1994. The company's income statement reveals that interest expense has almost doubled in the last year, and a quick ratio analysis of "number of times interest can be paid from income" shows a sharp decline from 7 times to about 4½ times in one year. Further examination of the cash flow statement reveals that the company purchased large amounts of treasury stock. This helps explain why stockholders' equity is low in comparison to total equities, which may make that 70% debt-to-total equity ratio more understandable.

2. This contrasts with minor stock repurchases that companies typically undertake to offer stock to employees in stock option plans; in such instances, modest treasury stock repurchases are offset by modest but comparable issuances of treasury stock.

3. An accounting change is just a "paper decision": it affects the way net income is presented, but it does not change the fundamental economic activity of the firm, so it does not affect cash receipts or cash expenditures.

4. Some possible answers are: (1) there have been losses in all three years; (2) depreciation charges have decreased; (3) capital expenditures are less than depreciation; (4) capital expenditures are less than disposals; (5) a big accounts receivable increase needs to be investigated; (6) inventories are decreasing; (7) segments of the business are being sold off; (8) the company has stopped paying dividends; (9) debt needs to be paid off with cash flow from operations; (10) there is much borrowing; (11) there is less borrowing this year. Are creditors trusting the company less?

References

Mohamed A. Rujoub, Doris M. Cook and Leon E. Hay, "Using Cash Flow Ratios To Predict Business Failures." *Journal of Managerial Issues*, Spring 1995, pp. 75–90.

"The Top 8 Reports," *Institutional Investor*, September 1995, pp. 123–129.

Julie H. Hertenstein is an associate professor of business administration at Northeastern University, Boston, Massachusetts, where **Sharon M. McKinnon** is a professor of business administration.

Characteristics of a Successful Entrepreneurial Management Team

Alexander L. M. Dingee, Brian Haslett and Leonard E. Smollen

What are the personal characteristics required to be a successful entrepreneur? Before making the personal sacrifices required to start and build a major enterprise, would-be entrepreneurs should engage in serious soul-searching to be sure they have what it takes to thrive in the toughest jungle of the business world.

To assist in this introspection, the following guidelines have been prepared by principals of Venture Founders Corporation (VFC). Founded in 1970 to design and apply new approaches to venture development and financing, VFC serves investor clients both in the United States and in the United Kingdom. These clients have committed capital to funds that finance new and young ventures that are found, evaluated and assisted by VFC.

Venture capitalists say they prefer a grade A entrepreneur with a grade B business idea to a grade B entrepreneur with a grade A idea. And it is generally a strong management team, not a lone entrepreneur that they back.

With that in mind, there are some initial questions that would-be entrepreneurs must consider: Do I have adequate *commitment, motivation* and *skills* to start and build a major business—to be a successful entrepreneur? Does my management team have the necessary skills to enable us to succeed in building a particular venture? And finally, do I have a viable idea?

If these questions can be answered affirmatively, then it may be wise to consider developing a business plan and beginning a search for venture capital. This, however, is only the first step of the entrepreneurial self-examination process.

Am I an Entrepreneur?

A good way to answer this question is by objectively comparing yourself to a successful entrepreneur. Begin by studying the following characteristics that successful entrepreneurs, venture capitalists and behavioral scientists say are important for success.

Drive and energy level: A successful entrepreneur must have the ability to work long hours for sustained periods with less than the normal amount of sleep.

Self-confidence: A belief in yourself and your ability to achieve your goals and a sense that events in your life are self-determined is essential.

Setting challenging but realistic goals: The ability to set clear goals and objectives that are challenging, yet realistic and attainable.

Long-term involvement: A commitment to projects that will reach completion in five to seven years and to work towards distant goals. This means total dedication to the business and to attaining these goals.

Using money as a performance measure: Money, in the form of salary, profits, or capital gains, should be viewed more as a measure of how the company is doing rather than as an end in itself.

Persistent problem solving: You must have an intense and determined desire to solve problems toward the completion of tasks.

Taking moderate risks: Entrepreneurial success is generally the result of calculated risk-taking that provides a reasonable and challenging chance of success.

Learning from failure: Understanding your role in a failure can be instrumental in avoiding similar problems in the future. A failure may be disappointing, but should not be discouraging.

Using criticism: You need to be able to seek and use criticism of the style and substance of your performance.

Taking initiative and seeking personal responsibility: You need to seize opportunities and put yourself in situations where you are personally responsible for success or failure. You should be able to take the initiative to solve problems or fill leadership vacuums. You should enjoy being involved in situations where your impact on a problem can be measured.

Making good use of resources: Can you identify and use expertise and assistance that is relevant to the accomplishment of your goals? You should not be so involved in the achievement of your goals and in independent accomplishment that you will not let anyone help you.

Competing against self-imposed standards: Do you tend to establish your own standard of performance, which is high yet realistic, and then compete with yourself?

No one individual possesses all these attributes. Weaknesses can be compensated for in other members of your management team. Do remember, though, *you* are the *most* critical risk. Rate yourself on each of these key characteristics "strong," "average," or "weak" compared with others you know and respect. Be as honest and accurate as you can. If you think you are average or weak on most of them, then do yourself, your family, and your would-be business associates a favor—do not start a business.

If you rate yourself high on most traits, this may be unrealistic and therefore you should review these ratings with people who know you well. Spouses, teachers, peers, and professional advisors are all likely to view you differently, both in terms of your past accomplishments and your potential. Take time with each reviewer to explain *why* you rate yourself as you do. Be prepared to alter your ratings in light of their opinions. If people you know tell you that you are likely to fail as an entrepreneur, they may be right. But both of you should be aware that making such an evaluation realistically is no quick-and-dirty task.

Once you believe you have an adequate assessment of yourself, think back on personal experiences that demanded entrepreneurial strengths. Reflect on these incidences and see if you acted in a manner consistent with your rating.

If you are convinced that you have the entrepreneurial wherewithal to start and build a business, you must now evaluate your management skills to determine your abilities and those that your management team must have. To this end, you should systematically audit your managerial experience and accomplishments in marketing and sales; operations; research, development, and engineering; finance and accounting; general management and administration; personnel; and the legal and tax aspects of business. To rate yourself, we suggest the following standards.

Strong = Know thoroughly and have proven ability
Average = Have limited knowledge and accomplishments and will need backup perhaps part-time
Weak = Unfamiliar and need someone's full-time skills

The different nature of each element makes it unlikely for individuals to be equally strong in all elements of these seven functions. For example, a powerful direct salesperson probably will not show equal strength in market research and evaluation.

Before giving yourself an overall rating on each of these functions, we suggest that you break them down to the principal elements and rate yourself on each element. Note that the critical elements of any function may vary with each venture: the marketing and sales function includes market research and evaluation and marketing planning as well as sales management and merchandising, direct selling, service, and distribution. The latter will not be critical if you market through distributors.

A listing and brief description of representative elements of all seven functions is presented at the end of this article.

For a more objective evaluation, you may want to review your management skills with former and current supervisors, peers and subordinates, who may all see a different side of you. After thoroughly evaluating your entrepreneurial traits and your management skills, you should be able to determine the personal risks you will run if you try to create a business.

If your dream is to build a multimillion-dollar business, it might also be wise to check your evaluation with one or more of the professionals who are active and respected in the fields of career counseling and entrepreneurial behavior. A man with a weak heart may only ask his wife about taking a gentle stroll up a small grassy hill, but he would be wise to consult a doctor before trying to climb a mountain.[1]

Does My Team Have the Necessary Complementary Skills?

Research into successful ventures shows that teams perform better than one individual. Knowing this, venture capitalists always look for a balanced team. So your next task is to analyze the business you are contemplating and determine what abilities and skills are critical to its success in the first two to three years. Then set about building a management team that includes people who are strong where you are weak.

In a new company, you may not want or be able to afford full-time staff to perform all functions. It is, however, important to choose part-time people carefully, since you may want some of them to come on board later. Avoid teaming up with a school friend whom you only know in casual situations or a colleague in the lab or office whose skills match your own. Although these collaborations are tempting, they rarely work out, and venture capitalists may be put off by a team that is made up of all engineers, salespeople or relatives.[2]

Do I Have a Viable Idea?

Imagine yourself a venture capitalist who has just analyzed the few hundred business proposals examined last year. Your analysis shows that you handled the various proposals in these ways.

1. Sixty percent were rejected after a 20-to-30 minute scanning.
2. Another quarter were discarded after a lengthier review.
3. About 15% were investigated in depth and two-thirds of those were dismissed because of serious flaws in the management team or the business plan that could not be easily resolved.
4. Of the 5% that were viable investment opportunities, terms acceptable to the entrepreneur(s) and other existing stock holders were negotiated in only 3%.

The 15% that were investigated in depth were presented by strong, well-balanced management teams who were able to show you relevant accomplishments in marketing, finance and operations and had developed (perhaps with some prodding by you) a comprehensive business plan.

As an entrepreneur, think what that venture capitalist's analysis means to you: there is a three-in-one-hundred chance of securing capital from any one source on terms acceptable to you and the investor and only a 15% chance of being considered seriously for investment, and a comprehensive business plan is usually required to qualify for such consideration.

So if you are really serious about going into business for yourself, you should start to develop a comprehensive business plan. If the plan is done properly and completely, it will probably take you 150 to 300 hours of intense work. Even when it is done, there is no guarantee that you will raise enough investment capital.

Is there any way to avoid going to all this effort only to have your plan rejected after a 20-minute perusal? Try seeing your business idea through the objective, critical eyes of a venture capitalist.

Before developing a business plan, it is important to answer the questions that venture capitalists may have on their minds when they review a plan to determine if it is worth studying and calling a meeting to discuss. The first question: What exactly will be sold to whom? Other key market questions are:

- Why will the customer buy your product?

- Who are the ultimate users and what influences on their purchasing habits are beyond your control?
- Who is the competition? Are they profitable now? Why do you think you can successfully compete with them?
- Is the market large and growing? Does it offer a multi-million-dollar potential for your company?
- Are you or will you be in a recognized growth industry?

You should then answer several questions about the other major aspects of the business you contemplate, questions about your team, your financial needs and the risks you are running. Such questions may include:

- What is the *maximum* amount of dollars and length of time that will be needed before your product is ready for market?
- What is the depth of your team's knowledge and extent of their reputations in the types of markets, technologies and operations in which you will be active?
- What are your team's management skills in the three key areas of marketing, finance and operations?
- How many unproven marketing, technical and manufacturing approaches do you contemplate?
- What are the strengths, weaknesses and major risks of your venture?

Careful thought about these areas should enable you to take a reasonable first look at your own venture ideas and to evaluate the potential for success as well as the major risks. The risks in any entrepreneurial venture are you, the entrepreneur, your team and any fundamental flaws in your venture idea. You should then be able to put together a business plan and avoid many of the early errors (for example, team inadequacies; underpricing; weak cash management) that so often cripple new ventures. You should also be able to improve your chances of securing financing and launching a successful venture.

Representative Elements of Seven Management Functions

1. Marketing and sales

a. *Market research and evaluation*: Ability to design and conduct market research studies and to analyze and interpret study results; familiarity with questionnaire design and sampling techniques.
b. *Strategic sales*: Experience in developing marketing strategies and establishing forces and then planning

appropriate sales, advertising and promotional programs and setting up an effective network distributor or sales representative organization.

c. *Sales management and merchandising*: Ability in organizing, supervising, motivating and providing merchandising support to a direct sales force; analyzing territory and sales potential; and managing a sales force to obtain a target share of the market.

d. *Direct sales*: Experience in identifying, meeting and developing new customers, demonstrated success in closing sales.

e. *Service*: Experience in identifying service needs of particular products and in determining service and spare parts requirements, handling customer complaints, and managing a service organization.

f. *Distribution management*: Ability to organize and manage the flow of the product from manufacturing through distribution channels to the ultimate customer, including familiarity with shipping costs, scheduling techniques, carriers, etc.

g. *Overall marketing skills*: Give yourself a combined rating reflecting your skill level across all of the above marketing areas.

2. Operations

a. *Manufacturing management*: Knowledge of the production processes, machines, manpower, and space requirements to produce the product; experience in managing production to produce products within time, cost, and quality constraints.

b. *Inventory control*: Familiarity with techniques of controlling in-process and finished goods inventories of materials.

c. *Quality control*: Ability to set up inspection systems and standards for effective control of quality in incoming, in-process and finished materials.

d. *Purchasing*: Ability to identify appropriate sources of supply, the amount of material in inventory, familiarity with economical order quantities and discount advantage.

e. *Overall operations skills*: Give yourself a combined rating reflecting your skill level across all of the above operations areas.

3. Research, development and engineering

a. *Direction and management of applied research*: Ability to distinguish and keep a prudent balance between long-range projects at the frontiers of your technology, which attract the most creative individuals, and shorter range research in support of current product development activity.

b. *Management of development*: Ability to plan and direct work of development engineers and to use time and cost budgets so that perfectionists do not ruin you and yet product performance, appearance, and production engineering needs can be met; ability to dis-

tinguish between bread-board, field and pre-production prototype programs.

c. *Management of engineering*: Ability to plan and direct engineers in the final design of a new product for manufacture and in the engineering and testing of the production process to manufacture that new product.

d. *Technical know-how*: Ability to contribute personally to research, development, and/or engineering because of up-to-date in-depth knowledge of the technologies in which your company is involved.

e. *Overall research, development, and engineering skills*: Give yourself a combined rating reflecting your skill level across the above areas.

4. Financial management

a. *Raising capital*: Ability to decide how best to acquire funds for startup and growth; ability to forecast the need for funds and to prepare budgets; familiarity with sources and vehicles of short- and long-term financing.

b. *Money management*: Ability to design, install, maintain, use financial controls; familiarity with accounting and control systems needed to manage; ability to set up a project cost control system, analyze overhead/contribution/absorption, prepare profit and loss and balance sheets, and manage a bookkeeper.

c. *Specific skills*: Cash flow analysis; break-even analysis; contribution analysis; budgeting and profit-planning techniques; profit and loss, balance sheet, and present value analysis of return on investment and payback.

d. *Overall financial skills*: Give yourself a combined rating reflecting your skill level across all of the above financial areas.

5. General management and administration

a. *Problem solving*: Ability to anticipate potential problems and plan to avoid them; ability to gather facts about problems, analyze them for real causes, and plan effective action to solve problems; thoroughness in dealing with the details of particular problems and in follow-through.

b. *Communications*: Ability to communicate effectively and clearly, both in speech and in writing, to the media, the public, customers, peers, and subordinates.

c. *Planning*: Ability to set realistic and attainable goals, identify obstacles to achieving the goals and develop detailed action plans to achieve those goals; ability to schedule own time very systematically.

d. *Decision making*: Ability to make decisions on your best analysis of incomplete data.

e. *Project management*: Skill in organizing project teams, setting project goals, defining project tasks, and monitoring task completion in the face of problems and cost/quality constraints.

f. *Negotiating*: Ability to work effectively in a negotiating situation; ability to quickly balance value given and value received.

g. *Personnel administration*: Ability to set up payroll, hiring, compensation, and training functions.

h. *Overall administrative skills*: Give yourself a combined rating reflecting your skill level across all of the above administrative areas.

6. Personnel management

a. *Leadership*: Ability to understand the relationships between tasks, the leader, and the followers; ability to lead in situations where it is appropriate; willingness to manage actively, supervise, and control activities of others through directions, suggestions, inspiration, and other techniques.

b. *Listening*: Ability to listen to and understand without interrupting or mentally preparing your own rebuttal at the expense of hearing the message.

c. *Helping*: Ability to ask for and provide help and to determine situations where assistance is warranted.

d. *Criticism*: Ability to provide performance and interpersonal criticism to others that they find useful; ability to receive feedback from others without becoming defensive or argumentative.

e. *Conflict resolution*: Ability to confront differences openly and to deal with them until resolution is obtained.

f. *Teamwork*: Ability to work well with others in pursuing common goals.

g. *Selecting and developing subordinates*: Ability to select and delegate responsibility to subordinates and to coach them in the development of their managerial capabilities.

h. *Climate building*: Ability to create, by the way you manage, a climate and spirit conducive to high performance; ability to press for higher performance while rewarding work well done.

i. *Overall interpersonal skills*: Give yourself a combined rating reflecting your skill level across all of the above personnel management areas.

7. Legal and tax aspects

a. *Corporate law*: Familiarity with legal issues relating to stock issues, incorporation, distribution agreements, leases, etc.

b. *Contract law*: Familiarity with contract procedures and requirements (government and commercial), including default, warranty, and incentive provisions; fee structures; overhead, general and administrative expenses allowable, and so forth.

c. *Patent law*: Experience with preparation and revision of patent applications; ability to recognize a strong patent; familiarity with claim requirements.

d. *Tax Law*: Familiarity with general state and federal reporting requirements for businesses and with special provisions concerning Subchapter S corporations, tax shelters, fringe benefits, etc.

e. *Overall legal and tax skills*: Give yourself a combined rating reflecting your skill level across all of the above legal and tax areas.

Notes

1. For a discussion and appraisal of such evaluations, see "Business Leadership Training: A Six-Month Evaluation," a paper by Jeffry A. Timmons, D.B.A., and John L. Hayes.
2. For further discussion, see "The Entrepreneurial Team: Formation and Development" by Jeffry A. Timmons, D.B.A., a competitive paper presented at the annual Academy of Management meeting in 1973.

Alexander L. M. Dingee is a cofounder and chairman of Venture Founders Corporation, Lexington, Massachusetts, which manages venture capital funds dedicated to creating and investing in seed, startup and first-stage situations. Previously he had successfully started two companies and now he also continues to cofound new ventures, Network Inc., a terabit router company, Marlboro, Massachusetts, and Cortec Inc., turnkey coinjection systems, Beverly, Massachusetts, for his own account.

Brian Haslett was a cofounder of Venture Founders Corporation and played a lead role in establishing its U.K. subsidiary and in helping many American and British entrepreneurs create and finance their new enterprises. He subsequently was a contributor to Venture Capital Journal. *Mr. Haslett died in 1985.*

Leonard E. Smollen was executive vice president and a cofounder of Venture Founders Corporation, a private company that manages venture capital funds. Currently Mr. Smollen provides consulting services to new ventures and venture capital partnerships.

From *Pratt's Guide to Venture Capital Sources*, 1997, pp. 23–28. © 1997 by Securities Data Publishing. Reprinted by permission.

Special Report—Breakaway: A Focus on Small Business

Going Outside

Advisory boards can provide straight talk, often at little cost

By CHRISTINA LE BEAU

Employees were slacking off, production was jammed up and entrepreneur Jeff Bizar was wondering what he had walked into. Yet he wanted the marriage to work. The party-decorations business he had just acquired seemed a natural fit for the entertainment company he started in 1992. Bizar Entertainment Inc. supplied DJs, motivational speakers and other entertainers, while the new addition produced backdrops, centerpieces and the like. What could be better?

But the new business "was less than 10% of my income and 99% of my headaches," says Mr. Bizar. So he took the issue to his advisory board, a group of fellow Chicago-area business owners. The entire staff would have to go, the group advised, and a whole new production system was in order. It wasn't unsalvageable, they believed, but it would take some work.

After hearing what it would take to save the business, Mr. Bizar realized that his heart wasn't in it. "I just wasn't passionate about that part of the business," he says. So 18 months after purchasing the decor business, he shuttered it. "It's not that I didn't see these things before," Mr. Bizar says, "but when you hear it from other people, well, I couldn't not believe it anymore."

Another Viewpoint

An outside perspective like that has saved more than a few small businesses from themselves. Though advisory boards seem particularly in vogue among tech entrepreneurs, the concept in fact was born long before most of them learned to walk. These boards carry no standard definition. Some are created by an owner for a specific company, while others, like Mr. Bizar's, are organized by a third party to serve each member's business. Some are hands-on, meeting monthly or more, even getting involved in the daily grind. Others meet quarterly, with an eye on the big picture. Many consist solely of interested outsiders, but a good number include investors as well.

What they all share is this: They are there to coach, evaluate, play devil's advocate and make introductions. These aren't boards of directors; they bear no fiduciary or legal responsibility and thus can focus on business advice in a way a company's directors may not have time for. And the price is just right for a small-business owner—typically a token stipend, if anything, though some do get stock options. Mr. Bizar pays $500 a quarter for monthly meetings through the Chicago-based President's Resource Organization. Pocket change, considering the potential payoff.

"If you think about it, where else in your life do you get absolutely straight, unvarnished talk?" says Robert Villency, chairman and CEO of Maurice Villency Inc., a furniture retailer based in Jericho, N.Y. Mr. Villency has relied on advisory boards since 1979, tapping them for wisdom on everything from expansion to handling the death of an executive. "Other people can look at your issues without ego and emotion getting in the way."

Consultants presumably could do the same thing, but "the formal structure of an advisory board gives you a sense of accountability," says Pittsburgh entrepreneur Anita Brattina, who has written about her experiences with an advisory board. "That puts a little more stake in the game for everyone at the table. Because if you're going to convene everyone, you want something to come out of it."

Of course there is the matter of choosing the people at that table. And here, too, there are few absolutes. Most draw the line at including customers or the company's banker, accountant or attorney, figuring that's cause for conflict at every turn. Instead they tap fellow entrepreneurs and vendors. Ms. Brattina, the president of Direct Response Marketing Inc., always seeks founder-CEOs—"people who've done it from scratch—who've been there, done that." Bogart Golf Inc., a rapidly growing chain of golf centers based in Bellevue, Wash., includes its architect and its advertising representative. "It gives them a vested interest in the company," says Scott Painter, Bogart's chairman and CEO. "They put more effort into us than if we were simply a client."

The Name Game

Taboo as it might seem, many businesspeople also turn to family and friends. Celebrities and industry icons get calls, too. Dermdex Inc. (www.dermadex.com), an online trading hub for skin-care supplies, tapped new-age musician and anti-aging guru John Tesh. "He knows the spa space very well," says Navroze Mehta, president and CEO of the Boca Raton, Fla., company. "And his wife, Connie Sellecca, is very involved in skin care and selling her own line. So clearly he can help in PR and promotions."

Yet if there's one myth about advisory boards, it's that names alone will open doors and unload pockets. "You've got to distinguish between advisory boards that are actually used by CEOs and advisory boards that are there to dress up a company," says John Sculley, the former Apple Computer Inc. CEO and now a venture capitalist, who turns down any offer that reeks of window dressing. "I think people see through that pretty quickly."

One offer Mr. Sculley didn't turn down—in fact one he embraced—came from InPhonic Inc., a wireless-networks provider in Washington, D.C. InPhonic CEO David A. Steinberg asked Mr. Sculley for a meeting after hearing him speak at a Young Presidents' Organization event. Nearly six hours after arriving for that meeting, Mr. Steinberg walked out with a commitment from Mr. Sculley to invest in the company and to serve on both its board of directors and its advisory board.

Though Mr. Steinberg had previously started two other businesses without advisers, this time he was building an infrastructure online—new terrain for him. Democratic National Convention Chairman Terry McAuliffe, another of InPhonic's four advisers, has helped open doors with organizations and trade groups—target markets. And Mr. Sculley at one point took off three days to fly to San Francisco and attend 12 meetings with Mr. Steinberg and potential clients, a trip that resulted in 10 deals, four of them on the spot.

"I expected to get some advice, but the reality is that these guys have just gone to bat for us, far beyond what we had actually hoped," says Mr. Steinberg, whose company now employs 74 people. Mr. Steinberg declined to reveal revenue.

Of course, Mr. Sculley did offer more than just time on that trip to San Francisco. "The first three pitches, I was really bad," says Mr. Steinberg, who started out selling way too hard for the West Coast crowd. "He critiqued me pretty rigorously."

That's brainpower that money just can't buy. "Who doesn't want nine other people thinking about your business?" asks Atlanta consultant Michelle Matthews, who started her solo organizational-development practice in 1999 after a career with the big consulting firms. Ms. Matthews, who counts her mother and

sister among her advisers, recalls a discussion with the board about accepting a retainer agreement from a client. She was ready to jump on it—it was guaranteed income, after all—but the board helped her slow down and work out an agreement that protected her from becoming a one-client consultant.

'Time for Reflection'

"I know I'm going to meet with them quarterly, so I've learned to allocate time for reflection about my goals," says Ms. Matthews, speaking not only about profitability, effectiveness and client mix, but also about finding a balance between work and life. "And both years I've exceeded my objectives."

The people at Reactive Search Inc. have other things in mind. Like attracting funding. "We're in a tough environment in terms of capital markets, so we perceived early on that we were going to have to prove a lot more," says Anthony Faulise, co-founder of this year-old e-commerce software maker from Durham, N.C. "So we went looking for the kind of experience we couldn't afford to pay cash for."

Mr. Faulise, who early on sought advice from Amazon.com founder and former Princeton University classmate Jeff Bezos, used "energetic networking" to build an advisory board that already includes Linda Watson, president of Egarden.com (www.egarden.com), and Alan Andreini, the executive chairman of eB2B Commerce Inc. Mr. Andreini, formerly vice chairman and CEO of InterWorld Corp., joined the advisory board after Mr. Faulise combed Princeton alumni magazines looking for people "old enough to have an influential position and young enough to be involved in technology."

For the price of stock options, Reactive Search has gained a dozen minds ready to weigh in on anything from hiring to funding. The company, which has eight paid employees and about as many unpaid Duke University interns, even tapped three advisers to serve as interim executives, including CEO. It's an arrangement that allows Mr. Faulise and his co-founder, Stephen Burnham, to focus on their strengths—sales and marketing, respectively—while steering toward an IPO and eventual profitability.

More money, no surprise, is almost always the ultimate goal. Using an advisory board to get there, however, means shedding fears and sharing weaknesses—"what one of my friends calls unbuttoning your kimono," says Ms. Brattina of Direct Response Marketing.

Ms. Brattina in 1991 applied for and won an advisory board for a year, courtesy of Pittsburgh's PowerLink Inc., a nonprofit business-development group that since has expanded nationwide under the auspices of the Athena Foundation, an East Lansing, Mich., women's leadership group. Ms. Brattina's then eight-year-old company was doing well enough—annual revenue of about $360,000—but real growth seemed elusive. How, she agonized, did any business grow to $1 million and beyond?

Initially reluctant to divulge too much to her advisers, Ms. Brattina wasn't finding many answers. But once she spilled, so did the solutions: Broaden services. Don't be afraid to use credit when necessary. Hire good managers and stay out of their faces.

It's something another PowerLink recipient, Ellen Ruddock, had to swallow as well. "I was five years in the business and dying when I got my panel," says Ms. Ruddock, who owns Career Dynamics, a leadership-training firm, and now serves as volunteer president for the Pittsburgh PowerLink group. "They helped me replace myself every step of the way in the business. Now I can see that we will become a million-dollar business shortly."

Ms. Brattina, 10 years after landing her PowerLink board, now employs 120 people—about half of them part time—and posts revenue exceeding $3 million. Her advisory board, constructed in part from that original group, is going strong. Next goal: $20 million. "There's no question that a president still has to lead the company and know where they want to take it, but it's very smart to use people who bring external insight," says Ms. Brattina. It doesn't hurt, she adds, if those people "really fall in love with your business."

Mr. Painter, the Washington golf executive, takes it one further. "I don't know if an advisory board embraces the company more," he says, "but there's definitely a love of the company that doesn't always come with the stiffness of a board of directors."

Ms. Le Beau is a writer in Rochester, N.Y
Write to Christina Le Beau at breakaway@wsj..com.

Advice at the Right Price

Small Business Administration

An old standby, the SBA still offers some of the most comprehensive free resources around. Check out www.sba.gov for guides to everything from starting, financing and marketing a business to tackling regulatory and tax issues. You'll find online courses and shareware, plus links to regional SBA offices and Small Business Development Centers. Call (800) 827-5722.

Local Business Groups

Don't overlook your local chamber of commerce, women's network, management council or any similar business group. Most hold regular programs that offer not only business advice, but also power networking. Check with your chamber for a list of other local business organizations.

Internet

Type "small business help" into any search engine, and you'll find no shortage of online resources, everything from articles and resource listings to services offering free Web hosting, file storage, e-mail and voice mail accounts, and shareware. One handy site is BenefitsLink, www.benefitslink.com, which tracks the latest employee-benefits developments, plus offers a benefits-centric search engine that delivers highly relevant links throughout the Web. Another useful site: Nolo.com, www.nolo.com, which features a comprehensive do-it-yourself center on small-business law. Of course, Nolo does publish legal books, software and forms, so you'll have to navigate some self-promotion.

Your Friendly Librarian

Before the Internet, we relied a lot more on our trusty reference librarians for answers to everything from geography queries to tax quandaries. The local library still offers an amazing depth of resources, from business books and CDs to directories and databases. You'll also find free, on-site Internet access at most locations.

Local Business Journals

For the price of a subscription (typically well under $100 a year), these weekly business newspapers offer how-to articles and sales leads, plus news of competitors and industry trends. Most publish annual "list" books, featuring the top 25 (or so) businesses in dozens of categories, such as law firms and real estate developers. Many also publish semiannual small-business and high-tech resource guides. Visit the Association of Area Business Publications Web site (www.bizpubs.org) for a directory of business journals nationwide.

—Christina Le Beau

UNIT 3

Financing the New Venture

Unit Selections

Key Points to Consider

- Why do entrepreneurs need to raise money to grow?

- How do startups determine how much initial capital they need?

- What factors affect the availability and cost of financing? Why are these factors critical?

- What are some important "deal-points" to an entrepreneur? To an investor?

- What do venture capitalists provide entrepreneurs, other than money?

- Why is a cash management strategy important for the startup venture?

- How does a startup venture determine how much capital is required to get going?

- What is the difference between debt and equity financing?

- What controls does the investor have on private companies?

- How can positive profits still result in negative cash flows?

 **Links: www.dushkin.com/online/**
These sites are annotated in the World Wide Web pages.

Entrepreneur Magazine/America's Business Funding Directory
   http://www.entrepreneurmag.com
Internet Resources for International Economics & Business
   http://dylee.keel.econ.ship.edu/econ/
U.S. Small Business Administration
   http://www.sba.gov

How do entrepreneurs finance their new ventures? The most successful entrepreneurs turn to the venture capital industry. The entrepreneur brings fresh ideas, management skills, and personal commitment while the venture capitalists (VCs) bring cash. Venture capital is provided by professionals who invest alongside management in young, rapidly growing companies that have the potential to develop into significant ventures.

The venture capital industry in the United States has grown to a size that could only be imagined in years past. In the last two years, venture capitalists have invested over $164 billion in new and growing businesses. Questions of how to raise money, when to raise money, and how to work with venture capitalists are frequent topics of concern with entrepreneurs today. This unit will describe some common sources of capital, provide information about the venture capital market, and offer guidance in approaching the venture capitalists and presenting the business plan.

Growth is an unavoidable fact of successful businesses. Growth due to an increase in sales requires product; in turn, additional product requires labor, inventory, raw materials, plant, property, and equipment. Since internally generated funds typically won't meet all expansion needs, most startups depend on outside capital to finance growth. In some instances, the entrepreneur may find that the new business does not begin to earn a profit until 2 or 3 years down the road. The entrepreneur therefore needs to secure the necessary capital to pioneer a new venture through the "financial Death Valley" and sustain the desired growth rate of the venture.

Financing the fast-growing venture tends be a time-consuming, complex task to the entrepreneur—who is most likely working heads-down on the daily needs. Typically, financing a new venture employs a combination of debt and equity financing. Debt is presumed to be lower-risk capital because it is repaid according to a set schedule of principal and interest. Debt financing involves an interest-bearing instrument usually called a loan. The payment is only indirectly related to the sales and profits of the new venture and typically, debt financing (also known as asset-based financing) requires some asset—for instance a vehicle, house, or other property/land—that will be used as collateral. Generally, lenders will allow ventures to borrow against their expected ability to generate the cash to repay the loan.

The entrepreneur with a new idea, when turned down by a bank, will often turn to a wealthy individual or several friends to back the business venture. In the United States "angel investors" commit some $30–60 billion per year in small businesses. But before receiving such "angelic support" many questions must first be answered. Certain critical elements must be present in a business plan before the venture will receive financing. Those who wish to be successful in dealing with outside investors should spend the time and effort to understand the objectives of their potential investors. Academic research on this topic has shown that in all too many cases startups don't get financed because the entrepreneur is not familiar with an investor's industry preferences, requirements, and specialization; risks and protection against losses; participation in management; or with the investor's "harvesting options" or "exit goals."

A good relationship between the entrepreneur and the venture capitalist is a vital element in a successful venture. Understanding this partnership is a necessary first step for the prospective entrepreneur. The entrepreneur must be prepared to compete successfully for the venture capitalists' dollars. It will be the task of the entrepreneur to select and approach the venture capitalist, most often with a complete business plan and strategic focus that supports an oral presentation. The presentation must demonstrate management's competence in knowing the following: (1) earning power/operating cash flows of the venture, (2) the potential terminal value of the business at exiting, (3) the value of the business model underlying the venture, (4) industry competitors and competitive advantages, and (5) how the management team intends to assess risks and create contingency plans.

When meeting with venture capitalists, the entrepreneurs need to be well prepared and "know their business numbers cold." Few analytical terms are more widely used and, at the same time, more poorly understood than the term cash flow. The cash flowing into a business venture is not the same as accounting profit. It is important for entrepreneurs to make weekly and monthly projections of cash received and disbursed. Such financial forecasts that relate to the future are called financial pro formas. This forecasting procedure is very difficult and perhaps that is why most entrepreneurs avoid it. As Mark Twain once said: "The art of prophecy is very difficult, especially with respect to the future."

Financial management is the cornerstone of the scorekeeping system for these investing and profit-making activities. A cash flow statement can help the entrepreneur come up with realistic estimates, determine financial requirements, understand the financial strategy framework, and craft a fund-raising strategy. The cash flow statement, also known as the statement of cash flows, is one of the most important financial planning tools that a startup venture can use. It is used to provide the entrepreneur with a clearer insight into the venture's cash management strategy: where funds come from and how they are disbursed, the amount of cash available, the amount of additional funds needed (AFN) to grow, and the general financial well-being of the new venture.

Finally, a well-prepared cash flow statement should also track the company's burn rate and top line revenue flow of cash into the business venture, which helps the investors recognize the true value of the venture. They prefer to see positive cash flows from operations, not just continual injections of cash and/or equity. A good financial plan for investors should not only show profit and cash flows, it should show how the business will pay back the money and make more money in the future. A comprehensive, investor-oriented business plan with complete financials will not guarantee success to the entrepreneur in raising funds for growing, but the lack of financials will ensure failure.

The Outlook

Will Venture Capital Come in From the Cold?

By Bernard Wysocki Jr.

The entrepreneurial economy, already hurting badly before the Sept. 11 terrorist attacks, has taken a sharp turn for the worse.

Entrepreneurs say their customers have entered a state of suspended animation, stunned by the terrorist attacks and their aftermath. Partnering deals are in limbo. But early-stage companies continue to burn through their precious cash, and some of the venture capitalists who back them wish for a "timeout" that they know is just wishful thinking.

"You almost want to take your companies and put them in a cryogenic freeze," says Todd Dagres, general partner at Battery Ventures and a board member at nine companies, including Akamai Technologies. Among start-ups, the next few months will bring slashed payrolls and even more tightening up to survive. Mr. Dagres sees a return to normalcy, but estimates it will take nine to 12 months. "Those who come out the other end with their teams together, the world will be their oyster. The weak will not be able to survive."

As in so much of the U.S. economy, the Sept. 11 attacks occurred at a delicate moment for early-stage, ambitious companies. The boom times of 1999 were a distant memory. First-round venture funding already had fallen to just $1.04 billion during the 2001 second quarter, down 87% from the year-earlier period, according to a survey by PriceWaterhouseCoopers. In September, just as some were detecting the faint signs of a rebound in confidence, this confidence disappeared on the terrible morning 13 days ago.

For some start-up companies, the "before and after" is stark. Great Plains Airlines, a Tulsa, Okla., start-up, was trying to raise $20 million from private institutional investors on top of $30 million raised in December. Interviewed days before the attacks, the head of Allegiance Capital Corp., David Mahmood, had noted that his finding risk-taking investors for Great Plains would be "unquestionably harder" than it might have been 18 months earlier. After the attacks, the prospect of funding any airline, never mind raising $20 million for a company with two 32-seat jets, is harder still.

"We had some people interested. But today I don't think they would invest in a kite factory," says Mr. Mahmood, who still thinks he has a 50-50 chance or better of finding funds.

In fact, what many of these early-stage companies face is uncertainty, not hopelessness. Great Plains is running 100% of its flights. In the first days after flights resumed, more than 60% of ticketed passengers showed up and traveled. The company could carve out a niche serving secondary markets, with smaller planes and shorter lines, even as the major carriers retrench. On the other hand, the airline, already a risky venture, could find itself unable to get the planes and financing it needs.

Looking ahead, will investors, executives and customers move away from the knee-jerk caution and start to embrace a more balanced—and more optimistic—view of the business landscape? They might. Venture capitalists talk of funding new technologies, e.g. those that provide security or video-conferencing. Even some start-ups grazed by the tragedy are still candidates for future funding.

At Everest Broadband Networks, which provides high-speed Internet service to office buildings, about 15 of the buildings it serves in lower Manhattan were initially without communications. (The number out of service has dropped to four.) It will hurt Everest's revenue a bit, but Chief Executive Jeffrey Feldman says the events of the past two weeks haven't derailed his negotiations for a fresh round of funding.

"I haven't gotten the final answer," says Mr. Feldman, who seeks $15 million to $20 million to last until the company's scheduled break-even point before the end of 2002. His negotiations continue today in California. Yet the events of the past two weeks, he adds, haven't "prompted the 'holy cow' reaction. It hasn't been a knockout punch."

Funded or not, most start-ups are keeping expenses to an absolute minimum. Some call it "hibernating" and just trying to hang on until a warmer climate loosens up funding and purchasing by potential customers.

Of course, this raises the question of whether would-be entrepreneurs will themselves hide from starting companies in a world economy that has gone from fragile to something worse. That would crimp innovation in America, surely. Paradoxically, though, the payroll slashing could bring new entrepreneurs to the scene.

"There's as much risk in the corporate world as in the entrepreneurial world," says Russ Medina, a Dallas-based telecom entrepreneur. He was CEO of a broadband start-up that failed in spring of 2001. But rather than get a job with an established concern, Mr. Medina just started another company, trying to establish a broadband company that offers wireless communication in public places.

Mr. Medina is undaunted in the aftermath of the attacks. "Does it make you turn around or does it make you proceed?" he asks. "We are continuing to persevere."

Write to Bernard Wysocki Jr. at bernie.wysocki@wsj.com

BASIC INSTINCT

THE MONEY'S STILL OUT THERE FOR THE RIGHT BUSINESS PLAN, BUT NOW MORE THAN EVER FUNDAMENTALS COUNT

By Bill Stensrud

There was once a time when every waiter in Hollywood seemed to have a movie script for sale. These days, the same waiter is also a would-be New Economy entrepreneur who has a business plan in the trunk of his car. The New Economy has brought out the entrepreneurial spirit in nearly everyone, and I applaud this development.

In the last few months, however, the bull market in venture capital has cooled. Venture capital firms are more selective than ever in picking startups they choose to fund. I have heard and read thousands of business plans and proposals. While some have promise, most fail because the entrepreneur does not understand what venture capitalists look for. And these aren't necessarily things you'll find in a book on how to write business proposals.

So how do you get VCs excited about your business proposition?

First the fundamentals:

Define your business. Precisely who is going to buy and precisely why? Who is your customer? Why will they buy your product or service? This is so fundamental that it is surprising sometimes how corporations, big and small, get it wrong. Cool products and great technologies don't create great businesses. Innovative solutions create great businesses when they solve real problems facing real people.

Target a rapidly growing market. Market growth creates an environment where it is much easier for a well run and focused business to thrive. Real examples of customer opportunities and specific needs are much more interesting that a consultant's projections of market size.

Offer a compelling differentiation to your customer. Why is your product or service significantly better than other solutions and competitors? The noise level is very high and you must be able to rise above it. Be able to explain this compelling difference simply and in very few words.

Have a sustainable advantage. It is hard to innovate and easy to emulate. Why is your business hard to copy? Great business models are sticky with the customer, making switching costs high. They also build barriers to competitors with technology that is strongly patented or with products or businesses that are hard to build and therefore copy.

Commit to management excellence. Great people create great businesses. Startups are not the place to learn a new job. Are you, the founder, the right CEO? If not, are you willing to relinquish the CEO position to someone who has the skills and experience to help you build a great business? Are you committed to work with your investors to build the best possible team to make the business successful? Either way, make it clear so there are no misunderstandings.

Do something you love. Many people are stuck in businesses for which they feel no passion. Others are doing it just for the money. Smart VCs are looking for entrepreneurs who are committed to their vision, will plow through the obstacles and get it done. VCs can sense your passion and excitement. These are the entrepreneurs who will succeed and these are the people VCs want to partner with.

Build to last. The "build a business and sell it" model will not be funded by a quality venture firm. If it doesn't sell, you have nothing. The company's business model must stand on its own. If you build a great company you may get acquired but it will be your choice, on your terms and at much higher price.

Second the tactics:

Perfect the elevator pitch (the executive summary). Imagine you find yourself in an elevator with your prospective investor and you have

10 floors to capture his or her attention. Can you create a compelling summary of your business opportunity within 60 seconds or in less than one page? And do it without using the words "leading" and "premier"? Dump the jargon. Don't explain that the Internet is growing, that more people are conducting business on the Net or that communication speeds are increasing (you simultaneously waste your prospective investor's time and insult his or her intelligence). Get to the point!

Target your investors. Money is available. But an investor should bring more. Acquire and show knowledge of the targeted VC firm, its successes and its specialties. How can the targeted VCs bring their expertise and entrepreneurial experience into play? Why is your opportunity a good fit for them? Why can they help you succeed?

Get Cindy Crawford on your board. I actually got a plan with this claim. I read it! All kidding aside, eStyle got a lot of media attention when it signed Cindy as their spokesperson last year. High profile affiliations can bring visibility, good advice and introductions to important partnership opportunities. In addition, few business plans get funded unless referred by someone known and respected by the VC firm.

There is no magic formula for getting a business funded. If you have a great business opportunity, solid people and an indomitable will you will succeed. If you are not getting through, there may be something wrong. Find out what it is and fix it.

There is at least one outcome worse than not getting funded. That is getting funded when you shouldn't. Spending three or four years of your life working 100-hour weeks on a poorly conceived business which ultimately fails is a great learning experience (I know because I did it) but it isn't much fun. A good venture partner will not only provide money. They are a good test of the quality of your business opportunity and, when you get funded, your investors should be great partners in helping you succeed.

Good hunting!

Bill Stensrud is a general partner at Enterprise Partners, a venture capital firm in Southern California with approximately $750 million under management. He can be reached at stensrud@ent.com.

RAISING MONEY

Ready Or Not?

Before you start shaking the trees for investors, make sure you're prepared to catch them.

BY DAVID R. EVANSON & ART BEROFF

If the purest excitement in business is that rare, big-sky idea, then *CD (pronounced "star CD") has enough firepower to light up even the most skeptical investor. The premise is simple: Allow consumers to immediately buy the music that's playing on their radios by dialing *CD on their cell phones. With one phone call, the service identifies the song, artist's name and CD title. If you like what you hear, you can buy it immediately by charging it to your cell phone bill or credit card.

It's this big idea that has George Searle, 35, and Humphrey Chen, 31, working 14-hour days building their Berwyn, Pennsylvania, company, ConneXus Corp., the developer of *CD. The idea itself is more than enough to excite investors, but the partners' Harvard MBAs add even more appeal.

Even so, Searle and Chen's initial pitch fell short with angel investors. They graduated in 1996 with a business plan for their idea but no funding. Searle returned with his wife and children to his family's farm in Indiana. Chen stayed on the East Coast, in West Orange, New Jersey, closer to the money that would eventually give life to their dream.

After tweaking their business plan, the pair worked a contact at Harvard into a meeting with Burr, Egan, Deleage & Co., the large Boston-based venture capital firm. The million dollars the partners sought was hardly worth the firm's bother. But the power of the idea, cou-

pled with Searle and Chen's earnestness, persuaded it to take a leap.

The initial injection of equity was enough for the partners to secure a venture lease on the computers and technology needed to pull off their *CD concept. A second round of venture capital has since been poured into the business and plans call for *CD to be rolled out in major metropolitan markets nationwide by year-end.

But the money-raising hasn't ended. In fact, it's just started. "It takes constant work to attract the capital required for a national launch," says Searle. "We're always refining ourselves and how we present the opportunity in order to find partners willing to fund our growth."

For companies like ConneXus, raising money from venture capitalists, or, for that matter, from angels and investment bankers, generally happens in four steps: identifying prospects, preparing to contact them, contacting them and closing them. According to Paul Rosenbaum, a managing partner with CEO-mentoring and capital-assistance firm Wayland Partners in Wayland, Massachusetts, "What frequently goes wrong in the process is entrepreneurs jump from step one to step three." Without proper groundwork, he says, their efforts are often for naught. What follows is a primer on getting everything ready to begin dialing for dollars.

1. Sharpen your focus. You must first set your sights on finding what is

called a lead investor. When you're raising money, you can find lots of investors willing to participate for small amounts of your deal. That will ultimately prove troublesome, however, because each investor will demand different terms and conditions, and in the end, the entire effort may consume more time than it's worth. By contrast, a lead investor is a marquee venture firm, investment banker or angel investor that's willing to kick in from 25 to 100 percent of the money; by its very presence in the deal, a lead investor gets all the fence-sitters and small fry to come in as well. When you're raising money, you must focus on finding your lead investor to the exclusion of any others.

2. Form an advisory board. A good strategy for tapping into the right vein of investors is to form an advisory board that contains industry or financial luminaries. Contact the executive director of your trade association, and ask him or her who might be willing candidates to advise and counsel your company through a critical period of growth and expansion.

Advisory boards can be toothless entities, or they can be extremely helpful to a company's development. One way to make them work better is to pay your advisory board members a fee for attending quarterly meetings. Once you've got them paying attention in a constructive manner, you'll find it's a very natural process for them to check their Rolodexes when you bring up the subject of raising money.

3. Secure legal counsel. The act of raising money almost always brings securities laws into play, which means you'll require the help of a lawyer. Hire one early in the process because he or she can help make introductions to the sources of capital you seek.

In fact, if you're a hotshot technology or Internet company, some law firms will actually defer their fees until funds are raised, further increasing the likelihood that your attorney will lead you to investors. In Searle and Chen's case, the partners were fortunate enough to be chosen for a program operated by Boston legal powerhouse Testa Hurwitz & Thibeault LLP. The firm agreed to defer its fees until funding was found for *CD. "They provided us with invaluable legal and business advice upfront for the opportunity to represent us as we grow," says Searle.

4. Figure out your sizzle. Before you speak with investors, you've got to figure out how to describe your company in a way that will make it stick in their minds. According to Rosenbaum, entrepreneurs are often caught off guard when investors ask what the company does, so they drone on about technology or market trends—losing the investor forever.

What does Searle say? "We went through a time when we would trip over how to explain our technology. Then we realized if we simply explained the consumer benefits of our service, investors understood immediately. Now we just say *CD lets you immediately buy the music you're hearing on the radio by picking up your cell phone and dialing *CD," says Searle. "If an investor wants to know more, we'll tell them. But it's not part of our elevator talk."

5. Write a business plan and a business-plan summary. You *must* have a business plan and a business-plan summary ready before you call any investors. "If your initial call is at all successful," Rosenbaum says, "the investor will ask you to send him or her a plan." He adds that your fund-raising efforts will almost certainly fail if you keep investors waiting eight weeks while you feverishly write the plan. In fact, when an investor requests more information, it's got to be there the next day—at the latest.

Another reason you must have a business plan before you talk to investors is that you can't possibly hope to answer the kinds of questions they're going to ask until you've been through the exercise of writing a plan. Most investors don't read business plans cover to cover, nor do they invest money on the basis of reading business plans alone. They invest, Rosenbaum says, after they've been formally and personally presented with the company and opportunity. Therefore, your business plan is more accurately the blueprint for presenting your company and your deal to investors.

A final tip about business plans from Rosenbaum: Never send out a copy of the entire plan after the first conversation, even if the investor asks for it. Send the executive summary instead. Then follow up. If the investor is interested, make sending out the full plan contingent upon meeting face to face.

6. Line up references. Who can vouch for your character? Former employment? Products or services? The time to find out is *before* you contact investors. The reason is simple: If, during your initial conversation, the investor asks to speak with customers or other references, you want to be able to spit out names and numbers right away, not say "I'll get back to you." You may be able to secure the references sure enough, but the question is, Will you be able to get the investor back on the phone again?

7. Get warm-body introductions. Raising money privately is probably dependent as much on personal relationships as it is on the underlying economics of the deal. As a result, you might identify a list of likely investors, but before you try to contact them, you need to work at getting some kind, any kind, of introduction. This personal introduction will lower their guard long enough for them to hear your pitch. Again, here's where advisory boards and the professionals you've retained can render invaluable assistance. For *CD, the introduction came from a professor at Harvard with an in at a venture capital firm. Obviously, you can't get the Good Housekeeping seal of approval with every investor, but some kind of introduction, no matter how distant it is, will dramatically increase your ability to get through to the people with money.

None of these strategies will by itself win the day, says Rosenbaum. But falling short on any one of them could very easily lose the day. "All your efforts must be focused on moving the process forward," he says. "If you're being reactive, you're probably not on the right track."

David R. Evanson's newest book about raising capital is called Where to Go When the Bank Says No: Alternatives for Financing Your Business *(Bloomberg Press). Call (800) 233-4830 for ordering information. He is a principal of Financial Communications Associates in Ardmore, Pennsylvania. Art Beroff, a principal of Beroff Associates in Howard Beach, New York, helps companies raise capital and go public.*

Venture Capitalists' Assessment of New Venture Survival

This study investigates whether VCs' assessment policies of new venture survival are consistent with those arising from the strategy literature (using two established strategy perspectives). Strategy scholars suggest the nature of the markets, competition, and decisions made by the management team affect a new venture's survival chances. The findings demonstrate that VCs' assessment policies are predominantly consistent with those proposed by strategy scholars—providing insight into why VCs consider certain criteria in their assessment of new venture survival as well as why some criteria are more important in their assessment than others. Through this increased understanding of venture capitalists' decision making, entrepreneurs seeking capital may be better able to address their requests for funding to those criteria venture capitalists find most critical to the survival of a new venture. Venture capitalists may use these findings to better understand their own decision making process, which, in turn, provides the opportunity to increase evaluation efficiency.

(Venture Capital; Decision Models; New Venture Strategy; Survival; Conjoint Analysis)

Dean A. Shepherd

Introduction

The majority of research on VCs' decision making has produced empirically derived lists of VCs' "espoused" criteria—criteria they report they use when evaluating either global measures of performance (c.f., MacMillan et al. 1987) or likely profitability (c.f., Roure and Keeley 1990). Few researchers have investigated VCs' assessment of new venture survival. This is surprising considering Tyebjee and Bruno's (1984) finding that VCs' investment decisions can be predicted from their perceptions of risk (new venture failure) and return. It appears that global measures of new venture performance may fail to capture the complexity of a VC's task. On the other hand, although studies investigating VCs' assessments of profitability are no doubt advancing the field, they need to be supplemented with studies of probability of survival assessments.

There is substantial evidence from strategy research that suggests strategic factors impact the survival chances of new ventures (c.f., Lieberman and Montgomery 1988, Bruderl et al. 1992). However, do VCs follow the decision logic reported in strategy research? The theory from the strategy literature used in this study is contingent upon the issues raised by the "industrial organization" (IO) and "population ecology" perspectives. The IO strategy perspective deals with the competitive positioning of the firm. The population ecology perspective deals with the firm's liabilities of newness—encapsulating those factors that have the greatest impact on new firm mortality. The concomitant consideration of these issues enables us to determine whether the VCs' assessment of a venture is consistent with whether the venture will actually survive (as predicted by strategy research). This approach addresses some of the theoretical limitations of previous research into VCs' decision making.

However, limitations of previous research into VC decision making also arise from the research methods used. Such limitations include problems of retrospective reporting (c.f., Tyebjee and Bruno 1984), use of questionnaire responses rather than actual evaluations (c.f., MacMillan et al. 1987) and biases and errors associated with self-reporting (c.f., Hisrich and Jankowitz 1990). Previous research has typically investigated what Argyris and Schon (1974) refer to as "espoused theories of action" as opposed to "theories in use."

Furthermore, few researchers to date have acknowledged that there may be a difference in a VC's decision policy for businesses in different stages of development. For example, we can expect that a VC's assessment policy for a new venture searching for seed, start up, or development capital may be different from the assessment policy for an established business searching for mezzanine capital.

This study addresses some of the theory and research method limitations of previous research into VC decision making by investigating whether VCs' *"in use" assessment policies of new venture survival are consistent with those arising from the strategy literature predominantly from an IO strategy perspective.*

The study proceeds as follows: First, the strategy literature is reviewed and hypotheses are generated and directed at the research question above. Second, data collection is discussed, including a description of the sample and the survey instrument used. Third, conjoint analysis is used to determine if the strategic considerations suggested by strategy scholars are actually those used by VCs to predict a venture's survival. Fourth, the results are reviewed and discussed in terms of the strategy literature and our understanding of VCs' decision making. Finally, the implications of this study to future research and to VCs and entrepreneurs are discussed.

Literature Review: Strategic Management

There is substantial evidence from the strategy literature that strategic factors impact the performance/survival chances of new ventures (c.f., Lieberman and Montgomery 1988). Central to IO strategy research is an understanding of the nature of the **markets** (Williamson 1985, Golder and Tellis 1993) in which a new venture will compete and the nature of **competitive** interactions between firms in those markets (Schmalensee 1982, Yip 1982). The **management** team must then decide where to position the new venture in order to achieve its competitive advantage (Besanko et al. 1996). In conjunction with this IO strategy perspective, we consider findings from a population ecology perspective of strategy that as new ventures learn over time about their internal and external environments they increase their probability of survival.

The literature review below addresses considerations of the market, considerations of competition, and finally the ability of management to choose and establish a viable position. A series of hypotheses are generated that propose VCs follow the decision logic proposed by strategy scholars. These hypotheses are then empirically investigated.

Market Considerations

IO strategy researchers propose that superior performance arises from a fit between the competencies of a venture and the key success factors of an industry (Andrews 1987). **Key success factors** *represent the requirements necessary for success within a particular industry.* Therefore a new venture team must commit to a number of key factors

they believe will lead to success within the competitive environment (Slater 1993). However, if the competitive environment changes, so too may the key success factors rendering the venture at a competitive disadvantage (Aaker and Day 1986, Golder and Tellis 1993). For example, if a new venture commits to a new technology, it faces the risk that as alternate technologies emerge, its technology will not perform as expected, and/or there will be little or no demand (Williamson 1985, Aaker and Day 1986). Similarly, shifts in consumers' tastes may place the new venture at a competitive disadvantage (Golder and Tellis 1993). Therefore if the key success factors are **unstable** (i.e., *requirements necessary for success will likely change radically during industry development*), a new venture is likely to face a high degree of technical and demand uncertainty (Nelson and Winter 1982).

If firms could readily adapt to changing key success factors, a "good fit" with the environment could be maintained. However, organizational inertia makes such change difficult (Boeker 1989). For example, there is a tendency to counter environmental threats by investing research funds into improving the current technology (Aaker and Day 1986), and/or solving new problems using inappropriate methods (Nelson and Winter 1982). These responses are often combined with a reluctance to withdraw too quickly from mature technologies that are highly profitable (Yip 1982).[1]

On the other hand, if key success factors within an industry remain **stable** (i.e., *requirements necessary for success are unlikely to change radically during industry development*), early commitment to a new technology and customers is likely to provide a sustainable competitive position and thereby a higher probability of survival. **Survival** is defined as: *the probability that this venture will continue to participate in the market.* The above discussion leads to Hypothesis 1.

HYPOTHESIS 1. *VCs' assessment of the probability of survival is significantly higher for ventures facing stable key success factors than those facing unstable key success factors.*[2]

Common wisdom from the strategy literature suggests that timing of entry, as well as key success factor stability, affects performance—pioneers have higher returns if they are successful (DeCastro and Chrisman 1995), but bear a higher risk of failure (Aaker and Day 1986, Mitchell 1991). A **pioneer** *enters a new industry first* and a **late follower** *enters an industry late in the industry's stage of development.* The higher risk of failure for pioneers, relative to later followers, is associated with higher levels of uncertainty. For instance, as a pioneer creates an industry, there is often uncertainty whether there will be sufficient market to sustain survival. Furthermore, customers may be reluctant to substitute out of a market in which they feel comfortable and into one whose future is uncertain (Lambkin and Day 1989).

Late followers are better able to recognize the attractiveness of a market and are able to minimize the costs of entry through cutting R&D corners and/or leap-frogging the pioneering technology (Yip 1982, Harrison and Fiet forthcoming). Some entrepreneurs decide not to pioneer with unproven technology or an unproven market, but wait until more information is available about customers' tastes and behavior so as to provide a product that better meets their needs (Peters and Waterman 1982). In doing so they learn from the pioneer's mistakes (Prahalad and Hamel 1990). This increased certainty, coupled with a reduced strain on resources, increases the probability of survival of later entrants over pioneers (Mitchell 1991).[3] The above discussion leads to Hypothesis 2:

HYPOTHESIS 2. *VCs' assessment of the probability of survival is higher for later followers than for pioneers.*

Competition Considerations

In newly established industries, pioneers need to create and develop entry barriers to avoid having their positions eroded by new competitors who can successfully imitate them. Entry barriers provide the pioneer an opportunity to operate in their industry for a grace period under conditions of limited competitive rivalry (with the possible exception of substitute products). Therefore barriers to entry initially provide a pioneer a lead time, and thereafter minimize competitive rivalry within the industry. **Lead time** *refers to the period of monopoly for the first entrant prior to competitors entering the industry* and **competitive rivalry** *refers to the level of competition among industry members during industry development.*

Together, lead time and subsequent competitive rivalry provide greater understanding of new venture performance by identifying how an advantage is obtained and the means by which it slowly reduces over time.[4] High barriers to entry can lengthen a new venture's lead time, providing important advantages including helping the venture strengthen its brand name (Schmalensee 1982), broaden its product line (Robinson and Fornell 1985), and achieve cost advantages through experience effects (Abell and Hammond 1979).

A long lead time (i.e., *an extended period of monopoly*) also provides time for a venture to learn new tasks, to invent and overcome conflict in new roles, to develop an informal structure, to create stable links with stakeholders, and to develop some organizational inertia and stability that will encourage customer trust. In other words, in the absence of industry competitors, lead time allows a new venture to increase its probability of survival (Freeman et al. 1983, Carroll and Huo 1986, Halliday et al. 1987). The subsequent level of competitive rivalry can also impact performance—as the level of competitive rivalry increases, so too does the risk of business failure (Keeley et al. 1996). This discussion is reflected in the following two hypotheses.

HYPOTHESIS 3. *VCs' assessment of the probability of survival is higher for long lead times than for short lead times.*

HYPOTHESIS 4. *VCs' assessment of the probability of survival is significantly higher for ventures facing low competitive rivalry than for those facing high competitive rivalry.*

Management Capability Considerations

As discussed under market considerations there is often considerable uncertainty about future demand (Fiet 1995). New ventures often need to educate the market about their product and persuade potential customers that the benefits of purchase are greater than the risks (Slater 1993). Once a frame of reference has been created and customers are convinced that product benefits outweigh the risks associated with newness, the new venture may have been able to establish a market presence and the legitimacy that comes with it.

However, a customer's frame of reference and market legitimacy can be difficult and costly (in terms of both human and financial resources) for the new venture to construct. If a venture already possesses these resources, it has educational capability that can be directed towards performing original market research and necessary market development (Stinchcombe 1965). Therefore **educational capability** *refers to the amount of resources and skills available to overcome market ignorance through education.*

Ventures with high educational capability can more rapidly develop stable links with stakeholders, decrease customer uncertainty, and engender customer trust, thereby increasing the firm's probability of survival (Stinchcombe 1965, Hannan and Freeman 1989). Furthermore, a strong effort at educating the market may also signal to customers the commitment of the new venture's managers to their product (Bradenburger and Nalebluff 1996). The above discussion leads to Hypothesis 5.

HYPOTHESIS 5. *VCs' assessment of the probability of survival is significantly higher for ventures with high educational capability than for those with low educational capability.*

Although VCs are expected to consider management's educational capability in their assessment of likely new venture survival, Dunne et al. (1989) propose that firms also need to be investigated in light of management experience in related industries. **Industry related competence** *refers to the level of experience and knowledge with the industry being entered, or a related industry.* It appears success is more likely to be achieved by those entering an industry in which the management team has prior experience (Roure and Maidique 1986, Cooper 1986). Roure and Maidique (1986) found that successful founders had experience in rapid growth firms that competed in the same industry as the start up. Opportunities often occur too quickly to be able to be grasped by someone from outside the industry; they must possess the necessary skills a priori (Feeser and Willard 1990). It appears industry specific human capital is a significant determinant of venture survival (Cooper et al. 1988, Bruderl et al. 1992). The above discussion leads to Hypothesis 6.

HYPOTHESIS 6. *VCs' assessment of the probability of survival is significantly higher for ventures with high industry related competence than for those with low industry related competence.*

Relative Importance of Decision Criteria

The current literature on VCs' decision making suggests the management team is important and often ranked as the most important criterion (c.f., Dixon 1991, MacMillan et al. 1987). Why is the quality of the management team so important to VCs? The strategy literature above suggests that uncertainty plays an important role in the survival chances of new ventures; for example, uncertainty over demand, technology, and competition as well as customers' uncertainty about a new venture's market offerings. We propose that while the market considerations (key success factor stability and timing) and competition considerations (lead time and competitive rivalry) are no doubt important, especially in retrospect, they are difficult for a VC to assess in prospect. They are difficult to predict due to the enormous environmental uncertainty typically surrounding a new venture. We propose one way a VC manages such uncertainty is to choose a management team they believe will be able to cope with expected and unexpected changes in the market and competitive environment, i.e., a management team with high educational capability and high industry related competence. This leads to the final hypothesis:

HYPOTHESIS 7(a). *In their assessment of new venture survival, VCs place higher importance on industry related competence than they do on key success factor stability, timing of entry, lead time, or competitive rivalry.*

HYPOTHESIS 7(b). *In their assessment of new venture survival, VCs place higher importance on educational capability than they do on key success factor stability, timing of entry, lead time, or competitive rivalry.*

In sum, strategy researchers (utilizing primarily an IO strategy perspective) suggest that the nature of the market, the competitive interactions between firms, and the abilities of the management team to establish a viable position in the market are central to understanding firm survival. This leads to a number of hypothesized relationships that we would expect VCs to consider if their decision policies are consistent with whether the venture actually will survive (as predicted by strategy research). Specifically, VCs' assessment of probability of survival is significantly higher for ventures facing high key success factor stability, that are late followers, have

long lead times, low competitive rivalry, high educational capability, and high industry related competence. The research method to empirically test the above hypothesized relationships is now described.

Research Method

Sampling Plan, Survey Method, and Sample. The 1996 Australian Venture Capital Guide (Pollitecon Publications 1996), a comprehensive guide to Australia's venture capital industry, and the 1995 Australian Development Capital Directory (Australian Department of Industry, Science and Technology 1995) were used to identify potential firms and participants. Firms listed in either guide and based in Australia with preferred investments in seed, start up, and/or development capital were considered as the sampling frame of VCs in Australia. The senior executives of each firm in the sampling plan were targeted for this study. It is estimated the Australian venture capital industry consists of 65 private venture capital firms with a total of 350 professional staff, $4 billion invested capital, $1 billion available capital, a current portfolio of 958 companies, with 655 completed investments (Pollitecon Publications 1996).[5]

Two methods of data collection were used: (1) experiment collected by author, and (2) experiment sent by mail. For reasons of resource efficiency the author personally collected only those responses from VCs located in Australia's three largest cities. Analysis of variance was performed on the importance weights of those responses collected through mail and those collected by the author. The two methods of data collection were not significantly different, consequently the two groups of responses were treated as one.

Sixty-six individual VCs representing 47 venture capital firms completed the survey capturing Australia's most senior VCs with Directors, Managing Directors, Executive Chairmen, General Managers, and CEOs representing 52% of the sample. Senior managers constitute a further 42% with only 6% of the sample accounted for by analysts. This represents a 65% response rate in terms of participating venture capital firms and a 19% response rate in terms of total professional VCs.[6] A comparison of VC firms in the study and those that did not participate reveal no significant difference in year established, number of professional staff, types of investment, total capital, completed divestments, and current number of portfolio companies (comparison data obtained from the Australian Venture Capital Guide (Pollitecon Publications 1996)). Given the similarity between participating and nonparticipating firms there is unlikely to be a nonresponse bias.

Attributes, Levels, and Dependent Variable. In this study, VCs evaluate a series of hypothetical conjoint profiles which describe new ventures in terms of eight attributes, each with two levels: (1) Stability of Key Success

Factors, (2) Timing of Entry, (3) Lead Time, (4) Competitive Rivalry, (5) Industry Related Competence, (6) Educational Capability, (7) Mimicry, and (8) Scope. The attributes of mimicry and scope were used as control variables. Attributes, levels, and definitions are provided earlier in the literature review. Attribute levels were chosen to represent variation that typically occurs in the decision environment of VCs, thereby maintaining believability and response validity. A pretest with VCs, accountants, and academics confirmed the face validity for both the attributes and their levels.

Survival (the probability that this venture will continue to participate in the market using a ten-year time horizon) is represented by an eleven-point scale with end anchors describing "very low probability of survival" and "very high probability of survival." Continued market participation is frequently used as a definition of survival (Lambkin and Day 1989). Biggadike (1979) and McDougall et al. (1994) find that, after eight years, new ventures begin to resemble the characteristics of an established venture. A ten-year time horizon was chosen, as it appears reasonable to assume ten years captures the transition from a new venture to an established business.[7]

Research Instrument and Experimental Design. The research instrument contained a cover letter, task instructions, the conjoint decision making experiment, and a post-experiment questionnaire that asked respondents to answer questions regarding characteristics of themselves and their firm. Relevant term definitions were also included on a detachable sheet that could be referred to while completing the survey. Once instructions were understood, respondents considered each conjoint venture description and provided a rating on an 11-point scale for the dependent measure—probability of survival.

For the conjoint experiment, an orthogonal fractional factorial design was used to reduce the number of attribute combinations and thus make the decision making task more manageable (Green and Srinivasan 1990). Each of the eight attributes was varied at two levels in a fractional factorial design consisting of 16 profiles (Hahn and Shapiro 1966). The original profiles were replicated to permit estimates of individual subject error for use in subsequent statistical analysis and allow a test-retest measure of reliability. These 32 profiles were randomly assigned to avoid order effects. A practice case and six hold-out cases were also used. The practice case familiarized respondents with the task and the six hold-out cases were used to test the models' predictive ability. Therefore the experiment presented VCs with 39 profiles to evaluate. The experimental design enabled both individual subject level and aggregate subject-level analyses.

Analysis. This study uses conjoint analysis to determine if strategic VC considerations reported by strategy scholars are actually those used to predict a new venture's survival. **Conjoint analysis** *is a general term referring to a technique that requires respondents to make a series of judgments based on a set of attributes (cues) from which the underlying structure of their cognitive system can be investigated* (Shepherd and Zacharakis 1997). From this series of judgments, the respondent's decisions can be decomposed, thus providing the researcher an opportunity to investigate the underlying structure of the decisions. Importantly, this technique avoids the use of retrospective and self-reported data by collecting information about a decision as that decision is made (Zacharakis and Meyer 1998).

Regression and analysis of variance (ANOVA) are the statistical techniques used to decompose the decision, e.g., regression decomposes an assessment into its underlying structure as represented by the independent variables and their corresponding beta coefficients. The conjoint technique allows analysis at both the individual and aggregate subject level, which improves the predictive ability of the research (c.f., Moore 1980).

To identify attributes statistically significant at the aggregate level, the regression coefficient (β) for each attribute (derived from the individual-subject level of analysis) are averaged across individuals with the sign of the β indicating the nature of the relationship (Vancouver and Morrison 1995). The mean βs represent a model of the sample's decision making. A **Z-statistic** *aggregates the t-statistics derived from the individual-subject analysis for that attribute to identify whether a particular attribute is significantly used by the sample* (Dechow et al. 1994).

Although two or more attributes may significantly affect the decision process, it is unlikely that those attributes will be of equal importance. Therefore the significance at the aggregate level of analysis is supplemented with a measure of relative importance—Hays' (1973) omega squared (ω^2). **Omega Squared** *is a measure of explained variance, and is used to assess the relative importance of the attributes.* The mean omega-squared values corresponding to all main effects were calculated. Predictive ability of individual and aggregate decision making models were tested using a Pearson R correlation between the observed score on six hold-out profiles and a predicted score calculated by the decision model(s). A VC's decision model contained a constant and a regression coefficient for each of the independent variables. Sixteen replicated profiles were used in a test-retest measure with the original 16 profiles using Pearson R correlations to test the consistency of responses for each respondent.

Results

Table 1 displays the aggregated regression coefficients for each factor, its corresponding Z score, and omega-squared value. At the aggregate level of analysis, the Z scores indicate that: Key success factor stability, timing, lead time, competitive rivalry, educational capability, and industry-related competence are significant in VCs' assessment of probability of survival, i.e., their Z scores exceed 1.645. The sign for the mean regression coefficient for each significant main effect indicates the variable level

VCs associated with higher probability of survival, i.e., high key success factor stability (Hypothesis 1), pioneering (H2), long lead time (H3), low competitive rivalry (H4), high educational capability (H5) and high industry-related competence (H6). Therefore Hypotheses 1, 3, 4, 5, and 6 are all supported. Hypothesis 2 was not supported. VCs' significantly used timing of entry in their decision making although in the opposite direction to that hypothesized, i.e., VCs assess a pioneering venture with a higher probability of survival than the probability of survival for a late follower.

Table 1   Significance and Importance of Decision Criteria

Decision Criteria	β Coefficient	Z Score	Omega Squared
Key Success Factor			
Stability	0.88	10.52*	0.05
Timing of Entry	0.69	3.57*	0.07
Lead Time	0.66	8.02*	0.03
Competitive Rivalry	0.97	12.14*	0.06
Educational Capability	1.15	14.04*	0.10
Industry Related Competence	2.14	37.77*	0.29
Control Variables			
Scope	0.04	0.18	0.02
Mimicry	0.23	2.46*	0.02

*significant $p < 0.05$

On average, the most important criteria for VCs in their assessment of a new venture's probability of survival is industry related competence ($\omega^2 = 0.29$), educational capability ($\omega^2 = 0.10$), timing ($\omega^2 = 0.07$), competitive rivalry ($\omega^2 = 0.06$), key success factor stability ($\omega^2 = 0.05$), and then lead time ($\omega^2 = 0.03$).[8] This supports Hypotheses 7(a) and 7(b) (i.e., VCs place higher importance on industry-related competence and educational capability than they do on key success factor stability, timing of entry, lead time, or competitive rivalry). The predictive ability of an individual model with its respective six hold-out profiles was significant for 73% of the VCs ($p < 0.05$), with a mean R^2 of 0.78. The aggregate model also demonstrated predictive ability, significantly predicting the decision policy of 75% of the VCs ($p < 0.05$) with a mean R^2 of 0.78. Ninety-two percent of VCs had significantly reliable responses. Mean test-retest correlation for the sample was 0.69 providing assurances that the new venture decision making task was performed consistently by the participants.

Discussion

This study utilized two perspectives of strategy to understand new venture survival—utilizing both the IO strategy and population ecology literatures provided a deeper understanding of new venture survival than if either literature was used alone. Common to both perspectives is the importance of uncertainty and its relationship with new venture survival (i.e., entrepreneur's uncertainty about the future market and competitors' behavior as well as customers' uncertainty over the newly created industry and the "new" business). These strategy perspectives were used to provide a theoretical framework from which to investigate and interpret VCs' assessments of new venture survival.

This study found considerable consistency between the proposed theoretical framework (based on strategy research) and the decision policies of VCs. Such consistency provided the opportunity to use theory to help us understand which attributes VCs consider and why. For example, VCs are likely to consider the probability of survival higher for those new ventures that have lower market and industry uncertainty. Furthermore, IO strategy scholars suggest the strategic choices that an entrepreneur makes can impact the survival chances of the firm—the environment will change in unexpected ways and it is important that the new venture be able to recognize those changes and respond appropriately. The need to deal with uncertainty provided insight into why VCs place such high importance on the abilities of the management team.

While VCs' assessment of new venture survival was found to be highly consistent with that proposed by strategy scholars, there was one exception. VCs assess a pioneer as having a higher probability of survival than a late follower, whereas strategy scholars, such as Mitchell (1991), suggest the opposite relationship. It appears that despite the issues of uncertainty and lack of legitimacy facing a pioneer, VCs believe the advantages of being early typically outweigh these initial disadvantages.

Does this represent an opportunity for VCs to improve their assessment of new venture survival (i.e., learn from, and conform with, the relationship between timing and new venture survival proposed by strategy scholars)? Alternatively, is there greater complexity in the relationship between timing and survival that VCs perceive yet is being missed by strategy scholars? For example, maybe the relationship between timing and new venture survival is contingent upon attributes not detailed in the strategy literature (and therefore not included in this study) yet are perceived and used by VCs. This question deserves further consideration by researchers of both strategy and VCs' decision making.

Possible Limitations

Conjoint analysis is used in this study because it accounts for a number of biases and errors that are pervasive in previous research. This study focuses on concurrent, rather than retrospective, techniques of obtaining and analyzing decision making. The technique itself has limitations. Through design of this study and its instrument, these limitations have been addressed (eliminated or minimized).

One such issue is this study's use of hypothetical ventures and environments. However, research into a variety of judgments provides evidence that hypothetical representations are useful for capturing real policies (c.f., Chaput de Saintonge and Hathaway 1981, Riquelme and Rickards 1992). "Professional judgment may therefore involve some abstract coding of the cues, similar to that provided by policy capturing tasks" (Brehmer and Brehmer 1988, p. 89). Use of hypothetical ventures and environments in conjoint analysis is still open to a threat of external validity but is a step towards actual decision making, i.e., more valid inferences can be made using conjoint analysis than those studies based on espoused criteria alone (Stewart 1993).

Sometimes an orthogonal cue set (as used in this study) can lead to the presentation of a profile that simply does not exist in the judge's experience, resulting in possible inconsistency. However, in the pretest all cases were deemed realistic.

There may also be questions regarding the generalizability of the results. The sample included only Australian VCs. Some study participants commented that Australian VCs are similar to those from the United States due to similarities in education,[9] training, types of investments, as well as the deregulation of the financial industry, which permitted a number of foreign VC firms to enter the Australian industry. However, other study participants commented that the Australian VC industry was relatively new (less than ten years old) and therefore not as mature as the VC industry in the United States or United Kingdom. Therefore, while Australian VCs are likely to be highly similar to those of the United States and United Kingdom, care must be taken in generalizing these results outside Australia.

Conclusion

This study investigated whether VCs' "in use" assessment policies of new venture survival are consistent with those proposed in the strategy literature. The primary finding of this study is that VCs' assessment policies are predominantly consistent with those proposed by strategy scholars. Such consistency provides an opportunity to utilize established theories to help us understand why VCs consider certain criteria in their assessment of new venture survival as well as why some criteria are more important in their assessment than others. VCs consider the level of uncertainty and the ability of the management team to minimize and/or deal with changes in the external environment in their assessment of new venture survival. This approach addressed some of the theoretical limitations of previous research into VCs' decision making.

This study also addressed research method limitations of previous research by (1) acknowledging potential differences in a VC's decision policy for business in different

stages of development and (2) investigating the "in-use" decision policies of VCs rather than their "espoused theories of action."

Therefore this study increases our understanding of how VCs assess a new venture in terms of its likely survival. Such an understanding could help entrepreneurs better address their requests for funding to those criteria VCs believe to be most important. Moreover, new ventures that lack a management team with industry-related competence and educational capability would be well advised to acquire these qualities before seeking venture capital or be prepared for the VC to require an appropriate management team be put in place. VCs may use these findings to better understand their own assessment policies, which, in turn, provides the opportunity to increase evaluation efficiency. A better understanding of the "in use" assessment policies of experienced VCs could also help train inexperienced VCs to make more accurate assessments of new venture proposals.

This study leads to other opportunities for future research, namely, more VC decision making scholars need to utilize theory to drive their research. This is the first study, to the author's knowledge, to use an overarching theory to derive the criteria to be investigated in VCs' assessment of new venture survival. However, we are not proposing that strategy is the only literature that can provide insight into VCs' decision policies; in fact we encourage the investigation of VCs' decisions from a number of different theoretical perspectives. Not only might the use of different theories provide a deeper understanding of VCs' decision policies but these different theories could provide avenues for VCs to improve the accuracy of their assessments. Similarly, using theoretical frameworks to study the "in-use" decision policies of expert VCs might provide important feedback to current theories suggesting the need for theory modifications and/or new theories.

Further research is still required into the "in-use" decision policies of VCs in their assessments of different aspects of performance and for businesses in different stages of development. We know that VCs' overall investment decision can be predicted from their risk and return perceptions, but little empirical research has been done into how VCs combine these two perceptions to form an overall evaluation of investment potential.

This study focuses on VCs' assessment of new ventures, i.e., investment proposals seeking seed to development capital. An interesting question then becomes: Do VCs weight criteria differently in their assessments of businesses in different stages of development? For example, where uncertainties over the future environmental conditions and the appropriateness of specific strategies are reduced (e.g., mezzanine financing or leveraged buyouts), do VCs rely less on the quality of the management team in their assessment of a firm's probability of survival? Do VCs use different criteria for their assessments of businesses in later stages of development? Do VCs weight and/or use different criteria for their assessments of likely profitability or for global measures of success? Much important research remains to be done.

Appendix A
Attributes, Levels, and Definitions

Criteria	Levels	Definition
Key Success Factor Stability	High	requirements necessary for success will not change radically during industry development
	Low	requirements necessary for success will change radically during industry development
Timing of Entry	Pioneer	enters a new industry first
	Late Follower	enters an industry late in the industry's stage of development
Lead Time	Long	an extended period of monopoly for the first entrant prior to competitors entering the industry
	Short	a minimal period of monopoly for the first entrant prior to competitors entering this industry
Competitive Rivalry	High	intense competition among industry members during industry development
	Low	little competition among industry members during industry development
Educational Capability	High	considerable resources and skills available to overcome market ignorance through education
	Low	few resources or skills available to overcome market ignorance through education
Industry Related Competence	High	venturer has considerable experience and knowledge with the industry being entered or a related industry
	Low	venturer has minimal experience and knowledge with the industry being entered or related industry
Control Variables		
Scope	Broad	a firm that spreads its resources across a wide spectrum of the market
	Narrow	a firm that concentrates on intensively exploiting a small segment of the market
Entry Wedge Mimicry	High	considerable limitation of the mechanisms used by other firms to enter this, or any other industry, e.g., a franchisee
	Low	minimal imitation of the mechanisms used by other firms to enter this, or any other industry e.g., introducing a new product

Appendix B
CASE 3: Venture AMN

1. This venture's entry wedge mimicry—*low*.
2. This venture's educational capability— *low*.
3. This venture's timing of entry—*late follower*.
4. This venture's market scope—*broad*.
5. This venture's industry related competence—*low*.
6. The industry's first entrant's lead time—*short*.
7. The industry's competitive rivalry—*low*.
8. The industry's key success factor stability—*high*.

Assessment 3: Probability of Survival

Based on the above venture description (using a 10 year time horizon), how would you rate the probability that this venture will survive? (Circle the number that best represents your response)

Very Low Probability of Survival   1 2 3 4 5 6 7 8 9 10 11   Very High Probability of Survival

References

Aaker, D. A., G. S. Day. 1986. The perils of high growth markets. *Strategic Management J.* **7** 409–421.

Abell, D. F., J. Hammond. 1979. *Strategic Market Planning: Problems and Analytical Approaches*. Prentice Hall, Englewood Cliffs, NJ.

Andrews, K. R. 1987. *The Concept of Corporate Strategy*. Irwin, Homewood, IL.

Argyris, C., D. Schon. 1974. *Theory in Practice*. Jossey-Bass, San Francisco, CA.

Australian Department of Industry, Science and Technology. 1995. *Australian Development Capital Directory*. Australian Government Publishing Service, Canberra, Australia.

Besanko, D., D. Dranove, M. Shanley. 1996. *Economics of Strategy*. Wiley, New York.

Biggadike, R. E. 1979. The risky business of diversification. *Harvard Bus. Rev.* **57**(3) 103–111.

Boeker, W. 1989. Strategic change: the effects of founding and history. *Acad. Management J.* **32** 489–515.

Brandenburger, A. M., B. J. Nalebluff. 1996. *Coopetition*. Doubleday, New York.

Brehmer, A., B. Brehmer. 1988. What have we learned about human judgment from thirty years of policy capturing? B. Brehmer, C. R. B. Joyce, eds. *Advances in Psychology* 54: *Human Judgment, the SJT View*. Elsevier Science Publishers, Amsterdam, 75–114.

Bruderl, J., P. Preisendorfer, R. Ziegler. 1992. Survival chances of newly founded business organizations. *Amer. Sociological Rev.* **57** 227–242.

Bruno, A. V., T. T. Tyebjee. 1986. The destinies of rejected venture capital deals. *Sloan Management Rev.* **27** 43–53.

Carroll, G. R., Y. P. Huo. 1986. Organizational task and institutional environments—an ecological perspective: Findings from the local newspaper industry. *Amer. J. Sociology* **91** 838–873.

Carter, N. M., T. M. Stearns, P. D. Reynolds, M. Williams. 1992. The effects of industry and founding strategy on new firm survival. *Frontiers of Entrepreneurship Research*. Babson College, Wellesley, MA, 161–172.

Chaput de Saintonge, D. M., H. R. Hathaway. 1981. Antibiotic use in otitis media: patient simulations as an aid to audit. *British Medical J.* **283** 883–884.

Cooper, A. 1986. Entrepreneurship and high technology. D. Sexton, R. Smilor, eds. *The Art and Science of Entrepreneurship*, Ballinger Publishing Company, Cambridge, MA, 153–180.

___, W. C. Dunkelberg, C. Y. Woo. 1988. Survival and failure: a longitudinal study. *Frontiers of Entrepreneurship Research*. Babson College, Wellesley, MA, 225–237.

DeCastro, J. O., J. J. Chrisman. 1995. Order of market entry, competitive strategy and financial performance. *J. Bus. Res.* **33** 165–177.

Dechow, P. M., M. R. Huson, R. G. Sloan. 1994. The effect of restructuring charges on executives' cash compensation. *Accounting Rev.* **69** 138–156.

Dixon, R. 1991. VCs and the appraisal of investments. *OMEGA Internat. J. Management Sci.* **19** 333–344.

Dunne, T., M. J. Roberts, L. Samuelson, D. T. Levy. 1989. Firm entry and post entry performance in the U.S. chemical industries: Comment. *J. Law and Econom.* **32** S233–S275.

Eisenhardt, K. M., C. B. Schoonhoven. 1990. Organizational growth: Linking founding team, strategy, environment, and growth among US semi-conductor ventures, 1978–1988. *Admin. Sci. Quart.* **35** 504–529.

Feeser, H. R., G. E. Willard. 1990. Founding strategy and performance: a comparison of high and low growth high tech firms. *Strategic Management J.* **11** 87–98.

Fiet, J. O. 1995. Risk avoidance strategies in venture capital markets. *J. Management Stud.* **32** 551–574.

Foster, N. 1982. A call for vision in managing technology. *McKinsey Quart.* **Summer** 26–36.

Freeman, J., G. R. Carroll, M. T. Hannan. 1983. The liability of newness: age dependence in organizational death rates. *Amer. Sociological Rev.* **48** 692–710.

Fried, V. H., R. D. Hisrich. 1988. Venture capital research: past, present, and future. *Entrepreneurship: Theory and Practice* **13** 15–28.

Golder, P. N., G. J. Tellis. 1993. Pioneer advantage: marketing logic or marketing legend? *J. Marketing Res.* **30** 158–170.

Green, P. E., V. Srinivasan. 1990. Conjoint analysis in marketing: new developments with implications for research and practice. *J. Marketing* **54**(4) 3–19.

Gross, I. 1979. Insights from pricing strategies. E. Baily, ed. *Pricing Practices and Procedures.* The Conference Board, New York.

Hahn, G., S. Shapiro. 1966. *A Catalogue and Computer Program for the Design and Analysis of Orthogonal Symmetric and Asymmetric Fractional Factorial Designs.* Report No. 66–C–165. General Electric Corporation, Schenectady, NY.

Halliday, T. C., M. J. Powell, M. W. Granfors. 1987. Minimalist organizations: vital events in state bar associations, 1870–1930. *Amer. Sociological Rev.* **52** 456–471.

Hannan, M. T., J. Freeman, 1984. Structural inertia and organizational change. *Amer. Sociological Rev.* **49** 149–164.

___, ___. 1989. *Organizational Ecology.* Harvard University Press, Cambridge, MA.

Harrison, J. S., J. O. Fiet. New CEOs pursue their own self interests by sacrificing shareholder value. *J. Bus. Ethics* (forthcoming).

Hays, W. 1973. *Statistics.* Holt, Rinehart and Winston, New York.

Hisrich, R. D., A. D. Jankowitz. 1990. Intuition in venture capital decisions: an exploratory study using a new technique. *J. Bus. Venturing* **5** 49–62.

Karakaya, F., B. Kobu. 1994. New product development process: an investigation of success and failure in high technology firms. *J. Bus. Venturing* **9** 49–66.

Keeley, R. H., R. Knapp, J. T. Rothe. 1996. High tech vs. non high tech, venture capital vs. non-venture capital: sorting out the effects. *Frontiers of Entrepreneurship Research.* Babson College, Wellesley, MA.

Lambkin, M., G. S. Day. 1989. Evolutionary processes in competitive markets: beyond the product life cycle. *J. Marketing* **53** 4–20.

Lieberman, M. B., D. B. Montgomery. 1988. First mover advantages. *Strategic Management J.* **9** 127–140.

MacMillan, I. C., L. Zemann, P. N. SubbaNarasimha. 1987. Criteria distinguishing successful from unsuccessful ventures in the venture screening process. *J. Bus. Venturing* **2** 123–137.

McDougall, P. P., J. G. Covin, R. B. Robinson, L. Herron. 1994. The effects of industry growth and strategic breadth on new venture performance and strategy content. *Strategic Management J.* **15** 537–554.

Miller, A., R. Wilson, W. Gartner. 1987. Entry strategies of corporate ventures in emerging and mature industries. *Frontiers of Entrepreneurship Research.* Babson College, Wellesley, MA, 496–509.

Mitchell, W. 1991. Dual clocks: entry order influences on incumbent and newcomer market share and survival when specialized assets retain their value. *Strategic Management J.* **12** 85–100.

Moore, W. L. 1980. Levels of aggregation in conjoint analysis: an empirical comparison. *J. Marketing Res.* **17** 516–523.

Muzyka, D., S. Birley, B. Leleux. 1996. Trade-offs in the investment decisions of European VCs. *J. Bus. Venturing* **11** 273–288.

Nelson, R. R., S. G. Winter. 1982. *An Evolutionary Theory of Economic Change.* Harvard University Press, Cambridge, MA.

Peters, T. J., R. H. Waterman. 1982. *In Search of Excellence.* Harper and Row, New York.

Pollitecon Publications 1996. *Australian Venture Capital Guide 1996.* Pollitecon Publications, Australia.

Prahalad, C. K., G. Hamel. 1990. The core competence of the corporation. *Harvard Bus. Rev.* **90**(3) 79–93.

Riquelme, H., T. Rickards. 1992. Hybrid conjoint analysis: an estimation probe in new venture decisions. *J. Bus. Venturing* **7** 505–518.

Robinson, W. T., C. Fornell. 1985. The sources of market pioneer advantages in consumer goods industries. *J. Marketing Res.* **222** 305–317.

Roure, J. B., R. H. Keeley. 1990. Predictors of success in new technology based ventures. *J. Bus. Venturing* **5** 201–220.

___, M. A. Maidique. 1986. Linking prefunding factors and high-technology venture success: an exploratory study. *J. Bus. Venturing* **1** 295–306.

Schmalensee, R. 1981. Economies of scale and barriers to entry. *J. Political Econom.* **89** 1228–1238.

___, 1982. Product differentiation advantages of pioneering brands. *Amer. Econom. Rev.* **72** 349–365.

Shepherd, D. A., A. Zacharakis. 1997. Conjoint analysis: a window of opportunity for entrepreneurship research. J. A. Katz, R. H. Brockhaus, eds. *Advances in Entrepreneurship, Firm Emergence and Growth, Volume 3.* JAI Press, Greenwich, CT, 203–248.

Slater, S. F. 1993. Competing in high velocity markets, *Indust. Marketing Management* **24** 255–268.

Stewart, T. R. 1993. *Notes of the Validity of Judgment Analysis.* Working Paper.

Stinchcombe, A. L. 1965. Social structures and organizations. J. G. March, ed. *Handbook of Organizations,* Rand McNally, Chicago, IL, 142–193.

Tang, M., Z. S. Zannetos. 1992. Competition under continuous technological change. *Managerial and Decision Econom.* **13**(2) 135–148.

Tyebjee. T., A. V. Bruno. 1981. Venture capital decision making: preliminary results from three empirical studies. *Frontiers of Entrepreneurship Research.* Babson College, Wellesley, MA, 316–334.

___, ___. 1984. A model of VC investment activity. *Management Sci.* **30** 1051–1066.

Vancouver, J. B., E. W. Morrison. 1995. Feedback inquiry: the effect of source attributions and individual differences. *Organ. Behavior and Human Decision Process* **62** 276–285.

Williamson, O. E. 1985. *The Economic Institutions of Capitalism: Firms, Markets, Relational Contracting.* Free Press, New York.

Yip, G. S. 1982. *Barriers to Entry.* Lexington Books, D. C. Heath and Company, Lexington, MA.

Zacharakis, A., G. D. Meyer. 1998. A lack of insight: do venture capitalists really understand their own decision processes? *J. Bus. Venturing* **13** 57–76.

Notes

1. Decisions to persist with outdated technology are often poor investments due to the law of diminishing returns (Foster 1982) and difficulty associated with transferring the link with old customers to new opportunities (Mitchell 1991).

2. The levels and definitions for all attributes are displayed in Appendix A.

3. Of course later entry may restrict the venture's upside potential (profitability), which is beyond the scope of this paper.

4. Barriers to entry provide a competitive shield (or act as an isolating mechanism) for industry members and may take many forms; for example, technological leadership (Lieberman and Montgomery 1988); consumer-based information advantages (Schmalensee 1982); and exclusive access to certain distribution channels (Karakaya and Kobu 1994).

5. There are also six government or semigovernment institutions involved in the equity funding of new ventures. These six firms were also included in the sampling plan. There was no significant difference in the decision making of private and public VCs, although small sample sizes for this statistical test would make it difficult to detect such a difference.

6. Some firms had more than one VC participate in the study. The results of this study did not vary significantly when the data were reanalyzed including the responses of only one VC per venture capital firm.

7. Although VCs typically harvest the business within eight years, they are often selling future cash flows extending to, and beyond, this ten-year period.

8. The control variables were relatively unimportant in VCs' assessments of survival.

9. A number of Australian VCs had MBAs from U.S. institutions. Furthermore, Australian business schools are modeled after their U.S. counterparts.

Accepted by Ralph Katz; received July 1997....

University of Colorado, College of Business, Campus Box 419, Boulder, Colorado 80309–0419 and Lally School of Management, Rensselaer Polytechnic Institute, Troy, New York 12180–3590 dean.shepherd@colorado.edu

From *Management Science*, May 1999, pp. 621-632. © 1999 by Dean A. Shepherd. Reprinted by permission.

Entrepreneur in residence

Five things to remember when raising money

By Ross Garber

When it comes to raising venture capital these days, it's silly season out there. There's too much capital to be invested, and valuations for companies are out of control at every stage. More than one VC has recently admitted to me that "in this market, anybody can get anything funded at any price." In effect, too much available cash has turned venture-backed financing into a faster-moving and sloppier game. As an adviser to several startups, I see this contributing to a decline in entrepreneurial discipline. At the same time, VCs are protecting themselves against high valuations by driving harsher terms of doing business.

So if you're tempted to play in the VC-funded startup arena, here are some thoughts I'd encourage you to consider.

Start with reality in mind. Fact: most startups fail. Raising venture capital isn't the same as getting on Who Wants to Be a Millionaire. And creating long-term, realizable value is not as easy as (1) raise a bunch of cash, (2) hire lots of people, (3) spend like mad on a brand, (4) take it public, and (5) get rich! The secret to successful fund-raising is to remember that you're trying to maximize the value of your company over a long period of time. So manage your fund-raising as a multiphase process, not as a one-time event.

This means that you must build a disciplined company. Even though you could conceivably raise capital without drafting a detailed business plan, write one anyway. It'll force you to think through your business and find the holes. Don't lie to yourself by showing revenues reaching a gazillion dollars in four years. It never happens. Create fund-raising start and finish dates, and stay active with the VCs only during that period.

Time your financing. The best times to fund-raise are when your company crosses major inflection points—events that significantly increase your valuation and thus reduce the cost of the capital you take. Always raise enough cash to get to the next inflection point, and don't mess up on execution and miss the deliverables. When my partner and I raised Vignette (Nasdaq: VIGN)'s seed round in 1995, we sold 16 percent of the company for $400,000 cash. At Vignette's current valuation, we each sacrificed $600 million in future wealth to get the company going. I'm sure glad that we finished our prototype in time to get the step-up in valuation on our next round.

Get the best deal, not the best price. Think one step ahead and optimize your current round so that it sets you up for the highest valuation on your next round. I call this the "moon-shot approach": rather than taking a straight-line trajectory, first whip around the Earth for maximum acceleration. And when it comes to the term sheet, avoid being abused on preferred stockholder rights like the infamous "preferred participation," or "double dip," feature; don't allow your board to be overrun with VC directors; and make sure that voting rights are structured so that all your VCs have an incentive to work together .

Pick the right investors—quickly. Entrepreneurs often spend way too much time schmoozing VCs, hoping to get the absolutely coolest firms into their deals. Don't worry so much about the VC beauty pageant. There's a group of VCs in the upper 25 percent of quality, and any one of them will get you to about the same place. Just pick the personalities you'll work best with, and get back to running your company.

Consider all your options. There are several mainstream financing alternatives that didn't exist a few years ago. For early-stage financing, VCs are your best choice: they know how to place the right people near you to assist in the company-building process. As your company matures, consider one of the crossover players like Attractor Investment Management or Pivotal Asset Management—one part VC and two parts public-markets money manager. They're less sensitive to valuation than traditional VCs and will be less likely to demand active roles in the oversight of your firm. For late-stage financing, investigate the investment banking option; they're best equipped to help you focus on IPO and public-company issues.

Ultimately, the entrepreneurs who create the most realizable value are those who approach each financing as if it's one in a series of football plays. A 50-yard bomb or a short-yardage pass may be the best call, depending on where you are in your drive downfield toward an IPO.

Ross Garber is the cofounder of Vignette, an e-business software vendor. Write to letters@redherring.com.

From *Red Herring*, March 2000, p. 92. © 2000 by Red Herring Communications.

CAPITAL

The VC On The Corner

Banks—and not just big banks—have started to eye growth companies as targets for private-equity investments

Jill Andresky Fraser

When you think about everything a good bank could offer you, are you focused on a credit line? If you are, it may be time to refocus your priorities.

That's because a growing number of banks—large and small—are setting up venture arms to invest in private-equity deals with entrepreneurial companies. At a time when volatility in the stock market, reduced venture-capital investment, and a range of other economic concerns have put some constraints on capital raising, banks' increased involvement as investors is one trend that is moving in the right direction for business owners.

"There are so many banks doing these kinds of deals now that they've quickly become a standard source of financing to pursue," says Gordon Tunstall, a financing intermediary whose firm, Tunstall Consulting Inc., is based in Tampa. When Tunstall recently raised $20 million for a software company that needed the funds to convert to an application-service-provider model that would substantially broaden its customer base, several banks were among the equity investors. "I'd have to say that they're interested in the same kind of deals that any other professional private-equity investor would consider: companies with at least a 20% to 30% growth rate, good profit potential, and a clear exit strategy, which might mean an IPO or a sale to a strategic partner," Tunstall says.

Although the trend developed relatively quickly, it seemed for a while as though it might be confined to the nation's largest banks, with Chase, Bank of America, and First Union emerging as big players. "Throughout much of the late 1990s, large banks were successful in finding legal ways around the regulatory restrictions that had limited their abilities to underwrite securities and make equity investments," explains Jerome Walker, a partner and banking regulatory expert at Salans, Hertzfeld, Heilbronn, Christy & Viener, a law firm in New York City. "They were looking for ways to move beyond the small, community-based investments that the government had been encouraging them to make for decades."

The logic behind the appeal of equity was irresistible. "The return that a bank can earn on a good private-equity investment is a lot more than the spread between the interest it pays for deposits and the interest it earns on loans," comments Sarah Miller, general counsel for the American Bankers Association Securities Association, based in Washington, D.C. "This is why we're no longer just seeing the top-tier banks getting involved in what we call 'merchant banking' activities. Even the smaller banks are interested, and many have started getting their feet wet."

A friendlier regulatory environment has also helped clear the path. Although legal restrictions still exist—largely to preserve the financial soundness of banks as they take on new risks—many types of investment opportunities are now possible, among them joint ventures or investing in common-stock deals, leveraged buyouts, and mezzanine (or interim) financing.

If you have a relationship with a lending institution, it's worth investigating whether that bank maintains a private-equity arm to invest in growth companies.

"As of now, what we've seen is two common forces driving banks into these deals," reports Jay Hachigian, a partner in the Waltham, Mass., office of Gunderson, Dettmer, Stough, Villeneuve, Franklin & Hachigian, a law firm that represents venture-capital funds and emerging growth companies. "It might be that a bank already has a lending relationship with a company, so now this becomes a way of broadening that relationship to include an investment component. But we've also seen cases where banks decide that the way to start their dealings with a young company is through an equity investment. And their thinking may be, as this company grows and becomes more mature—and therefore more able to sustain debt—the bank will also become a lender."

What's the bottom-line impact of all this for the owners of entrepreneurial ventures? More financing sources mean, at least in theory, better prospects for raising growth capital. But with a developing trend like this one, you'll need to be creative in figuring out how to tap into the market.

Certainly, if you have a relationship with a lending institution, it's worth investigating whether that bank maintains a private-equity arm to invest in customers or other growth companies. But don't be surprised if it's tough to get an answer to that question. Tunstall laughs as he notes, "I regularly bring deals to First Union Capital Partners. But if I went to the local branch of First Union and asked someone there about private-equity financing opportunities, it's a pretty good bet that he or she wouldn't know what I was talking about." If you have a relationship with a lending institution, it's worth investigating whether that bank maintains a private-equity arm to invest in growth companies.

Aggressive networking is, as always, a good idea. "The banks that have made private-equity investing a priority either have set up subsidiaries or acquired companies that know how to do it, so they're already out there following market trends and looking for good investment prospects," says Laurence Markowitz, a Salans partner who assists clients with private-equity placements and sometimes works with bank investors on equity deals. "If they haven't yet approached you, then you're best off working with some kind of middleman, whether it's an investment banker or your attorney or accountant, so long as they've got a proven record of dealing with banks as well as other sources of capital."

For any business owner who's been frustrated by the time-consuming loan-application process, there's some good news. When it comes to handling private-equity investments, banks are just as fast and efficient as any other players in the market are. That's because the decision makers in the banks' equity deals often gained their expertise working at traditional private-equity funds or investment banks.

If you're interested in pursuing this financing path, keep in mind a couple of caveats: Small-but-steady-growth companies need not apply. Also, if your growth model is very high risk, your prospects with bank investors may not be too strong, especially given the current state of the economy. Private-equity insiders say that the downturn in the Nasdaq market and, most especially, the dot-com

Prospecting Online

It's hard enough to come up with a list of investors that are worth approaching in the private-equity market. It's even harder when a new trend is developing, as is the case today with banks.

Although there's no comprehensive, up-to-date source of information regarding which banks are doing what in investing in growth companies, the Internet is always a valuable tool when you're hunting for capital. One site that provides a wealth of leads about both debt and equity options is www.businessfinance.com. There you can explore local microloan programs and all kinds of government financing opportunities (including those connected with the Small Business Administration). The site also covers equity options (with investors divided into different categories, based on the type of private-equity money you're seeking).

After that, try doing an Internet search using such word combinations as "banks and merchant banking" and "commercial banks and venture capital." You won't generate a bank vault full of leads, but you may come up with some interesting prospects that you haven't learned about elsewhere.

collapse have raised caution levels and made banks likelier to nix deals that lack very clear exit strategies.

That's not too surprising. After all, willing and able as bank investors may be, they are simply not the same as other private-equity players. According to Miller of the ABA Securities Association, many banks have been spooked by proposed Federal Reserve Board regulations that would require them to set aside large amounts in reserve against such risky investments.

"Banks have problems with these rules, especially as they were initially proposed by the Fed, since they would have needed to set aside reserves worth 50% of each investment," says Miller. "That's very different from the requirements that they're used to dealing with, which allow them leeway about which loans they make small or large reserves against." One way that the nation's largest banks have tried to cope with such restrictions is by wooing outside investors to put up some of the funds the banks will invest. Chase Capital Partners has been particularly active in that regard.

The bottom line for business owners: look for new and expanded opportunities on the bank-equity front. And keep in mind a lesson that you've probably already learned in your search for a line of credit: bankers can be a hard sell, at least the first time you approach them. So build a good business plan, concentrate on achieving your growth objectives, and keep knocking on those doors.

Jill Andresky Fraser is *Inc.*'s finance editor.

The Venture Capital Industry: An Overview

Venture capital is money provided by professionals who invest alongside management in young, rapidly growing companies that have the potential to develop into significant economic contributors. Venture capital is an important source of equity for start-up companies.

Professionally managed venture capital firms generally are private partnerships or closely-held corporations funded by private and public pension funds, endowment funds, foundations, corporations, wealthy individuals, foreign investors, and the venture capitalists themselves.

Venture capitalists generally:

- Finance new and rapidly growing companies;
- Purchase equity securities;
- Assist in the development of new products or services;
- Add value to the company through active participation;
- Take higher risks with the expectation of higher rewards;
- Have a long-term orientation

When considering an investment, venture capitalists carefully screen the technical and business merits of the proposed company. Venture capitalists only invest in a small percentage of the businesses they review and have a long-term perspective. Going forward, they actively work with the company's management by contributing their experience and business savvy gained from helping other companies with similar growth challenges.

Venture capitalists mitigate the risk of venture investing by developing a portfolio of young companies in a single venture fund. Many times they will co-invest with other professional venture capital firms. In addition, many venture partnerships will manage multiple funds simultaneously. For decades, venture capitalists have nurtured the growth of America's high technology and entrepreneurial communities resulting in significant job creation, economic growth and international competitiveness. Companies such as Digital Equipment Corporation, Apple, Federal Express, Compaq, Sun Microsystems, Intel, Microsoft and Genentech are famous examples of companies that received venture capital early in their development.

Private Equity Investing

Venture capital investing has grown from a small investment pool in the 1960s and early 1970s to a mainstream asset class that is a viable and significant part of the institutional and corporate investment portfolio. Recently, some investors have been referring to venture investing and buyout investing as "private equity investing." This term can be confusing because some in the investment industry use the term "private equity" to refer only to buyout fund investing. In any case, an institutional investor will allocate 2% to 3% of their institutional portfolio for investment in alternative assets such as private equity or venture capital as part of their overall asset allocation. Currently, over 50% of investments in venture capital/private equity comes from institutional public and private pension funds, with the balance coming from endowments, foundations, insurance companies, banks, individuals and other entities who seek to diversify their portfolio with this investment class.

What Is a Venture Capitalist?

The typical person-on-the-street depiction of a venture capitalist is that of a wealthy financier who wants to fund start-up companies. The perception is that a person who develops a brand new change-the-world invention needs capital; thus, if they can't get capital from a bank or from their own pockets, they enlist the help of a venture capitalist.

In truth, venture capital and private equity firms are pools of capital, typically organized as a limited partnership, that invests in companies that represent the opportunity for a high rate of return within five to seven years. The venture capitalist may look at several hundred investment opportunities before investing in only a few selected companies with favorable investment opportunities. Far from being simply passive financiers, venture capitalists foster growth in companies through their involvement in the management, strategic marketing and planning of their investee companies. They are entrepreneurs first and financiers second.

Even individuals may be venture capitalists. In the early days of venture capital investment, in the 1950s and 1960s, individual investors were the archetypal venture investor. While this type of individual investment did not totally disappear, the modern venture firm emerged as the dominant venture investment vehicle. However, in the last few years, individuals have again become a potent and increasingly larger part of the early stage start-up venture life cycle. These "angel investors" will mentor a company and provide needed capital and expertise to help develop companies. Angel investors may either be wealthy people with management expertise or retired business men and women who seek the opportunity for first-hand business development.

Investment Focus

Venture capitalists may be generalist or specialist investors depending on their investment strategy. Venture capitalists can be generalists, investing in various industry sectors, or various geographic locations, or various stages of a company's life. Alternatively, they may be specialists in one or two industry sectors, or may seek to invest in only a localized geographic area.

Not all venture capitalists invest in "start-ups." While venture firms will invest in companies that are in their initial start-up modes, venture capitalists will also invest in companies at various stages of the business life cycle. A venture capitalist may invest before there is a real product or company organized (so called "seed investing"), or may provide capital to start up a company in its first or second stages of development known as "early stage investing." Also, the venture capitalist may provide needed financing to help a company grow beyond a critical mass to become more successful ("expansion stage financing").

The venture capitalist may invest in a company throughout the company's life cycle and therefore some funds focus on later stage investing by providing financing to help the company grow to a critical mass to attract public financing through a stock offering. Alternatively, the venture capitalist may help the company attract a merger or acquisition with another company by providing liquidity and exit for the company's founders. At the other end of the spectrum, some venture funds specialize in the acquisition, turnaround or recapitalization of public and private companies that represent favorable investment opportunities.

There are venture funds that will be broadly diversified and will invest in companies in various industry sectors as diverse as semiconductors, software, retailing and restaurants and others that may be specialists in only one technology.

While high technology investment makes up most of the venture investing in the U.S., and the venture industry gets a lot of attention for its high technology investments, venture capitalists also invest in companies such as construction, industrial products, business services, etc. There are several firms that have specialized in retail company investment and others that have a focus in investing only in "socially responsible" start-up endeavors.

Venture firms come in various sizes from small seed specialist firms of only a few million dollars under management to firms with over a billion dollars in invested capital around the world. The common denominator in all of these types of venture investing is that the venture capitalist is not a passive investor, but has an active and vested interest in guiding, leading and growing the companies they have invested in. They seek to add value through their experience in investing in tens and hundreds of companies.

Some venture firms are successful by creating synergies between the various companies they have invested in; for example one company that has a great software product, but does not have adequate distribution technology, may be paired with another company or its management in the venture portfolio that has better distribution technology.

Length of Investment

Venture capitalists will help companies grow, but they eventually seek to exit the investment in three to seven years. An early stage investment make take seven to ten years to mature, while a later stage investment many only take a few years, so the appetite for the investment life cycle must be congruent with the limited partnerships' appetite for liquidity. The venture investment is neither a short term nor a liquid investment, but an investment that must be made with careful diligence and expertise.

Types of Firms

There are several types of venture capital firms, but most mainstream firms invest their capital through funds organized as limited partnerships in which the venture capital firm serves as the general partner. The most common type of venture firm is an independent venture firm that has no affiliations with any other financial institution. These are called "private independent firms." Venture firms may also be affiliates or subsidiaries of a commercial bank, investment bank or insurance company and make investments on behalf of outside investors or the parent firm's clients. Still other firms may be subsidiaries of non-financial, industrial corporations making investments on behalf of the parent itself. These latter firms are typically called "direct investors" or "corporate venture investors."

Other organizations may include government affiliated investment programs that help start up companies either through state, local or federal programs. One common vehicle is the Small Business Investment Company or SBIC program administered by the Small Business Administration, in which a venture capital firm may augment its own funds with federal funds and leverage its investment in qualified investee companies.

While the predominant form of organization is the limited partnership, in recent years the tax code has allowed the formation of either Limited Liability Partnerships, ("LLPs"), or Limited Liability Companies ("LLCs"), as alternative forms of organization. However, the limited partnership is still the predominant organizational form. The advantages and disadvantages of each has to do with liability, taxation issues and management responsibility.

The venture capital firm will organize its partnership as a pooled fund; that is, a fund made up of the general partner and the investors or limited partners. These funds are typically organized as fixed life partnerships, usually having a life of ten years. Each fund is capitalized by commitments of capital from the limited partners. Once the partnership has reached its target size, the partnership is closed to further investment from new investors or even existing investors so the fund has a fixed capital pool from which to make its investments.

Like a mutual fund company, a venture capital firm may have more than one fund in existence. A venture firm may raise another fund a few years after closing the first fund in order to continue to invest in companies and to provide more opportunities for existing and new investors. It is not uncommon to see a successful firm raise six or seven funds consecutively over the span of ten to fifteen years. Each fund is managed separately and has

its own investors or limited partners and its own general partner. These funds' investment strategy may be similar to other funds in the firm. However, the firm may have one fund with a specific focus and another with a different focus and yet another with a broadly diversified portfolio. This depends on the strategy and focus of the venture firm itself.

Corporate Venturing

One form of investing that was popular in the 1980s and is again very popular is corporate venturing. This is usually called "direct investing" in portfolio companies by venture capital programs or subsidiaries of nonfinancial corporations. These investment vehicles seek to find qualified investment opportunities that are congruent with the parent company's strategic technology or that provide synergy or cost savings.

These corporate venturing programs may be loosely organized programs affiliated with existing business development programs or may be self-contained entities with a strategic charter and mission to make investments congruent with the parent's strategic mission. There are some venture firms that specialize in advising, consulting and managing a corporation's venturing program.

The typical distinction between corporate venturing and other types of venture investment vehicles is that corporate venturing is usually performed with corporate strategic objectives in mind while other venture investment vehicles typically have investment return or financial objectives as their primary goal. This may be a generalization as corporate venture programs are not immune to financial considerations, but the distinction can be made.

The other distinction of corporate venture programs is that they usually invest their parent's capital while other venture investment vehicles invest outside investors' capital.

Commitments and Fund Raising

The process that venture firms go through in seeking investment commitments from investors is typically called "fund raising." This should not be confused with the actual investment in investee or "portfolio" companies by the venture capital firms, which is also sometimes called "fund raising" in some circles. The commitments of capital are raised from the investors during the formation of the fund. A venture firm will set out prospecting for investors with a target fund size. It will distribute a prospectus to potential investors and may take from several weeks to several months to raise the requisite capital. The fund will seek commitments of capital from institutional investors, endowments, foundations and individuals who seek to invest part of their portfolio in opportunities with a higher risk factor and commensurate opportunity for higher returns.

Because of the risk, length of investment and illiquidity involved in venture investing, and because the minimum commitment requirements are so high, venture capital fund investing is generally out of reach for the average individual. The venture fund will have from a few to almost 100 limited partners depending on the target size of the fund. Once the firm has raised enough commitments, it will start making investments in portfolio companies.

Capital Calls

Making investments in portfolio companies requires the venture firm to start "calling" its limited partner's commitments. The firm will collect or "call" the needed investment capital from the limited partner in a series of tranches commonly known as "capital calls." These capital calls from the limited partners to the venture fund are sometimes called "takedowns" or "paid-in capital." Some years ago, the venture firm would "call" this capital down in three equal installments over a three year period. More recently, venture firms have synchronized their funding cycles and call their capital on an as-needed basis for investment.

Illiquidity

Limited partners make these investments in venture funds knowing that the investment will be long-term. It may take several years before the first investments start to return proceeds; in many cases the invested capital may be tied up in an investment for seven to ten years. Limited partners understand that this illiquidity must be factored into their investment decision.

Other Types of Funds

Since venture firms are private firms, there is typically no way to exit before the partnership totally matures or expires. In recent years, a new form of venture firm has evolved: so-called "secondary" partnerships that specialize in purchasing the portfolios of investee company investments of an existing venture firm. This type of partnership provides some liquidity for the original investors. These secondary partnerships, expecting a large return, invest in what they consider to be undervalued companies.

Advisors and Fund of Funds

Evaluating which funds to invest in is akin to choosing a good stock manager or mutual fund, except the decision to invest is a long-term commitment. This investment decision takes considerable investment knowledge and time on the part of the limited partner investor. The larger institutions have investments in excess of 100 different venture capital and buyout funds and continually invest in new funds as they are formed.

Some limited partner investors may have neither the resources nor the expertise to manage and invest in many funds and thus, may seek to delegate this decision to an investment advisor or so-called "gatekeeper." This advisor will pool the assets of its various clients and invest these proceeds as a limited partner into a venture or buyout fund currently raising capital. Alternatively, an investor may invest in a "fund of funds," which is a partnership organized to invest in other partnerships, thus providing the limited partner investor with added diversification and the ability to invest smaller amounts into a variety of funds.

Disbursements

The investment by venture funds into investee portfolio companies is called "disbursements." A company will receive capital in one or more rounds of financing. A venture firm may make these disbursements by itself or in many cases will co-invest in a company with other venture firms ("co-investment" or "syndication"). This syndication provides more capital resources for the investee company. Firms co-invest because the company investment is congruent with the investment strategies of various venture firms and each firm will bring some competitive advantage to the investment.

The venture firm will provide capital and management expertise and will usually also take a seat on the board of the company to ensure that the investment has the best chance of being successful. A portfolio company may receive one round, or in many cases, several rounds of venture financing in its life as needed. A venture firm may not invest all of its committed capital, but will reserve some capital for later investment in some of its successful companies with additional capital needs.

Exits

Depending on the investment focus and strategy of the venture firm, it will seek to exit the investment in the portfolio company within three to five years of the initial investment. While the initial public offering may be the most glamourous and heralded type of exit for the venture capitalist and owners of the company, most successful exits of venture investments occur through a merger or acquisition of the company by either the original founders or another company. Again, the expertise of the venture firm in successfully exiting its investment will dictate the success of the exit for themselves and the owner of the company.

IPO

The initial public offering is the most glamourous and visible type of exit for a venture investment. In recent years technology IPOs have been in the limelight during the IPO boom of the last six years. At public offering, the venture firm is considered an insider and will receive stock in the company, but the firm is regulated and restricted in how that stock can be sold or liquidated for several years. Once this stock is freely tradable, usually after about two years, the venture fund will distribute this stock or cash to its limited partner investor who may then manage the public stock as a regular stock holding or may liquidate it upon receipt. Over the last twenty-five years, almost 3000 companies financed by venture funds have gone public.

Mergers and Acquisitions

Mergers and acquisitions represent the most common type of successful exit for venture investments. In the case of a merger or acquisition, the venture firm will receive stock or cash from the acquiring company and the venture investor will distribute the proceeds from the sale to its limited partners.

Valuations

Like a mutual fund, each venture fund has a net asset value, or the value of an investor's holdings in that fund at any given time. However, unlike a mutual fund, this value is not determined through a public market transaction, but through a valuation of the underlying portfolio. Remember, the investment is illiquid and at any

point, the partnership may have both private companies and the stock of public companies in its portfolio. These public stocks are usually subject to restrictions for a holding period and are thus subject to a liquidity discount in the portfolio valuation.

Each company is valued at an agreed-upon value between the venture firms when invested in by the venture fund or funds. In subsequent quarters, the venture investor will usually keep this valuation intact until a material event occurs to change the value. Venture investors try to conservatively value their investments using guidelines or standard industry practices and by terms outlined in the prospectus of the fund. The venture investor is usually conservative in the valuation of companies, but it is common to find that early stage funds may have an even more conservative valuation of their companies due to the long lives of their investments when compared to other funds with shorter investment cycles.

Management Fees

As an investment manager, the general partner will typically charge a management fee to cover the costs of managing the committed capital. The management fee will usually be paid quarterly for the life of the fund or it may be tapered or curtailed in the later stages of a fund's life. This is most often negotiated with investors upon formation of the fund in the terms and conditions of the investment.

Carried Interest

"Carried interest" is the term used to denote the profit split of proceeds to the general partner. This is the general partners' fee for carrying the management responsibility plus all the liability and for providing the needed expertise to successfully manage the investment. There are as many variations of this profit split both in the size and how it is calculated and accrued as there are firms.

The Midas List The 50 Most Powerful Dealmakers

The Man With the Golden Touch

At a time when the investing public has given up the venture capitalists for dead, the smart ones are busy funding the next round of technological innovation. Vinod Khosla is as busy as ever.

BY CARLEEN HAWN

THE NASDAQ STILL STRUGGLES after enduring its worst year ever. Initial public offerings have shut down. More than 40,000 people who joined dot-coms this past year have lost their jobs, and 91 Web companies have gone bust. Hints of recession are everywhere.

But have faith: The Internet Revolution is real, and it ain't anywhere close to being over. Right now dealmakers in Silicon Valley, Seattle, Boston and elsewhere are knee-deep in the capital stream, panning for the flecks of gold that could become the next Cisco, Microsoft or Oracle. Plenty of cash fuels their quest— some $37 billion still flowed into venture capital funds after technology stocks plunged last April. The capital invested in new companies rose 40% in the first nine months of last year to $52 billion. A total of 5,380 new companies got funded in 2000. Most of them will fail, as al-

ways, but from a few survivors enormous new wealth will flow.

> "The venture industry is larger today than ever before, in numbers and capital. Our ability to promote innovation and job creation is higher today than at any other point in our history."
>
> ROBERT EMERY, CHIEF EXECUTIVE, ROBERTSON STEPHENS

"This is a reckoning, but this is no time to retreat," says Vinod Khosla, superstar partner in VC firm Kleiner Perkins Caufield & Byers in Menlo Park, Calif. "The Tech Wreck is a stock-market phenomenon caused

by fear and greed. It doesn't change the underlying cycle of technology innovation. That's the Tech Trend."

Khosla, 46, has made a career of determining which companies will thrive. Lower-profile and less loquacious than John Doerr, his headline-happy partner, Khosla has rivaled Doerr's impressive record in 15 years in the business. Mining the extreme fringe, Khosla has funded some futuristic flops—pen-based computers, interactive games and such. But he also has backed some of the richest payoffs in high-tech.

In the past few years he has turned roughly $50 million in early investments into $15 billion on just half a dozen makers of breakthrough telecom gear— Juniper, Cerent, Corvis, Extreme Networks, Siara and Lightera. Khosla sees even bigger payoffs ahead. The future lies in broadband, so he bets on telecom infrastructure (Zambeel), optical net-

Tech's Best Venture Investors

Go to www.forbes.com/midas for the complete list of 100 names.

1 VINOD KHOSLA, 46, VC, Partner, Kleiner Perkins Caufield & Byers. DEALS: Juniper Networks, Extreme Networks, Cerent, Siara.

2 SETH NEIMAN, 46, VC, Managing Partner, Crosspoint Venture Partners. DEALS: Brocade, Foundry Networks.

3 L. JOHN DOERR, 49, VC, Partner, Kleiner Perkins Caufield & Byers. DEALS: Amazon, Netscape, Handspring.

4 LAWRENCE SONSINI, 60, LAWYER, Chairman, Wilson Sonsini Goodrich & Rosati. DEALS: Brocade, Palm, Agilent.

5 CHRISTOPHER SCHAEPE, 36, VC, General partner, Lightspeed Venture Partners. DEALS: Brocade, Ciena, Terayon.

6 DAVID COWAN, 34, VC, Managing Partner, Bessemer Venture Partners. DEALS: Ciena, VeriSign, Register.com.

7 RICHARD KRAMLICH, 65, VC, General Partner, New Enterprise Associates. DEALS: Healtheon/WebMD, Grand Junction Networks.

8 JAMES GAITHER, 63, VC, Managing Director, Sutter Hill Ventures. DEALS: Siebel, Nvidia, BroadVision.

9 GEOFFREY YANG, 41, VC, Founding Partner, Redpoint Ventures. DEALS: Foundry Networks, Shasta Networks.

10 ROBERT KAGLE, 45, VC, General Partner, Benchmark. DEALS: Ariba, Ebay, Synopsys.

11 FRANK QUATTRONE, 45, BANKER, Managing Director, Credit Suisse First Boston Technology Group. DEALS: Handspring, Corvis, Openwave.

12 THOMAS WEISEL, 59, BANKER, Chairman, Thomas Weisel Partners. DEALS: Yahoo,

Sycamore, JDS Uniphase, Siebel Systems.

13 MICHAEL MORITZ, 45, VC, Partner, Sequoia Capital. DEALS: Yahoo, Agile Software.

14 ANTHONY SUN, 48, VC, Managing General Partner, Venrock Associates. DEALS: Stratacom, Lightera Networks.

15 WILLIAM STENSRUD, 50, VC, General Partner, Enterprise Partners. DEALS: GlobeSpan, Juniper, Packeteer.

16 IRWIN FEDERMAN, 65, VC, General Partner, U.S. Venture partners. DEALS: Check Point Software, Nuance Communications.

17 GARY RIESCHEL, 44, VC, Executive Managing Director; Softbank Venture Capital. DEALS: VeriSign, Net2Phone.

18 ROGER MCNAMEE, 44, VC, General Partner, Integral Capital Partners. DEALS: Sycamore Networks, Inktomi.

19 BRADFORD KOENIG, 42, BANKER, Managing Director, Goldman Sachs. DEALS: Exodus, Kana, Actuate.

20 PAUL FERRI, 62, VC, General Partner, Matrix Partners. DEALS: Cascade Communications, Sycamore.

21 MICHAEL GRIMES, 34, BANKER, Managing Director, Morgan Stanley Dean Witter. DEALS: Agilent, Brocade Communications.

22 TERENCE GARNETT, 43, VC, Managing Director, Garnett Capital. DEALS: Siebel, Check Point Software, Niku.

23 JUDITH O'BRIEN, 50, LAWYER, Managing Director, Incubic. DEALS: Juniper, Granite Systems, Monterey Networks.

24 PROMOD HAQUE, 52, VC, General Partner, Norwest Venture Partners. DEALS: CoSine Commu-

nications, Advanced Fibre Networks.

25 JOHN MUMFORD, 57, VC, Founding Partner, Crosspoint Venture Partners. DEALS: Ariba, Connectify.

26 EFF MARTIN, 52, BANKER, Managing Director, Goldman Sachs. DEALS: Inktomi, Juniper.

27 JAY HOAG, 42, VC, General Partner, Technology Crossover Ventures. DEALS: Ariba, Cnet, Ascend.

28 ANDREW RACHLEFF, 42, VC, General Partner, Benchmark. DEALS: CacheFlow, Equinix.

29 CLIFFORD HIGGERSON, 61, VC, Partner, ComVentures. DEALS: Ciena, Digital Island.

30 CHARLES CORY, 45, BANKER, Managing Director, Morgan Stanley Dean Witter. DEALS: Applied Materials, Agilent.

31 MICHAEL HOMER, 42, ANGEL. DEALS: Netscape, Palm. TiVo.

32 GORDON DAVIDSON, 52, LAWYER, Chairman, Fenwick & West. DEALS: Exodus Communications, VeriSign.

33 ROBERT EMERY, 39, BANKER, Chief Executive, Robertson Stephens. DEALS: ONI systems, Vignette, Abgenix.

34 LAWRENCE CALCANO, 38, BANKER, COO, High Tech Group, Goldman Sachs. DEALS: Check Point, Ciena.

35 TODD BROOKS, 40, VC, General Partner, Mayfield Fund. DEALS: Brocade, Avanex.

36 TIMOTHY BARROWS, 43, VC, General Partner, Matrix Partners. DEALS: Sycamore Networks, SilverStream Software.

37 JAMES BREYER, 39, VC, Managing partner, Accel partners.

DEALS: Real Networks, Redback Networks.

38 ROBERT GUNDERSON JR., 49, LAWYER, Founding Partner, Gunderson Dettmer. DEALS: Redback, Ariba.

39 STEVEN KRAUSZ, 45, VC, U.S. Venture Partners. DEALS: Verity, Check Point.

40 PAUL CHAMBERLAIN, 37, BANKER, Managing Director, Morgan Stanley Dean Witter. DEALS: Ariba; Palm.

41 YOGEN DALAL, 50, VC, Managing Partner, Mayfield Fund. DEALS: Nuance Communications, BroadVision.

42 JAMES BARKSDALE, 58, VC, FOUNDER, The Barksdale Group. DEALS: Netscape, Palm.

43 WILLIAM SAVOY, 36, VC, President, Vulcan Ventures. DEALS: CNET, Charter Cable.

44 EDWARD ANDERSON, 51, VC, Managing General Partner, North Bridge Venture Partners. DEALS: Cascade, Arris Networks.

45 TENCH COXE, 43, VC, Managing Director, Sutter Hill Ventures. DEALS: Network Appliance, Alteon WebSystems.

46 JEFFREY CHRISTIAN, 45, RECRUITER, Chairman, Christian & Timbers. DEALS: Netscape, Ivillage, Yahoo.

47 JOHN DEAN, 53, BANKER, Chief Executive Officer, Silicon Valley Bank. DEALS: Ariba, Critical Path.

48 KANWAL REKHI, 55, ANGEL. DEALS: Exodus, Instantis.

49 ROGER EVANS, 55, VC, General Partner, Greylock. DEALS: Ascend, Openwave.

50 ROBERT DAVOLI, 52, VC, Managing Director, Sigma Partners. DEALS: Vignette, web-Methods, StarageNetworks.

working (Iolon) and software aided by networking (Asera).

Khosla's investment success, both for himself (he is a billionaire) and

his partners, is a key component of his appearance at the top of our Midas List of venture capital power brokers (see "Tech's Best Venture In-

vestors"). But it isn't just raw returns that earn these people a place on the list; the breadth and depth of involvement in successful ventures go

The Midas Rules

The rankings for the inaugural Midas List were based on extensive FORBES reporting and surveys sent to several hundred potential list members. For each member, we calculated the performance of all venture-backed companies through Dec. 29, 2000. Companies must have gone public, merged or been acquired after August 1995 to be eligible. We awarded points based on how involved candidates were in each company both before and after the primary liquidity event. We then multiplied scores by the market valuation of the company both at the time of the offering, merger or acqui-sition and on Dec. 29. The sum of these figures is a fairly accurate measure of a candidate's record of creating wealth. Carleen Hawn edited the list, which was produced by staffers Luisa Kroll, Erika Brown, Jennifer Godwin, Samatha Lee and Nicole Ridgway. Special consultant Jean Yaremchuk of research firm Venture-One calculated the rankings. Thanks to Silicon Valley bureau contributors Elizabeth Corcoran, Kerry Dolan, Quentin Hardy, intern Sara Henderson and IT consult-ant Brandon Russell.

into our formula. Midas members include entrepreneurs and the angel investors who nurture their ideas, the venture capitalists who fund them, the technical advisers who pass judgment on their technology and the lawyers who patent it, and the investment bankers who gift wrap the whole package and sell it to the public.

None is shrewder than Vinod Khosla (pronounced "vih-NODE KOE-sla"). He was born in 1955 into a military family in New Delhi, far from India's future "tech capital" of Bangalore. He earned degrees from some of the world's best tech-savvy institutions—the Indian Institute of Technology, Carnegie Mellon in Pittsburgh and the Stanford business school in northern California. After Stanford he and a Ph.D candidate, Andy Bechtolsheim, divined the idea that led them to found Sun Microsystems in 1982.

Khosla ran Sun until 1984, when he was eased out and was replaced by his M.B.A. classmate and pal, Scott McNealy. Just 30 at the time, Khosla could have retired, but Doerr persuaded him to work "part time" for Kleiner Perkins. "Staying at Kleiner was never in the plans," says Khosla, who had hoped to return to far-out research.

Then the first of Khosla's four children was born in 1988, and he decided a "stable" career in venture capital was a safer bet. He spent a de-cade at Kleiner as the firm pros-pered, and by 1995 Khosla, Doerr and other partners set off the race to the Internet bubble by backing Netscape. It went public 16 months after its founding.

Khosla also backed Web portal Excite, while Doerr pushed cable-modem marketer AtHome, Amazon.com and Healtheon (now Web MD). Excite and AtHome later joined in a Hail Mary merger, and a faltering Netscape sold out to America Online. Together Amazon, Web MD and ExciteAtHome have lost $52 billion of market value.

While Doerr ran into turbulence, Khosla has assembled a stable of lasting blockbusters the likes of which the venture community has rarely seen. Since summer 1999, Khosla has seen three of his optical networking outlets—Extreme Networks, Juniper and Corvis—go public on the Nasdaq. Even off 50% to 80% from their highs, their combined market cap approaches $60 billion.

The investing public is not very interested in this sector. Only 16 tech outfits went public in the fourth quarter of 2000, down from 67 in the first quarter, says Venture One Corp. But what looks dead from the outside is teeming with activity on the inside. Acquisitions of venture-backed firms jumped 26% to 365 last year. "Fundamentally, the technology market is strong, and it has had a huge impact on the economy. The innovation cycles are accelerating. What we saw in the last ten years is peanuts compared to what we'll see in the next ten," Khosla says.

> "The great successes are made by people who can see so far ahead they can't explain what's on the other side. We have a code phrase: 'the genetic defect.'"
>
> —SETH NEIMAN, MANAGING PARTNER, CROSSPOINT VENTURE PARTNERS

That perspective was missing in the Web frenzy, and the industry suffered for it, he says. Everyone tried to boot up and cash out; ventures with little intrinsic value clogged the markets. "We threw caution to the wind," he laments. "Discrimination was as visible as the Loch Ness monster."

In the aftermath dozens of tech companies have perished. But the high casualty rate is endemic to the life cycle of venture investing. As PCs began to take hold in early 1980s, hordes of makers swarmed after the business; only a handful survived, but they created huge wealth. Now is no time for wimpery. "Tremendous value will be created, but not through the mania of the dot-com world," Khosla says. "Businesses and technology-leads take time to build."

Khosla says the real revolution will take hold when old companies infuse their business with digital tools. His payoff comes in funding the firms that try to enable that. "Startups must make a fundamental economic contribution to be durable," he says. "If you build a company that does that, you power through the up and down cycles of the market."

So he is, if anything, doubling up on his bets. In 1999 he funded Corio, a so-called application service provider that hosts personnel and financial planning tasks for businesses. Corio went public in July. Its shares are down 72% from their high. Kleiner Perkins already owns 10% of the company, yet in November Khosla spent $3.1 million of his own money to buy shares worth another 2%.

"I'm not worried about risk," he explains. "The best thing that happened to Corio is that the category tanked. Its competition dried up! I am worried about people becoming gun-shy about funding. But one of the advantages of that is only good ventures get funded."

For now money is plentiful but talent isn't. Gone are the days of veteran chief executives vacating cushy corporate jobs for the promise of the big payoff of a public offering. This makes Khosla's job harder. "What matters now is experience, and coaching and mentoring of the entrepreneur. Talent is the scarcest commodity."

Last spring Khosla began pushing one of his protégés, Zaplet, to redouble its fundraising efforts. Zaplet peddles software for interactive e-mail, and Khosla thinks "Zaplets" could become an entirely new platform for enterprise software. Others concur: In October Zaplet raised $90 million. In these bleak times the money will have to last a year and a half.

Khosla sees Zaplets as the start of another trickle-down cycle. "People will use Zaplets because there is an economic return for their business. If Zaplets will be bought, then networks will be built, and if networks are built, then bandwidth will be bought. And if bandwidth is bought, then carriers will buy equipment to fund the growth."

Between now and then, the corporate casualties will almost certainly outnumber those who thrive. More people will lose money than make money. But in the end, more money will be made than lost. Investors should hang on. Those who steel themselves stand to be richly rewarded.

As Vinod Khosla puts it: "One Cisco makes up for a lot of losers."

Reprinted by permission from *Forbes,* magazine, February 19, 2001, pp. 86-90. © 2001 by Forbes, Inc.

Jackpot!

WHY BET THE FARM ON AN UNKNOWN VC WHEN YOU CAN FIND A SOURCE WITH THE FUNDS AND KNOW-HOW YOU NEED TO TAKE YOUR BUSINESS TO THE BIG-MONEY TABLE?

Do you see the glass as half empty or half full? If you're in the former camp, you may view the tech wreck as the death knell for early-stage funding. If you're in the latter camp, you probably see a much different picture. Despite the tumult, cash is still available. But you need to give investors a reason to invest.

Sunil Dhaliwal, a senior associate with Battery Ventures, a Wellesley, Massachusetts, venture capital firm with $1.8 billion under management, looks at a half-full glass. "If you believe early-stage funding can't be found, that's tantamount to saying there's no more innovation left to be funded," says Dhaliwal. "It's highly unlikely that 2001 is the year that innovation will cease to exist."

Of course, there are caveats. Investors want more experienced management teams, so first-time entrepreneurs will have a hard go. Also, investors are looking to capitalize on less crowded niches and are avoiding me-too companies. "The [best] candidates are those focusing on problems or opportunities that will crop up in [the next] 18 to 24 months," says Dhaliwal.

Tighter screening means fewer deals, but an optimist sees the silver lining. If the number of firms raising early-stage venture capital goes back to levels seen in 1996, '97 and '98, then 2001 could be the year when things finally return to normal. That's welcome news for businesses hoping to thrive in the post-New Economy.

The "PricewaterhouseCoopers MoneyTree Survey in Partnership With VentureOne," prepared exclusively for *Entrepreneur*, is proof that funding is still out there. By culling the firms with the most early-stage deals in 2000, we offer insight into the VC firms most likely to infuse your business with the cash it needs. (See "Top 100 Venture Capital Firms for Entrepreneurs")

Picking a VC firm, however, takes more than simply pointing at a name on a list. The most important thing is to find a firm that's a perfect fit with you and your business. The following three entrepreneurs did the legwork, and the following three investors liked what they saw—companies that complemented the investment strategies of their respective firms. When the two sides came together, they made very successful businesses—and that means everybody benefited.

—*David R. Evanson*

PLAYING HIS TUNE
Steve Wood & Gerry Langeler
DJANGOS RECORDS & OVP VENTURE PARTNERS

WHEN STEVE WOOD BOUGHT PORTLAND, OREGON-BASED Djangos Records in 1999, he envisioned a future for the store that went beyond used vinyl records and obscure indie bands. Wood, 36, wanted to turn Djangos into the industry's most successful independent retailer. But there was just one problem: He needed cash.

Meet Gerry Langeler of Kirkland, Washington-based OVP Venture Partners. Langeler had funded Wood's first venture— a software company—and liked Wood's entrepreneurial spirit. "We admire Steve's attitude and drive," says Langeler. "Steve is a scrappy competitor."

Djangos also represented an attractive opportunity for OVP. "This business will do better in a downturn because people are more price-sensitive," says Langeler. "[Djangos] is an investment that will retain value, because it has protection on the downside that we almost never see."

Thanks to lead investor OVP and a few other VC firms, Wood's company received $9 million in first-round financing last year. Djangos (named after legendary guitarist Django Reinhardt) now has 19 stores in five major metropolitan markets, a Web site that lets customers access all the stores' inventories, and projected revenue of $70 million for 2002. "What makes Djangos unique is our relationship with customers," Wood says. "They come to our store to buy and sell eclectic products that are out of print or hard to find."

Langeler's hands-off approach has worked out perfectly for Djangos. "The last thing we want to do is run the company," says Langeler, who is a Djangos board member. "We have a strong influence, not control. We're just here to write checks and pour fuel on the fire."

—*Peter Kooiman*

FINANCIAL SUPPORT

Check out which states boasted the most VC financing by number of deals and dollar amount in 2000.

STATE	DEALS	AMOUNT
CA	840	$8,421,105,000
NY	166	$2,979,470,000
MA	212	$2,116,424,000
TX	146	$1,510,988,000
CO	61	$1,439,885,000
NJ	56	$1,010,137,000
GA	87	$863,725,000
IL	46	$745,885,000
NC	54	$725,660,000
VA	86	$675,115,000
MD	46	$652,934,000
WA	94	$618,454,000
PA	63	$588,451,000
FL	43	$356,750,000
CT	40	$347,184,000
MO	5	$234,831,000
MN	32	$216,440,000
MI	20	$210,345,000
UT	10	$166,550,000
AZ	14	$148,850,000
OR	19	$144,400,000
IN	10	$128,500,000
NH	12	$112,110,000
TN	13	$69,100,000
OH	12	$67,450,000
DC	11	$59,650,000
KS	4	$49,000,000
ME	4	$42,500,000
AL	6	$40,300,000
KY	2	$25,200,000
LA	5	$24,050,000
RI	3	$21,000,000
DE	1	$20,000,000
MS	2	$13,600,000
WI	5	$13,100,000
NV	2	$10,000,000
HI	1	$6,000,000
NE	2	$5,500,000
OK	2	$5,500,000
ID	1	$5,000,000
SC	1	$2,500,000
NM	1	$2,000,000
WV	1	$500,000

Chart represents early-stage financing, which includes seed and first-round financing.
SOURCE: "PricewaterhouseCoopers MoneyTree Survey in Partnership With VentureOne

CLEANING UP
Kirk Huntsman & David Bogetz
DENTAL ONE & ABN AMRO PRIVATE EQUITY

GETTING MONEY IS LIKE PULLING TEETH. AT LEAST, IT FEELS that way. Thankfully for Kirk Huntsman, 43, getting expansion capital for his dental practice consolidation and management company, Dental One, wasn't nearly that painful. When David Bogetz of ABN AMRO Private Equity in Chicago came looking for Huntsman, he offered more than just the financing Dental One needed; he also brought plenty of business savvy to the table.

Designed to relieve management headaches, Dallas-based Dental One takes over dentists' daily business matters, such as hiring employees and negotiating leases. After starting the company in 1995, Huntsman and his co-founders realized they had tapped into a huge market and, more important, that their business model was working.

As it turns out, Bogetz and ABN AMRO were on the lookout for a dental practice consolidation company to invest in. Bogetz contacted Huntsman after hearing about Dental One through a Dallas health-care lender. The company and its principals had all the markings of a good investment for Bogetz: a proven business model, great business sense, and a stellar vision of the future. "We really liked that Dental One was run by businesspeople who had dental practice experience," says Bogetz. "Kirk has lots of ideas and energy—and he's moving this business forward. It's better than having a CEO who has no ideas and no vision. I've [experienced] it both ways, and [Kirk's] way makes successful companies. The other way is how you lose your money."

Dental One and ABN AMRO began negotiations in 1999, which led to $4 million in financing in March 2000. By year's end, Dental One's sales were $45 million. Who'd have guessed pulling teeth could be so lucrative?

—Nichole L. Torres

Take the Lead
Lucinda Duncalfe Holt & Henry Barratt Jr.
DESTINY WEBSOLUTIONS INC. &
BLUE WATER CAPITAL

ALTHOUGH HE REGULARLY ATTENDS VENTURE FORUMS, IT'S unusual for Henry D. Barratt Jr., managing director of Blue Water Capital, to find a company worth pursuing. So what moved him to not only inquire about Destiny WebSolutions, an Internet solutions provider, but to compete with others to fund the company? It had a lot to do with what Barratt saw in the company's president and CEO, Lucinda Duncalfe Holt.

"We first saw them at the Mid-Atlantic Venture Fair," explains Barratt. "[Duncalfe Holt] had a strong knowledge of leading people. She was a team-builder."

The team is the essence of Conshohocken, Pennsylvania-based Destiny's corporate culture. "It's [about] enabling everybody from senior management to associates and empowering them to do their jobs," says Duncalfe Holt.

REALITY CHECK

In the first quarter of 2001, early-stage, pre-IPO companies raised less money than they have since the second quarter of 1999. According to the "PricewaterhouseCoopers MoneyTree Survey in Partnership With VentureOne," total equity financings in venture-backed companies fell to $10.1 billion in the first quarter of 2001, a 40 percent drop from the last quarter of 2000. That represents the steepest quarter-to-quarter drop in history in terms of absolute dollars.

What does that mean for companies seeking financing? The number of businesses receiving early-stage funding dropped from 453 in fourth quarter 2000 to 235 in first quarter 2001, a 48 percent decline. Yet the median dollar amount each business received fell only 13 percent, from $10.9 million to $9.5 million per company (see below for first quarter investments for the last three years). So while it's more difficult for companies to get backing, those that do, get plenty of it to grow rapidly. Plus, industry sectors like networking, telecommunications, consumer and business services and software continue to attract huge amounts of funding compared to mid-1990s levels.

The dramatic drop-off in investing doesn't necessarily indicate a significant economic downturn. Setting aside the Internet gold rush of the last two years, the current climate is still more aggressive than historical norms and will likely remain that way. The bottom line is that entrepreneurs need more than just a new idea to get funding.

—*Tracy T. Lefterof, Global Managing Partner, Venture Capital Practice, PricewaterhouseCoopers*

Median Amount Invested per Round of Equity Financing ($M)

INDUSTRY	1999 Q1	2000 Q1	2001 Q1
Biopharmaceuticals	$7.40	$11.38	$13.00
Communications	$6.00	$16.50	$18.00
Consumer/Business Products	$4.14	$14.50	$3.10
Consumer/Business Services	$3.50	$10.00	$6.80
Electronics	$4.00	$8.70	$12.25
Health-Care Services	$5.75	$5.50	$6.50
Industrial	$3.55	$2.00	$5.00
Information Services	$6.00	$10.00	$9.00
Medical Devices	$4.00	$6.00	$9.70
Medical IS	$4.55	$14.00	$9.00
Retailers	$10.00	$20.50	$6.90
Semiconductors	$4.20	$10.00	$12.30
Software	$5.19	$9.00	$9.50
Grand Median	**$5.00**	**$10.00**	**$9.50**

Equity financings include cash investments by professional venture capital firms, corporations, private placement and individuals into companies that have received at least one round of professional venture capital.

SOURCE: "PricewaterhouseCoopers MoneyTree Survey in Partnership With VentureOne"

Barratt also appreciated Destiny's profitability. "They didn't need the money to make payroll," he says. "They needed it because they wanted to expand." Once Blue Water Capital pumped $750,000 into the company, Duncalfe Holt went after that expansion—2000 sales were $17.5 million.

Barratt says good communication is the cornerstone of their alliance. "We've [left] situations that were great investments but where we felt we couldn't communicate effectively with the management team," he says. "It's not the easy times we're concerned about; it's 'What if something hard happens—how will we work through it together?'"

—*Cynthia E. Griffin*

TOP 100 VENTURE CAPITAL FIRMS

VC Firm	Location of VC Firm	Early-Round* Deals in 2000	Web Site
J.P. Morgan Partners	New York	56	www.jpmorganpartners.com
Softbank Venture Capital	California	46	www.sbvc.com
Intel Corp.	California	45	www.intel.com
Angel Investors LP	California	38	www.svangel.com
New Enterprise Associates	California	35	www.nea.com
Bessemer Venture Partners	Massachusetts	31	www.bvp.com
BancBoston Ventures	Massachusetts	29	www.bancbostonventures.com
Austin Ventures	Texas	28	www.austinventures.com
Sequoia Capital	California	27	www.sequoiacap.com
Venrock Associates	New York	27	www.venrock.com
Sevin Rosen Funds	Texas	26	www.srfunds.com
U.S. Venture Partners	California	26	www.usvp.com
Mayfield Fund	California	25	www.mayfield.com
Accel Partners	California	24	www.accel.com
Battery Ventures	Massachusetts	24	www.battery.com
Greylock Partners	Massachusetts	24	www.greylock.com
Internet.com	Connecticut	22	http://internet.comvc.com
St. Paul Venture Capital	Minnesota	22	www.stpaulvc.com
VantagePoint Venture Partners	California	22	www.vpvp.com
Wilson Sonsini Goodrich & Rosati	California	22	www.wsgr.com
Crescendo Ventures	California	21	www.crescendoventures.com
Benchmark Capital	California	20	www.benchmark.com
Columbia Capital	Virginia	20	www.colcap.com
Crosspoint Venture Partners	California	20	www.cpvp.com
Draper Fisher Jurvetson	California	20	www.dfj.com
Draper Richards	California	20	www.draperrichards.com
Goldman Sachs Group	New York	20	www.goldmansachs.com
Pequot Capital Management	Connecticut	20	www.pequotcap.com
Redpoint Ventures	California	20	www.redpointventures.com
Charles River Ventures	Massachusetts	19	www.crv.com
Kleiner Perkins Caufield & Byers	California	19	www.kpcb.com
Madrona Venture Group	Washington	19	www.madrona.com
ARCH Venture Partners	Illinois	18	www.archventure.com
AV Labs	Texas	18	www.avlabs.com
Dominion Ventures	California	18	www.dominion.com
Matrix Partners	California	18	www.matrixpartners.com
PA Early Stage	Pennsylvania	18	www.paearlystage.com
TL Ventures	Pennsylvania	18	www.tlventures.com
Advanced Technology Ventures	Massachusetts	17	www.atvcapital.com
Polaris Venture Partners	Massachusetts	17	www.polarisventures.com
Trident Capital	California	16	www.tridentcap.com
Warburg Pincus	California	16	www.warburgpincus.com
Atlas Venture	Massachusetts	15	www.atlasventure.com
Draper Atlantic	Virginia	15	www.draperatlantic.com
Imlay Investments	Georgia	15	n/a
Lightspeed Venture Partners	California	15	www.lightspeedvc.com
Sprout Group	New York	15	www.sproutgroup.com
eCompanies-Evercore Venture Partners	California	14	www.ecompanies.com

TOP 100 VENTURE CAPITAL FIRMS (Table Continued)

VC Firm	Location of VC Firm	Early-Round* Deals in 2000	Web Site
Garage.com	California	14	www.garage.com
GE Capital, Equity Capital Group	Connecticut	14	www.equitycapital.com
Mellon Ventures	Pennsylvania	14	www.mellonventures.com
Canaan Partners	Connecticut	13	www.canaan.com
Dot Edu	California	13	www.doteduventures.com
InterWest Partners	California	13	www.interwest.com
Mid-Atlantic Venture Funds	Pennsylvania	13	www.mavf.com
Norwest Venture Partners	California	13	www.norwestvp.com
Adams Capital Management	Pennsylvania	12	www.acm.com
Patricof & Co. Ventures	New York	12	www.patricof.com
Prism Venture Partners	Massachusetts	12	n/a
Redleaf Group	California	12	www.redleaf.com
Ridgewood Capital	New Jersey	12	www.ridgewoodcapital.com
RRE Ventures	New York	12	www.rre.com
Sequel Venture Partners	Colorado	12	www.sequelvc.com
WI Harper Group	California	12	www.wiharper.com
ABS Ventures	Maryland	11	www.absventures.com
Advent International	Massachusetts	11	www.adventinternational.com
Alta Communications/Burr Egan Deleage	Massachusetts	11	n/a
Aurora Funds	North Carolina	11	www.aurorafunds.com
Blue Chip Venture Co.	Ohio	11	www.bcvc.com
Centennial Ventures	Colorado	11	www.centennial.com
CMEA Ventures	California	11	www.cmeaventures.com
Cordova Ventures	Georgia	11	www.cordovaventures.com
Flatiron Partners	New York	11	www.flatironpartners.com
Internet Capital Group	Pennsylvania	11	www.internetcapital.com
Menlo Ventures	California	11	www.menloventures.com
Morgenthaler Partners	California	11	www.morgenthaler.com
MPM Capital	Massachusetts	11	www.mpmcapital.com
Northwood Ventures	New York	11	www.northwoodventures.com
Oak Investment Partners	Connecticut	11	www.oakvc.com
OneLiberty Ventures	Massachusetts	11	www.oneliberty.com
Sigma Partners	California	11	www.sigmapartners.com
Staenberg Venture Partners	Washington	11	www.staenberg.com
Steve Walker & Associates	Maryland	11	www.stevewalker.com
TeleSoft Partners	California	11	www.telesoftvc.com
Whitney & Co.	Connecticut	11	www.whitney.com
CenterPoint Venture Partners	Texas	10	www.centerpointvp.com
Charter Venture Group	California	10	www.charterventures.com
ComVentures	California	10	n/a
Connecticut Innovations	Connecticut	10	www.ctinnovations.com
Dynafund Ventures	California	10	www.dynafundventures.com
Edison Venture Fund	New Jersey	10	www.edisonventure.com
Frazier & Co.	Washington	10	www.frazierco.com
Highland Capital Partners	Massachusetts	10	www.hcp.com
H.I.G. Ventures	Florida	10	www.higcapital.com
Madison Dearborn Capital Partners	Illinois	10	www.mdcp.com
Mohr, Davidow Ventures	California	10	www.mdv.com

TOP 100 VENTURE CAPITAL FIRMS (Table Continued)

VC Firm	Location of VC Firm	Early-Round* Deals in 2000	Web Site
Morgan Stanley Dean Witter Venture Partners	New York	10	n/a
Noro-Moseley Partners	Georgia	10	www.noro-moseley.com
Onset Ventures	California	10	www.onset.com
Oxford Bioscience Partners	Massachusetts	10	www.oxbio.com
Selby Venture Partners	California	10	www.selbyventures.com
Storm Ventures	California	10	www.stormventures.com
Summit Partners	Massachusetts	10	www.summitpartners.com
Wakefield Group	North Carolina	10	www.wakefieldgroup.com
Zero Stage Capital	Massachusetts	10	www.zerostage.com

*Early stage includes seed and first-round financing.

Note: Due to a 20-way tie for No. 86, there are actually 105 firms in our listing.

Doing the Numbers

RANKINGS ARE BASED ON THE NUMBER OF SEED AND FIRST-round financings made by venture capital firms and similar entities in calendar year 2000 as measured by the "PricewaterhouseCoopers MoneyTree Survey in Partnership With VentureOne" (www.pwcmoneytree.com). These early-stage investments typically represent the first time a company receives funding from a professional venture capital firm in exchange for equity.

Prior to obtaining venture capital, a company generally has received financing from the owners, employees, friends, family, or incubator or angel investors and may have taken on debt. Venture-backed companies may have been in operation for several years or may be true start-ups, in business for only a few months. At minimum, these companies have a fully developed business plan, a dedicated management team and extraordinary potential for rapid growth.

ROUNDTABLE

Not All VCs Are Created Equal

Five leading venture capitalists explain that even in today's tough economy, entrepreneurs should search for the "smart money."

Raising capital for new ventures may have suffered a setback when the dot-com bubble burst, but that has not impeded the flow of bright ideas that cry out for funding. A panel of venture-capital experts recently met at MIT—arguably innovation headquarters of the world—to discuss venture capital today and to answer questions from an audience of inventors, entrepreneurs and others. The panel discussion, appearing here in edited form, offers practical insights not only into what entrepreneurs should look for in a VC firm, but also what venture capitalists seek from startups.

Howard Anderson: What do entrepreneurs want from a venture-capital partner? Money, right? Is your money different?

Vernon Lobo: Money is money. Entrepreneurs need someone who'll help build the company, who has knowledge about the market space and access to similar companies, who understands financing.

Craig London: Our network of 300 companies helps young companies get customers and revenue faster. Startups that make "warm" calls instead of cold calls can get launched quicker.

Scott Lawin: Entrepreneurs need well-connected, experienced people dedicated to building the company. GS-Ventures wants to partner, not just invest. Look for value beyond cash.

Russell Siegelman: Kleiner Perkins offers operational experience. Any venture capitalist can write a check.

Howard Anderson: Sitting on startups' boards, maybe you get to one company's meetings six days a year. Is that what you offer?

Vernon Lobo: The question is: How much work do VCs do? Entrepreneurs should check references—even talk to portfolio companies that aren't stars and see how they're treated.

Craig London: The first criterion for choosing a VC is chemistry with your company—between the person you'll work with and your management team. Second is how the VC's technology fits your goals. Third is a network you can tap.

Scott Lawin: Add "alignment of interest." Does the VC want to enrich you, not just itself?

Audience member: Is it better to take the money or wait for the right partner?

Vernon Lobo: Wait. The wrong partner will cost more. Although if you're running out of cash, you have no choice.

Russell Siegelman: Don't wait forever. Deals can go dry. I'm wary of deals that have been marketed for six weeks. Take the best deal out of the first three weeks and move on.

Howard Anderson: Where can entrepreneurs get advice on the arcane aspects of proposals?

Vernon Lobo: A lawyer.

Russell Siegelman: Insist that you don't *want* something complex. The VC should be able to explain the term sheet in plain language.

Howard Anderson: Suppose the entrepreneur needs help filling the management team.

Craig London: Often the best managers are found through word of mouth. It's not necessarily value-added to have a VC do recruiting—unless it's for a CEO.

Russell Siegleman: Ask VCs if they have names that might be a good fit. Good venture people are always meeting people just to meet them. I think having VCs help recruit is value-added.

Scott Lawin: During the interview process, ask VCs, "What domain expertise do your partners have? Can they help find managers?"

> ## A venture capitalist makes three decisions. First, to invest and how much. Second and third, with the rest of the board, to hire or fire a CEO. Everything else is cajoling, persuading, presenting evidence.

Howard Anderson: Now, what do you want from startups? Before investing, how do VCs assess synergy with the startup's management team?

Russell Siegleman: I probe to find out how people got together. Is there a shared vision and culture? Some people may have strong technical dreams, and others may be completely different—a warning signal.

Craig London: Be sure you don't have two camps within the company. I even go to their offices and talk to the clerks.

Howard Anderson: What do you do about the B players on the management team?

Vernon Lobo: If we want to work with the company, we talk to the A-team players about the B players. When people have worked together before, the A team will have an informed perspective. We ask what they would do if the problems we anticipate materialize.

Vernon Lobo: I'd present a hypothetical problem to the A team. They might say, "He's never leaving; what we are doing is about more than building a company." Or they might say, "We'll do what's right for the company."

Scott Lawin: Entrepreneurs who are reasonable business people understand the difference between working with your friends and building a successful company. We try to be frank upfront.

Audience Member: How much operating control would your VC take on?

Craig London: We need at least 25% of the company. Most VCs take control of areas where they can add value.

Howard Anderson: OK. Now suppose an Internet grocer wants to build 10 warehouses for $1 billion. Would you try to change management's mind?

Russell Siegleman: I don't think VCs should have any political operating role. We're investors. We're betting on management to make operating decisions. However, if management is not making plan, that's different. A venture capitalist makes three decisions. First, to invest and how much. Second and third, with the rest of the board, to hire or fire a CEO. Everything else is cajoling, persuading, presenting evidence. Watch out for investors who want a significant role in operations.

Howard Anderson: And if the startup isn't meeting the business plan?

Scott Lawin: Cajole strongly without trying to run the company.

Russell Siegleman: If startups don't make plan, VCs have to do something. That's different from unilaterally making decisions.

Audience Member: Do most VCs want control of the board?

Scott Lawin: If we have majority ownership, we want comparable board seats.

Vernon Lobo: Usually our board representation is minority, like our investment. But the shareholder agreement gives us a say in large capital investments—and if there are changes in the business, the CEO or compensation.

> ## In the early stages, the equity holders should be people who are building the company.

Howard Anderson: As VCs, do you put money in, then tell people they don't own their stock anymore?

Craig London: They'd keep most of it. It depends on how good they are at negotiating.

Vernon Lobo: In the early stages, the equity holders should be people who are building the company. If a founder with 25% of the company leaves after six months, his replacement needs some equity. With reverse vesting, the remaining founders have a greater stake.

Russell Siegleman: Founders should think twice about splitting equity 50-50. One person may have the ability to add long-term value; the other may not. We tell companies we won't invest under that scenario. They rejigger the split or we walk. Face facts upfront. Once somebody's stock is vested, it's nearly impossible to rip it away. The idea and the reality of starting a company are different.

First-time entrepreneurs think, Wow, somebody's giving us money to do this great thing. Two years later, some partners bail. How much equity should they take?

Howard Anderson: I like to point out in the New Enterprise course I teach at MIT, that an unprofitable company is in disequilibrium. Something will go wrong: The business plan won't work; the product will be late, or it will be the wrong product; a crucial customer will make impossible demands. Some team members are used to large staffs to help with pricing models or whatever. There's a 75% probability the team won't be together in three years.

Audience Member: If a VC wants to turn our stock into an incentive stock-option agreement, how can we limit loss of stock?

Howard Anderson: Make the business plan. If you get in trouble, let your board know early and propose a solution.

Vernon Lobo: Do due diligence on what kind of people th VC partners are. Do they take unfair advantage of entrepreneurs when the going gets tough?

Audience Member: Should we choose a strategic investor or VC?

Craig London: Both. Strategic investors may become customers—even acquirers. Having a strategic investor validates your model. From an operations perspective, it might be better to go that route first.

Howard Anderson: Be careful, though. Strategic investors sometimes have hidden agendas. Intel might demand things a financial investor wouldn't. And if you deal first with a strategic investor who'll become a customer, other customers may avoid you.

Russell Siegelman: Get pure financial players first. Then the outside strategic investor will know it can't twist your arm. Also, the strategic investor's agenda may make it hard for VCs to come in later. Use a VC, then raise money from a strategic investor later at a higher valuation.

Vernon Lobo: Strategic investors make you jump through more hoops.

Russell Siegelman: If you think VCs' term sheets are complicated, try Intel's.

Howard Anderson: The experienced VC is used to problems and knows how to stick by companies. The strategic guy says, "Oh, problems? Time to run." The same with angel investors. On another topic, Scott, suppose Goldman Sachs has a strategic relationship with your startup and wants it to standardize its software. Would you be happy?

Scott Lawin: No. I'd want the entrepreneur to do many things with the software. Goldman Sachs wants a financial-service product, and that's it.

Russell Siegelman: Strategic players help with channel share, customers or even technology. But first, entrepreneurs should negotiate an operating agreement. Be sure that interests are aligned before you let the strategic guys invest.

Audience Member: What are the pros and cons of VCs who have invested in companies that could become your strategic partners and customers?

Vernon Lobo: That's a criterion. Investigate. If the VC has such contacts, you can say, "Here are ways you could get synergy between our company and your other companies."

Audience Member: What about building an investment syndicate: VC firms working with other VC firms?

Russell Siegelman: For you, there's value, but the venture guys might balk. Syndication makes it harder for us to get the right percentage of ownership. We'll join only if you're willing to sell 40% or 50% of your company.

Scott Lawin: In a syndicated deal, you need at least one VC who is committed to working with you when problems arise. Cut it up too fine, and the law of diminishing returns takes over.

Audience Member: If we gave up 50% of our company to syndicate with two good VC firms, would one get passive after a while? Would we be better off having just one VC?

Russell Siegelman: It depends. I've been on a board with Benchmark Capital for several years. We work equally hard. Frankly, if any board member isn't delivering, ask that person to leave.

Howard Anderson: Oh, the hardest thing is to get rid of VC board members. They stick around until they smell like last year's cheese.

Audience Member: Do VC firms ever have competing investments managed by different partners?

Russell Siegelman: We try not to. Sometimes we invest in a company that changes its business plan and ends up competing, but we wouldn't allow it going in. Life's too short.

Scott Lawin: Our pockets of investment dollars vary. Some are 100% Goldman Sachs money, some are less. We would not intentionally have 5% in one company and a big investment in an early-stage competitor, but we can live with it.

Howard Anderson: Do you sign nondisclosure agreements?

Scott Lawin: Later on in the process.

Howard Anderson: VCs do want to see that business plan first—the secret recipe.

Audience Member: Why should a soft market lower our valuation?

Russell Siegelman: Same reason a bull market raises valuations.

Howard Anderson: VCs look at what's comparable in the market. A soft market means it will take longer to get liquidity. Let me ask the panel, what was your internal rate of return on investment in 1999?

Discovering the Right VC Firm— and Getting Discovered

HOW TO INCREASE YOUR PROBABILITY OF SUCCESS WITH A VENTURE CAPITALIST

Find someone to refer you to a partner. In the insular venture world, prequalification through a referral will increase the chances of getting in the door.

Know your audience. Do research on the firm, the partners and the portfolio. Tailor your pitch accordingly.

Be succinct. Venture capitalists have notoriously short attention spans.

Be persistent. There is a fine line between persistence and annoyance, and it is that line that many successful entrepreneurs must walk.

Tell a credible story with a clear path to profitability and exit. Be prepared to defend your assumptions.

Engage in discussions with multiple venture firms. Competition breeds action.

WHAT ENTREPRENEURS SHOULD LOOK FOR IN A VENTURE FIRM

Strong network. The best venture partner will have strategic, financial and portfolio-company relationships they can leverage to the company's benefit.

Positive chemistry between entrepreneur and venture partner. Entrepreneurs should ask, do I want this person in a foxhole with me?

Venture partners with relevant operating experience. If they've done it before, they'll be able to help the company see around the corners.

Track record. How many IPOs or sales? How many write-offs?

Deep pockets and determination. Do they have the capital and the resolve to support the company financially in a market downturn?

Strong references. At the appropriate time, talk to CEOs of both successful and failed portfolio companies.

—*Venture capitalist Heberden Ryan*

Russell Siegelman: Ours was incredible. We had Juniper Networks.

Howard Anderson: 600%? You have to report it to your limited partners.

Russell Siegelman: You're not my limited, Howard.

Howard Anderson: Will your late '98 and early '99 investments have lower IRRs when they're liquid?

Russell Siegelman: Absolutely. Look how many companies trade below their IPO prices.

Audience Member: What is Safeguard's incubation strategy?

Craig London: Young companies need operations assistance. They have trouble getting and keeping qualified engineers. The Safeguard family has more than 40 "captive" engineers for software and hardware design. The value of incubating is not in providing shared T-1 services. That's ridiculous. The value is in captive resources and advice.

Howard Anderson: Don't discount angel investors. They're not as demanding as VCs, often have time to help and can tap their relationships.

Russell Siegelman: It's a detriment that angels "are not as demanding." I won't invest where angels have invested at a high valuation and done nothing.

Scott Lawin: It can get ugly when you're negotiating a VC round and angels demand a voice.

Howard Anderson: Some angels run away in tough times. VCs charge a little more, but they are long-term investors. If you need multiple rounds of financing, having a credible VC on your side carries clout.

Audience Member: Many VCs focus on minimizing their portfolio's downside. Shouldn't they be maximizing the upside?

Russell Siegelman: Yes. If VCs wanted mainly short-term dollars, we'd resign from underperformers' boards. We don't. Why? First, we're working with people we want to work with again. Second, we've seen $7 million write-offs that later gave us 300% returns.

Howard Anderson: We also have an emotional investment.

Vernon Lobo: And a reputation to uphold. If something goes awry, we blame ourselves, too, and want to help fix it.

Russell Siegelman: VCs shouldn't let underperforming companies suck up all their time, but we generally err on the side of staying involved.

Audience Member: Do you prefer entrepreneurs whose family and friends have already shown trust by investing?

Venture-Capitalist Terms Defined

Reverse vesting. With reverse vesting, the employee legally owns shares but agrees to sell a portion at a fair market-value price back to the company if leaving before the expiration of the vesting schedule. Reverse-vesting provisions are typically reserved for founders or other critical employees.

Incentive stock option. A stock option issued to an employee with an exercise price equal to or greater than the fair market value of the common stock at the time of issuance.

Strategic investor. A person or entity that derives additional value in a financial transaction beyond the pure economic return. Example: an automotive company investing in a tire company.

Financial investor. A person or entity that derives value in a financial transaction primarily through the pure economic return.

Term sheet. A nonbinding legal document that outlines the basic terms of an investment in a company.

Angels. Wealthy individuals who invest small amounts of their net worth in startup companies.

Syndicate. A consortium of venture firms that invests in a target company.

Nondisclosure agreement (NDA). A legal document proffered by a company to potential investors or partners prior to the dissemination of sensitive company information. The NDA obligates the signer to honor the company's request that the materials and ideas discussed in the business plan or meetings not be shared with any outside party without the express consent of the company.

Internal rate of return (IRR). The discount rate at which the present value of the future cash flows of an investment equal the cost of the investment: the most common measure of an investor's performance.

Initial public offering (IPO). A company's first offering of equity securities to the public market.

Incubator. A firm that provides various services (for example, shared communications and back-office infrastructure, and often shared office space) to early-stage companies, usually in return for an equity stake in the company.

Howard Anderson: Yes, it shows Mommy loves you. Seriously, people have to get started somehow. You may not be able to take a second mortgage or go without salary temporarily. But avoid VCs that are spread too thin. As the economy gets worse and liquidity becomes more difficult, VCs will spend more time and money on current portfolios. You might prefer a new fund. You need VCs with bandwidth and time.

Now it's time to thank the panel. Thanks for not just talking about how your money is better. Thanks for getting to substantive issues that really can help entrepreneurs.

Facilitator: *Howard Anderson, founding partner and senior managing director of YankeeTek Ventures of Cambridge, Massachusetts.*

Participants: *Scott Lawin, a founding member and COO of GSVentures in New York City; Vernon Lobo, managing director of Mosaic Venture Partners in Toronto; Craig London, vice president and general manager of Safeguard Scientifics in Palo Alto, California; and Russell Siegelman, general partner at Kleiner Perkins Caufield & Byers in Menlo Park, California. Contact the participants at*

handerson@yankeetek.com, scott.lawin@gs.com, vernon@mosaicvp.com, clondon@safeguard.com, rsiegelman@kpcb.com

---

Money Order

RAISING MONEY: VENTURE CAPITAL IS WITHIN REACH,
BUT YOU HAVE TO WORK FOR IT. FOLLOW THESE STEPS
TO THAT DEAL-CLOSING HANDSHAKE.

By David R. Evanson & Art Beroff

RAISING VENTURE CAPITAL IS A LOT like painting a room: The actual painting is the final step. What takes the most time is prepping the job—getting rid of old wallpaper, patching, sanding and cleaning.

In this vein, we understand our "Top 100 Venture Capital Firms for Entrepreneurs" list (page 62, *Entrepreneur,* July 2001) might provide irresistible fodder for capital-hungry entrepreneurs. But before you pick up the phone and start dialing for dollars, think about the prep work required to do a good job and be successful. Not sure how to start? The following steps will help:

1. Understand the mission. You need to know what you're looking for. First and foremost, you must find a lead investor. A lead investor is the firm that will either do the whole deal or orchestrate the participation of other venture firms, with their own capital commitments.

2. Form an advisory board. For better or for worse, a good number of deals that reach the closing table get there because of personal relationships somewhere along the line. Forming an advisory board decreases the degrees of separation between you and your potential investors by increasing the likelihood that one or more of the industry notables on your board has a relationship with, or is at least known to, your investors.

Sweet Talk: When investors ask what your company does, they don't want the five-minute soliloquy entrepreneurs typically give them. They want something short and sweet. The following description is a real yawner: "We provide solutions that enable our customers to achieve a substantial time-to-market and business flexibility advantage compared to companies that use traditional Web-based software application development tools...." Instead, try: "We make software that puts real economy in the New Economy," and see if the conversation doesn't go in a more productive direction.

3. Secure legal counsel. A good attorney who's experienced in venture capital transactions may be worth his or her weight in gold when it comes time to actually close the deal. But the reason to hire one from the outset, even before you begin negotiating with venture capital firms, is that retaining counsel gives you access to the attorney's Rolodex and provides entrée to more potential investors. In addition, your attorney's name will (hopefully) dress up

your business plan and, like the advisory board, provide a personal link between you and your investors.

4. Have a business plan and an executive summary at hand. If you're on the line with investors, there's a good chance they'll ask you for your business plan. You'd be wise to have it ready to go so you can send it out immediately. Another important reason to have a business plan available is that it forces you to think through the sort of nettling issues that investors raise, because they could start asking you all kinds of questions while you're on the phone. And you just won't be able to answer them with any degree of clarity or conviction unless you've gone through the discipline of writing a business plan.

Keep in mind, you shouldn't send your full business plan out to investors, even if they ask for it. Send an executive summary instead, and include summary projected financials. When you make follow-up calls, the trick is to make sending your full business plan a condition of meeting face to face. Here is how the call goes: "I appreciate that you want to see more based on our executive summary. I will send you our plan, but only under the condition that you agree to meet in person so I can present it to you."

Of course, the investor might want to meet with you after reading just the execu-

BUZZ

IN NEED OF CPR? Despite a tough market, untimely demise isn't the only possible fate for sound companies facing financial trouble. To avoid a sudden end, they can find resuscitative help in the "Emergency Room," a service recently launched by NVST Inc., a firm that provides research data, deal-making assistance and technology to private equity players and helps investors and entrepreneurs hook up via an online network.

The "E.R." was born as a response to requests from entrepreneurs who were having trouble closing financial deals, says NVST President and COO Samantha Wilkinson. Entrepreneurs—and only owners of established, revenue-producing companies need apply—can register for free at the NVST site, where they can explain their crises and why their companies are worth saving. NVST then matches them with investors who've reviewed the information and want in on the deal. "Many are viable companies," she says of the E.R. patients. "They have a good shot with a little help. So we said, 'Let's try to save as many as we can.'"

—C.J. Prince

tive summary. But as great as that would be, it doesn't obviate the need for writing the plan and deriving the benefits that would result from that exercise. Besides, your next investor might not be satisfied with only the executive summary.

5. Line up your references. Remember, luck is where opportunity and preparation meet. If an investor is itching and wants to talk to vendors, customers, employees, consultants or industry experts, the best solution to offer is a name and a phone number, not a vague "I'll get back to you." Once again, you have to do the groundwork. Call your allies ahead of time, tell them they might get a call, let them know what it's about, and, if it's practical, guide them toward what they should say.

6. Get warm-body introductions. If points one and two failed to drive the message home, then perhaps this one will: You'll get further faster with an introduction to investors than you will if you go after them without one. Maybe it's the saying "It's not what you know, but who you know." Maybe it's a conspiracy to make sure the rich get richer. Maybe it's just human nature. But whatever the reason, avoid contacting people out of the blue if at all possible.

DAVID R. EVANSON is a principal at Gregory FCA (www.devanson@gregoryfca.com), an investor relations firm.

Angel Investors Fill Void Left By Risk Capital

By BONNIE AZAB POWELL

LOS ALTOS, Calif.

Even in a gathering of some 70 people, spotting the money seekers was easy. They were the younger men huddled off to the sides, clutching glasses of mineral water and trying not to look anxious.

All around them, mostly gray-haired or balding Silicon Valley veterans in semiformal attire traded jokes and gossip over cocktails. It was early evening, but the mid-June sun still slanted through the picture window of the Los Altos Golf and Country Club's private dining hall, where the Band of Angels was convening again.

Begun in 1995, the band is an informal club of about 150 "angel" investors, or private financiers, who meet for dinner once a month to network with one another and to listen to representatives from three companies looking for seed capital. Before being invited, each start-up must find an angel from the group to serve as its sponsor (and the investors do not make themselves easy to find by listing the members' names anywhere).

Those seeking money must then pass the due diligence—or vetting—process and survive the final cut administered by Hans Severiens and Ian Sobieski, the band's managing directors. All for the chance to zoom through their PowerPoint presentation in the 20 minutes before the timer next to the podium flashes red.

But running the gantlet can definitely be worthwhile. If a company's presentation is well received, interested investors usually attend a follow-up luncheon a week later, where they may well write a $50,000 to $100,000 personal check in exchange for a small stake in the company.

In early 2000, it was still possible for a start-up to skip the angel stage and go directly to venture capitalists, taking home perhaps $5 million with few questions asked. In the heady days before the tech boom collapsed, the venture capitalists had billion-dollar funds raised from limited partners like universities and could easily afford to risk a pittance on early-stage concepts. No longer.

Venture capital financing fell from $26.1 billion in the first quarter of 2000 to just $10.2 billion for the first quarter of this year, according to PricewaterhouseCoopers/Venture One. What cash there was went mostly to struggling mid-stage companies already in the venture capitalists' portfolios; seed-stage financing plummeted to $32.9 million, down 75 percent from a year earlier.

Not only are venture capitalists shying away from start-ups just getting off the ground, they are also creating a bottleneck down the line for those angels still willing to take a chance. "The companies in the tough spot now are ones that have angel backing but no venture capital," said Steve Jurvetson, managing director of Draper Fisher Jurvetson, an early-stage venture capital fund. "When they need more money, it's difficult to get v.c.'s attention."

Last year the Band of Angels invested roughly $25 million in 23 companies, making the group one of the most active of the many angel networks in the United States. The Center for Venture Research at the University of New Hampshire puts the number of active angels in America at around 400,000. To be accredited, angel investors are required by the Securities and Exchange Commission to have assets of at least $1 million.

Angel investing has become one of the most popular activities for many wealthy people. But it is not a hobby for the impatient or the cautious: angels will not see their money again unless the company successfully goes public or is acquired. Given the youth of these companies, that can take a while even in an environment less hostile than the current one. Since its founding six years ago, fewer than 10 of the group's more than 100 investments have gone public, while about 15 have been acquired.

The group is also, in effect, a social club for Silicon Valley's elite. The Band is distinguished from other angel networks by the credentials of its members, many of them veterans of Intel, Sun Microsystems and other icons of technology development. That can make them an intimidating audience to a lot of struggling entrepreneurs—even more so now that the stock market's deflation has sewn up the purse strings of most other money sources.

"Times being what they are, we have to be realistic," said David Bandych, chief operating officer of the start-up Notiva, No. 2 in the evening lineup. Mr. Bandych and Tom Furphy, Notiva's chief executive, both left the East Coast supermarket chain Wegmans in early 2000 to found their software company, based in Rochester.

"I think it's a good thing we didn't get funding last year," Mr. Bandych added, not entirely convincingly. "We've had to get customers and prove ourselves first instead."

Sharply at 7:30 p.m., Mr. Severiens urged everyone to be seated. "If we don't get started now we'll all be here way past our bedtimes," he chastised the group, with the trace of a Dutch accent that remains even after half a century in the United States. Mr. Severiens' breadth of experience—a nuclear physicist who worked for Perkin-Elmer and the Atomic Energy Commission before becoming an investment banker at Morgan Stanley and other white shoe firms—is par for the course among members of this group.

He calls himself and Mr. Sobieski the Band's chefs, setting a smorgasbord of wine, food and good companies to nibble on.

But first comes the warm-up act from Fred Hoar, a co-founder of the group and a public relations maestro whose decades-long career has touched landmark technology companies from Fairchild Camera, whose later exiles founded Intel, to Apple Computer before it went public. Mr. Hoar began with a cheery "Greetings, Angels and Angelettes, Welcome to You Bet Your Assets, our monthly walk on the wild side of Wall Street."

He flashed a grin before taking aim at, among others, himself—regarding his rumpled cream suit, he joked, "Summer must be here: I look like a symphony in oatmeal." And he could not help noting the pain the group felt from the stock market. "As someone said," Mr. Hoar remarked, "I don't know whether to kill myself or go bowling."

Once the laughter died down and the salad course was cleared, the real business began in earnest. First up was Cardiac Focus, a medical device company developing a disposable vest that will help doctors screen and map cardiac arrythmias without surgery.

Craig McMullen, 57, recently recruited as the company's chief executive, is even balder than most of the angels, and delivered his PowerPoint presentation in a quietly urgent monotone. The company was on the prowl for $2 million to complete the development team, perform clinical trials, and file for Food and Drug Administration approval. Given the angels' own aging hearts and the company's sponsors before the group—among them Wally Buch, a heart surgeon, and Tom Fogarty, also a surgeon and the inventor of the first balloon catheter—it was no surprise that they paid close attention to the spiel.

Several hands went up for questions, particularly about regulatory issues, which were handled confidently by Terry Ransbury, 39, the company's co-founder and its chief technology officer.

Mr. Furphy, 35, of Notiva went next. He started off badly, with an audience participation trick—"Who's had a career in accounts payable?"—that elicited weary sighs. One angel took a look at Mr. Furphy's nearly shaved head and whispered, "Who'd trust someone with a haircut like that?" But as Mr. Furphy described the big retailers that are already using Notiva's software to automatically reconcile purchase orders, invoices, and shipping and receiving discrepancies, heads started nodding. The company's management team, with years of experience at Wegmans, also got the thumbs-up.

Then the 20-minute timer on the table turned yellow. With three minutes left, Mr. Furphy sped through his PowerPoint presentation like the pitchmen in the latest Toyota commercials, abandoning sentences halfway through. "We've thought about getting a hook for moments like these," Mr. Hoar confided.

The brief Q.& A. consisted mostly of questions about Notiva's venture capital financing. Notiva's team was hoping to raise $500,000 from the angels to tide them over until they secure $3 million to $5 million in venture capital.

The audience was tiring in spite of the regular coffee making the

rounds. And the final start-up, a developer of software platforms to allow wireless carriers to customize their mobile phone offerings, did not perk them back up. One investor even fell asleep over his apple tart.

Afterward, as people milled around, Mr. Furphy insisted that his timer malfunctioned. "I was robbed of a good seven minutes!" he laughed. He was not too troubled; apparently several angels indicated that they would show up for Notiva's follow-up lunch.

Before the chill in investing hit, two of the three companies that presented themselves to the Band could probably expect to get checks. Now, it's more likely to be one. But which?

As it turned out, no one but Notiva's sponsors and the two managing directors showed up for its lunch. The band's members were cautious, waiting to see if the company was indeed about to get a "term sheet," a venture capital contract. Others were less concerned. The morning of the follow-up, said Mark Brandt, the company's chief development officer, a single angel investor from outside the group committed to the entire sum.

The clear favorite of the evening was Cardiac Focus. In the week following the dinner, 10 members wrote checks, while another four rounded out the company's $2 million goal at its lunch.

"The mechanisms of the funding are pretty much the same, independent of product," Mr. Ransbury of Cardiac Focus, wrote in an e-mail the day after the dinner. "If you get critical mass with the investors whom the followers admire, then the deal happens. If not, it really doesn't matter, even if you have the cure for cancer."

But Cardiac Focus still faces many hurdles, including proving its device works well enough to get F.D.A. approval and eligibility for Medicare reimbursement.

At least now it has a greater chance of finding out. "The lust for entrepreneurship has not changed," said Mr. Severiens. "And now there are great bargains to be had."

FINANCE

The do's and don'ts of fund raising

Simple mistakes reduce chances of nailing a venture investment

It isn't David Letterman's Top 10 list, and entrepreneurs probably won't find it funny.

With venture funding harder to come by these days, entrepreneurs have to be twice as savvy as they were a couple of years ago when capital was flowing freely. Yet, start-ups seeking funding invariably make the same mistakes, experts say."

"It amazes me how many people we meet today who have not thought through what they are going to say when asking for funds," says Bethesda, MD-based BeaconVentureCapital.com managing director John Groth. With most VCs now more cautious with their money, he says, it is increasingly important to avoid pitfalls.

The venture market is more competitive than ever, says David Lavinsky, president of Los Angeles-based Growthink Inc., a fund-raising consultancy. Record-breaking numbers of companies are seeking venture capital, while at the same time, investors are getting skittish. "They are taking a hard look at the performance of their past investments and weighing whether their money is better spent on second-round financing for an existing venture, or taking a risk on a new one," Lavinsky says.

One of the biggest mistakes a growing business can make is to put forth a poorly constructed presentation to a VC, according to Donald F. Kuratko, Stoops Distinguished Professor of Business and founding director of Ball State University's entrepreneurship program. "Although VCs may be able to spot a diamond in the rough when it becomes a proposal for funds, it's never a good idea to make the person you are asking for money wade through typos, stammering, upside-down slides and other troubling signs of inattention to detail," Kuratko says.

In some cases, companies are paying attention to the wrong details, Lavinsky says. When pitching to a VC, enterprises (especially those in high tech) should emphasize the marketing of their particular technology, not the technology itself. "Many companies focus on having the best mousetrap," he says. "You can have the best mousetrap but still not get funding." He points to **Microsoft Corp.**, Redmond, WA, whose marketing prowess generally has rendered its software bugs moot.

Even before developing the next mousetrap, start-ups should survey their potential customer base and stake out a niche, Lavinsky advises. "There are too many mousetraps that don't meet customer needs, and no one will spend a dime on those."

If partnering seems like a good way to secure funding, entrepreneurs should nonetheless put a finite lifecycle on the pact,

---

TOP 10 REASONS
BUSINESSES DON'T GET FUNDING

1. **Making financial projections too aggressive**. Poorly reasoned, inconsistent or simply unrealistic figures on market penetration, operating margin or revenue-per-employee greatly damage the credibility of the entire business plan.

2. **Presenting large, generic market sizes**. Forget the trillion-dollar market. Business plans should determine the *relevant market size*, which equals a venture's sales if it were to capture 100% of its specific niche.

3. **Focusing too much on proprietary technology**. It's much more important to show how the technology satisfies a large, unfulfilled customer need.

4. **Stressing first-mover advantage**. Being first to market is great, but a business plan must demonstrate how the venture will create long-term barriers around its customers.

5. **Indiscriminately incorporating investor feedback into the business plan**. Investors, like everyone else, have different tastes. Incorporate only common concerns.

6. **Asking investors to sign an NDA**. Only proprietary technology is truly confidential, and the business plan should discuss the benefits—not the confidential aspects—of the technology.

7. **Not tailoring management biographies to the development phase**. Different management skill sets are needed to launch, grow and/or maintain a venture, and should be highlighted accordingly.

8. **Overemphasizing partnerships with well-known companies**. Partnerships by themselves have limited value. Business plans must delineate equitable and value-added partnership *terms*.

9. **Focusing too much on the future**. The best indicator of future performance is past performance. Business plans must demonstrate a venture's past track record.

10. **Excluding other successful companies from the competitive analysis**. Successful competitors can be a positive sign; they imply the market size is big and that the venture may have substantial profit and liquidity potential.

SOURCE: GROWTHINK INC.

---

experts say. "Plan on canceling a partnership if it doesn't bear fruit within a fixed period of time," Lavinsky says. Too many partnerships drag on, assuming one of the partners is winning customers. Finally, new ventures should plan on being financially conservative, but also realistic. Companies don't want to run out of funding—they may not get a second chance.

—Barbara Jorgensen

UNIT 4

Managing Growth and Creating Harvest Options

Unit Selections

Key Points to Consider

• What is the difference between entrepreneurial management and professional management?

• Why do so many owner-managed companies fail to escape their initial entrepreneurial phase?

• What exit options are available to entrepreneurs? What are the legal requirements for going public?

• How do entrepreneurs determine conditions that trigger a harvest or exit?

 **Links: www.dushkin.com/online/**
These sites are annotated in the World Wide Web pages.

American Civil Liberties Union
http://www.aclu.org/issues/worker/campaign.html

Center for Entrepreneurial Leadership Clearinghouse on Entrepreneurship Education
http://www.celcee.edu

Edward Lowe Foundation
http://www.lowe.org

High Performance Team
http://rampages.onramp.net/bodwell/home.htm

Sheffield University Management School
http://www.shef.ac.uk/uni/academic/I-M/mgt/research/research.html

U.S. Equal Employment Opportunity Commission
http://www.eeoc.gov

As profiled in the previous units, nimble and agile entrepreneurial companies have replaced the old-school business models with new leadership tactics, a hunger for creating value, and an obsession with opportunity that is unbeatable in the marketplace for talent and ideas. This unit looks at what happens after startup, such as managing rapid growth and creating harvest options. The set of changes that startups need to make as they rapidly grow is often termed the transition from entrepreneurial to professional management. This unit only begins to address the issues that startups must deal with in making the transition.

The growth of any new business venture is a product of both the opportunity selection and management factors. The true mark of a good venture is how it manages growth and whether it can sustain it. Centralized decision making and informal controls characterize entrepreneurial management. In startups, one person can comprehend all the information required for decision making and there is little need for formal procedures. The venture is small enough that business activity can be monitored via the supervision of the entrepreneur. The ventures that survive the growth phase have a disciplined team with intellectual honesty; they know what they know and do not know. Their honesty prevents a myopic vision that might be intoxicated by current success. They are also quick to delegate decision-making responsibility.

The entrepreneurial challenges of leadership and the job of management in a fast-growing venture can be complex and difficult. Entrepreneurs new at leadership often feel that they must have all the answers and must dictate policy or they will be seen as weak. But breaking through the growth wall requires an organization-wide transition from a culture of entrepreneurial doers and managers to entrepreneurial coaches and team leaders. Leadership is about knowing when to lead and when to step aside. Leaders should manage through directions, discussion, and suggestions.

Coordinating profitable, rapid growth requires a detailed plan and budget. Also, employees who are capable of delivering the desired outcomes in the growth plan must be hired. Entrepreneurs of startups should know that it is never too late to start developing smart tactics/practices for finding workers. Startups must be prepared, as they enter the battle for talented workers, with a plan, creative compensation packages, capital budgets with room for human capital investment, and other powerful strategic weaponry. Just as the most successful startup ventures have business plans, operational or manufacturing plans, and financial plans, companies that grow to the next level, breaking through the growth wall, also have internal plans for expansion.

The harvest of a business is the venture team's and investors' combined strategy for achieving the final cash rewards on their capital investment. In his book *The Seven Habits of Highly Effective People,* Steven Covey says that one of the keys to being effective in life is "beginning with the end in mind." To paraphrase Covey, entrepreneurs need to visualize the end of their venture and then develop a plan to make it happen even though it may take 5, 10, 15 years, or more to build a venture of significant net worth.

The harvest of a business venture can be a bittersweet experience. While it represents the ending of a long struggle to build financial values, it can also represent an emotional end to a rewarding experience. But a harvest decision does not always mean that the entrepreneur will leave the company. If the entrepreneur is successful, significant value will have been created. The issue then becomes harvesting and distributing that value. Quite often a harvest is triggered by outside investors who become a source of pressure on the venture team. The changes in lifestyle or other personal desires of the venture team may also begin to press for some form of harvest.

The structuring of a harvest strategy depends on options available to the entrepreneur. Many of these options depend on an assessment of the value of the business, which is a most difficult task. When it comes to developing a harvest strategy for the entrepreneur and the investors, the entrepreneur will need to attempt to value the company's assets for which a great amount of incomplete and conflicting information may exist. Based upon the valuation, there can be a number of alternatives available to the entrepreneur to end the venture—some are straightforward, others involve a more complex financial strategy. This unit presents the reader with a brief look at these options.

For almost all entrepreneurs, ending a venture is a huge undertaking. A venture worth harvesting is a venture that becomes a dominant part of their lives. Thus, the decision to harvest a venture cannot effectively be made apart from the entrepreneur's personal goals. Likewise, creating a harvest strategy should be a planned activity involving outside advisers and professionals, much like the preparation of a business plan. Creating such a strategy can never begin too early in the venture because, as with planning in other situations, the process itself is more important than the plan. For instance, venture capitalists prefer to invest in management teams with ideas for reaping profits, such as a merger or an initial public offering (IPO). They are critically interested in a mechanism that will allow them to exit the venture, liquidate their investment, and maximize after-tax cash flows. Entrepreneurs should look at the harvesting of a venture as a point in the future where preparation and opportunity meet, not necessarily when an opportunity is at an end.

"Are you built to grow?"

SETH GODIN

Is your company built to grow? I remember hiring my first, second, and third real employees. Whenever I hired someone, I was sure that person would be the last hire I'd ever make. I agonized over all three hires and spent months training them to put up with me. Since everyone I hired was going to be the very last person I would ever hire, each had to fit into the jigsaw puzzle of my company perfectly. If I needed a left-handed crochet specialist, well, that's what I hired. After all, this was it.

It became clear that I was fooling myself when I realized that there were seven people working in the attic of my house. And there were more people working in the guest bedroom. And there were even more people working in the dressing room. My wife tried to put a stop to the craziness after she discovered one too many containers of yogurt in the fridge. But the final straw was when I tried to convince her that it would be okay to have people work in our bedroom, "since they would be gone at night, and that's the only time *we* need it."

Once we moved to our first offices, it occurred to me that a subtle but very real change was happening to me—something that happens to an awful lot of bootstrapping entrepreneurs. Instead of building a company that would be profitable today, tomorrow, and forever, I was building a company that would grow. Almost none of the job growth in the United States over the past two decades has come from large, established companies. Big companies don't add jobs, but small companies do—especially new small companies.

It's not unusual to hear about a tech company that has 1,000 or more jobs to fill. Visit the Web sites of most aggressive startups, and you'll see plenty of help-wanted ads—even from companies that are in financial trouble. "Grow or die" is the slogan of the day.

But for a lot of these companies, the slogan should be something different: "Grow *and* die." Many of them probably *shouldn't* be growing so fast. Maybe they should slow down, focus, and get it right. But let's assume for a minute that hypergrowth is really necessary for your company. Let's assume that you've got your market by the tail and that the orders are going to go either to you or to a competitor—whoever grows faster.

So the question is, Are you built to grow? If you're basing your business's structure on the principles invented during the Industrial Revolution, it's not very likely. (But there is a lot to learn about the way that those old companies did their hiring.)

For 100 years, the key component in just about any company was the factory. The factory gated growth: It doesn't do any good to hire more workers until you've got a factory for them! And once a factory was built and staffed, the goal was to tweak it, tune it, and adjust it—not to overhaul it radically on a regular basis.

As a result of this heritage, most companies today have no idea how to organize for ongoing growth—especially ongoing growth of independent-thinking, white-collar types. Let's say that your goal is to add 200 people to your 400-person company this year. How should you go about doing that? Here are nine ways to think about the task.

Decentralize your hiring approach. If half of the people working for you are able to find someone better than they are to join the company, that can simultaneously solve your hiring problem and dramatically improve the quality of your workforce.

One word of caution: This approach will definitely *not* work if it's just another program, or if it's run by human resources (the least respected department in the company). If, on the other hand, you pay your employees a bonus equal to what you'd pay a headhunter ($30,000 a hire in some cases), and a big part of the CEO's job is to promote this program, *and* it's a critical part of job performance, then you may discover that the program fundamentally changes the way that you grow. After all, evangelical churches don't delegate converting heathens to the HR department—they charge every single parishioner with going out and preaching.

Don't just fill jobs—hire people. Advanced Micro Devices occasionally uses this approach: When executives find someone they really love, they hire first and find a job later. Some companies even offer hotshots a "gift certificate" that's good for a job anytime. (Hold on to that blue slip: Someday, you're going to want to work at Intel, and that slip will get you a job—instantly.)

Start a William Morris mail room. Barry Diller started there. So did many of the top agents in Hollywood. It's simple: If you want to break into agenting, get a job in the mail room at William Morris Talent Agency.

The beauty of this approach is that William Morris really can't make any horrible hires. After all, most people can do a pretty good job distributing the mail, and if they can't, well, firing the new guy and starting over won't cause a whole lot of service interruption.

By dramatically lowering the downside of a bad hire, the firm makes it easy to take chances, to get people in the door, and to let them prove themselves. Is it harder to get good people at first? No doubt. How many people want to tell their spouse that they are quitting their job to work in a mail room?

Start legends. One of the best ways to get people to want to come to work in your mail room is to make a big deal of the people who *used* to work there. There are plenty of companies that have famous CEOs but that keep their employees under wraps. Can you name three people who work for Cisco or Oracle?

By turning your employees into famed success stories, you run the risk of them leaving. But that's okay, because you make it more and more likely that dozens of other hotshots will come to take their place. It's worked for Jack Welch: Other companies raid his executive pool, and even more talent fills it back up.

All of these tips are fine, but what good are good people if you wreck them after hiring them or acquiring their company? If you're going to grow fast, that means that most of the time, the majority of the people in your company are new or are working with someone who's new. And that means new strategies.

Obsess over where people sit. Most companies allow their employees to get very comfortable with their spot in the office. It saves time and allows people to get into communication grooves. It can also ruin a fast-growing company. Here are the stories of two managers I know.

One manager took a hot, new hire and sat him *inside his own cube* for 60 days. That meant that every single person who came to visit the manager also met the new hire. It also meant that the manager and the new hire had

plenty of time for side chats and data exchange—a real-time indoctrination period.

The other manager took a recently acquired executive and sat her clear on the other side of the building for 60 days. He met with her four times—about once every two weeks.

Who's more likely to catch fire? Who's going to influence the company in a hurry?

If you're hiring hundreds of people, you should be reorganizing the desks in your office every week. Create cells or covens or hives or whatever you want to call them. Intermingle people. Don't sit all of the engineers together all the time—unless you want the marketing people to talk about "those guys in engineering."

Of course, it's not just about where people sit during the day. The company cafeteria can quickly become as segregated as the one in your old high school. Don't let all the jocks sit together. Why not offer old-timers a free lunch every time they invite a new person to eat with them?

Invite people over for dinner. How many kids does your boss's boss have? Is her husband a good cook? These are the little social cues that lead to long-term ease of communication. Knowing the people you work with helps make them feel more like family, which makes it far more likely that people are going to come to work with the attitude that you're looking for. It's way easier to lobby to have a new and challenging coworker thrown out of the company if you've never eaten a burger charred beyond recognition on his grill.

Publish a yearbook. Hire someone whose only job is to interview and profile new employees. Find out entertaining things about new employees. Brag about their past accomplishments. Take clever photographs. Turn your new hires into stars.

Distribute your findings in a book on an Internet-year basis, which for most companies is every month. And give your new hires back issues. That way, everybody has read a magazine-like profile of every single employee within a week of showing up for work. The result: People are more proud of the people they work with. The hiring process is much easier if you let prospective employees read past issues to help them decide whether to accept your job offer.

Note: If people aren't cool enough to brag about in the year-book, then don't hire them!

Send people to school. The best way to have amazing people is to help your current people grow into amazing people. And that means that everyone from the CEO on down takes two or more challenging courses a year. My favorites are the Dale Carnegie public-speaking class and Zig Ziglar's course on selling. Why? Because most employees are afraid to do one or the other. And because all employees can do better at speaking and selling—even if they're not in sales.

Just think: If you grow your own all-stars, you can go back to hiring for the mail room.

Make everyone wear a name tag—every day. That's my all-time favorite tactic. It's the real reason why I wrote this. Rule: If you forget your name tag, you are sent home to get it. The name tag is a powerful badge, the symbol of a fast-growing company. The name tag says that you are proud of your growth. And the name tag shows that you are serious about widespread interpersonal communication—up and down the organization.

I once ran a project with 90 new employees, all of whom started on the same day. We all wore painter's caps with our names on them. And we wore them until every single person knew everyone else's name. It took two weeks.

At Apple, everyone knows Steve Jobs. He doesn't need a name tag. But everyone else at the company does, because there's no way that Jobs knows everyone else! So he should wear one too. It's only fair.

"Hello! My name is…"

If you're serious about growing, put on a name tag today.

SETH GODIN (SGODIN@FASTCOMPANY.COM) IS THE AUTHOR OF *PERMISSION MARKETING: TURNING STRANGERS INTO FRIENDS, AND FRIENDS INTO CUSTOMERS* (SIMON & SCHUSTER, 1999) AND THE FOUNDER OF YOYODYNE ENTERTAINMENT.

MANAGING GROWTH

The set of changes that smaller, younger firms need to make as they grow is often termed *the transition from entrepreneurial to professional management*. This [article] addresses the issues that firms must deal with in making the transition:

•What is entrepreneurial management and how does it differ from professional management?

•What pressures force the firm to make the transition?

•How can entrepreneurs and their firms make the transition with a greater chance of success?

by Michael J. Roberts

Entrepreneurial and Professional Management

The terms *entrepreneurial* and *professional management* mean very different things to different people. To some, *entrepreneurial management* suggests creative people and an innovative and successful organization, while *professional management* implies a stifling bureaucracy. To others, entrepreneurs are associated with disorganization, and professional management offers efficiency and effectiveness. For the sake of this [article], however, *entrepreneurial* and *professional management* are merely descriptive terms and imply nothing about the creativity, innovation, or success of the organization.

Entrepreneurial Management

Entrepreneurial management is a style of management that is typically used when the firm is young and small. It is characterized by a number of features, including:
- *Centralized decision making*: In a small organization, the general manager can usually make most of the decisions required to manage the firm. The business is sufficiently small and simple enough that one person can comprehend all the information required for decision making.
- *Informal control*: The entrepreneurial firm is typically informal. There is little need for formal procedures, systems, and structures because the firm is small enough that activity can be moni-

tored via the personal supervision of the entrepreneur. Moreover, the firm is young and inexperienced and has not yet learned the routines required for success.

The entrepreneur's own ability to collect information, make decisions, and monitor their implementation reduces the need for formal structure, policies, and procedures.

Professional Management

Professional management is characterized by:
- *Delegation of decision-making responsibility*: Larger firms are sufficiently complex that one individual cannot make all of the decisions required to manage the firm. Therefore, the general manager must delegate responsibility to a hierarchy of middle managers. This pattern of delegation both determines and is determined by the firm's structure.
- *Use of formal control systems*: In response to the delegation of decision-making responsibility, formal systems are introduced. Because the general manager does not *personally* make all of the firm's decisions, there is a need for systems to guide and evaluate the performance of those who *are* making those decisions. These systems usually include a mechanism for setting objectives, monitoring performance against those objectives, and rewarding desired performance. In

addition, general managers also develop policies and standard procedures to guide the actions of those below.

The "Strategy of Coordination"

Just as the firm has an (explicit or implicit) strategy for its actions in the competitive marketplace, it also has an internal strategy for coordinating its efforts. Essentially, the dimensions of organization that we have been discussing are all elements of the way in which the firm chooses to coordinate its efforts.

There are two key dimensions to the strategy of coordination:

- The delegation of responsibility: whether the general manager makes the day-to-day operating decisions personally or delegates that decision-making responsibility to a hierarchy of middle managers.
- The use of formal control systems: whether the firm uses formal systems to set objectives, monitor performance, and control the activities of organization members.

These two dimensions describe a broad range of approaches to coordinating the firm's efforts. If we simply think in terms of the two-by-two matrix defined by these two dimensions, we can see that there are four archetypical strategies of coordination:

- Entrepreneurial management, which relies on centralized decision making and informal, personal control.
- Professional management, which utilizes the delegation of responsibility and extensive formal controls.
- Laissez-faire management, in which responsibilities are delegated, but control remains informal.
- Bureaucratic management, in which centralized decision making is supplemented with formal control.

		Use of Formal Control Mechanisms	
		Low	*High*
Delegation of Responsibility	**High**	Laissez-faire management	Professional management
	Low	Entrepreneurial management	Bureaucratic management

A *fundamental proposition* that underlies these ideas is that decisions regarding delegation and control have a strong influence on the firm's performance along two critical dimensions:

- Efficiency: the firm's ability to achieve its goals with a minimum of resources.
- Effectiveness: the firm's ability to adapt its goals and innovate to meet the changing needs of its environment.

Moreover, these two performance dimensions—and the decisions regarding delegation and control that underlie them—are fundamentally in *opposition*. Broadly speaking, choices that favor delegation have the potential to increase effectiveness, but simultaneously decrease efficiency; and the use of formal controls increases efficiency while reducing effectiveness. *Thus, the general manager's choices regarding delegation and control determine how these critical trade-offs are made.*

Making the Transition to Professional Management

When properly implemented, professional management offers an approach to coordinating the activities of a larger, more complex organization while avoiding the problems inherent in laissez-faire or bureaucratic management. There are several steps required for a successful transition to professional management.

Recognizing the Need for Change

The first step in the transition process is a recognition of the need for change. This is often extremely difficult because it is a by-product of success. Success reinforces beliefs and behavior that are appropriate to the entrepreneurial mode but that may not fit the needs of a larger, more complex firm.

Frequently, it is a crisis of some sort that highlights the need for change. Fortunately, knowledgeable outsiders can often help the entrepreneur see the need for such change before a crisis. Experienced board members or consultants can spot the early warning signs: lack of follow-up on details, incredible stress on the individual entrepreneur, and a sense of organizational disarray.

Once the entrepreneur has recognized the need for change, it is often difficult to know what to change *to*. Those who have successfully made the transition report that it requires a fundamental change in orientation: The manager must shift from getting personal satisfaction from direct action to a mode where that sense of accomplishment comes from achieving results *through others*.

Developing the Human Resources

Given this change of personal role in the organization, the entrepreneur needs to develop the human resources required to implement that model. Often, individuals who can accept and execute responsibility are not present in the entrepreneurial organization. The entrepreneur's style has made it difficult for aggressive, independent employees to survive. Moreover, many young firms simply lack the resources to attract and hire managerial talent.

In order to develop a competent managerial team, the entrepreneur must overcome personal loyalties that threaten the organization. In virtually every firm, the entrepreneur has a "right-hand person" without whom the business would not have survived in the early years. Unfortunately, many of these employees are unable to develop the more specialized skills needed to grow with the company. Entrepreneurs must overcome their personal loyalties and find more suitable employees for critical positions.

Delegating Responsibility

Once the entrepreneur has perceived the need for change and developed a management team, real delegation of responsibility can begin. The power of professional management lies in placing the responsibility close to the source of information required for sound decision making. Typically, this means delegating responsibility to managers who are close to customers, suppliers, and competitors. In the process of delegating, the general manager must be careful *not* to give up responsibility for key policy issues that require personal perspective. Moreover, delegation does not mean that the entrepreneur loses the opportunity to have *input* into the decision-making process; surely, the benefit of that experience should not be lost.

Developing Formal Controls

A final step in the transition process is the development of formal control mechanisms. Successful entrepreneurs realize that, with the onset of delegation, they can no longer control the behavior of individuals in the organization. It is important that the focus of the control system shifts to performance rather than behavior. In addition, successful firms realize the danger in simply adapting policies and procedures that are used at other firms. Firms that customize policies ensure that the practice makes sense for the organization. The process of devoting time and effort often inspires creative solutions, and builds commitment.

Conclusion

The reason why the transition to professional management is often so difficult is that it requires *far more* than changes in organizational systems and structures. It requires a *fundamental change in the attitudes and behaviors of the entrepreneur*. Merely creating organizational structures and systems accomplishes little if the entrepreneur is unwilling to truly delegate. Control systems are meaningless if the entrepreneur fails to use them. It is this need to fundamentally change the individual general manager's self-concept behavior that makes the transition process so difficult.

Managing Global Expansion: A Conceptual Framework

Anil K. Gupta and Vijay Govindarajan

There are at least five reasons why the need to become global has ceased to be a discretionary option and become a strategic imperative for virtually any medium-sized to large corporation.

1. *The Growth Imperative.* Companies have no choice but to persist in a neverending quest for growth if they wish to garner rewards from the capital markets and attract and retain top talent. For many industries, developed country markets are quite mature. Thus, the growth imperative generally requires companies to look to emerging markets for fresh opportunities.

Consider a supposedly mature industry such as paper. Per capita paper consumption in such developed markets as North America and Western Europe is around 600 pounds. In contrast, per capita consumption of paper in China and India is around 30 pounds. If you are a dominant European paper manufacturer such as UPM-Kymmene, can you really afford not to build market presence in places like China or India? If per capita paper consumption in both countries increased by just one pound over the next five years, demand would increase by 2.2 billion pounds, an amount that can keep five state-of-the-art paper mills running at peak capacity.

2. *The Efficiency Imperative.* Whenever the value chain sustains one or more activities in which the minimum efficient scale (of research facilities, production centers, and so on) exceeds the sales volume feasible within one country, a company with global presence will have the potential to create a cost advantage relative to a domestic player within that industry. The case of Mercedes-Benz, now a unit of DaimlerChrysler, illustrates this principle. Historically, Mercedes-Benz has concentrated its research and manufacturing operations in Germany and has derived around 20 percent of its revenues from the North American market. Given the highly scale-sensitive nature of the auto industry, it is easy to see that Mercedes-Benz's ability to

compete in Europe, or even Germany, hinges on its market position and revenues from the North American market.

3. *The Knowledge Imperative.* No two countries, even close neighbors such as Canada and the United States, are completely alike. So when a company expands its presence to more than one country, it must adapt at least some features of its products and/or processes to the local environment. This adaptation requires creating local know-how, some of which may be too idiosyncratic to be relevant outside the particular local market. However, in many cases, local product and/or process innovations are cutting-edge and have the potential to generate global advantage. GE India's innovations in making CT scanners simpler, transportable, and cheaper would appear to enjoy wide-ranging applicability, as would P&G Indonesia's innovations in reducing the cost structure for cough syrup.

> Going international needs no grand design, but neither should a company wander aimlessly into the global jungle.

4. *Globalization of Customers.* The term "globalization of customers" refers to customers that are worldwide corporations (such as the soft-drink companies served by advertising agencies) as well as those who are internationally mobile (such as the executives served by American Express or the globe-trotters serviced by Sheraton Hotels). When the customers of a domestic company start to globalize, the company must keep pace with them. Three reasons dictate such an alignment. First, the customer may strongly prefer worldwide consistency and coordination in the sourcing of products and services. Second, it may prefer

to deal with a small number of supply partners on a long-term basis. Third, allowing a customer to deal with different supplier(s) in other countries poses a serious risk that the customer may replace your firm with one of these suppliers even in the domestic market. Motivations such as these are driving GE Plastics to globalize. Historically, it supplied plastic pellets to largely U.S.-based telephone companies such as AT&T and GTE. As these firms globalized and set up manufacturing plants outside the U.S., GE Plastics had no choice but to follow them abroad.

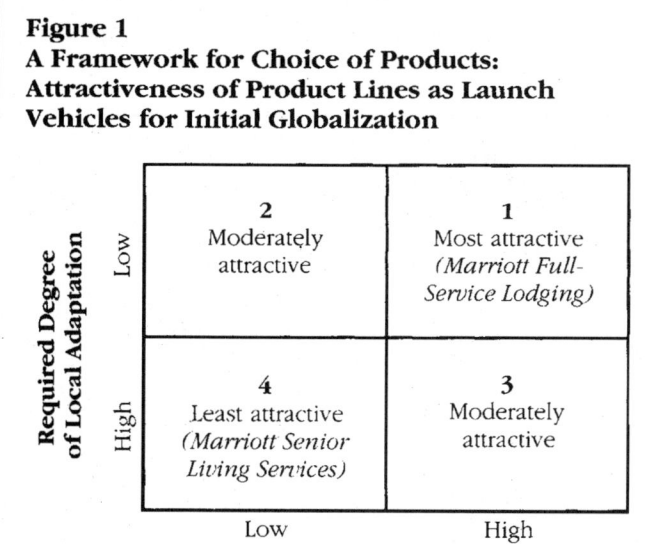

Figure 1
A Framework for Choice of Products: Attractiveness of Product Lines as Launch Vehicles for Initial Globalization

5. *Globalization of Competitors.* If your competitors start to globalize and you do not, they can use their global stronghold to attack you in at least two ways. First, they can develop a first-mover advantage in capturing market growth, pursuing global scale efficiencies, profiting from knowledge arbitrage, and providing a coordinated source of supply to global customers. Second, they can use multi-market presence to cross-subsidize and wage a more intense attack in your own home markets. It is dangerous to underestimate the rate at which competition can accelerate the pace of globalization. Look at Fuji's inroads into the U.S. market, historically dominated by Kodak. The trend is happening in other industries as well, such as in white goods, personal computers, and financial services.

In the emerging era, every industry must be considered a global industry. Today, globalization is no longer an option but a strategic imperative for all but the smallest firms. The following framework and set of conceptual ideas can guide firms in approaching the strategic challenge of casting their business lines overseas and building global presence:

- *How should a multiproduct firm choose the product line to launch it into the global market?*
- *What factors make some markets more strategic than others?*

- *What should companies consider in determining the right mode of entry?*
- *How should the enterprise transplant the corporate DNA as it enters new markets?*
- *What approaches should the company use to win the local battle?*
- *How rapidly should a company expand globally?*

CHOICE OF PRODUCTS

When any multiproduct firm chooses to go abroad, it must ask itself whether it should globalize the entire portfolio simultaneously or use a subset of product lines. Firms can make this choice randomly and opportunistically or in a well thought out and systematic manner.

Consider the case of Marriott Corporation, which was essentially a domestic company in the late 1980s. It had two principal lines of business: lodging and contract services. Besides other activities, the lodging sector included four distinct product lines: full-service hotels and resorts ("Marriott" brand), midprice hotels ("Courtyard" brand), budget hotels ("Fairfield Inn" brand), and long-term stay hotels ("Residence Inn" brand). On the other hand, contract services included the following three product lines: Marriott Management Services, Host/Travel Plazas, and Marriott Senior Living Services (retirement communities). As the company embarked on globalization, it had to confront the question of which one or more of these product lines should serve as the starting point for its globalization efforts.

Global expansion forces companies to develop at least three types of capabilities: learning about foreign markets, learning how to manage people in foreign locations, and learning how to manage foreign subsidiaries. Until firms develop these capabilities, they cannot avoid remaining strangers in a strange land, with global expansion posing a high risk. Engaging in simultaneous globalization across the entire portfolio of products compounds these risks dramatically. So it is often wiser to choose one or a small number of product lines as the initial launch vehicles for globalization. The choice should adhere to the twin goals of maximizing the returns while minimizing the risks associated with early moves abroad. These initial moves represent experiments with high learning potential. It is important that these experiments succeed for the firm because success creates psychological confidence, political credibility, and cash flow to fuel further rapid globalization.

Figure 1 presents a conceptual framework to identify those products, business units, or lines of business that might be preferred candidates for early globalization. Underlying this framework are two essential dimensions by which to evaluate each line of business in the company's portfolio—one pertaining to potential returns (expected payoffs) and the other to potential risks (required degree of local adaptation).

The first dimension focuses on the magnitude of globalization's payoffs, which tend to be higher when the five imperatives (listed at the beginning of the article) are stronger. Looking at the case of Marriott, it is clear that such imperatives are much stronger for full-service lodging than they are for the retirement community business. The primary customers of full-service lodging are globe-trotting corporate executives. In such a business, worldwide presence can create significant value by using a centralized reservation system, developing and diffusing globally consistent service concepts, and leveraging a well-known brand name that assures customers of high quality and service. In contrast, none of these factors is of high salience in the retirement community business, thereby rendering the imperatives for globalization much less urgent.

The second dimension of our framework concerns the extent to which different lines of business require local adaptation to succeed in foreign markets. The greater the extent of such adaptation, the greater the degree to which new product and/or service features would need to be developed locally rather than cloned from proven and preexisting concepts and capabilities. Because any new development involves risk, the greater the degree of required local adaptation, the greater the risks of failure—particularly when such development entails the already significant "liability of foreignness." Marriott exemplifies these principles. Compared with full-service lodging, the retirement community business is a very local business and thus requires more local adaptation.

Combining both dimensions, as indicated in Figure 1, full-service lodging emerges as a particularly attractive candidate for early globalization. As the spearhead for globalization moves, it provides Marriott with a high return/low risk laboratory for developing the knowledge and skills needed for foreign market entry and managing foreign subsidiaries. Having thus overcome the "liability of foreignness," Marriott would be better positioned to exploit the globalization potential of its other lines of business.

To reiterate, hardly any line of business today is devoid of the potential for exploitation on a global scale. However, any multiproduct firm that is starting to globalize must remember that a logically sequenced rather than random approach is likely to serve as a higher-return, lower-risk path toward full-scale globalization.

CHOICE OF STRATEGIC MARKETS

Not all markets are of equal strategic importance. This is a central tenet of the conceptual framework presented in **Figure 2**. The following two dimensions determine the strategic importance of a market: (1) *market potential*, and (2) *learning potential*.

The concept of market potential encompasses both current market size and growth expectations for a particular line of business. For instance, one of the critical markets for AOL is Japan because 45 percent of the PCs sold in Asia are there. It is important to remember that, notwithstanding the importance of the size of a country's economy, market potential does not always go hand in hand with the country's GDP. A blindness to this reality has led some authors to conclude that companies are not global unless they are present in the triad of Europe, Japan, and North America. Such simplistic conclusions can often be dramatically fallacious. If you are managing ABB's power plant business, the bulk of your market for new power plants lies outside the triad.

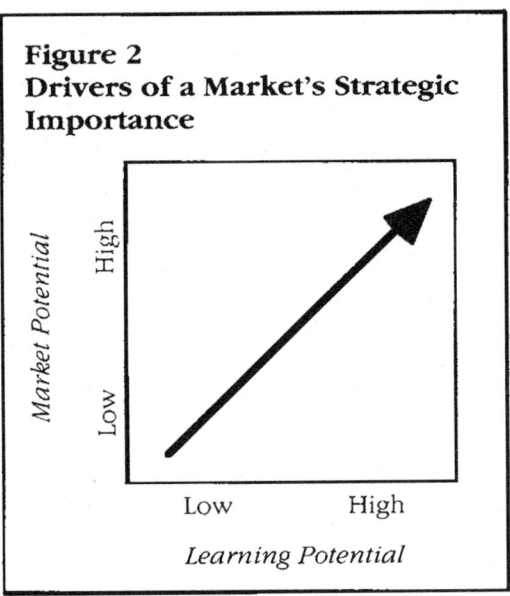

Figure 2
Drivers of a Market's Strategic Importance

Market Potential (Low to High, vertical axis)
Learning Potential (Low to High, horizontal axis)

There are two drivers of the learning potential of any market. The first is the presence of sophisticated and demanding customers for the particular product or service. Such customers (1) force a company to meet very tough standards for product and service quality, cost, cycle time, and a host of other attributes, (2) accelerate its learning regarding tomorrow's customer needs, and (3) force it to innovate constantly and continuously. France and Italy are leading-edge customer markets for the high fashion clothing industry—a fact of considerable importance to a company such as Du Pont, the manufacturer of Lycra and other textile fibers.

The second driver of a market's learning potential is the pace at which relevant technologies are evolving there. This technology evolution can emerge from one or more of several sources: leading-edge customers, innovative competitors, universities and other local research centers, and firms in related industries.

As indicated in Figure 2, the strategic importance of a market is a joint function of both market potential and learning potential. No firm is truly global unless it is present in all strategic markets. Nevertheless, despite their obvious importance, the timing of a firm's decision to enter strategic markets must also depend on its "ability to exploit" these markets. Going after a strategic market without such an ability is generally a fast track to disaster.

The ability to exploit a market is a function of two factors: (1) the height of entry barriers, and (2) the intensity of competition in the market. Entry barriers are likely to be lowest when there are no regulatory constraints on trade and investment (as in the case of regional economic blocks) and when new markets are geographically, culturally, and linguistically proximate to the domestic market. Even when there are low entry barriers, the intensity of competition can hinder a company's potential for exploiting a market. For example, the large U.S. market in the retailing industry has historically proven to be a graveyard for foreign entrants such as Marks & Spencer, precisely because of the intensity of local competition.

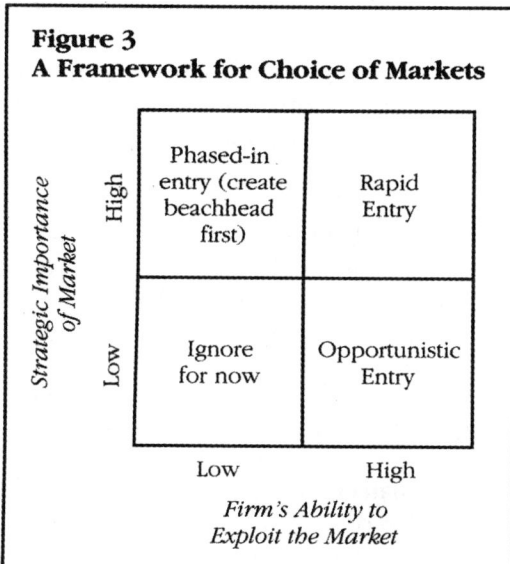

Figure 3
A Framework for Choice of Markets

Figure 3 presents a conceptual framework that combines the two key dimensions—"strategic importance of market" and "ability to exploit"—to offer guidelines on how a firm can engage in directed opportunism in its choice of markets. The firm's stance toward markets that have high strategic importance and high ability to exploit ought to be to enter rapidly. By comparison, the firm can afford to be much more opportunistic and ad hoc with respect to markets that have low strategic importance but are easier to exploit. In the case of markets that have high strategic importance but are also very difficult to exploit, we recommend an incremental phased approach in which the development of needed capabilities precedes market entry. One attractive way for a company to develop such capabilities is to first enter a *beachhead market*: one that closely resembles the targeted strategic market but provides a safer opportunity to learn how to enter and succeed there. Some commonly used examples of beachhead markets are Switzerland and/or Austria for Germany, Canada for the U.S., and Hong Kong or Taiwan for China. Finally, the firm

should stay away from those markets that are neither strategic nor easy to exploit.

MODE OF ENTRY

Once a company has selected the country or countries to enter and designated the product line(s) that will serve as the launch vehicles, it must determine the appropriate mode of entry. The entry mode issue rests on two fundamental questions. The first concerns the extent to which the firm will export or produce locally. Here, the firm has several choices. It can rely on 100 percent export of finished goods, export of components but localized assembly, 100 percent local production, and so on.

The second question deals with the extent of ownership control over activities that will be performed locally in the target market. Here also, the firm faces several choices: 0 percent ownership modes (licensing, franchising, and so on), partial ownership modes (joint ventures or affiliates), and 100 percent ownership modes (fully-owned greenfield operations or acquisitions). **Figure 4** uses these two dimensions to depict the array of choices regarding mode of entry that are open to any firm, and includes examples illustrating the variety of available options.

Choosing the right mode of entry is critical because the choice, once made, is often difficult and costly to alter. Inappropriate decisions can impose unwanted, unnecessary, and undesirable constraints on future development options.

Turning to the first question, greater reliance on local production would be appropriate under the following four conditions:

- *Size of local market is larger than minimum efficient scale of production.* The larger the size of the local market, the more completely local production will translate into scale economies for the firm while holding down tariff and transportation costs. One illustration of this argument is Bridgestone's entry into the U.S. market by acquiring the local production base of Firestone instead of exporting tires from Japan.

- *Shipping and tariff costs associated with exporting to the target market are so high* that they neutralize any cost advantages associated with producing in any country other than that market. This is why cement companies such as Cemex and Lafarge Coppee engage heavily in local production in every country they enter.

- *Need for local customization of product design is high.* Product customization requires two capabilities: a deep understanding of local market needs, and an ability to incorporate this understanding in the company's design and production decisions. Localizing production in the target market significantly enhances the firm's ability to respond to local market needs accurately and efficiently.

- *Local content requirements are strong.* This is one of the major reasons why foreign auto companies rely heavily on local production in markets such as the EU, China, and India.

Turning to the second question, given the differing costs and benefits of local market activities, neither alliances nor complete ownership are universally desirable in all situations. Unlike the complete ownership mode, alliance-based entry modes have the advantages of permitting the firm to share the costs and risks associated with market entry, allowing rapid access to local know-how, and giving managers the flexibility to respond more entrepreneurially and much more quickly to dynamic global competition than the conquer-the-world-by-yourself approach. However, a major downside of alliances is their potential for various types of conflict stemming from differences in corporate goals and cultures.

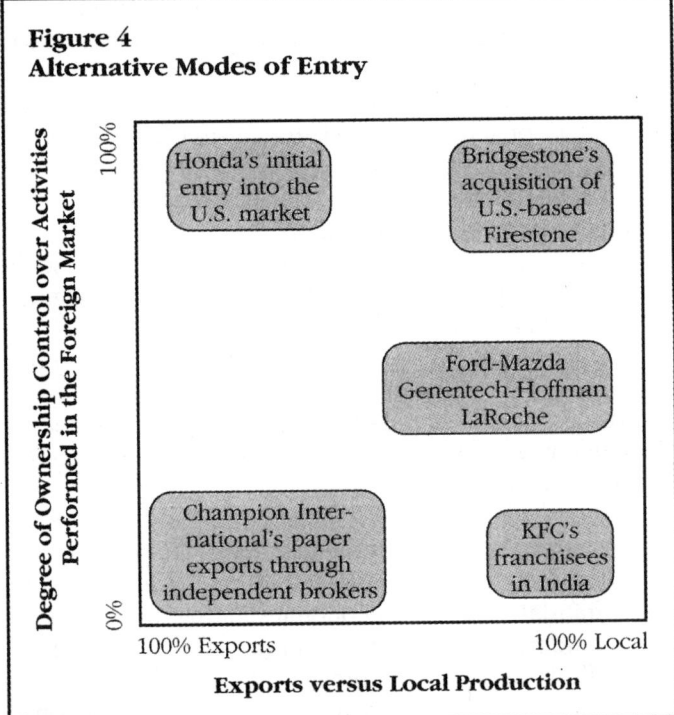

Figure 4
Alternative Modes of Entry

- Honda's initial entry into the U.S. market
- Bridgestone's acquisition of U.S.-based Firestone
- Ford-Mazda Genentech-Hoffman LaRoche
- Champion International's paper exports through independent brokers
- KFC's franchisees in India

Degree of Ownership Control over Activities Performed in the Foreign Market (0% to 100%)

Exports versus Local Production (100% Exports to 100% Local)

Taking into account the pros and cons, then, alliance-based entry modes are often more appropriate under the following conditions:

- *Physical, linguistic, and cultural distance between the home and host countries is high.* The more dissimilar and unfamiliar the target market, the greater the need for the firm to rely on a local partner to provide know-how and networks. Conceivably, the firm could obtain the requisite local knowledge and competencies through acquisition. However, in highly dissimilar and unfamiliar markets, its ability to manage an acquired subsidiary is often very limited. Ford's decision to enter the Indian market through the joint venture (JV) mode rested partly on the

company's need to rely on an experienced and respected local partner, Mahindra & Mahindra.

- *The subsidiary would have low operational integration with the rest of the multinational operations.* By definition, tighter integration between a subsidiary and the rest of the global network increases the degree of mutual interdependence between the subsidiary and the network. In this context of high interdependence, it becomes crucial for the subsidiary and the network to pursue shared goals, and for the firm to be able to reshape the subsidiary according to the changing needs of the rest of the network. Shared ownership of the subsidiary puts major constraints on the firm's ability to achieve such congruence in goals and have the requisite freedom to reshape subsidiary operations as needed.

- *The risk of asymmetric learning by the partner is (or can be kept) low.* In a typical JV, two partners pool different but complementary know-how into an alliance. Ongoing interaction between their core operations and the alliance gives each an opportunity to learn from the other and appropriate the other's complementary know-how. In effect, this dynamic implies that the alliance often is not just a cooperative relationship but also a learning race. If Firm A has the ability to learn at a faster rate than Firm B, the outcome is likely to be asymmetric learning in favor of Firm A. Thus, over time, Firm A may seek to dissolve the alliance in favor of going it alone in competition with a still-disadvantaged Firm B.

- *The company is short of capital.* Lack of capital underlay Xerox's decision in the 1950s to enter the European market through an alliance with the Rank Organization of the U.K.

- *Government regulations require local equity participation.* Historically, many countries with formidable market potentials, such as China and Brazil, have successfully imposed the JV option on foreign entrants, even when all other considerations might have favored the choice of a complete ownership mode.

A company that decides to enter the foreign market through local production rather than through exports faces a secondary decision. It must decide whether to set up greenfield operations or use an existing production base through a cross-border acquisition. A greenfield operation gives the company tremendous freedom to impose its own unique management policies, culture, and mode of operations on the new subsidiary. In contrast, a cross-border acquisition poses the much tougher challenge of cultural transformation and post-merger integration. However, setting up greenfield operations also has two potential liabilities: lower speed of entry, and more intense local competition caused by the addition of new production capacity as well as one more competitor. Taking into account both the pros and the cons, **Figure 5** provides a conceptual framework to determine when greenfield operations and/or cross-border acquisitions are likely to be the more appropriate entry modes.

This conceptual framework has two dimensions. The first pertains to the uniqueness of the globalizing company's culture. Nucor is a good example of a newly globalizing firm with a very strong and unique culture. It is significantly different from other steel producers in its human resource policies, egalitarian work environment, performance-based incentives, teamwork, decentralization, and business processes. The more committed a company is to preserving its unique culture, the more necessary it becomes to set up greenfield operations when entering foreign markets. This is because building and nurturing a unique culture from scratch (as would be feasible in the case of greenfield operations) is almost always much easier than transforming an entrenched culture (as would be necessary in the case of a cross-border acquisition).

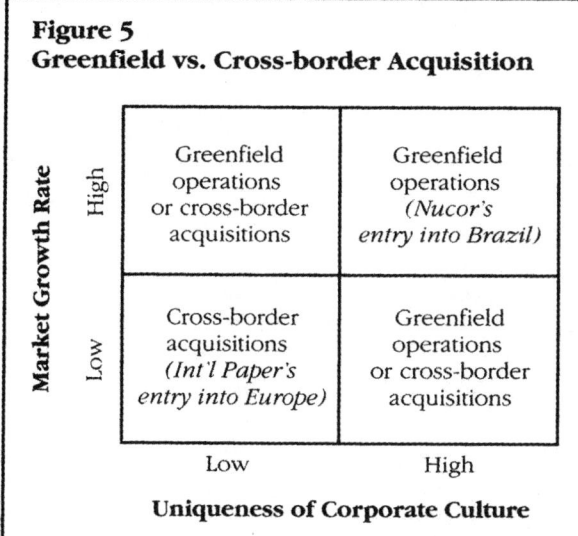

Figure 5
Greenfield vs. Cross-border Acquisition

		Uniqueness of Corporate Culture	
		Low	**High**
Market Growth Rate	**High**	Greenfield operations or cross-border acquisitions	Greenfield operations *(Nucor's entry into Brazil)*
	Low	Cross-border acquisitions *(Int'l Paper's entry into Europe)*	Greenfield operations or cross-border acquisitions

Aside from corporate culture considerations the impact of entry mode on the resulting intensity of local competition must also carry considerable weight in a firm's decisions. If the local market is in the emerging or high growth phase (such as the auto industry in China and India), new capacity additions would have little downside effect on the intensity of competition. In contrast, when the local market is mature (such as the tire industry in the U.S.), new capacity additions will only intensify an already high degree of local competition. Within the forest products industry, Indonesia-based Asia Pulp & Paper has used the greenfield mode for expanding into other high-growth Asian markets. In the same industry, the U.S.-based International Paper has pursued a different path and relied on the acquisition mode for its expansion into the mature European market.

TRANSPLANTING THE CORPORATE DNA

Having decided on a mode of entry for a particular product line into a particular target market, the challenge of building global presence moves on to implementing actual entry. Among the first issues the globalizing company must address is how to transplant the core elements of its business model, its core practices, and its core beliefs—in short, its DNA—to the new subsidiary. The following example illustrates the challenge of transplanting the corporate DNA.

After acquiring 2,000 employees from Yamaichi Securities, Merrill Lynch & Co. counted on an American-style investment advisor approach to build a high-trust image in the securities brokerage industry in Japan. Historically, says Sugawara (1999), the industry has been

> tainted by unsavory practices.... One well-known abuse... is "churning"—in which sales people persuade naive investors to buy and sell a lot of securities so the sales people can boost their commissions. Merrill Lynch promised that there would be no churning. Instead, its sales people were instructed to try to get an overall picture of customers' finances, ascertain their needs and then suggest investments. Something got lost in the translation, however. Japanese customers have complained that Merrill Lynch sales people are too nosy, asking questions about their investments instead of just telling them what stocks to buy.

As this example illustrates, obstacles to transplanting the corporate DNA can emerge from any of several sources: local employees, local customers, local regulations, and so forth. Given such obstacles, every company needs to develop clarity regarding what exactly its "core" (as distinct from "peripheral") beliefs and practices are. Such clarity is essential for knowing where the company should stay committed to its own beliefs and practices and where it should be willing to adapt. Having achieved this clarity, the company needs to build mechanisms to transfer core beliefs and practices to the new subsidiary. Finally, and most important, it needs to embed these beliefs and practices in the new subsidiary.

Clarifying and Defining the Core Beliefs and Practices

Core beliefs and practices can be defined at any of varying levels of abstraction. Take Wal-Mart's practice of promoting "Made in America" goods in its U.S. stores. Assuming that promoting the origin-of-manufacture is a core practice for Wal-Mart, the company can define the practice in more or less abstract terms. A more abstract definition would be, "Wherever we operate, we believe in promoting locally manufactured products." On the other hand, a less abstract definition would be, "We promote products that are made in America." As this example points out, defining core beliefs and practices in more abstract terms permits a higher degree of local adaptation. At the same time, if the core beliefs and practices become too abstract, they could lose much of their meaning and value.

Notwithstanding its criticality, the definition of what constitutes a company's core beliefs and practices is and must always be the result of learning and experimentation over time. This is because the answers will almost certainly vary across industries, across firms within an industry, and, for the same firm, across time. As observed astutely by a senior executive of a major global retailer, "Cut your chains and you become free. Cut your roots and you die. Note, however, that differentiating between the two requires good judgment, something that you acquire only through experience and over time."

Transplanting Core Beliefs and Practices to the New Subsidiary

Transplanting core beliefs and practices to a new subsidiary, whether a greenfield operation or an acquisition, is always a transformational event—the challenge of transformation being greater in the case of an acquisition. The likelihood is very high that the transplanted beliefs and practices are likely to be at best partially understood and, in the case of an acquisition, will often be seen as alien and questionable. As such, transferring core beliefs and practices to a new subsidiary almost always requires transferring a select group of committed believers ("the DNA carriers") to the new operation. The size of this group would depend largely on the scale of the desired transformation effort. If the goal is to engage in a wholesale replacement of an entire set of preexisting beliefs and practices (as in the case of ABB's acquisitions in Eastern Europe), then it may be necessary to send in a virtual army of DNA carriers. On the other hand, if the goal is to create a new business model (as in the case of Mercedes-Benz's Alabama plant), then the transplants would need to be much fewer in number and would need to be very carefully selected.

Obloj and Thomas (1998) describe rather vividly how the invasion process worked in the case of ABB Poland:

> The transformation began with an influx and invasion of external and internal ABB consultants that signaled clearly the introductory stage of organizational change. Their behavior was guided by their perception of the stereotypical behavior of an inefficient state-owned firm typically managed by a cadre of administrators who do not understand how to manage a firm in a market economy. They did not initially perform any sophisticated diagnosis or analysis of local conditions or develop a strategic vision for the transformation process. Rather, they forcefully implemented market enterprise discipline in the acquired former state-owned firms by a series

of high-speed actions. They implemented massive training efforts aimed at exposing employees and managers of acquired firms to the principles of the market economy, modern management principles, and the ABB management system. This was adopted in all acquired firms following Percy Barnevik's dictum that the key to competitiveness is education and reeducation.

Embedding the Core Beliefs and Practices

While the process of transplanting the corporate DNA starts with transferring a select group of DNA carriers to the new subsidiary, it can be regarded as successful only when the new beliefs and practices have become internalized in the mindsets and routines of employees at the new subsidiary. Achieving such internalization requires (1) visibly explicit and credible commitment by the parent company to its core beliefs and practices, (2) deepening the process of education and reeducation within the new organization right down to middle managers and the local work force, and (3) concrete demonstration that the new beliefs and practices yield individual as well as corporate success.

The approach taken by the Ritz-Carlton chain at its new hotel in Shanghai, China, illustrates how a company can go about successfully embedding its core beliefs and practices in a new subsidiary. Ritz-Carlton acquired the rights to manage this hotel, with a staff of about 1,000 people, under its own name as of January 1, 1998. The company believed that, consistent with its image and its corporate DNA, the entire operation required significant upgrading. As one would expect, the company brought in a sizable contingent of about 40 expatriates from other Ritz-Carlton units in Asia and around the world to transform and manage the new property. What is especially noteworthy, however, is the approach the managers took to embed the company's own standards of quality and service in the hearts, minds, and behavior of their local associates. Among its first actions in the very first week of operations under its own control, the company decided to start the renovation process from the employee's entrance and changing and wash rooms rather than from other starting points, such as the main lobby. As one executive explained, the logic was that, through this approach, every employee would see two radical changes in the very first week: one, that the new standards of quality and service would be dramatically higher, and two, that they, the employees, were among the most valued stakeholders in the company. This approach served as a very successful start to embedding the company's basic beliefs in every associate's mind: "We Are Ladies and Gentlemen Serving Ladies and Gentlemen."

WINNING THE LOCAL BATTLE

Winning the local battle requires the global enterprise to anticipate, shape, and respond to the needs and/or actions of three sets of host-country players: customers, competitors, and government.

Winning Host Country Customers

One of the ingredients in establishing local presence is to understand the uniqueness of the local market and decide which aspects of the firm's business model require little change, which require local adaptation, and which need to be reinvented. The global firm faces little need to adapt its business design if it targets a customer segment in a foreign market similar to the one it serves in its home market. However, if the firm wants to expand the customer base it serves in a foreign market, then adapting the business model to the unique demands of the local customers becomes mandatory.

Consider the case of FedEx when it entered China. As an element of its entry strategy, FedEx had to choose who its target customers should be: local Chinese companies or multinational corporations. The company chose to target multinational companies—a customer segment identical to the one it has historically served. Given the choice, FedEx was able to pretty much export the U.S. business model into China, including the use of its own aircraft, building a huge network of trucks and distribution centers, and adopting U.S.-style aggressive marketing and advertising. On the other hand, had FedEx selected local Chinese firms as its targeted customer segment, winning host country customers would have required a significantly greater degree of local adaptation of the business model.

Domino's Pizza is a good example of a company that has benefited from adapting its business model when it entered India. Unlike KFC, Domino's was successful in its initial entry into India, primarily because it tailored its approach to the Indian culture and lifestyle. Even though pepperoni pizza is one of the most popular items for Domino's in other markets, the company dropped it from the menu to show respect for the value Hindus place on the cow. Domino's also tailored other toppings, such as chicken, ginger, and lamb, to suit Indian taste buds.

Winning Against Host Country Competitors

Whenever a company enters a new country, it can expect retaliation from local competitors as well as from other multinationals already operating there. Successfully establishing local presence requires anticipating and responding to these competitive threats. Established local competitors enjoy several advantages: knowledge of the local market; working relationships with local customers; understanding of local distribution channels; and so on. In contrast, the new firm suffers from the "liability of newness." When a global firm enters a market, local competitors will feel threatened and will have a strong reason to retaliate and defend their positions. Such response constitutes entry barriers. In such a context, four possible options are available to the new invader:

1. Enter by acquiring a dominant local competitor.

2. Enter by acquiring a weak local competitor who can be quickly transformed and scaled up.

3. Enter a poorly defended niche.

4. Engage in a frontal attack on the dominant and entrenched incumbents.

Acquire a dominant local competitor. Acquiring a dominant local firm will prove to be successful if the following three conditions are met: (1) there is significant potential for synergies between the acquisition target and the global firm; (2) the global firm has the capability to create and capture such synergies; and (3) the global firm does not give away the synergies from a huge acquisition premium up-front.

A case of successful entry through acquisition of a dominant local competitor is Accor, the French hospitality company, which entered the U.S. market by acquiring Motel 6—the best managed market leader in the budget lodging category. On the other hand, Sony paid a huge premium to acquire Columbia Pictures; to date, however, it has had great difficulty in justifying this premium—despite the significant potential synergies between Sony's hardware competencies and the "content" expertise of Columbia Pictures.

Acquire a weak player. Acquiring a weak player in the foreign market is an attractive option under the following conditions:

1. The global firm possesses the capabilities that are required to transform the weak player into a dominant player; and

2. The global firm has the ability to transplant the corporate DNA in the acquired firm very quickly.

The sheer act of acquiring a weak player signals to other local competitors that they will soon be under attack. It is therefore to be expected that local competitors will retaliate. If the global firm is unable to transform the weak player within a very short time, the player could become even weaker under attack from local competitors.

Consider Whirlpool's entry into Europe in 1989 by acquiring the problem-ridden appliance division of Philips. Unfortunately, Whirlpool could not quickly embed the capabilities to turn around Philips's struggling appliance business. In the meantime, two European rivals—Sweden's Electrolux and Germany's Bosch-Siemens—got a wake-up call from Whirlpool's European entry. Quite naturally, the two invested very heavily in modernization, process improvements, new product introductions, and restructuring—all with a view to improving their competitiveness. The net result was a disappointment for Whirlpool in terms of its ambition to consolidate the white goods industry in Europe. By 1998, Whirlpool had 12 percent market share in Europe (half of its expected position) and was also underachieving in profitability. To quote Jeff Fettig, Whirlpool's head of European operations: "We underestimated the competition."

Enter a poorly defended niche. If acquisition candidates are either unavailable or too expensive, the global firm has no choice but to enter on its own. Under such circumstances, it should find a poorly defended niche for market entry under the following conditions:

1. Such a niche exists.

2. The global firm can use that niche as a platform for subsequent expansion into the mainstream segments of the local market. That is, the mobility barriers to move from the niche market to the mainstream segments are relatively low.

In the early 1970s, the Japanese car makers entered the U.S. market at the low end, a segment that was being ignored by the U.S. car companies and was thus a "loose brick" in their fortress. The Japanese companies used their dominance of the lower end segment to migrate to the middle and upper ends very effectively.

Frontal attack. The global company can choose a head-on attack on the dominant and entrenched incumbents provided it has a massive competitive advantage that can be leveraged outside its domestic market. If this were not true, taking on an 800-pound gorilla with all the liability of "newness" could prove suicidal. Lexus succeeded in its frontal attack on Mercedes and BMW in the U.S. market mainly because of a dominating competitive advantage in such areas as product quality and cost structure. For instance, Lexus enjoyed a 30 percent cost advantage. For Mercedes, given the high labor costs in Germany where it manufactured its automobiles, such a cost advantage could not be neutralized quickly.

Managing Relationships with the Host-Country Government

Local government can often be a key external stakeholder, particularly in emerging markets. Two points are worth noting in this context.

1. The global firm can ill afford to ignore non-market stakeholders such as the local government. For instance, the Chinese government recently banned direct selling. This action has an important bearing on such firms as Mary Kay Cosmetics and Avon, which depend on a highly personalized direct marketing approach.

2. Managing the non-market stakeholders should be seen as a dynamic process. Instead of simplistically reacting to existing government regulations, the firm should also anticipate likely future changes in the regulatory framework and even explore the possibility of helping shape the emerging framework. Instead of appeasement or confrontation, persistence and constructive dialogue with the local government are often critical elements of winning the local battle.

Enron's entry into India is a telling example of an active approach to transforming the entering firm's relationship with host governments. In 1995, mostly due to ideological and political reasons, the Maharashtra government put a sudden halt to Enron's partly built, $2.5 billion power plant. Yet by 1999, not only had Enron won back the original contract for the 826-megawatt unit, it even succeeded in getting a go-ahead to triple the capacity to 2,450 megawatts, representing India's largest foreign investment and Enron's biggest non-U.S. project. Instead of giving up, Enron persisted and helped shape evolving public policy. In the process, the company learned a lesson, but so did the Indian government.

SPEED OF GLOBAL EXPANSION

Having commenced the journey of globalization, a company must still address one major issue in building global presence: How fast should it expand globally? Microsoft's worldwide launch of Windows 95 *on the same day* epitomizes using globalization for aggressive growth. By moving quickly, a company can solidify its market position very rapidly.

However, rapid global expansion can also spread managerial, organizational, and financial resources too thin. The consequence can be to jeopardize the company's ability to defend and profit from the global presence thus created. Witness PepsiCo's helter-skelter rapid expansion in Latin America during the first part of the 1990s. In most cases, Pepsi's ambitious agenda resulted in market positions that have proven to be both indefensible and unprofitable.

Taking into account the pros and cons, an accelerated speed of global expansion is more appropriate under the following conditions:

- *It is easy for competitors to replicate your recipe for success.* This possibility is obvious for fast food and retailing companies such as KFC and Starbuck's, where it is easy for competitors to take a proven concept from one market and replicate it in another unoccupied market with a relatively small investment. However, this phenomenon is observable in other, very different types of industries as well, such as personal computers and software. The rapid globalization of companies like Compaq, Dell, and Microsoft reflects their determination to prevent replication and/or pirating of their product concepts in markets all around the world.

- *Scale economies are extremely important.* Very high economies of scale give the early and rapid globalizer massive first mover advantages and handicap the slower ones for long periods of time. This is precisely why rapid globalizers in the tire industry, such as Goodyear, Michelin, and Bridgestone, now hold considerable advantage over slower ones, such as Pirelli and Continental.

- *Management's capacity to manage (or learn how to manage) global operations is high.* Consider experienced global players like Coca-Cola, Citicorp, Unilever, and ABB. Should such a company successfully introduce a new product line in one country, it would be relatively easy and logical to globalize it rapidly to all potential markets around the world. Aside from the ability to manage global operations, the speed of globalization also depends on the company's ability to leverage its experience from one market to another. The faster the speed with which a firm can recycle its learning about market entry and market defense from one country to another, the lower the risk of spreading managerial and organizational capacity too thinly.

Becoming global is never exclusively the result of a grand design. At the same time, it would be naive to view it as little more than a sequence of incremental, ad-hoc, opportunistic, and random moves. The wisest approach would be one of *directed opportunism*—an approach that maintains opportunism and flexibility within a broad direction set by a systematic framework. Our goal here has been to provide such a framework.

References

D.A. Blackmon and D. Brady, "Just How Hard Should a U.S. Company Woo a Big Foreign Market?" *Wall Street Journal*, April 6, 1998, p. A1.

S. Ghoshal, "Global Strategy: An Organizing Framework," *Strategic Management Journal*, September–October 1987, pp. 425–440.

V. Govindarajan, "Note on the Global Paper Industry," case study, Dartmouth College, 1999.

G. Hamel and C.K. Prahalad, "Do You Really Have a Global Strategy?" *Harvard Business Review*, July–August 1985, pp. 139–148.

K. Iverson and T. Varian, *Plain Talk: Lessons from a Business Maverick* (New York: Wiley, 1997).

J.P. Jeannet and H.D. Hennessy, *Global Marketing Strategies* (Boston: Houghton Mifflin, 1998).

Jonathan Karp and Kathryn Kranhold, "Enron's Plant in India Was Dead: This Month, It Will Go on Stream," *Wall Street Journal*, February 5, 1999, p. A1.

T. Khanna, R. Gulati, and N. Nohria, "Alliances as Learning Races," *Proceedings of the Academy of Management Annual Meetings*, 1994, pp. 42–46.

K. Obloj and H. Thomas, "Transforming Former State-owned Companies into Market Competitors in Poland: The ABB Experience," *European Management Journal*, August 1998, pp. 390–399.

G. Steinmetz and C.J. Chipello, "Local Presence Is Key to European Deals," *Wall Street Journal*, June 30, 1998, p. A15.

G. Steinmetz and C. Quintanilla, "Whirlpool Expected Easy Going in Europe, and It Got a Big Shock," *Wall Street Journal*, April 10, 1998, p. A1.

S. Sugawara, "Japanese Shaken by Business U.S.-Style," *Washington Post*, February 9, 1999, p. E1.

R. Tomkins, "Battered PepsiCo Licks Its Wounds," *Financial Times*, May 30, 1997, p. 26.

"Xerox and Fuji Xerox," Case No. 9-391-156, Harvard Business School.

Anil K. Gupta is a professor of strategy and international business at the University of Maryland, College Park, Maryland. **Vijay Govindarajan** is the Earl C. Daum 1924 Professor of International Business at Dartmouth College, Hanover, New Hampshire.

Three Strategies for Managing Fast Growth

Managers can't leave growth to chance. They should have a strategy for growing as well as for applying new knowledge faster than their competitors.

George von Krogh and **Michael A. Cusumano**

Many companies approach growth management with no strategy other than to do what they did when they were new. New companies begin with a flourish. They have certain capabilities and knowledge. As they get caught up in short-term survival, they may cling to the same capabilities and knowledge. Or they may acquire the wrong kind of new knowledge and fail to grow the right capabilities. In the end, they may pour on new capabilities and knowledge—when it's too late.

The key to a long, healthy corporate life is steady growth. According to a 1998 survey, of the companies that enjoyed greater than 10% sales growth per year, about 78% were still around six years after starting. Of the companies with flat or decreasing sales, only 27.5% survived for six years.[1]

Growing Strategically

To grow steadily and avoid stagnation, a company must learn how to scale up and extend its business, lengthen its expansion phase, and accumulate and apply new knowledge to new products and markets faster than competitors.

Managers can't leave growth to chance. They must choose a plan that renders consistent sales growth for years, not just in short bursts. A good growth plan captures the vision for expanding the company. It addresses the product and market combinations the company intends to pursue, the size it hopes to achieve in a particular time frame, and most important, the know-how and organizational structures that will support expansion or diversification.

Such planning has an internal focus—rather than a focus on what competitors might do or what type of technological change might transform an industry. It is designed to help a company exert more control over its fate as it tackles outside challenges.[2] Implementation is easier for startup companies but possible for established enterprises, too. Company size should not drive the growth plan. Companies of all sizes need systems for creating, acquiring and sharing knowledge. Consider Netigy, a San-jose-based e-commerce service provider. Netigy has only 650 employees, but it already has invested in a chief knowledge officer and a knowledge-management system for 20,000 people. Netigy is prepared to handle its vision for growth.[3]

What does drive the growth plan is the company's set of capabilities. Managers must choose a plan that fits with the knowledge, learning skills and assets that the organization possesses or plans to develop. On the basis of the literature and our personal knowledge of fast-growing companies, we conclude that companies grow using three basic strategies: scaling, duplication and granulation. (See "About the Research.") There is no one best strategy. A growth plan may end up tapping more than one. The important thing is to include principles of organizational learning, knowledge acquisition and knowledge transfer.

Scaling: Doing More of What You're Good At

Scaling starts with a coherent vision of products, technologies and customers. The vision is the foundation for growth, at least until circumstances change significantly. The vision should reflect the company's commitment to growth, be brief and clear,

About the Research

We began our inquiry into growth strategies and capabilities by reflecting on cases of rapidly growing companies we knew. Michael Cusumano has written about Nissan, Toyota, Microsoft and Netscape.* Georg von Krogh has addressed learning, capability building and application of knowledge management in companies such as Skandia AFS, Sencorp, Shiseido, Sony, Siemens, Gemini Consulting, General Electric and Phonak AG.†

We also considered what authors in management and organization studies had to say about expansion strategies, the management of startups and young firms, the processes of knowledge creation and knowledge sharing—and organizational learning in general. We found that very few authors addressed the topics in combination and none attempted to integrate ideas about growth strategy, knowledge management, capabilities and organizational learning.

We concluded that companies must combine strategies for growth with explicit strategies for learning. They must base their growth strategies on their capabilities and market opportunities, then prepare their organizations to acquire or create specific knowledge about new technologies, customers and industries.

* M.A. Cusumano, "The Japanese Automobile Industry: Technology and Management at Nissan and Toyota," Harvard East Asian Monographs no. 122 (Cambridge, Massachusetts: Council on East Asian Studies, Harvard University, 1989); M.A. Cusumano and R.W. Selby, "Microsoft Secrets" (New York: Free Press/Simon & Schuster, 1995); and M.A. Cusumano and D.B. Yoffie, "Competing on Internet Time" (New York: Free Press/Simon & Schuster, 1998).

†G. von Krogh, K. Ichijo and I. Nonaka, "Enabling Knowledge Creation: How to Unlock the Mystery of Tacit Knowledge and Release the Power of Innovation" (New York: Oxford University Press, 2000); and G. von Krogh and J. Roos, "Organizational Epistemology" (London: MacMillan, 1995).

and be understood by all employees. The focus should be on a concrete product, technology and customer segment.[4]

Netscape's founders believed that the Internet would revolutionize the way people worked and interacted.[5] Their vision was to build infrastructure software that would put the company at the heart of the new, networked world and let it ride the Internet wave while experimenting with new products, technologies and markets.

Scaling requires a company to implement its vision quickly. As co-founder Jim Clark observed, "An axiom of motorcycle racing applies precisely to the technology business: Move fast, keep going—or end up on your butt. Slow down on the throttle and you'll be off the road and into the trees."[6] In two years, Netscape went from a basic browser for surfing the Internet to more sophisticated browsers for corporate customers. It kept up the momentum by quickly adding a variety of servers, then opening up new markets for corporate intranets and extranets (the latter being intranets extended to select customers or sup-

pliers). Next it moved to electronic commerce, adding new servers and applications tools and creating Netcenter.com—all within four years of starting. When America Online acquired it in fall 1998, Netscape had a value of more than $10 billion.

Invest Aggressively To grow by scaling, a company expands product development around core technologies and offerings, expands product lines and increases the intensity of marketing by using existing distribution channels to reach new customer groups with related needs. It must increase manufacturing capacity and enlarge corporate infrastructure—for example, by building bigger and better information systems and setting up central human-resource-management systems to recruit and train employees quickly. (See "Is Scaling the Right Strategy?")

Companies must pursue aggressive investment—often *before* sales growth becomes apparent. Netscape invested in growth, knowing that without growth, it would face far more serious problems than overinvesting. And Netscape grew—even more quickly than it anticipated.

Specialize and Standardize Companies that grow fast often centralize and standardize administrative areas such as finance and accounting to handle the increased transactions. Initially, they have simple functional structures, with manufacturing, marketing, sales, product development, finance and accounting all separate. As they grow, they duplicate the functional departments within divisions tied to particular products or geographic markets. Smaller teams then focus on specific customer segments and control the resources they need. Netscape moved from one small research-and-development group to separate R&D divisions for its browser and server products—and later for its e-commerce tools and Web site.

Hire the Right Mix To refine and exploit existing products, processes and market know-how, key people must learn quickly and share their insights and technical knowledge. Netscape co-founder Mark Andreessen and a core group of programmers gained invaluable design experience and market insights from working at the University of Illinois on Mosaic, Navigator's predecessor. They distributed 2 million copies of Mosaic and learned how the networked world of the Internet could function, with hot links potentially connecting every computer and database worldwide.[7]

But although Andreessen and the other programmers had most of the essential concepts and technical skills, they lacked the money, managerial insights and organizational skills needed. Jim Clark, who had founded Silicon Graphics a few years earlier and knew how to make a technology into a viable business, served as a Pied Piper in attracting other talent and resources.[8]

Netscape had to learn quickly. Its customers changed from savvy Internet users of a single product—the browser—to more-conservative corporate users who wanted an array of products that were rock-solid reliable. Netscape had to figure out how to design, document, test, sell and support mission-critical products in a more professional way.

At the same time, it had to absorb many new people. Clark hired young programmers who had worked on Web browsers

NETSCAPE

1994: Founded by Jim Clark and Marc Andreessen
1995: $80 million in sales
1998: Approximately $500 million in revenues and more than 3,000 employees

Is Scaling the Right Strategy?

Growth by scaling works best when:
- The market is potentially large enough for rapid growth in a focused product line.
- The product creates unique value in the customers' view.
- The company can distribute products widely at low cost. Netscape used the Internet to overcome traditional entry barriers that software producers faced, such as bundling software with hardware or relying on software retail stores. Customers simply downloaded software from the Netscape Web site.

Scaling requires a company to learn about mass manufacturing and new manufacturing techniques. If the product is related to software or services, the company must become expert in the latest relevant technologies and standards, information systems and hardware trends. Knowledge of mass marketing is important, but when competition intensifies, individualized customer information becomes the strategic weapon. Learning how to offer technical support for an increasing customer group is critical for companies that are scaling. So are new routines (for procedures, quality standards, planning, milestones and goals), without which a company can become increasingly chaotic and unprofessional—and ultimately hurt product quality and service.

IKEA

1954: Starts as a small, domestic furniture manufacturer and retailer in Sweden with sales of 2 million Dutch guilder.
1984: Sales grow to 2,679 billion guilder.
1999: Sales grow to 16,954 billion guilder. Is franchiser and direct owner of many stores; operates out of Denmark. Has a presence in 25 countries, with 50,000 employees worldwide; 80% of sales are in Europe and 14% in the United States.

and added seasoned managers, engineers, and sales and marketing experts from computer and telecommunications industries. Recruiting from a veritable Who's Who of U.S. high-tech companies, Netscape leveraged the experts' knowledge to train the less seasoned.

Adapt the Structures For knowledge to be shared, a company must set up the right organizational structures, processes and culture. As Netscape grew, it sought to maintain the creativity

and innovative capabilities typical of small organizations; in late 1996, it reorganized the product divisions into minidivisions, or *divlets*. Each divlet reported to its own general manager and worked on a specific product release or server product.

The arrangement had certain flaws: poor cooperation, redundant work and mistakes that could have been avoided through collective brainstorming. In 1997, after Netscape failed to rewrite Navigator/Communicator in Java, Barksdale decided to make the divlets report directly to Andreessen. As chief technology officer, Andreessen had been without formal product responsibilities. Barksdale's move effectively centralized product planning and gave Andreessen authority to cancel projects and to force more knowledge sharing among the browser and server teams.

Find Ways to Learn From Customers Early Netscape discovered the intranet market by learning from its customers. A major bank in Switzerland had begun using Netscape's browser and server technology for its internal corporate network to allow employees to share information easily by using the Internet communications protocols. Netscape quickly identified intranets as a new opportunity and extended the idea to create extranets.

Netscape also learned to cultivate lead users and to have them test early versions of its products and give rapid feedback to developers. It started internal initiatives to find new ways to apply its technology to corporate markets. It used its own technology to create extranets that linked Netscape engineers, sales, marketing and support personnel to independent software vendors, content providers, Internet-service providers and computer manufacturers.

Duplication: Repeat the Business Model in New Regions

Like scaling, duplication starts with a coherent vision of products, technologies and customer segments. But unlike scaling, the vision must include goals for geographical expansion. The vision of IKEA founder Ingvard Kamprad was to go beyond Sweden and democratize the furniture industry throughout Europe by making new products affordable to the masses. Kamprad's vision relied on Swedish design skills and a store ambiance that could communicate an appealing lifestyle to young people everywhere. (See "Is Duplication the Right Strategy?")

Balance Standardization and Adaptation Duplication typically involves packaging the company's entrepreneurial know-how for new geographic areas—for example, by setting up overseas subsidiaries or franchising a business concept.[9] A carefully orchestrated tension balances standardization (keeping processes and organizational details close to the way they are done in the original location) and adaptation (changing the organization and processes to address the needs of the local region).

Duplicating marketing in overseas markets is important, but responsiveness to local market conditions is key to long-term success. In new geographic areas, companies may choose to centralize manufacturing and administrative functions, duplicate the functions or both. Centralized manufacturing reduces manufacturing costs, but duplicated manufacturing increases flexibility.

Duplicated businesses should follow similar human-resource-management practices. By standardizing staffing, training and remuneration plans, a company can rotate employees among subsidiaries instead of having to hire and train new people when work in one locale increases. With HR duplication, employees also share new ideas and experience smoothly while providing consistent service to customers.

Hire Flexible, Independent Managers Companies must give managers the independence they need to balance adaptation to local markets with preserving what made the original business successful. IKEA did that well, although its senior country and regional managers often were Swedish or familiar with the Swedish language. Eventually, however, a truly global company must train foreign managers in its practices and values, as IKEA has been doing gradually in the United States and China.

Duplicate Key Parts of the Infrastructure Geographical expansion calls for simple procedures and for work processes robust enough to handle varied employee backgrounds. During expansion, informal sharing of experience usually is not the best learning mechanism. Senior managers have less control over local recruiting and human-resource development than those using scaling. Growing by duplication requires that a company externalize, or transfer, key elements of its infrastructure.[10] Some companies use *black-boxing*—whatever mechanism they can set up to share their *black boxes* (critical data at various levels of detail in ready-to-use form, such as written or online manuals or video presentations).

Black boxes must be available at a moment's notice to help employees and managers worldwide to accomplish important tasks. A single black box at one level of detail may help in establishing a new subsidiary in a new territory. It might include checklists on choosing a site, using legal counsel, selecting and training personnel, laying out a store and purchasing manuals. A box at another level might include detailed instructions on how to service clients outside business hours or how to set up a store-maintenance program.

IKEA used black-boxing. The European expansion group it organized to jump-start its duplication in Switzerland, Germany, France, Italy, Denmark, Norway and Austria bought land, hired people, constructed furniture outlets and decided on the new outlets' decor. Two months before opening a new store, a first-year operations group would move in while the expansion group moved on to the next site. The first-year group would take charge, train people, arrange the store opening and set up the operations. Then IKEA would establish a local country organization to run the operations. The international expansion group, IKEA's "Knowledge Marines," represented the ideal mechanism for accumulating know-how from each new site and spreading the knowledge to newer operations.

Duplicate Entrepreneurial Knowledge IKEA learned how to blackbox entrepreneurial knowledge, too. The preferred site for new stores was always relatively cheap land on the outskirts of a city. The stores were simple and functional, most often two-story buildings with displays on the second floor and warehousing on the first. IKEA standardized and documented products, catalog format, logo use (although in Norway the company used red and white instead of the traditional blue and yellow), and personnel selection and training. The custodian of the entrepreneurial knowledge was the international expansion group.

IKEA also used *devoted practice* to duplicate its corporate vision. Local employees would devote themselves to learning certain tasks by studying manuals and attending training courses. Kamprad acted like a field commander, communicating the vision to new employees, visiting new stores, taking notes on store operations and discussing procedures and improvements directly with employees. Through such attention to detail, the black box can become a local routine. Employees then use it as a foundation for devising new and better solutions.

Be Aware of the Limitations It would be naive to expect black-boxing to be consistently successful. Customer tastes and employee backgrounds are too diverse for one set of processes and programs to fit all situations. When IKEA expanded to the United States in 1986, it found that U.S. customers had subtle but important differences in tastes and shopping habits from Europeans. They wanted shelves, but for televisions, not books. European sheets did not fit American beds. European cups, plates and drawers seemed small to Americans.[11]

In addition, black boxes may not be sensitive to new requirements. A company that grows through duplication must be able to learn quickly, fixing procedures and products that don't work and making the people who created them aware of the new requirements. That is especially true of young high-growth companies expanding abroad in highly competitive markets. Senior executives and central-management systems must have the openness and flexibility necessary for modifying a formula that was a winner back home.

SAP

1972: Is founded by former IBM software engineers in Mannheim, Germany.

1992: Launches resource-planning software R/3 and makes its name.

1996: Begins developing industry-specific solutions. Introduces AcceleratedSAP methodology.

1998: Delivers services map for complete life-cycle solutions and support. Has 22,000 employees in more than 50 countries. Hires 2,400 employees in this year alone.

1999: Delivers mySAP.com. Reports total sales of $5 billion, a one-year increase of 18%.

IKEA had a slow start in the United States, but it learned quickly.[12] The company now adapts fully one-third of its product designs to U.S. tastes. Combining black-boxing and local learning has helped IKEA improve duplication of its business and remain competitive over time in many markets.

Is Duplication the Right Strategy?

Growth by duplication works best when:

- The business requires physical presence and the company can repeat its business model in new geographic markets. Home furnishings, for example, include items that customers want to see before purchasing. For services such as consulting, architecture and customized software development, personal contact and trust building are essential.

- There is a need for better distribution. A company might shift from a scaling to a duplicating strategy when distribution channels are underdeveloped or when it can build up a unique set of local distributors that would be costly for potential competitors to imitate.

- The company can adapt its experience in product development, manufacturing and marketing approaches fairly easily. Unique information about local customers and new trends from foreign markets may lead to better market segmentation and targeted marketing than smaller local companies can offer.

Duplication requires several kinds of learning. To set up new subsidiaries abroad, a company must learn about local market conditions and apply the knowledge in adapting products, marketing and operations. Duplicating, like scaling, may require learning about mass manufacturing or mass marketing, but it is also likely to need individualized communication flowing between central management and local management, product-development staff, local marketing staff, sales staff and customers. Duplicating involves learning about new competitors, regulatory differences, the best ways to handle logistics and currency-related risks. Alliances with local companies can expand knowledge because they provide access to local insights about marketing, manufacturing capacity and product development. Acquisitions are an option, but integration into the existing organization may be problematic, especially if the acquired company is in another country.

Granulation: Growing Select Business Cells

There are limits to scaling and duplicating. A company's product line may run out of steam, too many low-cost competitors may copy it, or there may be no new foreign markets to conquer. At that point, the best strategy could be granulation distinguishing the cells, or smaller granules, of the business and growing them aggressively.

SAP, now one of the largest software companies in the world, went through both scaling and duplication before attempting granulation. The company initially specialized in enterprise-resource-planning (ERP) systems that let clients track and plan financial and other resource flows. Its early product, R/1, supported only a few resource flows. In 1989, SAP launched R/2, which offered new features and more than doubled the company's sales over the next three years. In 1992, it launched R/3, which integrated resource planning across functions and customer-suppliers, allowing customers to manage more than 1,500 business processes. R/3 made SAP a global name in software.

Toward the end of 1997, SAP embarked on duplication. In 1998 it reorganized into industry business units, with a core development unit for new technologies and services plus a global sales-and-marketing unit. As custodians of specialized know-how in industry-specific resource planning, the units transformed SAP from a one-product company to a multiple-product company. SAP now builds on the R/3 platform whatever the customer needs, while integrating component software from other suppliers.[13] It continues to improve R/3 and shares knowledge by training in-house personnel and representatives from local IT consultancies. Approximately 150 instructors now teach more than 200 courses at 85 training centers worldwide. SAP is adding remote training programs, too. Such enhancements and SAP's extensive implementation expertise have enabled it to add Chevron, Eastman Chemical and Microsoft to its long customer list.

Balance the Old and New Granulation is like the other strategies in starting with a strong, coherent vision for growth, but its focus is on developing unique capabilities and creating new businesses. A company uses its resources and knowledge to explore new territory with new, autonomous business units, independent subsidiaries or corporate spinoffs. Granulation is risky; business units may not leverage fully the company's existing knowledge and asset base. Although individual entrepreneurs learn from working on local technologies with local customers and local staff, they work better when they have access to information, expertise and resources from other parts of the company.[14] Each new cell, therefore, should reuse existing product technologies, manufacturing processes, organizational processes and consumer information but combine those assets in new ways. (See "Is Granulation the Right Strategy?")

In 1996, SAP released R/3 Version 3.1, which had Web interfaces. The launch inspired further exploration of e-business solutions at SAP and led to a new growth strategy. The company began developing new business groups to create technologies for both individuals and small to midsize firms. It then launched mySAP.com, a portal-based marketplace that facilitates transactions among customers with different transaction volumes. In March 2000, SAP formed SAPMarkets, a separate venture for electronic market activities.

Balance the Informal and Formal Both informal and formal methods are required for knowledge to flow between entrepreneurial cells. Informal personal ties help people in different groups establish trust and share experiences. SAP favors a "football team" style of work over hierarchies. Communication frequently occurs spontaneously, making SAP seem almost like a university.[15]

However, informal ties generally center on short-term issues.[16] Fast-growing companies need to complement informal mechanisms with more-formal knowledge sharing, such as strategic-planning processes that encourage regular discussions among managers and employees from different cells. Companies also can hold periodic conferences or rotate experienced personnel among company units.

Evaluate and Monitor Companies benefit from selectively evaluating and monitoring new business opportunities the way venture capitalists do. First, local entrepreneurs conceive business ideas, draft business plans, organize a venture team and form entrepreneurial cells. Then senior-management representatives act as investors, with both a monitoring and advising role. The entrepreneurial model also lets companies invest successfully in outside enterprises with attractive technologies, products, services or customer bases.

Learn From Customers, Partners and Competitors At SAP, the business units' chore is to dig up industry knowledge. Often knowledge comes from customer feedback or lead users. SAP has gathered interested customers to work with company developers on some 50 projects. A strategic alliance with Nokia—to extend mySAP.com to a wireless mobile work force—is likely to generate useful learning, too.

When a company grows through granulation, its competitors may be unknown, but they are probably not inactive. The company must establish systems to gather and analyze intelligence on existing and potential competitors—and speed it to decision makers.

Acquiring smaller companies with expertise in the new technology and forming alliances are two ways to acquire external knowledge. Both need routines for sharing knowledge between the acquisition or alliance partner and the rest of the company. Sharing mechanisms may include integration teams (for acquisitions), shared management responsibilities, periodic conferences and meetings, or shared access to databases and knowledge bases.

Combining Strategies

To identify the strategy with the best fit, a company should start with a bird's eye view of the comparative strengths of scaling, duplicating and granulating. (See "Strategies for Growing and Learning.") The scaling strategy is simplest: A company merely learns how to do more of what it already does. Duplication is more complex, requiring a company to learn how to apply what it knows to new geographical markets. The most demanding in terms of knowledge acquisition, granulation requires a company to gather substantial information about new competitors and new product and market opportunities. But it also enables gradual diversification from related businesses into unrelated technologies, products and markets.

Is Granulation the Right Strategy?

Growth by granulation works best when:

- Growth through scaling and duplicating has clear limits. The company has conquered all relevant markets, product demand is flattening out, customers are changing their preferences, or increasing competition for market share makes further growth too expensive.
- A new technology is flourishing that could become a substitute for the company's products or a new business opportunity. Companies must explore and experiment with new technologies that are adjacent but outside current knowledge areas, routines and capabilities.
- The company is sufficiently mature to monitor new business activities, share knowledge internally and learn effectively about new markets and competitive scenarios.

Granulation requires that a company obtain knowledge outside itself and its operations, especially about its industry. Initially, a new cell, or business unit, might benefit from employees' internal experiences, but as it ventures into an unknown market with new products and learns from the experience available to the industry at large, it will move away from the parent company's core know-how.* Skill at acquiring industry experience rapidly should become a generic skill for entrepreneurs throughout a company.

*P. Ingram and J.A.C. Baum, "Opportunity Constraint: Organizations' Learning From Operating and Competitive Experiences of Industries," Strategic Management Journal 18 (1997): 75–98.

Johnson & Johnson, with its emphasis on creating subsidiaries, is a classic example of granulation.[17] Founded to provide surgical supplies to doctors, the company grew by expanding into related healthcare markets for hospitals and home consumers. Early on, management created separate companies (usually wholly owned by J&J) for each distinct market and allowed them considerable independence. When necessary, the separate companies collaborate—for example, in providing joint distribution services to the hospital industry. By 1999, the company had 190 subsidiaries, 98,000 employees, operations in 51 countries and approximately $24 billion in sales (divided among the hospital, pharmaceutical and consumer health-care sectors). It remains one of the fastest-growing large companies in the world.[18]

Large companies with business units or subsidiaries in different growth stages may want to tackle scaling, duplication and granulation simultaneously. For most early-stage companies, though, it is best if managers implement the three growth strategies sequentially, with some overlapping, as SAP did. A successful firm might first try scaling up its basic business. As it reaches the limits of scaling, it might start duplicating its successful business model abroad, while still emphasizing scaling as much as possible. Eventually the company should be able to pursue granulation, using new business units or spinoffs to diversify in its home market and, later, abroad.

Strategies for Growing and Learning

Means of Learning	Scaling **Netscape**	Duplicating **IKEA**	Granulating **SAP**
Experience sharing	Sharing the core business knowledge	Sharing the know-how of selecting entrepreneurs and managers	Sharing entrepreneurial knowledge in new business cells for new markets
Externalization: Making experiences explicit	Making entrepreneurial know-how in product development, manufacturing, marketing and sales explicit	Black-boxing entrepreneurial know-how and applying it across new markets	Making the knowledge of entrepreneurs in new cells explicit
Formal sharing of knowledge	Sharing within and between functions, such as product development or marketing	Sharing knowledge about procedures that work and those that don't work	Building on and recombining explicit knowledge across cells in order to enhance creativity and generate new business
Devoted practice: Learning by doing	Developing different routines, practices, functions and disciplines	Applying black-box procedures and knowledge	Devoting attention to evaluation and monitoring of new business opportunities
External knowledge acquisition	Establishing formal market connections to ensure customer feedback to product development	Acquiring knowledge about the appropriateness of products, services and processes in the local context	Developing procedures for industry learning

The road will not always be smooth. SAP learned from early customer feedback that it had overengineered R/3: Implementation at customer sites required considerable time, effort and money. The company responded by launching its AcceleratedSAP rapid-implementation technology, which speeds up the introduction and use of its software systems. It also started to provide best-practice cases of business processes so that its clients could benchmark and improve their own operations.[19]

For most early-stage companies, though, it is best if managers implement the three growth strategies sequentially, with some overlapping.

Managing and sharing knowledge is vital. Both IKEA, with its Knowledge Marines, and SAP, with its aggressive training program, worked hard to mobilize local staff to sell and implement products in different markets. But however a company chooses to apply its knowledge and whatever strategy it chooses, it must be committed to continued growth. It can't afford to become complacent. Companies that aren't steadily growing might very well be on their way to steadily dying.

ACKNOWLEDGMENTS

For their helpful comments, we wish to thank three anonymous reviewers; also Simon Grand, Peter Gomez, Yvonne Wicki and Mark Macus of the University of St. Gallen, and Harbir Singh of the University of Pennsylvania's Wharton School. In addition, we thank participants at the Conference on Knowledge and Innovation (Helsinki School of Economics and Business Administration, Helsinki, Finland, May 26–27, 2000), including James G. March, Ikujiro Nonaka, Patrick Reinmoeller and Giovanni Dosi. Andreas Seufert at the University of St. Gallen assisted in the research on SAP.

ADDITIONAL RESOURCES

Many companies have deep corporate knowledge but are not sure how to use it to competitive advantage. "Working Knowledge: How Organizations Manage What They Know," by Thomas Davenport and Lawrence Prusak (Cambridge, Massachusetts: Harvard Business School Press, 1997), and "Enabling Knowledge Creation: How To Unlock the Mystery of Tacit Knowledge and Release the Power of Innovation," by Georg von Krogh, Kazuo Ichijo and Ikujiro Nonaka (New York: Oxford University Press, 2000), provide ample guidelines. The KnowledgeSource Web site (http://www.knowledgesource.org/) offers additional links and information.

Reading about lessons learned from successful companies is a good way to avoid pitfalls and duplicate what works. "Competing on Internet Time: Lessons From Netscape and Its Battle With Microsoft," by Michael Cusumano and David Yoffie (New York: Free Press, 1998), and "Microsoft Secrets: How the World's Most Powerful Software Company Creates Technology, Shapes Markets and Manages People," by Michael Cusumano and Richard Selby (New York: Free Press/Simon & Schuster, 1995), capture lessons from rapidly growing companies. Robert Spector tells Amazon.com's story in "Amazon.com—Get Big Fast: Inside the Revolutionary Business Model That Changed the World" (New York: Harper Business, 2000).

John Nesheim's "High Tech Start Up: The Complete Handbook for Creating Successful New High Tech Companies" (New York: Free Press, 2000) gives good pointers, particularly on how to deal with risk.

REFERENCES

1. J. Timmons, "New Venture Creation" (Burr Ridge, Illinois: Irwin, 1998), 14.

2. We concur with S.L. Brown and K.M. Eisenhardt's notion in "Competing on the Edge: Strategy as Structured Chaos" (Boston: Harvard Business School Press, 1998) that growth should be organically driven by the internal pace of the company rather than external factors.

3. Chuck Salter, "Built To Scale," Fast Company, July 2000, 348–354.

4. J.R. Baum, E.A. Locke and S.A. Kirkpatrick, "A Longitudinal Study of the Relation of Vision and Vision Communication to Venture Growth in Entrepreneurial Firms," Journal of Applied Psychology 83, no. 1 (1998): 43–54.

5. M. Cusumano and D. Yoffie, "Competing on Internet Time: Lessons From Netscape and Its Battle With Microsoft" (New York: Free Press, 1998).

6. J. Clark, "Netscape Time: The Making of the Billion-Dollar Start-Up That Took on Microsoft" (New York: St. Martin's Press, 1999), 60.

7. Marc Andreessen often jumped from one topic to another during conversations but showed a remarkable ability to connect seemingly diverse ideas. As chief legal counsel of Netscape, Roberta Katz, commented, 'The browser is a map of his brain." Cusumano and Yoffie, "Competing on Internet Time," 18.

8. Clark, "Netscape Time."

9. S.G. Winter and G. Szulanski, "Replication as Strategy," working paper 98.10, Wharton School, Philadelphia, Pennsylvania, 1999.

10. G. von Krogh, K. Ichijo and I. Nonaka, "Enabling Knowledge Creation: How to Unlock the Mystery of Tacit Knowledge and Release the Power of Innovation" (New York: Oxford University Press, 2000); and M. Boisot, "Knowledge Assets: Securing Competitive Advantage in the Information Economy" (New York: Oxford University Press, 1998).

11. "IKEA: Furnishing the World," The Economist (Nov. 19, 1994): 79–80; and also see C.A. Bartlett and A. Nada, "Inguardkamprad and IKEA," Harvard Business School case 390-132 (Boston: Harvard Business School Publishing Corp., 1990).

12. www.ikea.com/about_ikea/timeline/fullstory.asp.

13. J. Rieker, "Die drei von der Baustelle," Manager Magazin, April 1998, 114–126.

14. R.N. Yeaple, "Why Are Small Research and Development Organizations More Productive?" IEEE Transactions on Engineering Management 39, no. 4 (1992): 332–346.

15. "Die Regeln der SAP," Manager Magazin, May 1998, 238.

16. M.W.H. Weenig, "Communication Networks in the Diffusion of an Innovation in an Organization," Journal of Applied Social Psychology 25, no. 5 (1999): 1072–1092.

17. Another is Thermo Electron, whose growth is described in C.Y. Baldwin and J. Forsyth, "Thermo Electron," Harvard Business School case no. 9-292-104 (Boston: Harvard Business School Publishing Corp., 1992). Unlike Johnson & Johnson, Thermo Electron generally sold public stock in its subsidiaries to take advantage of the capital markets—an important tactic for raising money.

18. "Dusting the Opposition," The Economist, April 29, 1995, 71–72; and www.jnj.com/annual/99_annual//jj_99_ar.pdf.

19. www.sap.com/service/asap_rm.htm; and A. Seufert, "SAP: The German Software Giant" (presentation at the MIT Sloan School of Management, Cambridge, Massachusetts, Nov. 5, 1999).

Georg von Krogh is a professor of management at the University of St. Gallen in Switzerland and director of its Institute of Management. **Michael A. Cusumano** is a professor of management at the MIT Sloan School of Management in Cambridge, Massachusetts. Contact the authors at georg.vonkrogh@unisg.ch and cusumano@mit.edu.

Insular Culture Helped Yahoo! Grow, But Has Now Hurt It in the Long Run

By MYLENE MANGALINDAN and SUEIN L. HWANG
Staff Reporters of THE WALL STREET JOURNAL

SANTA CLARA, Calif.—They were the most successful sextet of the Internet boom. The first was Jerry Yang, who created a clever new service for searching the fledgling World Wide Web with his friend David Filo in 1994. They brought on Tim Brady, a friend from Stanford. Anil Singh signed on as the first sales employee.

Ellen Siminoff, a recent Stanford M.B.A. graduate, came aboard to plot the business's expansion. A recruiter tapped Jeff Mallett, then a vice president at Novell, to head business operations. The same recruiter also brought in a little-known high-tech executive named Tim Koogle, who came to work in their 800-square-foot office in the summer of 1995.

Their company, Yahoo! Inc., rocketed to a market value of $134 billion, and the young leaders became legends, defining Silicon Valley start-up life. They worked furiously at their jobs but played as well, getting together to watch football games and having one another over for dinner. In an amazingly short time, the six—Mr. Filo faded into the background, as chief engineer—transformed Yahoo into one of the best-known brand names on the Internet, now used by 185 million people worldwide. From day one, the group adopted a defiant, anticorporate image, wearing jeans, putting their feet on their desks and eating at taco joints.

On Wednesday, the game abruptly ended. With its stock down 92% from its peak and advertising sales plunging, Yahoo said it would launch a search for a new chief executive from outside the company. Mr. Koogle will remain as chairman. The unexpected move amounted to a humbling acknowledgment of something people close to Yahoo have increasingly been saying: that the tightknit, us-against-the-world management style that fueled Yahoo's astronomical rise may also have exacerbated its decline.

"Their culture helped them build a superb site and a really edgy brand, but it also held them back from making forward-looking business decisions," says Holly Becker, an analyst at Lehman Brothers. "The culture that served them so incredibly well until the middle of last year is now letting them down."

Business partners and former executives say the small group's intense closeness made it hard for Yahoo to retain or attract experienced managers. Over a long acquisition spree, Yahoo spent billions to buy GeoCities Inc., Broadcast.com, and numerous smaller companies—yet many of the targets' top executives wound up leaving Yahoo, unable to penetrate its inner sanctum. Yahoo's top European and Asian executives and a slew of middle managers also left, amid complaints that the top team wouldn't delegate authority.

"They're very insular," says Stephen Hansen, former chief financial officer at GeoCities, a company acquired by Yahoo in 1999. "They see the world through the Yahoo lens."

A Yahoo spokeswoman strongly disagrees, saying the company has always brought in and retained talented executives. She says that Yahoo is always open to new ideas and that it has been working particularly hard in recent years to further strengthen its ranks. "If we have a reputation for being closed-minded, we wouldn't see all these excited new executives who want to come here," adds the spokeswoman, Nicki Dugan.

In a particularly painful lost opportunity, Yahoo bungled a chance last March to buy eBay, the auction company that today is one of the few profitable Internet companies. Yahoo, which serves like a giant Yellow Pages for the Web, offers its directory free and makes its money primarily by selling advertising and other marketing programs targeted at its Web audience. It has recently been diversifying by running online stores for retailers, creating Web sites for corporations and offering a number of other online transaction services.

Yahoo had realized that its own auction site, which it started after eBay, was lagging behind its rival. The companies began exploring a possible deal. But people familiar with the matter say the talks foundered on disagreement over the role that would be played by Meg Whitman, eBay's CEO. Ms. Whitman wanted to report directly to Mr. Koogle, these people say, adding that while Mr. Koogle had no problem with that, Mr. Mallett insisted the veteran Hasbro executive should report to him.

eBay declines to comment on the talks, as does Yahoo. Bob Kagle, an eBay director and a general partner at Silicon Valley venture firm Benchmark Capital, declines to discuss the talks but says: "Yahoo had a very defined culture that they're very proud of and comfortable with. Among other things, they were not comfortable with the impact that integrating another large and successful company might have on that culture."

Mr. Koogle, asked about critics' suggestions that Yahoo's top-management insularity is now a weakness, said in an interview Wednesday that the CEO search was the answer. "This should address that head-on," he said.

The search adds to the growing list of challenges facing Yahoo. Its sales force is struggling to replace the tens of millions of ad dollars dot-coms were lavishing on the portal just a little over a year ago. Some of its international operations, considered critical to growth, are in turmoil: The heads of four Yahoo international units have resigned in the last month.

The fall in Yahoo's stock, the currency that attracted workers and business partners when it was soaring, has cut the company's market value to below $10 billion. The stock fell $3.25 to $17.69 in 4 p.m. Nasdaq trading [yesterday], a trend that leaves the company vulnerable to a takeover attempt. Last week, it adopted a shareholder-rights plan to fend off any such attempt.

From the start, Yahoo's casual, thumb-your-nose image was more than a way of life. Executives codified it into a marketing machine. They realized they had more than a technology: They were creating a media brand name. They came up with funny publicity stunts and aired irreverent commercials featuring quirky characters using their search engine in unusual ways.

Gooey Yahoo

For all their intensity, the brass exploited the irreverent image internally as well, creating offbeat job titles Chief Yahoo, for a founder, and Gooey Yahoo, for an employee whose aim was making the site warm and fuzzy. They wrapped everything with their trademark yellow and purple.

The top-down style worked fine in a rising market. Yahoo had no trouble luring talent. It was still small enough that top executives could be personally involved in many matters. As recently as a couple of years ago, Ms. Siminoff and Mr. Singh were negotiating all the ad deals themselves, sometimes bringing in Mr. Mallett to close them, ad executives say.

"Yahoo culture used to be what everyone imagined the Internet to be," says Jim Meskauskas, chief Internet strategist at online media-buying firm Mediasmith Inc.

When the dot-com boom arrived, Yahoo was besieged by companies begging to advertise on its site. It went on a hiring binge. From 386 employees in 1997, it went to 803 in 1998 and 1,992 in 1999.

That's when Yahoo's management style began to look like a liability, some advertisers say. A sense developed that decisions always had to go to the top. New employees, often fresh out of school and sometimes ill-informed, were always having to check with higher-ups before agreeing to terms. "You can't run a 3,000-person company, a $2 billion company, with a core management team of four or five people," says Bill Bishop, co-founder and executive vice president of CBS Marketwatch Inc., a Yahoo advertiser. "It doesn't work."

The Yahoo spokeswoman notes that several of the company's general managers are responsible for the financials of their units. She says Yahoo believes very strongly in "pushing decision-making down to the lower levels."

Yahoo acquired lots of other Internet companies, but it became apparent to executives at these companies that their input wasn't welcome in the inner circle. The result was that Yahoo lost some of the sort of talent that it badly needs today, now that Old Economy realities are hitting the young company.

Take Thomas Evans, chief executive of GeoCities, a company that operated a network of personal home pages. Yahoo bought it for $4.7 billion in 1999. A former president of U.S. News & World Report, Fast Company and Atlantic Monthly magazines, Mr. Evans was a veteran of the advertising and media business. In several meetings, Yahoo's top brass tried to persuade Mr. Evans to accept a midlevel job developing relationships with advertisers, people familiar with the situation say, offering him far less responsibility than he had hoped.

In one meeting, they say, Mr. Evans warned the young executives they were alienating the clients they would someday need the most. "Ad sales are a cyclical business," he said to Yahoo's president, Mr. Mallett, according to two people at the meeting. Referring to the company's aggressive sales tactics, he said: "People hate you. You're arrogant and condescending. When there's a downturn in the market, they'll cut you first." People who were present say Mr. Mallett exploded in anger, retorting: "You don't get it. You're old media." Mr. Evans left GeoCities—and Yahoo—when the acquisition was closed.

Asked about the incident, Mr. Evans says all he wishes to say is that "I didn't think I would be able to have the kind of impact that would have helped the situation or changed their thinking."

Michael Barrett, another former GeoCities executive, says, "If you look at any talented executive at any company [Yahoo] bought, the positions they offered them were so far below the position they had that it spoke volumes. The not-built-here mentality has driven their culture."

The Yahoo spokeswoman declines to comment on the incident but notes that Yahoo acquired several smaller companies in specific areas, and some of their executives didn't necessarily have the right skills for a larger corporation.

A few months later, Yahoo paid $5.7 billion for Web broadcasting concern Broadcast.com. It appeared the pattern might be broken when Yahoo executives seemed to take a liking to Broadcast's president, Todd Wagner. "He walked like Mallett, he talked like Mallett," says one former Broadcast executive. It didn't last. Mr. Wagner, like the rest of Broadcast's top brass, left shortly after the acquisition was closed. Mr. Wagner didn't respond to an e-mail seeking comment. The Yahoo spokeswoman says Mr. Wagner left on good terms.

Starting to Change

Yahoo was one of the first Internet companies to expand abroad. As managing director of Yahoo Europe, it hired Fabiola Arredondo, a veteran of JP Morgan and BMG, the entertainment arm of Bertelsmann AG. But it wasn't long before she butted heads with officials in Yahoo's Santa Clara headquarters, and a decision to pull Yahoo Europe's IPO was made against her wishes. Ms. Arredondo said in mid-February that she is quitting the company. Yahoo declines to comment.

Yahoo now appears to be making some progress in growing out of its prolonged adolescence. Last year it brought on Sue Decker, former research chief at Donaldson Lufkin & Jenrette, as chief financial officer. Agency executives say Yahoo is hiring scores of new sales-staff members, but this time people with experience in the ad industry. "They have been very proactive in saying they need to grow to the next level and are going to have to bring very senior people in from the outside," says Jana Rich, a recruiter for Korn/Ferry International.

Yahoo points out that it has been bringing in such new talent as its financial chief and Jim Brock, senior vice president of major initiatives. People familiar with the company say its founder, Mr. Yang, is reasserting himself. For most of its history, he was content serving as Yahoo's unofficial ambassador, speaking at conferences and schmoozing with business partners. Now he is taking a bigger role, such as directly addressing investors, analysts and the media on the Wednesday conference call announcing the search for a new CEO. He has hired people to work directly for him.

At a board meeting Feb. 27, Yahoo directors debated whether they could risk bypassing Mr. Mallett for the CEO spot. "They were wrestling over the risks of losing Jeff versus the benefits of putting someone new in," says one informed person.

Their decision highlights a shift in what has long been a laid-back board, which operated with few formal procedures or prepared materials. This person says Yahoo directors used to get only a one-page agenda with a few bullet points before meetings, rather than the extensive briefing materials prepared at most companies ahead of such sessions. Now, under CFO Ms. Decker, directors 0are given detailed presentations about operational results.

Write to Mylene Mangalindan at mylene.mangalindan@wsj.com and Suein L. Hwang at suein.hwang@wsj.com

---

—Joann S. Lublin contributed to this article.

the decision

Wouldn't that extra $100 million help your business move along at a faster pace? With so many IPOs flying high, why not you?

It has become a story of our times.

Buy.com, an Aliso Viejo, CA-based retailer that sells its wares over the Internet, raised $182 million through an initial public offering in mid-February—not bad for a company that lost $146 million in 1999 and can't predict when it will become profitable. The stock was priced at $13 a share but closed out its first day of trading on the Nasdaq Stock Market at a little over $25 a share. Some analysts have questioned whether the company has a viable business model, but investors don't seem to care. Buy.com's "pop"—the gain in its stock price during the first day of trading—of nearly 100 percent is characteristic of many IPOs today.

It's hard to imagine such a thing happening even a few short years ago, but the IPO market is unlike anything Wall Street analysts, bankers, or investors have ever seen before. New offerings raised more than $69 billion last year, according to Thomson Financial Securities Data, 39 percent greater than in 1996, the previous record. Technology companies—including the red-hot Internet services sector—accounted for the vast majority of those offerings.

The IPO market is driven in large measure by the strong performance of the technology-heavy Nasdaq, which surpassed 5,100 in the first quarter of 2000. There is a strong demand among investors of all stripes for tech stocks, and this has brought many technology companies into the market for the first time. Market observers expect IPO activity to remain strong this year so long as the Nasdaq holds up. "When the Nasdaq does well, IPOs are booming," says Jeffrey R. Hirschkorn, a senior market analyst at IPO.com, a Website that tracks new-issue activity.

Some well-established names came to the market for the first time last year, including The Goldman Sachs Group, United Parcel Service, and Charter Communications. But according to IPO.com, 57 percent of all IPOs in 1999 were brought by companies that had been in business for less than five years. Also, 81 percent of all companies with new issues last year had sales of less than $100 million, a lower sales base than in previous years. In other words, the apples being picked from the tree are smaller and greener than before.

This perception is underscored by another telling statistic: 73 percent of all companies that came to market for the first time in 1999 had no earnings. Indeed, profitability no longer seems to matter very much to investors. Not knowing which companies will be the winners, many large institutional investors have put money into as many new companies as possible. If it has a promising business model and looks like it might be a survivor, a company can attract a high valuation even though it has yet to report any earnings. "Are compa-

nies coming out sooner than we've ever seen? Absolutely," says Merrill Lynch & Co. analyst Edward McCabe, who covers the business-to-business technology sector. "Arguably, this is venture capital investing in the public market. There will be many more losers than winners. Winners will create tremendous value. Losers could be close to worthless."

Okay, so here you are, running a small private company with a great idea and an insatiable appetite for capital. Wouldn't an extra $100 million make your business move along at a faster pace? Oh yes, you say, like a turbocharger on a minibike. And so, you wonder, why not me?

Why not indeed. Clearly the traditional criteria for taking a company public have changed. It used to be that you needed to show eight consecutive profitable quarters as validation that your business model works, but that's no longer the case. Last year, investment bank Robertson Stephens took Santa Monica, CA-based Stamps.com public despite two risk factors that would have killed the deal just a few years ago. The company is developing an online postage service, but at the time of the IPO, the U.S. Postal Service hadn't approved its product idea, and another company claimed to own the technology. Investors still lined up for the shares, which were priced at $11 but eventually shot up to $98.50 before settling in around

$30 in mid-February. All this despite the fact that "the business model hadn't yet been established," says Christopher Bulger, the head of technology investment banking at Robertson Stephens.

JUPITER'S JOURNEY

In the Beginning
Winter 1998–99

Founded in 1986, New York City-based Jupiter Communications sought to help its clients understand and seize the potential of Internet commerce—a specialty that dovetailed nicely with the explosion of the Net in the mid-'90s, as Jupiter became one of the most prominent providers of research on the Internet economy. Having analyzed an industry that has brought renewed excitement to IPOs, Jupiter was well-prepared to contemplate its future as a public company and had looked toward 1999 as the year it would happen. That contemplation got more serious during early 1999, and by March, when CFO Jean Robinson came on board, the company had begun to aggressively pursue its goal. "There's a huge amount of work that goes on," says Robinson. It involved maintaining both an external and internal focus. Jupiter's team talked about the company during informal discussions with a bunch of banks and also worked to get its shareholders on board, while at the same time spearheading the normal pre-IPO effort to get its house in order.

There are several compelling arguments in favor of going public. New companies need capital to fund their growth, and at some point the venture capitalists who nurtured them through their early years will give way to the vastly larger financing capacity of the public market. The money can be used to fund new product development or build brand awareness through extensive marketing. The availability of stock options is a critical factor in recruiting and retaining employees, while the availability of stock as a currency can enable a company to grow through acquisitions.

Companies that go public share most if not all of these motivations. U.S. Interactive, an Internet marketing, consulting, and technology firm, based in King of Prussia, PA, wanted to repair itself to nearly triple in size this year. U.S. Interactive had revenues of $38 million in 1999 but expects to hit $100 million in 2000. President and chief executive Steve Zarrilli raised $46 million in August of last year, and some of that money has been used to build out departments like human resources, the legal department, and a wide array of other corporate functions. Zarrilli wanted working capital "so we could continue to expand the infrastructure of the company," he explains.

Look Before You Leap

Jupiter Communications, a New York-based research firm that specializes in Internet commerce, wanted to be able to reward long-time employees who had been working at below-market compensation levels for a few years with an equity stake in the company. Jupiter chief financial officer Jean Robinson also says the firm's IPO was a highly valuable branding event, "and a big part of our asset is our brand name."

And often, companies will go public because they see an opportunity in the marketplace that can only be exploited through access to a deep pool of capital. David T. Blair, CEO at Rockville, MD-based Health-Extras Inc., which sells a variety of insurance programs directly over the Internet, cites the importance of the "first mover advantage"—being the first company to occupy space in an emerging industry. Blair thought he saw that opportunity last year and ultimately raised $60 million through an IPO in December. "There was just this tremendous advantage

that we didn't want to let slip by," says Blair.

If the reasons for going public are compelling, it's not a decision that should be made lightly—more so today than ever. There is, first of all, the grueling nature of an IPO, and "grueling" is a word that veterans often use to describe it. The process places extraordinary demands on senior management, particularly the CEO and CFO, and it's important to make sure your team has enough bandwidth to run the company and put together an offering simultaneously. In the case of Jupiter Communications, the company hired Robinson, who had been an investment banker for J. P. Morgan & Co. doing public offerings including IPOs, seven months prior to its deal. "From the moment I came in, all I did was the IPO," she says.

Are You **Really Sure** About This?

If you're a CEO who's contemplating an IPO, walk over to a mirror and take a long, hard look. The person you see there—does he or she have the right stuff? Taking a company public is a grueling affair, especially since the process occurs while you're also trying to manage its day-to-day affairs—a big enough job in itself. Perhaps the senior management team needs to be strengthened first through additional hires. Also, has your company's business model been thoroughly validated? Failing to meet Wall Street's expectations can be a fatal mistake for a new public company. The smartest decision you ever make may be to delay the IPO for a few quarters.

There are also the added demands of running a public company. There are Securities and Exchange Commission (SEC) disclosure requirements that must be met through various quarterly and annual filings.

And it's critically important that new public companies maintain strong ties with Wall Street securities analysts and their new investor base, all of whom will be watching their every move with the close attention of a country sheriff at a hippie revival.

Missing your numbers is seen as a marker for a bigger problem.

Most important, if the barriers to the IPO market have never been lower, the risks of failure have never been higher. It's difficult to watch the level of new issue activity and not want to take advantage of a historic opportunity to raise capital, build your company, and become wealthy in the bargain. "*Everyone* wants to go public," says securities attorney Andrew Tucker at McLean, VA-based Shaw Pittman. "Everybody looks at a 4,600 Nasdaq and says my personal wealth could go through the roof."

But analysts and investors have little patience with a new company that doesn't meet or exceed its revenue and earnings projections during its first year of operation. Investors will quickly dump the stock, and the company may find itself in a weaker position than before it went public. Institutional shareholders who were less than discriminating when making their initial decisions will flat out abandon a company that can't deliver consistent performance. "Missing your numbers is not just viewed as an operational issue, but as a strategic issue," says Stephan J. Mallenbaum, head of the technology issues practice at Jones, Day, Reavis & Pogue in New York. "Missing your numbers is seen as a marker for a much bigger problem." What worries investors, Mallenbaum explains, is that your business model might be invalid.

A new company that has disappointed Wall Street suddenly finds itself in a tenuous position. Its stock may be trading below the IPO price, rendering all those employee stock options worthless and poisoning morale. It also might become an acquisition target for a competitor.

"When you go public, you've bet your business," says Merrill Lynch's McCabe. "And if you missed your forecast, you lose."

And yet, while failure would be painful for the company's senior managers, some good might still come of it. "The companies that stumble will get merged or consolidated," says Mallenbaum. "But they will be better off for having gone public."

For some companies, the smartest decision is to wait until their business model has been more thoroughly validated and their forecasting skills honed. Of course, the IPO market might turn against them and an opportunity to raise capital would be lost. But there are worse things. "People go public too soon," says Tucker. "They rarely go public too late."

From *The Survival Guide to IPOs*, pp. 2-5. © 2000 by American Lawyer Media, Inc.

THE INITIAL PUBLIC OFFERING
EARLY PLANNING CONSIDERATION

By Michael D. Donahue

The Importance of Early Planning

The initial public offering ("IPO") for the emerging growth company usually will be the most complex, time consuming and legally intensive transaction the company has experienced to that date. Management will be required to respond to extensive requests for documents, information and interviews from its auditors, attorneys and underwriters and its underwriters' attorneys. These due diligence inquiries will examine the business, financial and legal affairs of the company in greater detail than management has previously experienced. This process will usually identify several "corporate cleanup" matters that will require modifying and, possibly, renegotiating structural and contractual arrangements. The underwriters or auditors may require that prior transactions or arrangements be modified or reversed and a number of material problems may exist or arise that must be solved before going public.

Delays in responding to these inquiries and solving these problems may delay or jeopardize the successful completion of the public offering, reduce the valuation of the company and impact the interests of the company's principals. Many early planning considerations can avoid these potential problems and enhance the value of the company and the interests of its principals.

Management considering an IPO must start preparation several months in advance. In addition, some thought and planning should start at least two years in advance of the proposed IPO. Management decisions and corporate transactions as much as three years in advance of an IPO can create or avoid significant problems. Since many new internet and technology companies are now going public within 24 months of being founded, these ventures need to commence this planning at the time they are started.

The Management Team

A strong management team is obviously important in attracting an underwriter and completing an IPO. An ex-perienced CFO is a particularly important member of this team. A CFO with CPA or public company experience is important. The advice and services of the CFO are important as early as two years before the IPO to establish accounting, control and reporting systems and advise the company on business decisions and transactions that can affect the financial results of the company and the financial statements that will appear in the prospectus.

If the company does not acquire a strong CFO at an early stage, it should consider obtaining advice from an accounting firm experienced in these matters and engaging a financial consultant to provide advice and, possibly, act as a "part-time CFO." This is particularly important for the start-up internet company that may be launching the "sprint" to the IPO. These ventures may not attract a high-level, full-time CFO at the inception, but they should obtain professional accounting and financial guidance at the outset from outside accountants and consultants.

Other Members of the Team

The company will engage attorneys and accountants experienced in public offerings to handle its IPO. Obtaining these services at an early date will assist in these early planning considerations. Adding members to the board of directors or to a board of advisers who are prominent members of the business community and obtaining their guidance at an early stage will be beneficial. An important advantage of obtaining financing from professional venture capitalists is that their expertise is highly valuable in preparing for the public offering.

Audited Financial Statements/Accounting Firm

Audited financial statements of the company for the prior two or three years (depending upon the type of registration form used for the offering) will be required in the prospectus. These financial statements must conform not only to generally accepted accounting principles ("GAAP") but also to extensive additional requirements promulgated by the Securities and Exchange Commission ("SEC") in its Regulation S-X.

The company will need auditors who are expert in these SEC requirements and experienced with IPO's. This will not necessarily require a Big Six accounting firm. Other national firms and many regional firms have the expertise and experience for these engagements. However, some underwriters may prefer a national or Big Six firm, particularly for larger IPO's (over $40 million). The company should seriously consider engaging the auditors whose report will appear in the prospectus as much as three years in advance of the proposed IPO to audit the company's financial statements. If the company waits until closer to the IPO to engage its auditors, it may find it is not possible to obtain the audit reports it will require for the prospectus or it may discover that certain matters will not be reflected on its financial statement as it had expected.

If the company does not obtain these audit services at this early stage, it should consider engaging the accounting firm at least for the limited purpose of providing advice and preliminary services. In some situations, the auditors can perform limited audit steps at the close of a fiscal year with a view towards completing the audit and rendering an opinion at a later time when the company is more certain it will need this for a public offering. In addition, the auditors can provide consulting and review services to advise the company on its accounting and control systems and the accounting treatment of certain transactions.

Commencing the audit process several years in advance is important not only to obtain the required audited financial statements but it also assists the company to develop and maintain the accounting and control systems necessary to provide reliable financial information on a timely basis which is critical to successfully completing the IPO and complying with the reporting requirements of a public company. This can also significantly reduce the burden of management and the extent of legal fees at the time of the IPO.

Financial and Accounting Advice

Generally Accepted Accounting Principles (GAAP) and SEC accounting rules provide detailed requirements on revenue and expense recognition, capitalization expensing and expenses, treatment of acquisitions of assets and businesses and the accounting impact of several types of transactions including stock options, repricing stock options, stock for services and other matters. These rules can have a dramatic impact on a company's earnings and balance sheet particularly for technology, software and start-up companies. Management needs to know these rules and their impact on the company's financial statements prior to and at the time of entering into these transactions. The impact of these rules on the company's reported financial statements can have a signifi-

cant impact on the valuation of the company, the ability of the company to secure a particular underwriter and the ability of the company to qualify for listing on NASDAQ or various stock exchanges.

In addition, when a company is preparing its written business plan and projections and is in the process of seeking an underwriter or other capital source, the company needs reliable information on what its financial statements will look like after adjustments for GAAP and SEC accounting rules.

Material Transactions

Transactions as much as three years prior to a public offering can affect the prospects of attracting an underwriter and the valuation the company obtains on the IPO. These transactions can also impact the amount of management time and legal and accounting expense incurred for the public offering and the nature of the disclosures that appear in the prospectus. Some of the matters to be considered are as follows:

Related Party Transactions. Related party transactions as far back as three years may be required to be disclosed in the prospectus. These disclosures may be objectionable to the company, the other parties to these transactions and to the underwriter. Transactions and arrangements in private companies often involve conflicts of interest that are unacceptable or unworkable in a public offering. In some situations amending or unwinding these transactions may be necessary or desirable.

Management Compensation. The SEC requires detailed disclosure of executive compensation during the issuer's prior fiscal year (see SEC Regulation S-K, Item 402). Some compensation arrangements, particularly some "perks" that are found in private companies are not viewed favorably in public companies.

Material Acquisitions. An acquisition of another business may require audited financial statements of the acquired business to be included in the prospectus. In some situations, financial statements for the acquired business may not be available, let alone audited financial statements. This problem may be avoided if the transaction is an acquisition of assets as opposed to the acquisition of a business and it may be possible to structure and document the transaction to produce the desired result. However, advice from professionals familiar with the SEC positions on this should be obtained at the time of the transaction.

Financial Reporting and Tax Considerations. Management should obtain advice on the financial reporting and tax effects of transactions and operations for periods that will be included in the prospectus including commending and terminating business operations; acquiring or disposing of businesses or assets; issuance of cheap stock or stock options to acquire securities; research and development activities; and material lease transactions. The acquisition of a business may be treated for financial reporting purposes as a "pooling of interests" or an "acquisition" with dramatically different results on the company's financial statements. Product shipping and sales practices and product return and refund policies can affect recognition of revenues and the timing of this recognition. Management should be apprised as early as possible of the position their auditors and the SEC will take on these matters.

Structure and Organization

Various structural and organizational aspects of the corporation may need to be amended in anticipation of becoming a public company. These can include:

Corporate Structure. It may be necessary or desirable to eliminate certain classes of stock with different rights, preferences and privileges; redeem securities with conversion rights or renegotiate terms with holders; eliminate or modify preemptive rights, shareholder agreements, buy-sell agreements; modify the articles of incorporation or bylaws; consider certain anti-takeover provisions; reincorporate in another state; review and improve provisions for indemnifying officers and directors; complete a stock split to adjust the number of shares outstanding and price per share to be consistent with the terms of the proposed underwriting; and establish employee incentive plans including stock option and stock bonus plans and pension and profit sharing plans.

Business Structure. In some private businesses, all assets or operations material to the business may not be held or carried on in the same entity. Certain assets may be held by the principals or by a related company; certain activities may have been carried out by another entity such as a research and development partnership; the company's business may be closely associated with a company owned or controlled by the same principals such as a distributor, supplier, franchisee, franchiser, licensee or licensor; and certain material aspects of the business may be carried on through joint ventures with other entities that may be affiliated with management. These arrangements may need to be restructured to be combined in the public company and to eliminate conflicts of interest and disclosure problems.

Other Disclosure Matters

Early consideration of a number of disclosure matters will assist in cleaning-up problems that could result in objectionable disclosures or in jeopardizing the public offering. Some problems can be so serious that it is necessary that the problem be eliminated rather than disclosed. Problems that are considered reasonable "business risks"

to owners of a private company may not be acceptable to an underwriter or the public marketplace. The company's lawyers will be required to deliver an opinion of counsel to the underwriters at the closing that various legal matters with respect to the company are in order and this may require resolution of problems not previously considered by management.

Addressing and resolving these problems at an early stage may avoid delaying the progress of the public offering. If the resolution requires renegotiating arrangements or resolving disputes, it may be more difficult and expensive to do this if the other side realizes the resolution is critical for the success of a public offering. On the other hand, in some cases, the entry of the underwriter on the scene may assist in resolving old problems, particularly where the public offering will benefit the other parties. These matters can include:

Legal Proceedings. Pending and threatened legal proceedings are required to be disclosed where the risk to the company is material. In some cases the potential financial exposure of the company or impact on its business from an adverse result makes it so material that the offering cannot proceed without resolution of all or part of the dispute.

Contingent Liabilities. Even where legal proceedings are not threatened, contingent liabilities of the company could have a material adverse affect on its financial condition or business operations. These risks may be required to be disclosed and their potential impact may be so great that they are required to be resolved. In some cases, merely the possibility of such liabilities arising may be required to be disclosed and the disclosure itself could be damaging to the company. In such cases it may be necessary to clean up the problem before the IPO and this may require time. These can include failure to comply with legal or regulatory requirements applicable to the business or products of the company; potential income, withholding, excise or other tax liabilities; environmental and toxic clean-up matters; prior issuances of securities in violation of state or Federal securities laws; violations of antitrust, franchise or unfair business practice laws; defaults on covenants or conditions of debt or lease provisions; violations of the Foreign Corrupt Practices Act; patent, trademark or copyright infringement; or the unenforceability of contractual arrangements important to the company's business.

Dependence Upon Customers, Suppliers, Licensees, Licensors, etc. Where a material part of the company's business is dependant upon another entity such as a customer, supplier, licensee, or licensor, disclosure of this will be included in the prospectus matter. However, if there is a problem with the financial, business or legal instability of the other entity or there is a dispute with that entity or there is a question as to the enforceability or validity of the contractual arrangements with that entity, solutions to these matters may need to be addressed.

Regulatory Matters. Where the company is subject to governmental regulation or its products or services are subject to governmental or industry association approvals, potential regulatory or approval problems typically need to be resolved. If any governmental investigation is in process, it may be necessary to reach a final disposition prior to proceeding with the offering unless it is possible to satisfactorily assess the potential impact of the final disposition.

Tax Liabilities. Potential liabilities to state, Federal, local and foreign taxation authorities would be required to be assessed for disclosure purposes and may need to be resolved. This can include state sales tax, employee withholding provisions and tax treatment of foreign operations and international transactions.

Adding Value

Early planning not only avoids problems but can add value to the company for its public offering. This can include:

Management/Board of Directors. Underwriters will tell you the most important consideration in selecting a company is the quality of its management. Attracting a strong management team and board of directors can help attract an underwriter and sell a company.

Employee Benefit Plans. Employee incentive plans, particularly stock option and bonus plans, can improve employee performance and morale. Underwriters and investors like companies with attractive employee incentive plans. Tax and GAAP problems can be created if incentive options or stock are granted close in time to the IPO. It is important to create and implement these a sufficient time before the IPO to avoid these problems.

Improving the Balance Sheet. Companies experiencing dramatic growth in revenues may also be generating significant payables and other current liabilities, which can produce an unattractive balance sheet. Refinancing current liabilities with a bridge loan or other type of loan that converts current liabilities into long-term liabilities can improve the balance sheet.

Business Acquisitions/Combinations. The business may lack an important element the addition of which may increase its value or eliminate a risk or negative aspect of the business. The acquisition of another business, additional technology, or the establishment of additional suppliers or customers may have a significant positive impact on the value of the company for purposes of a public offering.

Finding and Selecting the Underwriter

It is obviously important to the company to find and attract a quality underwriter. It is also important to select an underwriter that is the right size for the company's proposed offering and it would be beneficial to engage an underwriter with experience in the company's industry. In selecting the underwriters to approach, it is important to know in advance whether the company will meet those firms' underwriting criteria.

In searching for an underwriter, the company should try to avoid being "shopped around." Being previously turned down by a number of underwriters is not usually a positive factor in meeting with additional prospective underwriters. The company's attorneys, accountants, board members and other professional advisers can assist in identifying the correct underwriters and in making introductions. If the company has venture capital investors, they will provide important assistance and may control the process.

In selecting an underwriter, the issues the company should consider are: the reputation and financial resources of the underwriter; the types and sizes of prior underwritings; the initial price range compared to the final pricing of the underwriter's prior offerings; the mix of retail and wholesale investors the company can expect; the research, market-making and financial consulting services the underwriter can provide after the offering; the performance of the stocks previously underwritten; the nature and quality of the syndicate, if any, that will be organized by the underwriter and the identity of any co-manager that may be involved. If the potential offering and proposed underwriters being considered are small in size, the company should inquire into the numbers of prior public offerings the underwriter has completed and consider the risk of the underwriter not successfully selling the offering.

Companies should focus not only on the proposed valuation and pricing that is discussed by the underwriter in preliminary negotiations and set forth in the letter of intent. These can change prior to the final pricing. The company should also be concerned with the market performance of the company's stock after the offering because companies almost always require substantial additional capital subsequent to the IPO and principals of the company typically are unable to sell their shares publicly in a registered secondary offering until after the IPO. The reception the company and its selling shareholders receive from the investment banking community for subsequent public offerings will be affected by the performance of the company's stock after the IPO.

Finders and Consultants. The company may engage consultants to assist in preparing the business plan and finding an underwriter. The compensation agreements for these arrangements often involve a finder's fee or "success fee" consisting of a percentage of funds raised and/or equity in the company. Companies should consult securities counsel in entering into these kinds of agreements and make sure they are carefully drafted. These agreements are often unclear or open-ended with respect to when and under what circumstances they terminate and the scope of the transactions to which they apply. In such cases the compensation terms may be objectionable to underwriters. The National Association of Securities Dealers, Inc. regulates underwriters' compensation and some state securities commissioners regulate underwriter compensation and selling costs. These arrangements may create problems with these regulations. If these arrangements are not carefully structured and documented, they can result in disputes at the time of the public offering.

Companies should exercise some control over the activities of finders and consultants to prevent inadvisable "shopping" and should obtain detailed information on their activities so that the company is aware of the identity of firms that were contacted and the results of those contacts.

Pre-Filing Publicity—Gun Jumping

The Securities Act of 1933 (the "1933 Act") prohibits any offer to sell any security in a public offering prior to the filing of a registration statement with the SEC and regulates the offers that may be made after the filing of the registration statement. The SEC takes the position that any publicity or communications which have the effect of conditioning the public or arousing public interest in the securities of the issuer may constitute an offer for these purposes. These types of activities are called "gun jumping" and are violations of Section 5 of the 1933 Act.

These prohibitions do not apply to preliminary negotiations with underwriters and to not prohibit communications with shareholders that are necessary to negotiate and obtain approvals for various corporate matters required for the public offering. Required communications with shareholders can include notification pursuant to "piggyback" registration rights and solicitation of shareholder approvals required for various corporate restructuring. SEC Rule 135 permits a pre-filing press release that is strictly limited to the information permitted by Rule 135.

Publicity about the company's business or products can constitute gun jumping if the SEC deems them to be conditioning the market for the company's securities. This can include interviews with journalists and speeches by the company's management. Companies considering public offerings are not expected to cease all corporate and product advertisements and announcements but should carefully monitor these activities for compliance with these requirements.

Companies considering public offerings should consult with securities counsel for guidance on this issue. The SEC can require a delay of as much as six months to the effectiveness of a registration as a "cooling off" period if it determines that inappropriate publicity occurred. In extreme cases, the SEC may bring an enforcement action for gun jumping.

Legal Counsel

The Company's securities counsel will be an important part of the company's team in carrying out an IPO and will usually be the primary quarterback leading the team. It is obviously important to use legal counsel experienced in public offerings. Experienced legal counsel can also be important in guiding and advising the Company on these early planning considerations. The company should also seek legal counsel who can provide practical business guidance, help locate and attract other members of the team and help locate, meet and select the right underwriter.

Mr. Donahue is a corporate and securities lawyer and concentrates on representing emerging growth companies, securities broker/dealers, investment banking firms, venture capital firms and investment advisers. He is a member of the law firm of Donahue & Mesereau, LLP and was previously a staff attorney and Branch Chief with the United States Securities and Exchange Commission. He is active in a number of industry associations, is a member of the Board of Directors and a past-president of the Los Angeles Venture Association and has been Chairman of its Investment Capital Conference since its inception in 1994.

Prepared for The Investment Capital Conference 2001 March 14, 2001

Harvesting Firm Value: Process and Results

J. WILLIAM PETTY

FOR MOST WITHIN THE ACADEMIC COMMUNITY, entrepreneurship has come to be viewed as a process involving the relentless pursuit of a potential investment opportunity without regard to resources currently owned (Stevenson and Gumpert, 1985; Stevenson and Sahlman, 1987). The objective of this pursuit depends in part on the nature of the opportunity itself. For micro-firms, the goal is mostly to provide a "preferred" lifestyle. For mega-firms, or entrepreneurial firms, on the other hand, the objective is to create economic value. Although micro- and mega-firms have some similarities, there are real differences between them, an important one being the opportunity for the mega-firm to harvest a terminal value from the investment that is not present for the micro-firm. Thus mega-firms are of primary interest to us within the context of harvesting a venture.

Most of the academic literature in entrepreneurship has concentrated on the earlier stages of the entrepreneurship process, namely, identifying and exploiting an opportunity. Little attention has been given to exiting or what has come to be called *harvesting the business*, which is the focus of this chapter.

Harvesting an entrepreneurial firm is the approach taken by the owners and investors to realize terminal after-tax cash flows on their investment. It defines how they will extract some or all of the economic value (cash flows) from the investment. Also, from the entrepreneur's perspective, the issue of harvesting is about more than money, involving personal and nonfinancial aspects of the harvest as well. Even an entrepreneur who realizes an acceptable value for a firm may come away disappointed with the overall outcome of the harvest.

How Important Is Harvesting?

There is little in the way of hard evidence as to the exact significance of the harvest; that is, it cannot be said precisely how much of the value realized from a venture is attributable to a successfully implemented harvest strategy. However, from intuition alone, one would expect that few events in the life of the entrepreneur, and for the firm itself, are more significant than the harvest.

In one sense, the harvest is not as important as successfully identifying an opportunity or even growing the firm. These two phases of the entrepreneurial process are without question the primary value-creating activities. However, *the availability and effectiveness of the exit ultimately determine the value to be realized from the venture.* While value must first be created, it must then be realized for any real benefit. Thus, the terminal liquidity, or lack thereof, provided by the harvest will ultimately determine the value received from the venture. The inability to harvest at a *fair* value would be much like buying a stock, watching its value increase over time, but not being allowed to capture the value by selling the stock. However, the stock analogy fails to capture the complexity of the harvest relative to selling a publicly traded stock.

The significance of the problem may also be viewed from a macro perspective by considering the large number of family-owned firms that will be faced with the prospects of the harvest. It has been estimated that 18 percent of the financial assets held by U.S. households, or $2.4 trillion, is invested in privately held firms, mostly family-owned businesses—$300 billion more than these same households have invested in publicly traded companies (Paré, 1990). Many of these privately owned firms were founded by entrepreneurs in the 1950s and 1960s who are or soon will be contemplating and executing a harvest or exit strategy. The same situation also exists in Europe. As many as 17,000 European companies received equity venture capital during the past decade (Batchelor, 1992). Most of those investments have yet to be harvested.

The harvest is also of prime importance to outside investors. These investors typically have a priori expectations about their investment that include either taking the firm public or being acquired by other investors (Freear et al., 1990). Investors, be they professional venture capitalists or private informal investors, have an obvious vested interest in the exit mechanism used to liquidate their investment. While not having the same personal significance for the firm's investors as it does for the entrepreneur, the effectiveness of the harvest affects the amount and timing of the after-tax cash flows to be received, which in turn determines the eventual return earned on the investment. From experience, they realize that time can exact a fierce penalty on the rate of return. A successful entrepreneurial venture returns at least 40 percent compounded annually to investors over a holding period of four to five years. To achieve such a return requires a terminal cash-flow multiple of 5.4 times the original investment. However, the same yield over 10 years requires 28.9 times the original investment. Thus, an investment in a high-risk venture that is unrealized after 10 years is thought to be long past its "sell-by" date in all but a few rare instances. Consequently, venture capitalists are reluctant to make an investment without having some idea as to how an exit will be arranged.

In short, the opportunity to exit successfully from a venture is thought to be a significant factor in the entrepreneurial process, both for the entrepreneur and for any investors providing risk capital.

In examining the literature on harvesting the venture, there are four areas of interest:

1. Developing a strategy.
2. The value-creating process.
3. The process of the harvest.
4. The European experience in harvesting.

When Does the Harvest Begin?

The typical prescription for developing a harvest strategy is simple: *Now, not later.* Timmons (1994) suggests that entrepreneurs build a great company but do not forget the harvest; he also advises that entrepreneurs should keep harvest options open and think of harvesting as a vehicle for reducing risk and for creating future entrepreneurial choices and options. Thus, crafting a harvest strategy is viewed as something to be done early on and as an ongoing process along with growing the business, even well before the impending need or desire to harvest.

Given the conventional wisdom of the need for a harvest strategy even before the event, a natural question would be, Do entrepreneurs ever follow this advice? To answer this question, one must rely on limited empirical evidence. Holmburg (1991) surveyed CEOs at computer software firms that went public between 1980 and 1990. He found that 15 percent had a written harvest strategy as part of the original business plan; 5 percent developed a formal exit strategy subsequent to preparing the business plan; 40 percent had given some thought to the harvest; and the final 40 percent did not give any consideration to the harvest beforehand (Figure 1). Similar results were found in another study where 40 percent of the CEOs surveyed did not consider the harvest at the outset of the venture (Hyatt, 1990). Thus, it can be concluded—based on our limited information—that roughly 60 percent give some advance thought to the harvest, either informally or

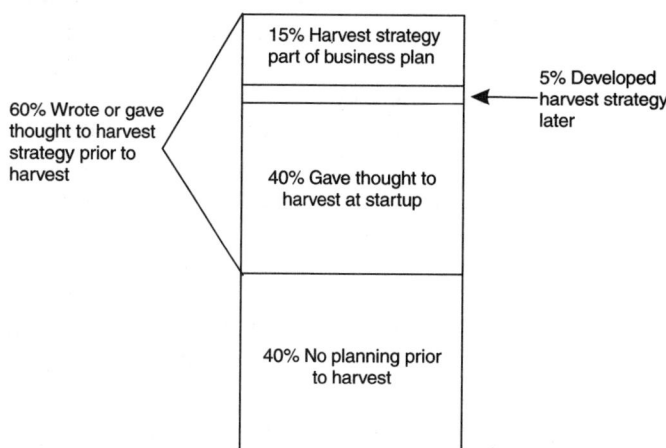

FIGURE 1
Developing the Harvest Strategy

formally. However, only 20 percent appear serious in their efforts.

You Cannot Harvest What You Have Not Created

Valuing a firm when the stock is not traded in the marketplace is difficult in the best of circumstances. But even worse is forecasting the value of a startup some five or 10 years into the future. Financial contracting requires some estimate of the venture's terminal value and an assumed horizon date for the harvest (Sahlman and Summer, 1988). The problem is one of assigning value to an asset for which the greatest amount of incomplete and conflicting information exists. To be even more precise, founders and early-stage investors are in reality purchasing an option on the future cash flows to be exercised if the firm does well; the option characteristics are especially apparent when staged commitments are allowed.

The possible approaches for determining a company's value are legion. However, most investors in entrepreneurial firms rely on some multiple of earnings, be it net income, operating income, or earnings before interest, taxes, depreciation, and amortization (EBITDA). For instance, a multiple of EBITDA plus the firm's cash is often used to estimate firm value. Outstanding debt is subtracted to determine the value of the equity. This approach, while simple, begs an important question: What *should* determine harvest value? Two basic perspectives can be used in answering the question: either the accountant's "map of the territory" or the economist's. An accountant would say that earnings drive firm value—the larger the earnings, the greater the firm value. The economist's map of firm value, on the other hand, is based on the present value of future cash flows.

To the extent that a willing buyer is prepared to pay some multiple of earnings for a firm, value—at least from all appearances—is based on earnings. But there is little in the way of an economic rationale or any empirical evidence to suggest that a firm's value is closely linked to earnings (Brennan, 1995). Instead, many believe that value ought to be determined by finding the present value of future cash flows discounted at the opportunity cost of funds for the given level of risk (Copeland et al., 1994). Nevertheless, the conventional wisdom that earnings matter continues to carry the day for most investors.

The issue of valuation as it relates to the harvest strategy is important; one cannot structure the deal without some notion of what the harvest value will be. However, the issue can be expressed more fundamentally by asking, Will economic value be created with the capital that is being invested in the venture? Given that a start-up company is not traded publicly, one cannot depend on the capital markets for that information. Even so, firm value can correctly be represented as the capital invested in the business plus any value created by earning economic rates of return that exceed the cost of capital; or stated negatively, firm value is equal to the capital invested, less the value destroyed by earning rates of return less than the firm's opportunity cost of funds.

As a firm moves in time toward the harvest, there are two questions that are of primary importance. First, are the current owners and managers effectively creating firm value? The answer to this question can be answered easily from historical financial data by estimating the economic value added (EVA) over time. The economic value added from a firm's operations in year t (EVA_t) could be estimated as follows (Stewart, 1991):

$$EVA_t = (\text{return on capital}_t - \text{cost of capital}_t) \times \text{invested capital}_t$$

where return on capital is measured as *economic* income divided by the amount of capital (cash) invested in the company over its life, and cost of capital is the investors' opportunity cost of funds—a concept almost totally alien to most entrepreneurs. This single measurement of economic value added, which is seldom considered by large companies (much less smaller companies), can tell us a great deal about the value-creating ability of a company, an issue of import if there is to be any value to harvest.

The second and related question is, Could new owners do more with the company than the founders? If so, then the firm would have greater value in the hands of new owners. That is, growing a venture to the point of diminishing returns and then selling it to others better able to carry it to the next level is a proven way to create value. How this incremental value will be shared between the old and the new owners largely depends on the relative strengths of each party in the negotiations, i.e., who wants the deal the most.

With the foregoing as a backdrop, the next step is to examine the actual harvesting process.

The Harvesting Process

For the most part, designing a harvest strategy is limited to one of several options. The more common ways to harvest include the following:

- Restructuring the company's goals and strategies in order to increase the cash flows extracted from the business by the owners and investors.
- Being acquired by or merged into another, usually larger, company.
- Private sale for cash, debt, and/or equity to: (1) another company or group of investors; (2) management, frequently through a leveraged management buyout; (3) employees, usually in the form of an employee stock option plan; or (4) family members.
- Public stock offering.

How do entrepreneurs view these options? Again drawing on Holmburg's (1991) study of the computer software CEOs who took their firms public, each respondent was asked to reflect back to the start-up stage of the company and to rank the probability at that time that the firm would use one of four alternative harvest strategies at some point in the future. The options included an initial public offering, being acquired by a larger company, merging with another firm, and a leveraged buyout by employees. Somewhat of a surprise, 65 percent of the CEOs considered an initial public offering as their most likely choice; 30 percent assigned the highest probability to being acquired by a larger company, and the remaining 5 percent thought a leveraged buyout by employees would occur. These results are supported by another recent survey of 100 CEOs where more than half planned on going public from the initial start-up phase (Hyatt, 1990). The discussion that follows briefly explains several of the above options.

Increasing the Firm's Free Cash Flows

A firm's free cash flows represent the amount of cash that can be distributed to its investors—debt and equity—after all operating needs have been met. Specifically,

$$\text{Free cash flows} = \text{operating profits after tax} + \text{depreciation} - \text{investments required to grow the firm}$$

In a firm's early years, everything goes into growing the company. All available cash is devoted to growth, which means that the last term in the above equation is large. For most growth firms, the free cash flows are significantly negative in the early years. As a firm and its industry mature, the opportunity to grow declines, which can result in sizable amounts of free cash flows.

Many of the fights in the 1980s between management and corporate raiders occurred in mature industries, such as oil and steel, over the use of the firm's cash flows. Management was using them to invest in unrelated businesses, usually with dismal results, while the raiders thought the newly acquired firms should not have been acquired because the result was a loss of focus. So the raiders attempted to take over these widely diversified businesses in an attempt to return them to their core businesses—and to return the cash flows to the investors. A substantial part of the academic literature in this area focused on this debate (e.g., Donaldson, 1994; Bhide, 1989).

Within the context of harvesting, the concern is not so much about the battle over the use of the free cash flows as it is in converting them into a way of harvesting an entrepreneurial firm. Specifically, at some point, an entrepreneur and any investors in the venture may decide to slow or even discontinue the company's sales growth rate. Rather than reinvesting all the cash flows back into the company, the owners begin cashing out of their investment. Only the amount of cash is retained that is necessary to maintain current markets—there is no effort to grow the present markets or expand into new markets. The free cash flows can then be harvested without affecting current operations. For many ventures, this event may occur as a natural consequence of maturing markets where competition has removed any growth opportunities that earn returns greater than the firm's cost of capital. The mistake at this point is for the entrepreneur not to harvest. Thus, restricting a company's growth is a viable strategy for harvesting the venture, but it requires some time to accomplish.

Increasing the firm's free cash flows has two potential advantages. First, the owners can retain the ownership of the company if they are not ready to sell. Second, the strategy is not dependent on finding an interested buyer and going through the often time-consuming and energy-draining experience of negotiating the sale, nor does the owner face the exciting, but at times frustrating, process of a public stock offering.

There are, however, some disadvantages as well. In harvesting the business, the desire is to maximize the after-tax cash flows going to the company's owners and investors. If the firm simply distributes the cash flows as dividends, the income will be taxed both as corporate income and again as personal dividend income to the stockholders. There are ways, within limits, to avoid this problem, but it may not provide the entrepreneur as much discretionary cash flow as an outright sale. Another disadvantage of this strategy is the chance that the firm may not be able to sustain its competitive advantage while simultaneously harvesting the venture. If so, the end result may be an unintended liquidation. Finally, for the entrepreneur who is simply tired of the day-to-day operations, harvesting the venture by siphoning off the free cash flows over time may be asking for too much in the way of patience. Unless there are other individuals within the company who are qualified to provide the needed managerial leadership, then the strategy may be too emotionally draining.

Merging or Being Acquired

In terms of mergers and acquisitions, the literature has mostly been concerned with the rationale and success of acquiring or merging with another company, especially in an unrelated business (Weston et al., 1990). The predominant question has been, What can management accomplish through corporate diversification that the owners cannot achieve through their own diversification and with a lot more ease?

The 1980s came to be known as the decade of the deals and as a time of hostile takeovers, which to many instinctively felt wasteful and harmful. But not all was bad about the 1980s. The decade's merger and acquisition (M&A) activity allowed the shareholders of a significant number of privately held companies to realize the value "locked-up" in their companies via a market-based transaction. In other words, the M&A activity of the 1980s allowed many entrepreneurs the opportunity to harvest their investment that might not have otherwise been possible.

The financial issues related to selling a firm are basically the same with any exit strategy, namely, how to value the company for the purpose of the sale and how to structure the payment. However, financial matters, while not insignificant by any means, are not the only issues of importance when it comes to selling the firm and may not even be the primary concern.

To gain some understanding into this process, Petty et al. (1994) collected a sample of acquisition transactions of privately held companies reported in *Mergerstat Review* between 1984 and 1990. The sample was limited to acquisitions valued between $5 million and $100 million. Also, 278 venture-backed companies that were acquired between the years of 1987 and 1990 were identified through the *Venture Economics* database, which included the names of venture capitalists who had participated in the financing. With this combined listing, background information about the buyer and seller and about the acquisition itself was collected from the Dow Jones News Retrieval Service.

The issues addressed in the study fell into one of three areas: 1) the decision to sell, 2) the selling process, and 3) the post sale. Using these issues as guidelines, phone interviews were conducted of a limited sample of the entrepreneurs—efforts to interview venture capitalists were essentially unsuccessful. Some of the conclusions reached from the interviews were as follows:

1. Some of the entrepreneurs were significantly disappointed with the acquisition process and the final outcome. They came to realize that the firm served

as the base for much of what they did, both in and out of the business arena. This sentiment existed more with owners of the low-tech firms, especially service firms, than with the high-tech companies.

2. The most prevalent reason for selling the company related to estate planning and the opportunity to diversify their investments. A second reason for the sale related to the need for financing growth, which the firm or the owner did not have the capacity to provide.

3. The harvest did provide the long-sought-after liquidity, but some entrepreneurs found managing money more difficult, and less enjoyable, than they had expected and less rewarding than operating their own company.

4. The disillusionment of selling the firm was particularly evident when the entrepreneur continued in the management of the company but under the supervision of the acquiring owners. The differences in corporate culture became a significant problem for both companies involved in the transaction, but more so for the selling entrepreneur.

5. A number of the selling owners were disappointed in the advising they received from the "experts." After the fact, they wish they had talked to other entrepreneurs who had been through the experience of a company sale.

6. Most entrepreneurs relied on their staff and advisors to determine a fair price for their company. Thus, they would talk in terms of cash flows and earnings, most often the capitalization or multiple of the earnings or cash flows, and seldom the present value of future cash flows. However, most of the entrepreneurs felt they had a sense of what they would accept for the firm, and that instinct had a greater influence than did the supporting computations. Most often, the price was not a serious issue.

7. There is considerable downside risk if the acquisition is not consummated. During the negotiations, management's focus and attention shifts from company operations to consummating the sale. Members of the existing management team may be promised promotions after the acquisition, which are not fulfilled after the negotiations fail. Hence, there is a real risk of losing part of the management team and certainly taking several months to regain the firm's focus.

In addition to selling the firm or being acquired by independent purchasers or acquirers, the harvest strategy can be accomplished by selling to the firm's own management or its employees, as described in the following two sections.

Management Buyout

As already observed, the 1980s will long be remembered—not so favorably by some managers and employees—for the unfriendly takeovers and corporate restructurings, involving corporate raiders and takeover artists, such as Carl Icahn and T. Boone Pickens. These paragons—or parasites some might say—popularized financial engineering, in which an attempt to buy a company is made for the purpose of restructuring it and selling it off in pieces to the highest bidder. To finance the deal, heavy amounts of debt are incurred, with as much as 90 percent of the financing coming from high-yield debt, thus the name *leveraged buyout*. If the leveraged buyout is performed not by outsiders but by the firm's own management, we have a *management buyout* (MBO).

The MBO has been used by some to thwart outside raiders and by others to refocus current management's vision. The evidence is clear that MBOs can contribute significantly to a firm's operating performance by increasing management's focus and intensity and that the benefits accruing from MBOs are not short-term in duration. (See Kaplan, 1989 and 1991, for an analysis of the operating effects of large-firm MBOs, and Wright et al., 1992b, for smaller-firm MBOs.)

Given the empirical evidence of increased efficiencies produced from an MBO and the proven longevity of these benefits, an MBO should be considered a potentially viable means for transferring firm ownership—both for large and small businesses. In like manner, an MBO can serve as a possible means for harvesting a venture. While the managers within many entrepreneurial businesses frequently have a strong interest and incentive to buy the business, they often lack the financial capacity to do so. An MBO can resolve this intractability. It simply means that they must be prepared to live in a glass house and with the unforgiving nature of debt financing.

If an MBO is used to consummate the sale, not only is the new owner exposed to financial risk, so is the selling owner. Also, to the extent that the entrepreneur accepts debt in consideration for the company, there is a potential complication to be resolved. The deal must then be structured to minimize potential agency problems. Specifically, if the new owners have placed little if any of their own money in the deal, they may be inclined to take risks that are not in the best interest of the selling entrepreneur; they simply have nothing to lose if the company fails. Also, if the terms of the deal include an earnout where the final amount of the payment depends in part on the subsequent profit performance of the company, the buying owners have an incentive to do things that lower the firm's profits during the earnout period. Thus, the entrepreneur needs to take great care in structuring the deal; otherwise, there will most likely be disappointment with the outcome.

In addition to their recent popularity in the United States, management buyouts have come to be used in Europe as well. In Europe, the venture capital industry has had a significant role in MBOs, especially for smaller firms. Wright et al. (1992a) evaluated a sample of 182 venture-backed MBOs and found the same improvement in operating efficiencies and longevity as did researchers in the United States. Also, European managers who undertake MBOs typically anticipate their exit to be in the form of a public offering, but almost invariably the firm is sold to a third party. This last finding will become clearer at a later point in the chapter.

Employee Stock Ownership Plan

Employee stock ownership plans (ESOPs) were designed to increase productivity by linking employee compensation to company performance and by giving employees a role in management through their voting rights as shareholders. The research to date suggests that ESOPs have indeed been effective toward these ends. For instance, using both Tobin's (Tobin, 1969) and accounting performance variables, Park and Song (1995) found that average performance significantly increases after establishing or expanding an ESOP (see also Beatty, 1995). There are also tax advantages with ESOPs that are not available with other retirement plans.

In response to the above benefits, owners of small and midsize firms have been the primary users of ESOPs when they are ready to sell (Englander, 1993). The opportunity for employees to invest in employer stock and the significant tax savings not available with other retirement plans—for employers and employees alike—makes the ESOP potentially attractive as a way to harvest the venture (Beatty, 1995).

A *leveraged* ESOP particularly fits the needs of an entrepreneur wanting to harvest a venture. This type of ESOP borrows money to buy the company's stock. By having access to borrowed money, the leveraged ESOP can make large purchases of the stock at one time, conceivably purchasing the entire company. Figure 2 presents a flow

FIGURE 2
The Harvest: Using the Leveraged ESOP

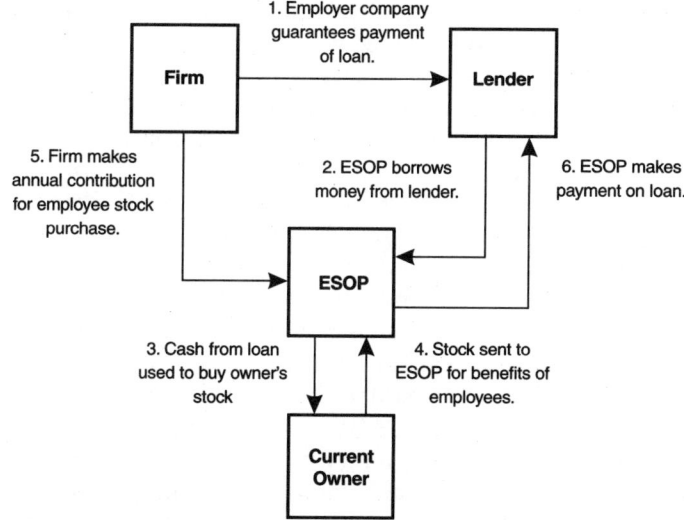

Adapted from D. R. Garner, R. R. Owen, and R. P. Conway, *The Ernst & Young Guide to Raising Capital.* New York: John Wiley & Sons, 1991, p. 282.

chart of the sequence of events when a leveraged ESOP is used to provide an employee retirement plan and, in conjunction, to allow the present owners to sell their stock. The firm first establishes an ESOP and guarantees any debt borrowed by the ESOP for the purpose of buying the company's stock. Next, the ESOP borrows money from a lender, and the cash is used to buy the owner's stock. The shares are held by a trust, and the company makes annual tax-deductible contributions to the trust so it can pay off the loan. As the loan is paid off, shares are released and allocated to the employees.

While an ESOP benefits the owner by providing a market for selling stock, it also carries with it some tax advantages that make the approach attractive to owner and employee alike. Some of the benefits are as follows:

1. If the ESOP owns at least 30 percent of the firm after purchasing the shares, the seller can avoid current tax on the gain by using the proceeds to buy other securities.
2. If the ESOP owns more than 50 percent of the company, those who lend money to the ESOP are taxed on only 50 percent of the income received from such loans. Thus, the lender can afford to offer a lower interest rate, usually about 1½ percentage points below a company's normal borrowing cost.
3. The dividends that a business pays on the stock held by the ESOP are allowed as a tax-deductible expense; that is, the dividends are treated like interest expense when it comes to taxes.

Despite the advantages ESOPs offer, they are not appropriate for all companies. If the entrepreneur does not want the employees to have control of the company, then an ESOP is not an option. Also, the ESOP must cover all employees, and the owners are required to disclose certain information about the company, such as its performance, and its key executives' salaries, which for some entrepreneurs is not palatable. Finally, using an ESOP can place the employees in double jeopardy, where both their jobs and their retirement funds depend on the success of a single business. Even so, an ESOP has considerable potential when crafting a harvest strategy.

The next section looks at the option for harvesting the venture that most would love to attain, but few do.

Initial Public Offerings

An initial public offering (IPO) is not in and of itself a primary means for harvesting a venture. While founders and the shareholders clearly benefit from an IPO, its principal purpose in most situations is to facilitate the raising of future capital. Simply put, publicly traded stock provides for greater liquidity, which allows the company to raise capital on more favorable terms than if it were privately held. These perceptions are borne out in Holmburg's (1991) study, where he asked the CEOs of firms that had gone public to indicate the level of importance of some 17 different possible motivations for the public offering. The items receiving the highest percentage of "very important" responses are as follows:

Raise capital for growth	85%
Raise capital to increase working capital	65%
Facilitate acquiring another firm	40%
Establish a market value for the firm	35%
Enhance the firm's ability to raise capital	35%

For all practical purposes, the CEOs clearly considered financing future growth as the primary impetus for going public. Without a strong IPO market, young high-growth firms would have limited access to the public capital markets, but equally bad, they would have less access to private investors who rely on the IPO market to harvest their investment. However, at the same time, the IPO market is beneficial to the founding entrepreneur in the form of increased liquidity and the enhancement of future options, both of which reduce the investor's risk exposure. So it may not be a pure harvest in the same way of other approaches where cash is received, but the investor captures some of the same advantages accruing to the firm.

Understanding the IPO Process

The IPO process can be one of the most exhilarating, but also frustrating and exhausting, experiences an entrepreneur will encounter (Sutton and Beneddetto, 1990). Managements of large companies, much less small ones, do not like being exposed to the vicissitudes of the capital markets and to the world of investment bankers.

In a survey of the *Inc.* magazine's top 100 firms, the CEOs who had participated in public offerings indicated they spent 33 hours per week on the offering for 4 months (Brokaw, 1993). The cost of the IPO process seemed excessive and exorbitant to many. They found themselves not being understood and having little influence in the decisions being made. Disillusionment with the investment bankers, and much of the entire process itself frequently occurred. At some point, the owners wondered where they had lost control of the process, a feeling generally held by most entrepreneurs involved in a public offering.

The chronology of a public offering is relatively straightforward, namely:

- The management decides to go public.
- An investment banker is selected to serve as the underwriter, who in turn brings together a group of investment houses to help sell the shares.
- A prospectus is prepared.

- The managers, along with the investment banker, go on the road to tell the firm's story to the brokers who will be selling the stock.
- On the day before the offering is released to the public, the decision is made about the actual offering price.
- All the work, which by now has been months, comes to fruition in a single event—offering the stock to the public and waiting for the consequence.

During this process, the firm's owners and managers are answering such questions as:

- What do we need to do in advance of going public?
- What are the legal requirements?
- Who should be responsible for the different activities and how should we structure our team to make it all happen?
- How do we choose an investment banker?
- How do we determine an appropriate price for the offering?
- How is life different after we are a public company?

While the foregoing issues are important, they do not represent the complete story. The missing element is the shift in power that occurs during the process. When the chain of events begins, the company's management is in control. They can dictate whether or not to go public and who the investment banker will be. However, after the prospectus has been prepared and the road show is underway, the firm's management, including the entrepreneur, is no longer the primary decision-maker. Now the investment banker has control of the decisions. Finally, the marketplace, in complement with the investment banker, begins to take over, and ultimately it is the market that dictates the final outcome.

In addition to the issue of who controls the events and decisions in the IPO process, one other matter is important—understanding the investment banker's motivations in the IPO process. Stated differently, who is the investor banker's primary customer here? Clearly, the issue firm is rewarding the underwriter for the services being performed through the fees paid and a participation in the deal. But the economics for helping with an IPO may not be as rewarding for the investment banker as other activities, such as involvement with corporate acquisitions. The investment bank is also selling the securities to its customers on the other side of the trade. Thus, it becomes unclear as to what is driving the pricing decision by the investment banker (Sahlman, 1988). This potential agency problem may be one of the reasons for the upfront underpricing of IPOs (Welch, 1996).

While the process of going public may prove frustrating and exasperating, the eventual outcome frequently is not. In a survey of firms listed on the French *Second Marché* (secondary market), most CEOs were very satisfied with their decision (Desroches and Belletante, 1992).

The firm owners thought the external image of the firm was improved in the eyes of the suppliers, customers, and others after the offering, along with an increased effectiveness in the level of communications, strategy, and other internal management-related aspects. They disliked, however, the fluctuations in the firm's share price, which they did not believe reflected firm performance. Similar results were observed by Desroches and Jog (1989) in a study of 194 firms that went public in Canada. They concluded that CEOs do not convey a significant loss of control and actually welcome the more structured decision-making which resulted from going public. Although they did not like the valuation of their shares by the marketplace, their conclusion was that going public does imply significant and positive changes to the status of the firm, management structure, and the entrepreneur.

While the Canadians were overwhelmingly pleased with the outcome of going public, they like the French, disliked the feeling of powerlessness about the firm's stock price and the belief that the market price does not reflect the true value of the firm. This view is one that is held by managers across the board, without respect to firm size. The perception is that the capital markets are myopic; that management is under pressure for short-term performance and can no longer look to the shareholder's long-term best interests (Jones et al., 1992).

While there are certainly anomalies, as explained in the next section, there is absolutely no empirical evidence that the capital markets are short-sighted, while management can see more clearly into the long-term future. If anything, it is management that is myopic, not the markets (Miller, 1994).

Understanding the IPO Market

If contemplating a public offering, management needs to have an understanding of the basic nature and peculiarities of the new-issues market. In this area, there is no lack of empirical work about the outcomes of new offerings. Specifically, three anomalies have been found:

1. There is a large amount of empirical literature validating IPO underpricing, dating back 20 years—all finding that the distribution of initial returns to be highly skewed, with significant positive means (Ibbotson, 1975). The average first-day return of a new issue falls somewhere between 10 percent and 15 percent. These results are even more pronounced for smaller, younger companies going public than for their older, more established counterparts. For instance, the average initial return on IPOs with an offering price of less than $3.00 was found to be an amazing 42.8 percent, whereas the average initial return on IPOs with an offering price of $3.00 or more was only 8.6 percent (Chalk and Peavy, 1987). Moreover, underpricing persists in every country

with a stock market, although the amount of underpricing is different from country to country (Loughran et al., 1994).

2. There are cycles in both the volume of new issues and the magnitude of first-day returns. The periods of high average initial returns are known as "hot issue" markets. (Hot issue markets were first identified by Ibbotson and Jaffe, 1975.) The cycles in underpricing allow one to predict next month's average initial return based upon the current month's average with a high degree of accuracy, i.e., the first-order autocorrelation of monthly average initial is 0.66. Likewise, high-volume months are almost always followed by high-volume months, where the autocorrelation is 0.89 (Ibbotson et al., 1994).

3. New issues tend to underperform for up to five years after the offering (Loughran, 1993). For IPOs during the period 1975 to 1984, the total return from the end of the first day of trading to three years later was 34.5 percent, compared with the return on the NYSE of 61.9 percent (Ritter, 1991). Again these findings were even more pronounced for younger firms than for established firms. There is also reason to believe that the earnings per share of companies going public typically grows rapidly in the years before going public, but then actually declines in the first several years after the IPO (Jain and Kini, forthcoming).

Ibbotson et al. (1994) described the IPO market pricing as a puzzle to those who otherwise believe in efficient capital markets and argued that the anomalies are interrelated by periodic overoptimism by investors which causes many firms to rush to market, resulting in disappointing returns to long-term investors when the issuers fail to live up to overly optimistic expectations. They also found that firms that issue during low-volume periods typically experience neither high initial price run-ups nor subsequent long-run underperformance and that the patterns are much more pronounced for smaller, younger companies going public than for their older, more established counterparts. Their finding is consistent with evidence by Hanley and Ritter (1993) suggesting inefficiencies in markets for smaller-cap stocks.

In short, the IPO market has somewhat a personality of its own and one that acts a bit different from the rest of the capital markets—a fact that needs to be understood by an entrepreneur wanting to take a firm public.

A Venture Capital Perspective of IPOs

Many venture capitalists believe that an IPO produces a higher price than an outright sale. That belief is encouraged by the fact that the average valuation of IPOs between 1988 and 1992 was $106.9 million versus $37.4 million for private sales. But the companies floating IPOs are mostly stars or potential stars, whereas those that are sold include not only stars but also many mediocrities with no hope of going public.

The gains realized through IPOs were almost five times greater than the next most profitable method of harvesting the venture, according to a study of how 26 venture capital funds exited 442 investments from 1970 to 1982 (Soja and Reyes, 1990). That study found that 30 percent of the exits were through IPOs, 23 percent private sales, 6 percent company buyouts, 9 percent secondary sales, 6 percent liquidations and 26 percent write-offs.

A study of 77 high-tech companies backed by venture capital that had IPOs between 1979 and 1988 found that the times returns (amount returned ÷ amount invested) on the venture capital investment at the initial offering price was 22.5 times for the first round; 10 times for the second round; and 3.7 times for the third round (Bygrave and Stein, 1989). Four years after the IPO the times return was 62.7 times for the first round, 38.1 times for the second, and 13.5 times for the third.

The average compound annual rate of return for the first round of venture capital at the time of the IPO was 220 percent; four years after the IPO (about seven years after the first round of venture capital), it had declined to 57 percent. So although the times return increased from 22.5 times to 62.7 times, the rate of return declined because of the longer holding period—another indication of underpricing of new issues.

According to industry wisdom, venture capitalists financing seed and start-up high-technology companies are looking for compound annual returns of 50 percent or more; for second-stage financings they tend to look for 30 to 40 percent; while third-round investors may expect returns of 25 to 30 percent (Morris, 1985).

A rule of thumb is a return in five years of seven times the first venture capital (a compound rate of return of 48 percent). The evidence in the above studies gives some credence to these expected returns. However, in the latter 1980s, the returns of funds started in the 1980s fell far short of expectations, mainly owing to the public's loss of interest in speculative IPOs during the latter 1980s. As a result, many venture-backed companies were unable to go public. Thus, venture funds were unable to reap their expected harvests. The return of a "hot" IPO market in the 1990s has provided hopes of a return to the earlier years. However, based on limited evidence, the returns probably have only returned to the 15 to 20 percent range.

The European Experience with Harvesting

To understand the environment for harvesting in Europe, one can draw on the comprehensive work edited by Bygrave et al. (1994). In this study, realizing investment value is the result of collective efforts of a group of researchers who carefully examined the harvesting process across Europe.

The organized venture capital industry in Europe is little more than 12 years old, in contrast to 50 years for the U.S. industry. There were a few players in Europe before 1980, most notably the U.K. firm now named 3i, and at least one unsuccessful American-style venture capital firm that was set up in the 1960s. But it was during the entrepreneurial era of the 1980s that European venture capital grew explosively. From 1984 through 1992, the venture capital funds under management in Europe grew from ECU 3.6 billion to ECU 38.5 billion (EVCA, 1991–93). More recently, the total capital under management in Europe approximates that of the United States.

Unlike the United States, however, where entries and harvests have been roughly in balance, the amount of money being invested in portfolio companies by European venture capital funds far exceeds the amount being divested. For instance, over five years (1988 to 1992), ECU 21.2 billion was invested in portfolio companies but only ECU 9.4 billion was divested. Of course, some of that imbalance is because the total pool of venture capital continues to grow. But that is only a partial explanation because the amount of new funds raised has been declining since it peaked in 1989. If the 1990 to 1992 trend continues, a log jam of unrealized investments is building up.

By the end of 1992, most people within the European venture capital industry agreed that much of the investment-divestment imbalance was due to the relative scarcity of viable harvest options. For instance, of 158 MBOs completed in the period 1983 to 1985 in the United Kingdom, more than 70 percent had not been harvested successfully by June 1992 (Wright et al., 1992a). That lack of successful exits is particularly acute with smaller MBOs.

At the start of the 1990s, frustration on the part of venture capitalists in the United Kingdom and the Netherlands over the lack of exit options gave rise to a number of new initiatives designed to facilitate harvesting. Among them were proposals for a pan-European private secondary market for venture capital investments and for a local participation market for Dutch venture capital investment. (Onians, 1993; Elbertse, 1993).

During the 1980s, a number of European countries set up second- and third-tier stock markets in order to facilitate IPOs by small companies that could not meet the requirements of the main markets. These markets include the Unlisted Securities Market (USM) in the United Kingdom, the *Second Marché* in France, and the Parallel Market in the Netherlands. A surge in venture capital in the United Kingdom, France, and the Netherlands coincided with a boom in these countries' secondary markets. However, despite these efforts to create equity markets for private firms, the results have been unsuccessful. For instance, the USM is to be closed at the end of 1996 to be replaced by the Alternative Investment Market (AIM). In addition, a pan-European exchange is being formed called the EASDAQ in an effort to create the equivalent of the NASDAQ in the United States. So at the present, Europe continues to lack a well-established market for IPOs.

Given the limited accessibility to the IPO market as an exit strategy, venture capitalists in Europe have primarily resorted to company sales as their exit mechanism of choice—41 percent of all exits in Europe come through the company being sold, compared with 10 percent exits through IPOs. Here too, however, the number of corporate sales has decreased in recent years. In the United Kingdom, the number of sales of MBOs averaged 39 per year from 1981 through 1988, but fell to 15 in 1989, 8 in 1990, and 3 in 1991. Fortunately, trade sales in other European nations have not been as severely affected. Even so, the European venture industry, along with the entrepreneurs in whose companies they have invested, is experiencing severe problems in realizing the value created through its investments.

Current State of Affairs and the Need for Research

Based on the prior research, several things can be said about harvesting with reasonable certitude:

- To harvest value, it must first be created. Whether a firm is high-tech or low-tech, small or large, economic value is created only by earning rates of return that exceed the investors' opportunity cost of the funds—including the owners'. Value is destroyed by earning rates of return that are less than the opportunity cost of the funds—again including the equity owners. Creating value and capturing the value are not the same thing. Without the opportunity to harvest, a firm's owners and investors will be denied a significant amount of the value that has been created over the firm's life.

- Harvesting is more than merely selling and leaving a business. It is about capturing value (cash flows), reducing risk, and creating future options.

- There are four fundamental approaches to harvesting a venture: 1) Restructuring the company's goals and strategies in order to increase the cash flows extracted from the business by the owners and investors; 2) selling to outsiders, management, employees, and/or family members; 3) being acquired or merged into another business; or 4) issuing stock to the public.

- Investors providing high-risk capital—particularly venture capitalists—generally insist on an exit strategy as part of the terms of the deal. As a result, the accessibility to venture capital is driven by the availability of harvest options.

- Return distributions resulting from venture-backed harvests and IPOs are known.

- The window of opportunity for harvesting quickly opens and closes. That is, there are waves of IPOs and merger and acquisition opportunities.

Besides what is known about harvesting an entrepreneurial firm, there are also some impressions based on intuition and anecdotal evidence, including:

- Few events in the life of the entrepreneur, and for the firm itself, are more significant than the harvest.
- Some entrepreneurs are averse to thinking about the harvest, while others begin the venture to harvest it.
- The decision to harvest is frequently the result of an unexpected crisis rather than a well-conceived strategy.

Finally, some things are still not known about the harvest. The following questions are begging further research:

- How much difference does an effective harvest strategy make in releasing the value within the firm for the benefit of the owners and investors?
- What is the entrepreneur's perspective about the harvest? How do these expectations compare to the final outcome?
- How important is timing in the harvest? How does the entrepreneur know when to harvest?
- What can be done to increase the effectiveness of the harvest?
- How do the entrepreneur's personal preferences and situation affect the harvest?
- What can be done by the entrepreneur to enhance the probability of a successful harvest?
- A better understanding of the actual process of the harvest is needed. Some things are known about the outcomes but little about the process, e.g., 1) What are the catalysts that bring the entrepreneur and investors to the decision to harvest? 2) How do they make a choice as to the approach to be taken in harvesting? 3) What does the entrepreneur need to know before going through an IPO?

These questions and many others go unanswered. There is so much that could be done. The primary limitations are the researcher's own creativity and the limited availability of quality data. Gaining access to the needed information is no small matter in this area. Nevertheless, given some creativity and diligence, numerous research questions could be addressed, and the importance of the topic calls us to take up the challenge.

REFERENCES

Batchelor, C. 1992. Enterprise looks for a way out. *Financial Times*, December 22.

Beatty, A. 1995. The cash flow and informational effects of employee stock ownership plans. *Journal of Financial Economics* 38(2):211–230.

Bhide, A. 1989. The causes and consequences of hostile takeovers. *Journal of Applied Corporate Finance* 2(2):n36–59.

Brennan, M.J. 1995. A perspective on accounting and stock prices. *Journal of Applied Corporate Finance* 8(1):43–52.

Brokaw, L. 1993. The first day of the rest of your life. *Inc.* 15(5):144.

Bygrave, W.D., and M. Stein. 1989. A time to buy and a time to sell: A study of venture capital investments in 77 companies that went public. In N.C. Churchill et al. (eds.): *Frontiers of Entrepreneurship Research*. Wellesley, MA: Babson College, 288–303.

Bygrave, W. D., M. Hay, and J. B. Peeters, (eds.). 1994. *Realizing Investment Value*. London: Pitman Publishing.

Chalk, A., and J. Peavy. 1987. Initial public offerings: Daily returns, offering types and the price effect. *Financial Analyst Journal* 27(4): 65–69.

Copeland, T., T. T. Koller, and J. Murrin. 1994. *Valuation: Measuring and Managing the Value of Companies*. New York: John Wiley and Sons.

Desroches, J. J-Y., and B. Belletante. 1992. The positive impact of going public on entrepreneurs and their firms: Evidence from listing on the "Second Marché" in France. In N. C. Churchill et al. (eds.): *Frontiers of Entrepreneurship Research*. Wellesley, MA: Babson College, 466–480.

Donaldson, G. 1994. *Corporate Restructuring: Managing the Change Process from Within*. Cambridge, MA: Harvard Business School Press.

Elbertse, E. 1993. Developing exit mechanism in your market. Presentation at European Venture Capital Association business seminar on exiting in Europe, Venice, February 11–12.

Englander, D. W. 1993. Cashing out through ESOPs. *Small Business Reports* 18(10):43–45.

European Venture Capital Association (EVCA). 1991–93. *Venture Capital in Europe: EVCA Yearbooks*. Zaveman, Belgium.

Freear, J., J. A. Sohl, and W. E. Wetzel. 1990. Raising venture capital: Entrepreneurs' views of the process. *Frontiers of Entrepreneurship Research*, 223–265.

Holmburg, S. 1991. Value creation and capture: Entrepreneurship harvest and IPO strategies. In N. C. Churchill et al. (eds.): *Frontiers of Entrepreneurship Research*. Wellesley, MA: Babson College, 191–204.

Hyatt, H. 1990. The dark side (of going public). *Inc.* 12(6):46–56.

Ibbotson, R.G. 1975. Price performance of common stock new issues. *Journal of Financial Economics* 2(3):235–272.

Ibbotson, R. G., and J. F. Jaffe. 1975. Hot issue markets. *Journal of Finance* 30(4):1027–1042.

Ibbotson, R.G., J.L. Sindelar, and J.R. Ritter. 1994. The market's problems with the pricing of initial public offerings. *Journal of Applied Corporate Finance* 7(1):66–74.

Ibbotson, R.G., J.L. Sindelar, and J.R. Ritter. 1993. Initial public offerings. *Journal of Applied Corporate Finance* 1(2):37–45.

Jain, B. and O. Kini (Forthcoming). The post-issue operating performance of IPOs. *Journal of Finance*.

Jones, S., M. B. Cohen, and V. V. Coppola. 1992. Going public. In Sahlman, W. A., and Stevenson, H. H. (eds.): *The Entrepreneurial Venture*. Cambridge, MA: Harvard Business School Publications.

Kaplan, S. 1989. The effects of management buy-outs on operating performance and value. *Journal of Financial Economics* 24:217–254.

Kaplan, S. 1991. The staying power of leverage buyouts. *Journal of Financial Economics* 29:287–313.

Loughran, T. 1993. NYSE vs. Nasdaq returns: Market microstructure or the poor performance of IPOs? *Journal of Financial Economics* 33: 241–260.

Loughran, T., J. Ritter, and K. Rydqvist. 1994. Initial public offerings: International insights. *Pacific-Basin Finance Journal* 2(3):165–199.

Miller, M. 1994. Is American corporate governance fatally flawed? *Journal of Applied Corporate Finance* 6(4):32–39.

Morris, J.K. 1985. The pricing of a venture capital investment. In S. E. Pratt and J. K. Morris (eds.): *Pratt's Guide to Venture Capital Sources*, 9th edition. Wellesley Hills, MA: Venture Economics.

Onians, R. 1993. A European secondary market. Presented at EVCA business seminar on Exiting in Europe, Venice, February 11–12.

Paré, T. P. 1990. Passing on the family business. *Fortune* 127(9):50.

Park, S., and M.H. Song. 1995. Employee stock ownership plans, firm performance, and monitoring by outside blockholders. *Financial Management* 24(4):52–65.

Petty, J.W., B.E. Bygrave, and J.M. Shulman. 1994. Harvesting the entrepreneurial venture: A time for creating value. *Journal of Applied Corporate Finance* 7(9):48–58.

Ritter, J. 1991. The long-run performance of initial public offerings. *Journal of Finance* 46(3):3–27.

Sahlman, W. A. 1988. Aspects of financial contracting in venture capital. *Journal of Applied Corporate Finance* 1 (4): 23–36.

Sahlman, W. A. 1989. Teaching notes accompanying CML Group, Inc. *Going Public*. Cambridge, MA: Harvard Business School Publishing Division.

Soja, T.A., and J.E. Reyes. 1990. *Investment Benchmarks: Venture Capital*. Needham, MA: Venture Economics.

Stevenson, H.E., and D.E. Gumpert. 1985. The heart of entrepreneurship. *Harvard Business Review* 63(2):85–94.

Stevenson, H.E., and W.A. Sahlman. 1987. Entrepreneurship: A process, not a person. Working paper 87-06, pp. 1–49.

Stewart, G.B., III. 1991. *The Quest for Value*. New York: Harper-Collins, pp. 136–140.

Sutton, D.P., and M.W. Beneddetto. 1990. *Initial Public Offerings*. Chicago: Probus Publishing Company.

Timmons, J. 1994. *New Venture Creation*. Chicago: Irwin, p. 654.

Toben, J. 1969. A general equilibrium approach to monetary theory. *Journal of Money, Credit, and Banking* 1:15–29.

Welch, I. 1996. Equity offerings following the IPO: Theory and evidence. *Journal of Corporate Finance* 2:227–259.

Weston, J.F., K. Chung, and S. Hoag. 1990. Theories of mergers and tender offers. In *Mergers, Restructuring and Corporate Control*. Englewood-Cliffs, NJ: Prentice Hall, 190–222.

Wright, M., K. Robbie, Y. Romanet, S. Thompson, R. Joachimsson, J. Bruining, and A. Herst. 1992a. Realizations, longevity and the life-cycle of management buy-outs and buy-ins: A four-country study. Presented at the European Federal for Economic Research (EFER) Forum, London Business School, December 12–14.

Wright, M., S. Thompson, and K. Robbie. 1992b. Venture capital and management-led buyouts: European evidence. *Journal of Business Venturing* 7(1):47–71.

Wright, M., S. Thompson, K. Robbie, and P. Wong. 1992c. Management buy-outs in the short and long term. In N. C. Churchill et al. (eds.): *Frontiers of Entrepreneurship Research*. Wellesley, MA: Babson College, 302–316.

Choosing Your Exit Strategy

by William H. Payne

Your exit strategy impacts many directions that you might choose in growing your business. Not considering your exit strategy early may indeed limit your options in the future. It is not a matter of whether you will sell, or otherwise dispose of, your interest in this business. Your only decisions are when and how.

It Pays to Plan Ahead

It's always a good idea to plan your exit strategy early. It's also important that your founding operating partners and investors agree with it. If you wish to sell the business in five years, but your operating partner wants to own and manage it with you for 15 years, you have a problem. If you suggest to key employees that you have no plans to exit the company and then sell within two years, they are likely to be dissatisfied and could disrupt the sale. If you decide you would like to give your shares to your heirs, angel investors may object and choose an exit strategy that does not complement your future plans.

If you wish to share equity with employees or with heirs, it helps to start early, when the company valuation (and share price) is low. U.S. tax laws severely limit gifts to heirs; hence, it will take many years to pass the business on to your children. Assuming the company experiences consistent growth, sharing equity with employees can be rewarding at any stage in the business cycle. However, transferring total ownership to the employees, including the sale of your shares, is more easily accomplished and costs less when you start early.

If you choose to fund the early growth of your company using venture capital (VC), you are usually setting out on a course leading to an initial public offering (IPO), or to the sale of the company. Before seeking VC funding, it is mandatory that the entrepreneur contemplate the management and control issues that accompany VC funding and eventual public ownership.

Finally, if you plan to seek a business partner and/or outside financing from angel investors, banks or venture capitalists, someone will surely ask about your long-term plans regarding the business, and specifically, how long you plan to be with it. You need to have a thoughtful response.

Is Selling the Best Way Out?

Liquidation of ownership in your business is a very personal decision, and it is yours to make as the entrepreneur. Some founders say that creating a business and selling it within a few years is a travesty to the employees who helped build it. Others have said they couldn't possibly go public, because a "big brother" would constantly be looking over their shoulders. From my perspective, there is no incorrect exit strategy. You, your partners, your investors and your employees are building a business. Your exit strategy is simply a very important part of your business plan.

Selling your business to another individual or independent business is one of four usual choices for liquidating your equity. It's a huge decision and generally one that is difficult to make. One day you own the company, and the next day you do not. To optimize the terms of the sale, the new owner may insist you continue to operate the business for an agreed-upon period of time. From another perspective, then, you move from controlling owner to employee in one quick step.

Proceeds from the sale of a private company usually consist of cash, shares of a public company, shares of a private company or a combination of the above. This is generally a move toward greater liquidity in your personal estate. You are selling illiquid shares of your private company for cash and/or shares of a company that will eventually become liquid.

This allows the successful entrepreneur, who often has nearly 100 percent of his or her assets tied up in the business, the option of diversifying his or her portfolio of investments. Some entrepreneurs sell to other private companies and achieve asset diversification by becoming part of the larger, merged business. While immediate liquidity may not be their primary driver, founders who take this course usually move closer to a liquidation opportunity.

The disadvantages of selling your business are also obvious. You have given up your "baby." You are no longer in control. You may have passed up the opportunity to grow the business (and the value of your shares) in the future.

When Should You Sell?

It may be time to begin working on selling your business when you are losing sleep (or your hair) because you realize one or more of the following:

- Your business is a very valuable asset.
- Ownership represents nearly 100 percent of your net worth.

- Some power outside your control (competitor, government, act of God, etc.) could take that away from you.

Personally, I like investing in small, well-run companies positioned to be "discovered" by an attractive buyer. As an investor, I prefer niche or boutique businesses in which:

- The investment required to achieve break-even in cash flow is less than $500,000.
- The annual revenue potential within the first five to ten years is $5 million to $20 million.
- The likelihood that a large public company might be interested in purchasing the company is significant. In other words, these companies plan to sell to an attractive public company as the business approaches a preset valuation.

Is Going Public Better Than Being Acquired?

Offering shares of your company to the public markets is viewed by some as an exit strategy. In my opinion, it is not. Initial public offerings, or IPOs, involve issuing new shares for cash at a time when the business is challenged with an opportunity to grow, which would be facilitated with an infusion of cash. However, going public generally limits your exit options and, by default, defines your exit strategy. Once the shares trade in public markets, significant employee ownership (that is, more than 50 percent) or control by your heirs is unlikely.

Selling ownership to public markets generally provides the cash for growth, while offering the principals of the company the promise of some future liquidity of their shares. Liquidation by the entrepreneur can be accomplished, but it is likely to require many years, unless, of course, the entire company is subsequently sold. Control by the founders is generally possible, but the company acquires a new set of investors with a short-term perspective on defining success. Dealing with the demands of the market makers and the Securities and Exchange Commission (SEC) will become a reality. And, in volatile markets, it may not be desirable.

Selling to Your Employees

Employee ownership can be very rewarding and can take several forms. Most of us are familiar with Employee Stock Ownership Plans, or ESOPs, which are managed like a pension plan with all company contributions used to buy company stock. But, an ESOP is only one arrow in the equity-compensation quiver.

Motivated employees can be given appropriate incentives through other forms of equity, such as stock options, stock-purchase plans and performance-based stock bonuses. These plans generally allow the founder to maintain control of the company as his or her shares are diluted by those shares made available to the employees. Equity compensation as part of a corporate culture fosters a great working environment conducive to a high-growth business.

Under certain conditions, it is possible for the founder to sell shares back to the company, or to the ESOP. However, the legal ramifications of this strategy are many and should be explored well in advance.

Passing Control to Your Heirs

Transferring ownership to the founder's heirs is more common than most entrepreneurs might imagine, although tax laws in the United States limit this option. It requires patience and endurance. Gifts by a single U.S. citizen to each heir, without paying gift tax, are limited to $10,000 a year, and the tax implications of passing a business to your heirs through your estate are daunting. It's best to take action early in the life of the business, when the share price is low and the entrepreneur has many years to give some of it away.

For high-tech entrepreneurs, this option may not be feasible, because high-tech products may have limited life spans. However, there are plenty of entrepreneurs building significant businesses outside of the high-technology arena. The long-term prospects for a well-run commodities business, for example, justify planning to pass ownership along to the following generation.

If you haven't done so already, I suggest you develop your exit strategy now. Get a good understanding of your options. Then, talk to your spouse, parents, friends and business advisors. Use all these insights to develop a strategy that meets your needs. Once you have developed your plan, think about structuring your company to meet those needs.

The Race to Embrace

Companies are getting hitched in record numbers. Yet most mergers fail. Here are lessons from the 200 Best Small Companies in America on how to improve the odds.

BY LUISA KROLL

WHAT WAS JAMES R. SWARTWOUT doing on top of a 20-foot ladder? The 54-year-old chief executive of Torrance, Calif.-based plastics component manufacturer Summa Industries was checking out an acquisition target. An odd way of kicking the tires, perhaps—unlike that of any of the seven previous potential buyers who visited privately held Plastron Industries, the maker of "bobbins," thermoplastic parts for wound electronic components such as coils. But Swartwout had his reasons. "Roofs are expensive," he says. "They have to be replaced every 20 years and should be reflected in a transaction price."

To crunch the numbers, most acquirers physically inspect crunchy-hard assets. But due diligence for Summa—which makes plastic components like filters, valves and conveyor belts for lighting, electrical devices and food processing—is a devotional exercise. For four months Swartwout and two other executives learned all they could about Plastron, reviewing reams of financial documents, meeting with its largest customers, talking to plant workers, hiring an environmental consultant to evaluate the site. They also commissioned a $10,000-plus marketing study to evaluate Plastron's market position.

Finally, in March 1999, Summa put money on the table, buying Plastron for $20 million in cash and warrants. The acquisition made Summa the largest U.S. supplier of bobbins—and considerably stronger in a highly competitive industry. Now it ranks number 110 on our list of the 200 Best Small Companies in America, (*Forbes*, October 30, 2000, pp.224–264) in which companies are scored by growth in sales and earnings.

When Swartwout arrived at Summa 12 years ago, it was a decrepit equipment manufacturer that had lost money for a decade. He sold off the ailing business, and in the past five years he has acquired ten plastics companies. Since 1996 sales have grown from $8 million to $107 million, and earnings per share from 23 cents to $1.46.

U.S. companies last year shelled out a total $1.6 trillion acquiring others.

There are hundreds of reasons to merge—quick growth, competitive advantage with suppliers and distributors, adding valuable customers or technology, global expansion, survival, panic, just to name a few. And many causes for divorce: Fact is, most mergers fail, according to a recent study by consulting firm KPMG. It cites shoddy due diligence, a lack of synergy between the two companies, too little planning and lousy execution of deals. That doesn't mean companies are dropping out of the race to embrace. U.S. companies last year shelled out a total $1.6 trillion acquiring others.

Bigger mergers tend to fail more spectacularly because there's more at stake—witness Mattel's purchase of Learning Co. or Quaker's purchase of Snapple. Acquisitions made to prop up a sagging underlying business usually bomb—as Compaq learned to its chagrin with Digital Equipment. Even apparently well-conceived unions, like AOL and Time Warner or MCI/WorldCom and Sprint, can get held up or even undone by antitrust regulators. The KPMG report concludes that more than half of all deals destroy shareholder value, and an additional third have no benefit.

Small companies have their share of hideous marriages. Still, "their averages are clearly better," says Mark L. Sirower, a mergers and acquisitions adviser at the Boston Consulting Group and author of *The Synergy Trap*. He estimates that the success rate of the mergers between small and midsize companies (with sales of $350 million and below) is close to one out of two, compared with one out of three for larger companies.

Why the slightly better odds? Small companies usually merge with small outfits, and can get their arms around a problem faster. They are less likely to do a deal merely to impress the public, opines Daniel J. Donoghue, managing director of mergers and acquisitions at U.S. Bancorp Piper Jaffray in Minneapolis; rather, they use acquisitions to buy the talent and technology they need. Large corporations, Donoghue claims, "have more arrogance about it. Small companies view acquisitions as ways to strengthen the management team. They're more apt to embrace them and learn from the deal."

That's a good thing, given how active small companies are in the merger market (see chart). If they keep up the pace of the first nine months, public companies with

Gotcha: Pushing The Limits of Due Diligence

As a journalist, James Mulvaney investigated Irish terrorists, mobsters, O.J. Simpson and Ferdinand Marcos. He headed the team that won the 1996 Pulitzer Prize for uncovering fraudulent practices at a fertility clinic and writing stories that led to federal indictments and the largest malpractice settlement in California history.

Now, as head of KPMG's investigative due-diligence practice, he digs up dirt on companies that are about to be acquired. For $4,000 to $10,000, Mulvaney and team will pull documents from courthouses, sift through databases and check out every item on a résumé. Pay up to $50,000, and they'll track down former spouses and colleagues and interview the competition. Nowadays, when the most important acquired asset may be talent, you can't stop the snooping with a target's financials.

While most investigations end happily, a few turn up deal-killing information. In a recent case a computer company hired Mulvaney to look into the backgrounds of directors at an acquisition candidate. One board member, he discovered, was going through an acrimonious divorce—a fact the director had never mentioned. Why such a big deal? The wife stood a good chance of collecting a lot of his stock and of using those shares to insist on a board seat. The client didn't want to get embroiled in that struggle, and walked away from the deal.

Another time, the KPMG private eyes looked into a targeted company that appeared clean until they checked the criminal courts and learned that half its board members were involved with organized crime. A third takeover candidate seemed okay until a media search revealed that the company had been banned from doing business in Florida, a key territory for the buyer.

Perhaps the most established M&A snoop is Strang Hayes Consulting in New York. It draws its staff from the alumni of the CIA, Secret Service, FBI and the Drug Enforcement Administration. Since its inception in 1989 it has conducted more than 3,000 due-diligence investigations. In the past three to four years, more than half of that business has come from companies making merger-related transactions. For $10,000 Strang Hayes will do a complete background check—short of surveillance work—in less than two weeks. The same service involving cross-border executives costs $15,000 and takes up to three weeks.

"There are so many ugly stories," says President Robert Strang. One chief executive had hidden five sexual harassment lawsuits filed against him. Another executive failed to mention that he held a significant amount of stock in a competitor—which led the potential buyer to assume that the guy might not have his own company's best interest in mind. Another time the investigators discovered that roughly half the top executives of a company were unindicted co-conspirators in a fraudulent deal. From what the could tell, the company had changed its name in order to conceal that fact.

All this work is legal, mind you, but it is usually done on the sly, often without the knowledge of the targeted company. Investigators work quietly so as not to scare off the intended merger partner, disrupt the negotiations or risk being sued for libel. In fact, potential acquirers often have their lawyers hire investigators to ensure that all information is protected under attorney-client privilege. When dirt is unearthed, the potential buyer usually backs off without explaining. Let some other hapless buyer—perhaps a competitor—unearth the bad news the hard way.　　　　—L.K.

revenues below $350 million will spend 8.3% of their market value this year buying other companies; large corporations will only put up 5.6%.

What makes a successful partnership? A few simple things that bear repetition, starting with a well-planned and carefully implemented deal. This year's list of the 200 Best is a good place to mine lessons for happy—and not so happy—marriages.

DON'T WAIT FOR A DEAL TO COME TO YOU. Boulder, Colo.-based Carrier Access (number 7) made that mistake initially. "We waited a year too long," says cofounder Nancy Pierce. "If we had acted sooner we could have grown faster."

Launched eight years ago by Pierce and her husband, Chief Executive Roger Koenig, Carrier Access sells broadband equipment that allows phone companies, Internet service providers and wireless carriers to offer customers local and long-distance service, high-speed connections and video over that fabled "last mile." The company, which reported a 126% increase in sales last year to $109 million, was an early player, but it faced daunting competition from much larger firms. To keep its edge, Carrier Access needed to develop new products fast. Pierce and Koenig thought they could pull it off by increasing their R&D budget. Then they realized they had to start acquiring engineering talent and technology.

So they contacted investment bankers about bringing in deals. They sat through several nice PowerPoint presentations of companies that missed the mark. Some prospects didn't stretch them out far enough. Others had been shopped to death. A couple were based in Silicon Valley, where costs and turnover were too high. Carrier Access bid on them anyway—and lost out to Cisco and Nortel.

Pierce talks to everybody about merger candidates.

Time to take the situation into their own hands. "We had to be more innovative and crafty," says Pierce, who has looked at 25 deals in the past year, often in small cities where the cost of living and employee turnover are low. Gregarious and charismatic, Pierce talks to everybody she knows about merger candidates, phoning venture capitalists, chatting up customers—even asking employees to name the companies they fear most. One deal she is currently negotiating came from a Carrier Access vice president, who heard about the company from an old friend he ran into at the airport. Pierce pounced within 24 hours, interrupting discussions the target was having with another potential acquirer, and stopped the company from signing a no-shop clause.

Carrier Access found its first mate while on a consulting project. A customer recommended Millennia Systems, which designs broadband communications equipment, to help Carrier integrate a microchip into a new product. Koenig hired the firm in April for a short-term project but liked what he saw. Millennia had 20 engineers with considerable talent in optics and Internet protocol. Plus, it was based in affordable Roanoke, Va., 50 minutes from

Virginia Tech University. Though the company wasn't for sale at the time, Koenig persuaded the owners to sell out in August for $13 million in stock and cash (and the assumption of $224,000 in debt).

STICK TO YOUR KNITTING. The cliché needs to be repeated again and again. Acquiring a company just to diversify your product or service base is asking for trouble. Which is why a company like Fairfield, N.J.-based Measurement Specialties (number 23) never looks outside its rather narrow specialty: making electronic sensors for such products as washing machines, scales and electronic pressure gauges. The top four executives have 80 years of experience in sensor technology among them. Chief Executive Joseph R. Mallon Jr., now age 55, started in the industry when he was 20 and served as president of a sensor-technology company in Silicon Valley before joining Measurement Specialties in 1995. Three years elapsed before he started buying; since 1998, the company has made three acquisitions, all complementary products.

One of them was AMP Sensors, a money losing division of electronic-connectors giant AMP. Measurement Specialties bought the tiny division for $3.8 million in August 1998, shortly before AMP sold out to conglomerate Tyco International. Because its production was so similar to Measurement Specialties' method of light-electronic assembly, Mallon had little trouble shifting the AMP production line from Valley Forge, Pa. to his Shenzhen plant in China's Guangdong province.

Looking beyond the balance sheets and financial statements is a requisite skill.

"I can't imagine buying something that doesn't fit with what we already know," says Mallon. He's doing something right. Since March 1998 sales have doubled, earnings are up sevenfold and the stock is up tenfold.

KNOW WHAT YOU'RE BUYING. You'd be crazy not to run the numbers backwards, forwards and sideways. But looking beyond the balance sheets and financial statements is a requisite skill. Summa Industries' Swartwout doesn't just poke around at perilous heights to get to know his acquisition target. When he learned that one candidate got 60% of its revenues from eight customers, he made sure he sat down with every one of them. Another time Summa commissioned an

outside environmental consultancy to check out a potential mate's factory. The firm gave it a thumbs up. But Swartwout had to see for himself, inspecting the grass and looking for recently patched asphalt. Not satisfied, he ordered another assessment by a different environmental firm and found a problem, as he suspected—residue from an old fuel tank that hadn't been properly cleaned. (Summa had to eat the cost itself.)

Swartwout doesn't do all the snooping himself. Summa recently hired a Spanish-speaking personnel director, who has already visited one company, where she learned about management-labor relations and safety procedures from its mostly Hispanic plant workers.

Due diligence shouldn't be confused with dawdling. "As soon as you start, you're damaging the company you're acquiring," says Power-One Chief Executive Steven Goldman. Why? "Because you're taking management's attention away from the business."

Power-One (number 105) does not waste any time. The Camarillo, Calif. company makes power-conversion products—boxes costing $15 to $4,000 that convert alternating current to direct current. Its customers are Internet service providers and manufacturers of datacom and telecom equipment. Power-One, which has made four acquisitions in 24 months, uses a homemade quickie system for reviewing a target in seven days. Rather than sending a typical 20-page questionnaire, it delivers an Excel spreadsheet with blanks to fill in. The data generate an estimated acquisition price based on dozens of factors, including product mix, future sales and R&D expenses. The program has a built-in litmus test: Companies that can't complete all the relevant information within 48 hours send up a red flag.

LEARN THEIR TRIBAL CUSTOMS. You've heard a lot on the subject of culture clashes—the fact that they do business a whole lot differently than we do. Behind the clichés are some real friction points, and they go way beyond how people dress or what company dining rooms look like. Plantronics (number 43), a telephone headset maker, had its eye on Clearvox, which produces cellular headsets. But the Santa Cruz, Calif. company wanted to make sure that its target shared its obsession with customer service. Plantronics took special pride that callers waited a maximum of only 8 seconds to reach a live body at the complaint desk. So it talked with Clearvox accounts and learned the company was even willing to lose money on a transaction to keep

More Deals, More $$

Small company spending for acquisitions has been rocketing.

Transaction Value ($bil)

Note: Total transaction value is consistently under-reported, as not all companies report transaction value. All buyers with $350 million in revenues or less. May not reflect private buyers who don't report revenues. Year 2000 numbers are nine-month annualized. Sources: U.S. Bancorp Piper Jaffray; Thomson Financial Securities Data.

Grabby, Grabby

The 200 Best Small Companies are an acquisitive lot. Mergers help them nab key people and technology—as well as survive. Among the top dealmakers:

Company	Number of acquisitions[1]	Value ($mil)
Applied Micro Circuits	6	$4,781
Qlogic	3	1,797
Diamond Technology	3	1,075
Ebay	10	730
Macrovision	3	666
Razorfish	8	639

[1]Completed or pending acquisitions from January 1998 through September 2000. Source: Thomson Financial Securities Data.

customers happy. The estimated $10 million takeover went ahead.

Acquiring a foreign company brings a different set of challenges. Power-One hired an industrial psychologist to work with executives at two of its acquisitions, Zurich-based Melcher and Boston-based IPD. At IPD 90% of employees were of Chinese descent. Over a two-day session at a country club in Camarillo, 20 top managers from both companies and Power-One participated in workshops on conflict and communication. The U.S. executives, unsurprisingly, tended to make decisions on the spot, while the Swiss liked to sleep on it overnight and then regroup. Power-One's boss Goldman has incorporated that lesson into his management style. The Chinese, on the other hand, felt slighted if certain people were left out of discussions; they leaned heavily toward consensus. Gold-

Accident ... Or Merger?

A historian once described the merger of two ailing railroads as "two drunks helping one another home." Nowadays it's a pretty apt description of what is doing on in Internet land. Trying to combine content and commerce can be an effective recipe for failure. Ivillage, a Web site for women, tried to change its business model in part by acquiring e-retailer Ibaby for a total $12.3 million in cash and stock. The problem: not enough eyeballs to make the commerce side profitable; Ivillage also discovered the headaches that come with taking and delivering orders. "It was a diversion that was not going to get us to scale," admits Jay C. Hoad, an Ivillage board member and a partner at Technology Crossover Ventures. In July Ivillage sold Ibaby for a minimal profit—some equity and ad banners.

Hitching to the Internet has been perilous for some companies looking to diversify. Whittman-Hart, which earned $30 million on $481 million in revenue last year, had a solid business as a technology consultant to manufacturing, retail, health care (and some Internet) companies with $50 million to $500 million in sales. But the Web was hot. Whittman-Hart envied USWeb/CKS, which had a thriving business setting up e-commerce sites. Whittman-Hart grabbed it for $6.5 billion in stock, and renamed the combined entity Marchfirst.

Then came the correction. Marchfirst insists that selling to new ventures accounts for only 8% of its revenues. Still, its stock has sunk from $48, when the deal closed on Mar. 1, to $11.

What happens when you acquire a company for its technology—and then discover you don't really want the rest of the company? Hollywood Entertainment, which rents tapes, was interested in Reel.com for its software that sold videos to folks based on a history of their tastes and purchases. The $90 million deal in cash and stock two years ago got two thumbs up. But competition from Amazon.com and Buy.com proved overwhelming: Reel lost money on every sale, and burned $4 million in cash per month. Hollywood filed for a public offering of Reel shares—valued between $600 and $800 million—but retracted when the market soured. Hollywood ended up shuttering Reel in June, firing all 120 people.

Last month Webvan bough Homegrocer for $550 million in stock. The combination hasn't solved Webvan's basic cost problem: how to increase the number of deliveries per hour. There are no economies when your drivers operate in disparate regions (Webvan in Chicago and Atlanta; Homegrocer on the West Coast). Webvan has $525 million in cash but is torching $125 million of it per quarter, estimates Jeetil Patel, an analyst at Deutsche Bank Alex. Brown. Upgrading Homegrocer's computer systems will only add more oxygen to the fire. Not good news in a very stingy capital market.

Now, deals that don't stop the flow of read ink are doomed. In January golf equipment retailer Chipshot.com bought GolfServ, a site that licenses its handicap-tracking, tee-time booking and instruction services to more than 250 sites, for about $20 million in cash and stock. Great service, but GolfServ was more than a year away from profitability. The union proved to be something of a three-putt. Strapped for cash following the crash, Chipshot sold GolfServ back to its founders for $500,000 in cash in August.

"We've had seven offers since the divorce to take over other companies," says GolfServ President Kathryn Savarese. "We've declined them all." At least somebody learned something.

—*Brett Nelson*

man now makes sure he talks to all key people at that operation and gets them on board for big decisions. "They won't support it if they don't feel good about it," he says.

And they might not support it if they don't understand it. Ebay's $260 million acquisition in May 1999 of 135-year-old Butterfield & Butterfield is a case study in mutual inscrutability and failed expectations. The world's largest online flea market thought it could revolutionize the traditional art auction business by creating a vast new class of customers who would bid on high-ticket items, but over the Internet.

It never happened. Few executives at Ebay (number 46) had ever been to a live auction. For three months after the deal Ebay sent teams up from San Jose to San Francisco to learn about Butterfield's business. "Ebay had no idea what they were getting themselves into," says a former Butterfield executive who has since left, along with other top managers. Today the auctioneer still sells the old-fashioned way. But its online presence is barely a silhouette. You can find its wares—books, fine art, memorabilia, Native American craft—under one of ten auction house cat-egories on a Web site called Ebay Great Collections. The site apparently isn't bowling over anyone. "We haven't heard much—and assume it's not doing well," says Jeetil Patel, an analyst at Deutsche Bank Alex. Brown. "Butterfield has been completely de-emphasized. Ebay's moved on."

START INTEGRATION WELL BEFORE THE DEAL IS CLOSED. It's easy to put off the messy details of combining assets and jobs. But delays create bigger problems—starting with the anxiety of employees, who don't know if their days are numbered, and the inevitable guilt of survivors. "Integration shouldn't start on day one," advises Boston Consulting Group's Sirower. "It should start on day negative 30 or day negative 50."

Westford, Mass.-based NetScout Systems (number 22)—which makes data-collection devices that monitor the performance of computer networks—has the transition process down. Fearful that he might have problems ironing out the kinks of incompatibility, Chief Executive Anil Singhal had already turned down two potential candidates. He settled on NextPoint, whose performance-analysis products and reporting applications complemented NetScout's line. It was also just across town, which made it easy to get to know the company from the inside—top managers on down to engineers.

In the weeks before the $60 million deal (stock and cash) was consummated in July, NetScout warmed up its welcoming committee. On the day of the announcement Singhal himself went over to NextPoint to tell employees. He left it to his second in command, President Narendra Popat, to inform NetScout's staff. When NextPoint moved into NetScout offices two weeks later, the employees found a big Welcome sign. Everyone received a benefits package; telephone and IT systems were already hooked up. A NetScout "buddy" was paired with each new employee for the first few weeks. "It was like moving into a new house where everything was taken care of," says Singhal.

NetScout had also evaluated the jobs of all NextPoint's 60 employees. Anyone whose position turned out to be redundant was redeployed elsewhere in the company.

Some salespeople were assigned to new regions. Singhal says that 90% chose to stay.

Layoffs, everyone agrees, are the nastiest part of integration. Mishandled, everyone suffers: Morale plunges, productivity flat-lines and the employees you want to keep start looking for the exit signs. Coming clean counts for a lot—even if you're just delivering bad news.

Measurement Specialties never hid the fact it would have to let some people go when it acquired AMP Sensors, and said so during its first meeting with new employees. It did try to cushion the blow. Anyone who stayed through the transition would get two months' notice, a severance package of one week's salary per year of service and a bonus of four weeks' pay.

NEVER TAKE YOUR EYE OFF AN ACQUISITION. Orem, Utah-based Mity-Lite did—and it probably cost the company a spot on the 200 Best (where it had landed five of the six previous years).

Mity-Lite (recently renamed Mity Enterprises) was accustomed to delivering consistent 20% annual earnings growth. The company, which makes institutional furniture for niche industries, had done successful acquisitions in the past, including a turnaround. So it didn't blink when it bought CenterCore, which produces circular call-center units with dividers, in a bank foreclosure last April for $5.3 million.

"We figured the savings would get us through."

The strategy may have been sound on paper, but the execution was abysmal. To save an estimated $1 million a year, Mity-Lite folded CenterCore's New Jersey operations into the underutilized Arkansas plant of a different division. "Money hides a lot of mistakes," says Bradley Nielson, the chief financial officer. "We knew we'd have a tough time, but figured the savings would get us through the transition."

Hardly. For starters, not one person from CenterCore agreed to relocate to Arkansas. Mity-Lite contracted with a half-dozen consultants, who decided not to join the combined company and had little incentive to smooth out the transition. Worse, Mity-Lite entrusted its 49%-owned Arkansas affiliate, DO Group, to handle integration—but without designating goals and responsibilities. Integration became a third-tier chore.

Things started to unravel in the fall, as the combining of computer systems fell apart. CenterCore ran on a proprietary Hewlett-Packard network, and had written its own code; DO Group had to merge it with its IBM system, so it could read how to build the furniture. The switchover took place at CenterCore's busiest time of year,

when its big military customers placed orders. Without the system up and running, the group took to building the units by hand. Orders were delayed and sent out damaged or incomplete. Inventory, which couldn't be correctly forecast, piled up dangerously high.

By December the managers in Orem began to pay attention. But until they took over the last 51% of DO Group, there was little they could do on the ground. As soon as the paperwork was complete in April, Chief Executive Gregory Wilson sent a general manager to Arkansas. After two months he left, overwhelmed.

The distractions hit the bottom line. First-quarter earnings were down 20%—the first such drop in eight years. Without the acquisition problems the company would have reported a 30% increase. That's when Chief Financial Officer Bradley Nielson offered to tackle the Arkansas fiasco. In early September he uprooted his family and headed south for what he hopes is a 9- to 12-month stay, tackling the system issues and trying to mend damaged customer relationships. He's optimistic, but both he and Wilson aren't taking any chances. If they can't turn things around within six months, they'll cut their losses and either sell or liquidate.

"We kick ourselves for not putting our own people in sooner," says Nielson. Wilson has a bleaker view of the acquisition: "We shouldn't have done it at all."

Business for Sale Update

THE
FLIP SIDE OF THE
BOOM

Buyers have an unusually high number of solid companies to choose from. Your best bet is to get your business in tip-top shape before taking it to market

by JILL ANDRESKY FRASER

HAS THERE EVER BEEN A TIME THIS fabulous for selling a company?

Not even the postmillennial one-two punch of declining stock prices and rising interest rates could blunt the mergers-and-acquisitions trend that first began heating up in 1997. Solid private companies are selling for good—and sometimes even great—prices. The momentum is coming from the deepening pool of buyers—cashed-out entrepreneurs, well-heeled investors, corporate refugees with severance packages or stock-option profits to burn, and, of course, all those companies on the prowl for strategic acquisitions.

A survey of the 12 companies that appeared in *Inc.*'s Business for Sale column from April 1999 through March 2000 reveals that 42% have been sold, in the majority of cases for their asking prices or even more. (See "Where Are They Now?" below.) That's impressive, since histori-

cally only about one-quarter to one-third of all private companies ever manage to find a buyer.

For companies with strong financials, well-prepared documentation, and a proven customer base, sales prospects often turned out to be brighter than one might have expected. The Southeastern nautical bookstore, which had lost out on a deal a year earlier (when a buyer who had signed a letter of intent pulled out because he lacked the financial wherewithal), ended up with three serious bids, which pushed the sales price to $2.5 million, from a listing of $2.25 million. The seller and his wife celebrated with a six-month cruise to Maine and Canada on their 42-foot yacht.

"One of the things that made our lives as buyers so simple was that the bookstore's seller, Milt Baker, had put together a highly detailed package of information about the company," recalls Vivien Godfrey, an *Inc.*

subscriber who purchased the bookstore with her husband, John Mann. "ninety five percent of the time, if we had a question for him, he knew the answer and could quickly provide us with the backup we needed."

Typically, big companies sell far more easily than small ones do, and most investment bankers won't waste their time on a company with less than $3 million in sales—and for some the minimum is $5 million. Some business brokers won't handle companies with revenues below $500,000 or even $1 million. But in the current overheated market, size seems irrelevant. The packager and distributor of safe-sex products, our tiniest contender with just $104,000 in sales, and the business-to-business Web site with $123,000 in revenues attracted between them about 350 inquiries from potential buyers. Both companies ended up closing great deals. In the case of the condom packager, it was

WHERE ARE THEY NOW?

The fates of the companies featured in the Business for Sale column from April 1999 through March 2000

Company	Date featured	Annual sales	Asking price	Number of inquiries	Result
TEXAS MINICHAIN OF PIZZERIAS	April 1999	$1.8 million	$705,000	10 to 15	Several deals stalled because the seller refused to sign a noncompete agreement
EAST COAST TENT-RENTAL COMPANY	May 1999	$1.2 million	$1.1 million	80 to 90	Got plenty of interest, but out-of-date financials discouraged bids
PACKAGER AND DISTRIBUTOR OF SAFE-SEX PRODUCTS	June 1999	$104,000	$75,000	About 150	Sold to an *Inc.* reader in August 1999 for asking price
MID-ATLANTIC VIOLIN SHOP	July 1999	$384,000	$295,000	20+	Is still on the market after partnership breakup disrupted sales
ROCKY MOUNTAIN WINDOW CLEANERS	August 1999	$556,000	$439,000	25 to 30	Sold in September for $430,000 to someone who read an advertisement in the local newspaper
SOUTHEASTERN RETAILER OF NAUTICAL BOOKS AND CHARTS	September 1999	$3.9 million	$2.25 million	498	Received three offers and was sold to an *Inc.* reader in February for $2.5 million
BUSINESS-TO-BUSINESS WEB SITE	October 1999	$123,000	$229,000	About 200	Sold to a customer (before the article appeared) for the asking price
TEXAS LIQUOR RETAILER AND WHOLESALER	November 1999	$6.8 million	$3.75 million	100	A $3-million deal fell through in February; revenues have dropped to $4 million; the company is still on the market at a reduced price of $2.5 million
HOLIDAY-PRODUCTS MANUFACTURER	December 1999	$1.8 million	$1.8 million	75+	Is still on the market
CARPET-AND-UPHOLSTERY-CLEANING FRANCHISES	January 2000	$235,000	$290,000	323	Is still on the market
MID-ATLANTIC VENDING ROUTE	February 2000	$450,000	$490,000	About 15	Is still on the market
PAYROLL SERVICE AND SOFTWARE DEVELOPER	March 2000	$450,000	$2.1 million	42	In May the company sold its customer list to a competitor for $900,000; rights to software are still on the market for $1 million

clear, said broker Marc Dosik, who handled the sale at VR Business Brokers, that "people really responded to a successful home-based business that could be relocated anywhere."

Sometimes, of course, outside events can overtake the most carefully laid plans. That was the case with the Texas liquor retailer and wholesaler, which promised to be sold quickly with sales at $6.8 million, a superfast growth record, and a not-too-high price tag of $3.75 million. The company attracted about 100 callers; within a month, the seller had a deal for $3 million with a local resident who owned some restaurants and viewed the business as a good strategic fit.

The deal appeared finalized, but—as often is the case—was contingent upon financing. And while the buyer was looking for capital, all hell broke loose. As Eric White, the listing broker at Empire Business Brokers, describes it: "A huge competitor moved into town who had deep pockets and began lowering prices beyond the level that my company was even pay-ing for its supplies. It's just unbelievable how quickly things began to unravel." The competitor managed to acquire a wholesale liquor license far more expeditiously than White and his client ever imagined possible, so the company's wholesale division collapsed as well. "To give you a sense of how bad things got," White reports, "annual sales dropped from $6.8 million to about $4 million. I'm hoping they have finally stabilized now."

But that wasn't the seller's only problem. With a $3-million price tag, the deal was too large to qualify for Small Business Administration financing, so the would-be purchaser had to pursue conventional bank financing. "The buyer was looking for about four months," notes White, "because banks just weren't willing to assess very much value to the company's $1 million in inventory. Maybe they were afraid that someone could just drive a truck up to the door and unload all that liquor if things really turned bad."

By the time financing finally seemed possible, this past February, the situation looked so bleak the buyer pulled out. The retailer is still on the market at the reduced price of $2.5 million, but White doesn't expect much action in the near future. "The price probably has to drop much lower, or the company needs to prove over a longer period of time that the decline is over, before a sale can happen," he concludes.

EVEN MORE REVEALING, PERHAPS, ARE the stories behind the companies that failed to change hands during the past year even though they appeared to be likely candidates for successful sales. Their plight, of course, is the flip side of the current boom. Robust selling rates and high deal prices have brought lots of strong businesses to the selling block, which gives buyers an abundance of attractive options. Companies not up to snuff in one way or another are likely to get passed over.

Two of our 12 recent businesses for sale lost out on tremendous opportunities because of problems on the paperwork front. The East Coast tent-rental company, for example, attracted more than 80 inquiries, but the company's failure to provide up-to-date and accurate financial statements kept scaring potential bidders away. As the broker complained, "It's a great company, but the owners just can't seem to give me a financial statement that accurately reflects what's going on in the business right now." And the holiday-products manufacturer—a dynamo with $1.8 million in sales, a thriving market niche, and more than 75 inquiries—has an unusual and off-putting corporate structure (nonprofit status for what appears to be a profit-making venture) that so far has prevented it from making the cut as well.

Realistic pricing should be a given even in this hot market. No matter how many

times a seller says, "Make me an offer," the truth is, bidders get scared off when the price tag seems out of line. The carpet-and-upholstery cleaning business ($235,000 in sales and a $290,000 price tag) attracted more than 300 visitors to a Web site it had set up solely to handle inquiries from *Inc.* readers. Not a single one of those visitors asked for more information. And no one made a bid, although the operation is profitable. Frankly, it's priced too high, and that's why the company is still on the market.

With so many healthy companies available, buyers are smart to be picky. Therein lie some lessons for would-be sellers:

•*Keep financial reports and tax filings current.* Although there may be nothing wrong with your company, you'll scare off bidders with tax-reporting extensions or excessively delayed financial statements. If you've had trouble staying current in the past, upgrade your accounting software or consider switching accounting firms.

•*Strive for accuracy.* Serious bidders will demand a high level of comfort, especially about the accuracy of cash-flow statements, accounts-receivable lists, and the assessed value of fixtures, equipment, and inventory. This is a time when it may really pay off to invest in audited financial statements.

•*Time your deal right.* Although it always makes sense to try to sell during a hot market like this one, it's even more important to pay attention to what's going on within your company and industry. The bottom line: Don't try to sell during a significant downturn (unless you absolutely don't have any other options and are prepared to accept a rock-bottom price).

That's a mistake the sellers of the mid-Atlantic violin shop made. They wanted to sell because of a partnership dispute and breakup, but those factors disrupted sales and profit margins, which scared off potential buyers. The current owner is working hard to restore results to their former robust levels, but that probably should have happened before the company hung up its For Sale sign.

•*Keep things simple.* Anything unusual—such as the holiday-products manufacturer's use of nonprofit status—is bad news when it comes time to sell your company. So look at your business the way a

stranger would, and eliminate complications before you try to sell.

•*Accept reality.* If you're operating in a highly competitive market, there's no doubt that your buyer will insist on a noncompete agreement (and perhaps even a clause in the sales contract that states that you will not try to hire key staffers for any new business operation at all). If you're not prepared to make such concessions, your company probably won't sell.

That's what happened with the seller of the Texas minichain of pizzerias. "He thought he would get a naïve buyer who wouldn't raise the noncompete issue—so that he could go off and buy another pizza franchise instead—but that was one of the first questions that prospects raised," recalls broker Luke Lammert of Southwest Business Services. Since the seller wouldn't agree, the company has ultimately proved unsellable, at least for now.

•*Put a realistic price tag on your company.* A good rule of thumb is that only on the rarest of occasions do companies sell for a price that's as high as one times revenues. If you're trying to sell for more than that, as was the case with the mid-Atlantic vending route, be prepared for your financials to be examined under a microscope. "This company wanted top dollar, but the problem was, some of its machines just weren't generating as much profit as others were," explains the broker, Marc Dosik. "The seller needed to either lower the price to a more realistic level or go through and eliminate less profitable locations."

SO IS THIS THE TIME TO SELL YOUR company? If it's market-ready and not priced in the stratosphere, you may want to act soon, before this three-year-old cycle peaks, which it inevitably will. But if your company is plagued by glitches that only a founder could love, don't expect to unload it any faster now than you ever would have. You'll be better off taking the time to polish up your business before hanging up a For Sale sign, even if that means risking a slowdown in the market.

Jill Andresky Fraser (incfraser@aol.com) is Inc.'s finance editor.

Passing the Baton Peacefully

Startups are finding the qualities that make a great founder don't always make a great CEO. Here's how to smooth the transition of power

Four years ago, when serial entrepreneur Michael Lyons sought inspiration for launching his next business, he had only to search as far as his computer screen. Like many Net surfers, Lyons was overwhelmed by all the text in cyberspace—more so because he's dyslexic. An Internet search engine based on images instead of words might sell, he thought. So the 49-year-old Boston University MBA founded his fourth company—ditto.com—and started building such a product.

Then last year, ditto.com launched a more traditional search—for a CEO to replace Lyons. Board members were beginning to question whether they had the right team to ensure the company's future. And with more than $30 million on the line, venture-capital backers were becoming anxious as they watched other dot-coms crash. So Lyons stepped aside for an outside CEO—Wayne Willis—and retreated to the role of chairman.

FAMILIAR TALE. Such handovers of power have become almost a ritual of the startup culture, amplified by the recent tidal wave of dot-com failures. Technical or marketing visionary starts company. After initial success, company falters and backers seek someone to blame. With few exceptions—Bill Gates and Michael Dell come to mind—founder steps aside for professional manager and often leaves company.

Indeed, in a study of recent management changes at 173 high-tech companies in Silicon Valley, professors Thomas Hellmann and Manju Puri of Stanford University's Graduate School of Business found that more than half moved their founders aside within six years on average—and that nearly 60% of the founders subsequently left. "If they aren't happy with the turn in the company or think things are too tense or aren't going well, they just leave," Puri says. "They still have equity. It's not like they are leaving with nothing."

More fascinating are the reasonably rare nonquitters—those who find a useful niche and work with a successor to help make their original dream come true. For the founder, doing so means

swallowing plenty of pride. "Let's be real," Lyons says. "Nobody gives up this job willingly. You've been here since Day One, and [now] you have to say, 'I'm going to let somebody else do that.'" And "that" can include sea changes in strategy—and cutting loose original employees who are friends and family of the founder.

PAYING LIP SERVICE. In an environment with so much potential for tension, the company also runs a risk. "Many of the qualities that you need to be an entrepreneur—passion, charisma, self-confidence—can make it hard to subordinate yourself to the CEO of your own company," says Scott Gordon, who, as managing director of the Internet practice at executive-search firm Spencer Stuart, places CEOs who displace founders. "Many companies have been destroyed because the founder pays lip service to being just a member of the team but never gives up the reins."

If such time bombs can be disarmed, however, keeping the company's creator on board may be beneficial for both parties. For the founder, there's the money. "It's a matter of weighing your self-worth against your net worth," says Alan Hu, founder of software company Collabria in San Mateo, Calif., who was bumped by an outside CEO last year. "You want your shares to be worth something." It also can be a relief to stop spreading yourself too thin. "Every time I needed to go out and raise a round [of funding], the operations suffered," Hu recalls.

For the company, there's the advantage of retaining someone who likely knows more about the core product than anyone else—and is committed to it. In his new role, Lyons has been concentrating on finding new places to license ditto.com. Of late, he has been jetting back and forth between the U.S. and Japan, where he's in talks with several potential partners about bringing visual-search technology to Web portals.

HATEFUL STUFF. Lyons says that after taking stock—essentially, asking himself if he was still having fun—he began to realize in January, 2000, that his days as CEO were numbered. Ditto.com had grown from a handful of acolytes to nearly 30 full-time employees and more than 60 part-timers, leaving Lyons with less time to do what he liked best: come up with new ideas. "When you get a company of 50 to 100 people, by definition the CEO is going to sit in management meetings the whole time," he says. "And you have to do things like budgets and employee manuals. I hate that stuff."

This was no revelation to the company's directors. "We knew from the beginning that Michael was the perfect person to take [ditto.com] to a certain stage," says Giorgio Ronchi, an adviser to the company's board and CEO of ETF Group, the European venture-capital firm that is ditto.com's lead backer. "He's a visionary. But when the company gets bigger, and he really has to manage, he isn't as happy. He is not the best person for this." Thus, the board—composed mainly of outsiders—reached a consensus on replacing Lyons.

Once decided, the board let the founder (who owns less than 10% of the company) help choose his successor—a wise move. Lyons himself established the criteria for what kind of candidate would fill his shoes. He wanted an operations wizard with an ability to work with investors and the board. "If the founder is going to stay on, there has to be a personal fit as well as a background fit," Lyons says.

SENIOR-MANAGER MATERIAL. Although the board didn't set a deadline for the changing of the guard, it was clear sooner was better than later, Lyons says. Another adviser to the company introduced Lyons to Willis, 53, who had held a string of senior-management positions in high-tech companies, including a four-and-a-half-year stint as president of Voice-Tel, an interactive voice-messaging company. Voice-Tel was sold to Premiere Technologies in 1997 for about $200 million.

Lyons and the board liked what they saw in Willis, who holds a law degree from Yale University. But Willis says he didn't agree to climb into the driver's seat until Lyons assured him he'd also get the keys. He says he knew that for the management team to succeed with the founder still on board, the chain of command had to be established at the outset. "It doesn't work if somebody's going to say, 'Well, you come in and take care of the details, and you're responsible for everything, but I get to make all the decisions,'" Willis says. "This is, by the way, what a lot of founders say."

When a founder does remain, in fact, the relationship between the entrepreneur and the new CEO becomes a critical management test. Executives who have experienced this liken it to an arranged marriage, since love is rarely part of the mix—at least at first. What matters, rather, is a willingness to work out differences for the good of the child—the fledgling company whose survival depends on the availability of venture capital. Founders, therefore, must check their ego at the door, even as the outside CEO plays to the sometimes-capricious demands of the company's financiers. Not surprisingly, the likelihood that founders will be replaced increases by 15%, on average, when a firm is backed by VC money, Stanford's Puri and Hellmann found.

"CAREENING OUT OF CONTROL." In sizing up the situation at ditto.com, Willis drew on past experience: He'd once been asked by a board to help rescue a company in the midst of a funding crisis—and quickly realized the problems stemmed largely from a nasty conflict between the founder and the new CEO. "The founder was keeping his hands on the levers, and the CEO couldn't drive," Willis says. "They were just careening out of control. At that point, I negotiated an exit for the founder."

After joining ditto.com last March, Willis wasted no time in taking a hard look at the company's business plan. Soon came the first test of ditto.com's founder-CEO relationship: Willis proposed changing the direction of the company.

Lyons had envisioned ditto.com as a consumer Web site on the order of Yahoo! and other search engines. (Typing in the word "Bush," for instance, calls up pictures of the British rock group Bush, President George W. Bush, the President's mother Barbara, and an azalea bush.) Ads had been developed for such a site, and the staff was revved up for expansion.

GOING B2B. Willis concluded, however, that the company's advertising-based revenue model wouldn't lead ditto.com to profitability. He quickly realized he had a sales job to do: persuading Lyons and the rest of the team that the search engine should be marketed to Web portals and other sites to implement as part of their existing services—a business-to-business product rather than business-to-consumer. In essence, Willis' task entailed remaining true to the founder's vision, while adapting the plan to the changing dot-com market. "It was about being able to apply a fresh set of eyes to something and having the founder trust someone to nurture his baby," Willis says.

Lyons recalls that as a trying time. It took him about a month to come around to Willis' way of thinking: That the dot-com landscape had been transformed, making the world a frightfully inhospitable place for stand-alone Web sites. Before Lyons signed on to the change, scores of meetings were held. And outside advisers were brought in. "Basically, we had to come to terms with the fact that it was not the time to brand our own site but to license our index to the top players around the world," Lyons says. "That's a fundamental shift. And that took some doing."

Fortunately for ditto, the new strategy shows signs of working: Its technology—which competes with Alta Vista, a search engine owned by Internet investment company CMGI—is now being used by such sites as NBCi, Momma, Dogpile, and MetaCrawler. Lyons and Willis decline to discuss the company's finances. But Lydia Loizides, an analyst at Jupiter Media Metrix, an Internet consulting company, says ditto.com has a solid business model and calls the company "one of the leaders" in the field. "They have been at this for quite a while and have, in my opinion, a robust offering that can really provide value to people who are trying to improve Web searching," Loizides says.

WHY BREAKUPS HAPPEN. Venture capitalists say the founder's willingness to support a major tweaking of the business plan is perhaps the biggest test of the founder-CEO relationship. "Breakups mostly have to do with differences over what to do with the direction of the company," says Roland Van der Meer, a partner in ComVentures, a Palo Alto (Calif.) venture-capital firm with $1.2 billion under management. "Everything else is noise."

Still, Willis hasn't embarked on a cakewalk. With a change in command inevitably comes the reviewing of the troops. Sometimes, the friends or family of a founder don't fit in as the company matures. Or they're made vice-presidents but aren't qualified to do the job. Laying off the loyalists is one of the most distasteful tasks an outside CEO faces, but it can be necessary—and Willis played hatchet man on several occasions.

"They've built the company through the first phase, which is very hard, and I have a lot of respect for that," says Willis of the casualties. "I try to find another seat for them either in or outside the company. But it's my decision." (Ditto.com now has 47 full-time staffers, as people have been hired to implement its new strategy.) Notes Lyons, who saw several of his early employees fired: "That's a hard thing for me, O.K. Because let me tell you, I've got a bunch of combat troops."

SHARING RESPONSIBILITY. Ego is the enemy that can turn friction over such moves into a war. And both Lyons and Willis admit to having healthy egos. The key to managing ego, Willis says, is to transform governance of the company from the exclusive preserve of the founder into a shared responsibility. "You need to have decision making and leadership derived from the enthusiasm of the entire management of the company, including the board," Willis says. "Then no one's ego is dominant."

Indeed, companies in which the founder-CEO relationship appears to work have controls that keep entrepreneurs from overstepping. At ditto.com, Lyons doesn't commit the company's resources until the management team has given its O.K. "It works because he has the authority to represent the company in a complete way, but he also has boundaries," Willis says.

During the 75% of his time when he isn't seeking overseas customers, Lyons pitches ditto.com's technology to corporate Web sites. "In general, it has been a positive shift in my role in that it allows me to do what I am best at," Lyons says. "If I had to manage the day-to-day operations, I would not have been able to do this."

MAXIMIZING FACE TIME. In fact, Willis and Lyons are working well together despite a major logistical challenge: Much of the time, they're 2,000 miles apart, Lyons at ditto.com's technology center in Naperville, Ill., where the company was founded, and Willis at the firm's Burlingame (Calif.) headquarters, which the company opened when it discovered that the marketing and business-development talent it needed was clustered in Silicon Valley. The execs frequently shuttle between offices to maximize face time.

Despite the relatively smooth road so far, Lyons concedes there are bumps. To help him deal with the occasional frustration, he depends on his peers at the Young President's Organization, a group of CEOs and former CEOs in noncompeting businesses. Four hours every month, the band gets together to compare notes and occasionally let off steam—a sort of group therapy for execs. It was Lyons' YPO cohorts who persuaded him the time had come to pass the baton. "These folks know me better than most anyone on the planet," Lyons says. "They helped me focus. They helped me differentiate between ego and vision."

Lyons doesn't hide the fact that he may leave ditto.com one day. "I am perpetually thinking about a new venture," he says. But he maintains this has nothing to do with his new role. In fact, leaving the CEO chair has helped him come to terms with his limitations, he says—and, in the future, will help him prepare earlier for the leadership transition. (In fact, he wonders if his company might have died had it clung to its original business model.)

"My other advice is take a vacation," Lyons adds. "Let the other guy run it for a minute. Seriously, founders are neurotic. They do not take vacations. It'll give you a little perspective."

By Eric Wahlgren in New York

Company for sale by owner— or maybe not

*Who should sell your company? You? A business broker?
An investment banker? How to make the call*

BY JILL ANDRESKY FRASER

A MERGERS-AND-ACQUISITIONS MARKET as overheated as today's, it's no surprise that many of you are asking yourselves, "How much could I sell my company for?" If the potential payoff is great enough, the next question often is, "Could I sell it myself?"

As with so many decisions in business it all depends on the circumstances. When AdOne Classified Network, an Internet-based classified-advertising company, sold itself last year for close to $20 million to a consortium financed by five major media corporations, the company's CEO played a major role. "An entrepreneur must take ownership in the process. You cannot abrogate that," says Brendan Burns, the president and CEO of the original company and now CEO of the new venture, AdOne LLC, headquartered in New York City. "I handled all the contacts with potential buyers myself, which was really an exercise in networking but very important in getting it all done right. Then I relied on an investment banker to help me hammer out the best structure for the transaction."

In some situations, all that a sale-oriented adviser adds is more expense and an unnecessary level of bureaucracy. In other situations, though, it's tough to imagine how a deal could get done well without an independent expert equipped with a Rolodex full of networking contacts.

"One very big consideration is the kind of industry you're in—and how knowl-

edgeable you are about it," says Marc Rubenstein, a partner in the Boston law firm Palmer & Dodge LLP. "In some industries, business owners know all their competitors. They run into them all the time, and they're the most likely purchasers. Or there are only a handful of financial firms that invest in a business's niche, and again, the owners know them all."

In such cases, you can make the initial approach and even handle the negotiations if one of your contacts is interested in a possible deal. (To gauge whether that's wise, see box, "The Do-It-Yourself Test.") Assuming your company's accountant and lawyer are up to the challenge, they can prepare the necessary financial reports for prospective buyers, facilitate due diligence, and draft term sheets and other legal documents.

Then again, many owners—even those with good contacts—should not attempt to go it alone and instead should rely on a sales expert. "Some people just don't feel confident about picking up the phone and calling someone to say that they're thinking about selling their company. That means they're really not the best people to make the approach," says Rubenstein. "Other times, people are just great at running their businesses, but they don't have a clue about how best to package them for possible sale." That's when an M&A adviser can add value that really pays off.

When it comes to going it alone, you're in the best position if you have the right contacts and some relevant experience. "Maybe you've already sold a business before or you've been in a corporate position that allowed you to closely observe a sale," says Jonathan Layne, a Los Angeles-based partner and cochair of the corporate-transactions practice of law firm Gibson, Dunn & Crutcher LLP.

But even then, you may need help. "Especially in those deals where the owner is going to stay on for a while, either working as a consultant or as a high-level employee of the buyer, it can be very difficult to go head-to-head in bloody negotiations and then plan to show up for work for the next few years," says Layne. "It's better to have an adviser handle that kind of negotiation for you, so that you can maintain good relations throughout the whole experience."

That's a strategy Burns found useful during AdOne's complex and multistage sale process. "Having an investment banker involved helped a great deal at a couple of points," he recalls, "when we needed to defuse the tension and just step into the background for a while. I'd say that he was instrumental at those points in moving things along in the best possible way."

For business owners who conclude that they want—or need—some level of assistance with a company sale, there are generally two ways to go: with a business broker

Tax issues

Yikes. It's complicated enough to decide when and how to sell your company. But thanks to a recent change in the tax laws, selling is now more painful than ever—that is, if you're being paid in installments.

"The federal government used to allow sellers who received their payments over time to pay the taxes associated with the sale over time," explains Mark G. Bosswick of David Berdon & Co. "Now you can't choose to do that if you're an accrual-method taxpayer, which is the category most businesses fall into. In most cases, they've got to pay the full tax bill for the year in which the sale closes, no matter when they receive the payment."

For many small-business owners, that is a potential disaster, since they may not have the cash up front (or may not want to spend it on taxes). According to one estimate, as many as 260,000 businesses a year may be affected by the rule change.

Still, there are a couple of ways to get around the tax man. "You may be able to delay the tax bite by accepting stock instead of cash, but of course there's a risk involved, since the stock may decline in value before you sell it," says Bosswick. "You also don't achieve much in the way of diversification," he adds, "unless your investment banker designs some kind of stock-hedging strategy to accompany the sale."

An easier course of action is simply to require full payment up front. If that's your plan, shop for a business broker with proven contacts and expertise in the financing arena, so that you won't discourage potential buyers who may not have a wallet full of cash.

The do-it-yourself test

Don't decide to sell your company by yourself before you answer these four questions:

1. Do you have a fairly good sense of how much your company is worth?

If not, it pays either to get an independent appraisal or to rely on a business broker or investment banker. Otherwise, you risk underpricing the company or discouraging potential buyers by pricing it too high.

2. Can you draw up a list of likely buyers?

Depending upon your company's niche, your prospects might be competitors, suppliers, strategic partners, or customers. Don't cheat here. If you really don't have a clue, you're better off relying on a professional who has already gone this route.

3. Do you really have the time to do this?

"It's incredibly time-consuming to do the networking yourself, so you've got to have the internal organization to support you," emphasizes Brendan Burns of AdOne. "The important thing is to keep your company moving forward through the whole process." If you know in your heart that you and your staff) won't be able to manage both the sale and the company's operations, don't try to go it alone.

4. Can you do a better job than anyone else?

If you're articulate, passionate about your company, and—above all—not self-conscious about pitching it for sale, then the answer is probably yes. But if you suspect that your emotions or anxieties could get in the way, step aside.

---

or with an investment banker. (Some real estate brokers also have a sideline as business brokers, but they're not worth considering if your company has assets and selling points beyond buildings and property.)

Business brokers saturate the low end of the M&A marketplace. They get involved in small deals, even those with price tags well below $1 million. They'll take on selling companies that haven't yet tapped into their growth potential, as well as fully mature businesses in less-than-sexy industries. For many low-tech entrepreneurs, brokers are the only game in town.

Good brokers can bring three assets to the table: current knowledge of the marketplace, which helps them price companies at high but achievable levels; expertise at drumming up potential buyers; and contacts with sources of financing. In cases in which the seller isn't willing to accept an extended payment schedule (see box, "Tax Issues"), a well-connected broker may be able to keep a deal from tanking by hooking the buyer up with the right lender.

Still, there's a vast range in quality among business brokers. Some try to make up for their own lack of contacts by relying on an advertising or a direct-mail-marketing blitz, which can be risky. George D. Shaw, a certified public accountant and partner in charge of corporate finance advisory services at Grant Thornton LLP in Boston, warns: "Business brokers may market a company so widely that the owner basically has no other option but to sell, whatever the price, because the competitors find out, the employees find out,

and the company no longer is feasible as an independent business. That's the worst possible position to be in when you're thinking about selling."

To minimize such a risk, check out potential business brokers as carefully as you would a company hire. "It's very important to look for a broker who is heavily involved in your industry and has sold companies like yours in the past, advises John Sjoholm, a senior tax partner at Nykiel, Carlin & Co., an accounting firm in Schaumburg, Ill. "Most of our entrepreneurial clients have interviewed somewhere between three and seven brokers before deciding which one to hire."

The other option is to hire an investment banker, but investment banks generally are interested in handling only significant transactions. "Significant" can

Money, money, money

If you hire an expert to help you through the sale process, what can you expect to pay?

Business brokers

Although their fees vary, most charge a commission tied to the final sale price, generally about 10%. A growing trend among brokers is to also assess an up-front fee—which could run as high as $10,000—for the preparation of marketing materials. (Tip: Beware of one scam technique in which brokers come up with wildly optimistic pricing estimates and use them to hook unsuspecting sellers into paying high upfront marketing fees.)

Investment bankers

Surprisingly enough, despite their higher level of service, most bankers charge lower percentage commissions than brokers do (mainly because they're working on deals of a much bigger scale). And there's more payment variation in this end of the marketplace. Typical fees may range from 3% to 6% of the total sale price. Performance incentives sometimes get added. On deals that are more complex (or potentially more time-consuming), some bankers charge a monthly retainer as well.

mean the sale of a large private company. It can also mean the sale of a small company in a niche that attracts interest either from professional investment groups or from larger strategic partners. Although investment bankers' thresholds of interest vary, many won't consider a deal with a price tag below $3 million. (For differences in the ways that business brokers and investment bankers get compensated, see box, "Money, Money, Money.")

In certain transactions, investment bankers can add key advantages. "When deals are more complicated and there are significant tax and payment issues to be addressed, an investment banker can help with the structure," says Mark G. Bosswick, a senior tax partner, lawyer, and CPA with David Berdon & Co. LLP, an accounting firm in New York City. That might be true particularly in cases in which multiple categories of stock or other financial instruments (such as hedging devices) are involved.

> In some situations, all that a sale-oriented adviser adds is more expense and bureaucracy. In other situations, it's tough to imagine how a deal could get done well without an independent expert equipped with a Rolodex full of networking contacts.

Since bankers often possess better potential contacts than most brokers do, their participation can streamline the sales process. The most successful investment bankers specialize in a short list of industries, so it pays to shop around for one with a track record and networking base that are relevant to your company.

These days, Shaw of Grant Thornton adds, "it also makes sense to look for an investment banker with the capability to sell your company internationally, because that's a growing outlet for many entrepreneurial firms." Still, he warns, "there's a big difference between an investment banker who just has an international database of prospective leads and one that has real distribution capabilities overseas." (The latter includes international offices and close affiliations with foreign investment- or merchant-banking firms.) If you think your company could attract international interest, pay special attention to that issue when interviewing bankers.

Another way an investment banker might add value is simply by accepting your company as a client. "If a well-respected banker takes your company on, then that may be a form of credential, because it's a sign to the outside world that you've been vetted by an independent expert," comments Rubenstein. "But it can be a tough call to make because some companies don't need it. We've got a client right now," he says, "who's trying to assess whether hiring someone will add or detract value from the final deal. This is a case in which the seller knows how much his company is worth, and he already knows all the possible players who might want to buy it. He can pick up the phone himself or hire someone to do it. Will an investment banker's involvement raise the price enough to justify the fee? There's no easy answer. We're trying to figure it out right now."

One final point: whether you hire an investment banker or a business broker, the issue of Internet marketing probably will be raised either by you or by your adviser. Is promoting your company's sale on-line a helpful strategy?

Here again, the answer depends on your company's situation. If it's small, quirky, or otherwise likely a hard sell, you can only benefit from being marketed to the broadest possible audience (so long as your Web description manages to protect your confidentiality). Growing numbers of business brokers, especially those with national affiliations, are experimenting with this advertising medium; expect the trend to continue.

Still, with upper-end deals—the kind in which the buyers are large companies or professional investment groups rather than individuals or other small companies—one-on-one networking matters so much that it's hard to imagine that buyers would even check out an Internet site. Rubenstein may put it best: "I will buy a PalmPilot from the Internet. But I'm not going to buy a company from it. This is one business activity that really depends upon the Rolodex, the personal contacts, and a willingness to hit the pavement."

Jill Andresky Fraser (incfraser@aol.com) is Inc.'s *finance editor.*

Index

Index

Test Your Knowledge Form

We encourage you to photocopy and use this page as a tool to assess how the articles in *Annual Editions* expand on the information in your textbook. By reflecting on the articles you will gain enhanced text information. You can also access this useful form on a product's book support Web site at *http://www.dushkin.com/online/*.

NAME: _____   DATE: _____

TITLE AND NUMBER OF ARTICLE: _____

BRIEFLY STATE THE MAIN IDEA OF THIS ARTICLE:

_____

LIST THREE IMPORTANT FACTS THAT THE AUTHOR USES TO SUPPORT THE MAIN IDEA:

_____

WHAT INFORMATION OR IDEAS DISCUSSED IN THIS ARTICLE ARE ALSO DISCUSSED IN YOUR TEXTBOOK OR OTHER READINGS THAT YOU HAVE DONE? LIST THE TEXTBOOK CHAPTERS AND PAGE NUMBERS:

_____

LIST ANY EXAMPLES OF BIAS OR FAULTY REASONING THAT YOU FOUND IN THE ARTICLE:

_____

LIST ANY NEW TERMS/CONCEPTS THAT WERE DISCUSSED IN THE ARTICLE, AND WRITE A SHORT DEFINITION:

We Want Your Advice

ANNUAL EDITIONS revisions depend on two major opinion sources: one is our Advisory Board, listed in the front of this volume, which works with us in scanning the thousands of articles published in the public press each year; the other is you—the person a ctually using the book. Please help us and the users of the next edition by completing the prepaid article rating form on this page and returning it to us. Thank you for your help!

ANNUAL EDITIONS: Entrepreneurship 02/03

ARTICLE RATING FORM

Here is an opportunity for you to have direct input into the next revision of this volume.
We would like you to rate each of the articles listed below, using the following scale:

1. **Excellent: should definitely be retained**
2. **Above average: should probably be retained**
3. **Below average: should probably be deleted**
4. **Poor: should definitely be deleted**

Your ratings will play a vital part in the next revision.
Please mail this prepaid form to us as soon as possible.
Thanks for your help!

RATING	ARTICLE	RATING	ARTICLE
	1. The Origin of the Entrepreneurial Species		35. Angel Investors Fill Void Left By Risk Capital
	2. Who Are the Self-Employed?		36. The Do's and Don'ts of Fund Raising
	3. How a Start-Up Evolves		37. "Are You Built to Grow?"
	4. What It Takes to Start a Startup		38. Managing Growth
	5. Top Ten Entrepreneurs		39. Managing Global Expansion: A Conceptual Framework
	6. The Man and His Money		40. Three Strategies for Managing Fast Growth
	7. Michael Dell		41. Insular Culture Helped Yahoo! Grow, But Has Now Hurt It in the Long Run
	8. Success Rules!		42. The Decision,
	9. 10 Stupid Things Entrepreneurs Do!		43. The Initial Public Offering: Early Planning Considerations
	10. Go Global		44. Harvesting Firm Value: Process and Results
	11. Lights Amid the Gloom		45. Choosing Your Exit Strategy
	12. One More Time… Should Small Companies Attempt Strategic Planning?		46. The Race to Embrace
	13. How Entrepreneurs Craft Strategies That Work		47. The Flip Side of the Boom
	14. The Success Start-Up Guide		48. Passing the Baton Peacefully
	15. Preliminary Legal Considerations in Forming a New Enterprise		49. Company for Sale by Owner—Or Maybe Not
	16. How to Write a Great Business Plan		
	17. Outline for a Business Plan: A Proven Approach for Entrepreneurs Only		
	18. Finding Your Competitive Edge		
	19. Bear Opportunities		
	20. Get Smart Fast—Or Else		
	21. Solving the Puzzle of the Cash Flow Statement		
	22. Characteristics of a Successful Entrepreneurial Management Team		
	23. Going Outside		
	24. Will Venture Capital Come in From the Cold?		
	25. Basic Instinct		
	26. Ready or Not?		
	27. Venture Capitalists' Assessment of New Venture Survival		
	28. Five Things to Remember When Raising Money		
	29. The VC On the Corner		
	30. The Venture Capital Industry: An Overview		
	31. The Man With the Golden Touch		
	32. Jackpot!		
	33. Not All VCs Are Created Equal		
	34. Money Order		

(Continued on next page)

BUSINESS REPLY MAIL
FIRST-CLASS MAIL PERMIT NO. 84 GUILFORD CT

POSTAGE WILL BE PAID BY ADDRESSEE

McGraw-Hill/Dushkin
530 Old Whitfield Street
Guilford, Ct 06437-9989

ABOUT YOU

Name   Date
_____   _____

Are you a teacher? ☐   A student? ☐
Your school's name
_____

Department
_____

Address   City   State   Zip
_____

School telephone #
_____

YOUR COMMENTS ARE IMPORTANT TO US!

Please fill in the following information:
For which course did you use this book?
_____

Did you use a text with this ANNUAL EDITION?   ☐ yes ☐ no
What was the title of the text?
_____

What are your general reactions to the *Annual Editions* concept?
_____

Have you read any pertinent articles recently that you think should be included in the next edition? Explain.
_____

Are there any articles that you feel should be replaced in the next edition? Why?
_____

Are there any World Wide Web sites that you feel should be included in the next edition? Please annotate.
_____

May we contact you for editorial input?   ☐ yes ☐ no
May we quote your comments?   ☐ yes ☐ no